Financing Economic Development in the 21st Century

Financing Economic Development in the 21st Century

SECOND EDITION

Sammis B. White and Zenia Z. Kotval, Editors

M.E.Sharpe
Armonk, New York
London, England

Library of Congress Cataloging-in-Publication Data

Financing economic development in the 21st century / edited by Sammis B. White and Zenia Z. Kotval. —2nd ed.
p. cm.
Includes bibliographical references and index.
ISBN 978-0-7656-2782-7 (cloth : alk. paper) — ISBN 978-0-7656-2783-4 (pbk. : alk. paper)
1. United States—Economic conditions—2001–2009. 2. United States—Economic conditions—2009
3. Venture capital—United States. 4. Finance, Public—United States. 5. New business enterprises—United States—Finance. I. White, Sammis B. II. Kotval, Zenia, 1964–

HC106.83.F557 2012
338.973—dc23 2012000154

Printed in the United States of America

The paper used in this publication meets the minimum requirements of American National Standard for Information Sciences Permanence of Paper for Printed Library Materials, ANSI Z 39.48-1984.

IBT (c) 10 9 8 7 6 5 4 3 2 1
IBT (p) 10 9 8 7 6 5 4 3 2 1

Contents

Foreword

Economic Development Finance: Practice Leading Theory

Edward (Ned) *Hill*

The practice of economic development in the United States began as the republic was founded, with infrastructure finance tied to a view of economic development playing a central role in its politics. Local and state governments and their residents searched for ways to connect to the larger trans-Atlantic and transcontinental economies, attract employers, and especially to pay for transportation infrastructure improvements.

Parts of Ron Chernow's 2004 biography of Alexander Hamilton can be offered up as a primer and history of the roots of industrial and manufacturing policy in the United States. Chernow notes Madison's negative reaction to Hamilton's *Report on Manufacturing*—the first attempt to define a manufacturing policy in the United States. However, Madison was in favor of legislation to promote the nation's economic development—which was nearly synonymous with promoting the nation's westward internal development. Madison joined John Quincy Adams, Henry Clay, and the last of the Federalists in this desire when the National Republican Party, which quickly became known as the Whig Party, was formed in the early 1830s (Merry 2009).

As the Federalists became Whigs the stage was set for decades of struggle between Jeffersonian Democrats and Clay's Whigs over the issue of financing internal improvements (roads, canals, and harbors) and Clay's advocacy for his American System—an economic development policy of internal improvements, high tariffs, and even a national university. Joseph Ellis spends time on the reaction of the Jeffersonian Democrats in his 1998 biography of Jefferson.

Politics in pre–Civil War America was a blend of argument over states' rights, the power of the federal government to regulate and stimulate commerce between the states, slavery, and a public political struggle for control over specie (paper money) and credit. It was a debate over the path economic development was to take in the nation that was subsumed under the meaning of Union.

Andrew Jackson's election was aided by his opposition to both interstate internal improvements and to the Second Bank of the United States (Meacham 2008). Polk followed in his patron's opposition to the federal finance of internal improvements, frustrating Clay's presidential ambitions and his political support for building a nation through internal improvements (Merry 2009).

Frequently lost in political biographies of Lincoln are his political roots as a Whig and his admiration of Clay and his American System. These sentiments worked their way into the platform of the newly formed Republican Party. David Donald's 1995 biography of Lincoln makes the connection between Lincoln's and Clay's philosophies for national development through internal improvements. It is no surprise that Lincoln supported economic development public policies that look familiar today, with his support for railroads in general and transcontinental railroads, in particular. His other signature economic development achievement was in his support for public university education and for the practical sciences from the establishment of land grant universities through the Morrill Land-Grant Act of 1862. Of course, it was during Lincoln's tenure of the Civil War that the northern states became industrialized, and with the demands of war and the vitalization of the bond and stock markets, this triggered international flows of capital to the United States from Britain.

The rush to invest in transportation infrastructure that connected the West to the East Coast began in earnest after the 1825 opening of the Erie Canal. Canals allowed for population movement and the development of cities as break-in-bulk points, resulting in the growth of wholesale and retail agglomerations. The drive to be on the route was reinforced with the expansion of steam railroads in the 1840s and 1850s. Railroads reduced the cost of hauling both freight and people and made investors both understand the returns that could take place through network effects and relish the returns that come from developing real estate near the intersections of a transportation system.

Railroad entrepreneurs became adept at acquiring financing by selling stocks and bonds to cities, towns, and villages that were on a proposed rail line. They were also very good at watering down stocks and going bankrupt. The result was that state and local finances were put under stress and states began to amend their constitutions prohibiting state and local governments from owning shares in companies or issuing bonds in their behalf. Schoettle covers these constitutional prohibitions as they stood in 1990.

Beginning with the Great Depression, many states hired teams of lawyers to narrow the application of these prohibitions. Among the earliest and most inventive were a group of Depression-era lawyers in Mississippi led by Governor Hugh Lawson White.

Practice again led economic development theory during the Great Depression when the Mississippi Industrial Act passed in 1936. Hugh White conceived the need to engage in industrial recruiting while he was mayor of Columbia, Mississippi, in 1929, and he moved the Mississippi Industrial Act through the legislature during his first year as governor in 1936.

Connie Lester's (2004) short history of the evolution of publicly financed industrial recruiting in Mississippi begins with Mayor White "surveying the sawmill graveyards . . . and deciding that Columbia would not disappear like other lumbermill towns." He encouraged the Marion County Chamber of Commerce to begin industrial recruiting. The Chamber employed Chicago-based Fantus, the first site location and economic development consulting firm, to recruit a factory to come to Columbia (LeRoy 2005). The quid pro quo reached was that Reliance Manufacturing would locate an apparel company in Columbia that would employ 300 workers in return for a loan guarantee made to a New Orleans bank to back an $85,000 loan needed to build the factory.

There was nothing unique about going to the local business community to provide a start-up loan to a recruited company. Akron, Ohio recruited what evolved into the rubber industry in 1869 by offering $13,600 in finance raised by subscription from the local business community to allow Dr. B.F. Goodrich to move his newly formed Goodrich & Tew Company from Hastings-on-Hudson, New York, where the company Goodrich acquired and renamed was originally located. What was new was that Mayor White invented a loan loss guarantee, or insurance, indirectly made by local government that allowed a bank to fund a loan that it perceived as being risky.

Mayor White did not stop at inventing loan loss insurance as an economic development finance tool; he also started a training school using the recruited company's supervisors as teachers and trained the potential workers on the company's equipment. Alabama did the same to recruit Honda to Lincoln, Alabama decades later.

The outlines of modern economic development attraction strategies emerge from what an energetic mayor put together. Mayor White had the Chamber work with an industrial site location consultant, provided a public loan loss guarantee, and recruited and trained the labor force for the employer. In terms of the economics behind this flurry of invention—he tackled information failures, removed the risk of making a loan due to a lack of information about the borrower, and then he removed labor market uncertainties. In other words, much of the work of the public sector was to remove transactions costs and information imperfections that inhibited private investment. Mayor White also laid the foundation for what he would do in his next job, when he became Governor White.

Governor Hugh White's consulting lawyers invented what has become the most commonly used economic development finance tool, the public-purpose tax-exempt economic development bond. But a way had to be found around the Mississippi Constitution's prohibition of state government investing in private firms and from municipalities subscribing to the capital stock of companies. The lawyers used the general welfare clause of the Constitution as a vehicle by including employment in its list of considerations.

The Mississippi Industrial Act allowed Mississippi's cities and towns to finance land purchases and factory construction. The Act established what has become a common practice in state and local economic development. It also established what has become a well-received form of federalism in the operation of state and local economic development programs: the state sponsors and directs the program, and localities provide the financing and retain local land use and regulatory control.

The state advertised and recruited firms, received 3,000 inquiries, narrowed the list to 60 eligible projects, issued 21 certificates, and 12 companies ended up opening plants in Mississippi (Lester 2004). Thus began the industrialization of the South, the invention of economic development finance and, as some would later put it, the second War Between the States.

Bingham (1998) presents U.S. industrial policy as a set of very pragmatic public policy reactions to either economic crisis, especially as it affects industries that are central to the economy, or to demands to support the development of new industries or new employers at the local level. What this short history attempts to do is to demonstrate that economic development finance has been a part of American political tradition, but it has been a controversial part.

Kenneth P. Thomas found that state and local governments allocate $70 billion in business incentives, of which over 70 percent are location incentives (White 2012). This is not a trivial sum of money. The chapters in this volume offer ways to evaluate the effectiveness of these expenditures and provide viewpoints on both the efficacy of these expenditures and insights on how these development tools work. This is important because, in a federalist system of government, these tools are here to stay.

These chapters should be read while remembering both the short history related here and the fantastic financial events associated with the Great Recession of 2007 and the freeze of the global credit markets that took place in September 2008. Government intervened strongly in the functioning of the credit market when two of the Detroit Three collapsed. Fraud in an unregulated and smug credit market created a crisis in the housing markets that local and state governments now have to correct one swipe of a bulldozer's blade at a time.

Coincidently, new research cited by White (2012) is also changing our understanding of what sorts of businesses create jobs. This research demonstrates that it is not small business that creates jobs, but new businesses.

These facts bring new insight into the role of private-public partnerships in the arena of economic development finance:

- State and local government are frequently best positioned to intervene in failing property markets dominated by abandonment because they are the only entity that can bear the costs of cleanup and be in a position to realize a return due to their very long-term horizons.
- When new land uses are proposed, governments frequently bear the risk private markets cannot bear because the risk has not been demonstrated.
- If state and local governments dominate the lending or investing, then political concerns may subvert balance sheet realities. To provide a barrier to political factors or corruption influencing the decision making, the intermediaries are frequently public-private partnerships.
- Economic development has to be practiced through the income statement of private firms. If a location does not affect the income statement or if the location does not offer access to globally scarce and highly specialized labor, then money will be wasted.
- Economic development cannot be directly about jobs. It is true that the desired outcomes from business development activities are both income and work. However, these two outcomes are derived only indirectly through the sale of products—goods and services.

Therefore, a regional economy is a portfolio of products. The vibrancy and growth of the economy depends on the composition of products within the portfolio. Growing economies are entrepreneurial with a disproportionate share of their product portfolio made up of firms with products in the early stages of the product life cycle. Small companies do not grow jobs. Companies with young products grow jobs. Young companies are also the most risky to finance.

Please keep these observations about economic development in mind as you read and learn from the chapters that follow.

References

Bingham, Richard D. 1998. *Industrial Policy American Style: From Hamilton to HDTV*. Armonk, NY: M.E. Sharpe.

Blackford, Mansel G., and K. Austin Kerr. 1996. *BFGoodrich: Traditions and Transformations, 1870–1995*. Columbus: Ohio State University Press.

Chernow, Ron. 2004. *Alexander Hamilton*. New York: Penguin Press.

Cobb, James C. 1982. *The Selling of the South: The Southern Crusade for Industrial Development, 1936–1980*. Baton Rouge: Louisiana State University Press.

Donald, David Herbert. 1995. *Lincoln*. New York: Simon & Schuster.

Ellis, Joseph J. 1998. *American Sphinx: The Character of Thomas Jefferson*. New York: Alfred A. Knopf.

———. 2004. *His Excellency: George Washington*. New York: Alfred A. Knopf.

Lester, Connie. 2004. Economic development in the 1930s: Balance agriculture with industry. *Mississippi History Now* (Mississippi Historical Society), May. http://mshistory.k12.ms.us/articles/224/economic-development-in-the-1930s-balance-agriculture-with-industry (accessed February 12, 2012).

LeRoy, Greg. 2005. *The Great American Jobs Scam: Corporate Tax Dodging and the Myth of Job Creation*. San Francisco: Berrett-Koehler.

Meacham, Jon. 2008. *American Lion: Andrew Jackson in the White House*. New York: Random House.

Merry, Robert W. 2009. *A Country of Vast Designs: James K. Polk, the Mexican War, and the Conquest of the American Continent*. New York: Simon & Schuster.

Schoettle, Ferdinand P. 1990. What public finance do state constitutions allow? In *Financing Economic Development in the 21st Century*, ed. Sammis B. White, Richard D. Bingham, and Edward W. Hill, 27–49. Armonk, NY: M.E. Sharpe.

Shanahan, James L., and Richard Goe. 1988. Akron, Ohio: Regional economy at the turning point. In *Economic Restructuring of the American Midwest: Proceedings of the Midwest Economic Restructuring Conference of the Federal Reserve Bank of Cleveland*, ed. Richard D. Bingham and Randall W. Eberts. Norwell, MA: Kluwer Academic.

White, Sammis B. 2012. Perspectives on economic development. In *Financing Economic Development in the 21st Century* (2d ed.), ed. Sammis B. White and Zenia Z. Kotval. Armonk, NY: M.E. Sharpe.

Preface

In a nation in which the mantra "jobs, jobs, jobs" is heard daily in every state and in the nation's capital, there is ample reason to explore the merits of stimulating job growth. There are steps that can be taken at the national level, but there are also many options that can be utilized at the state and local levels. Just as there is debate about the best measures for creating jobs through federal policies and programs, there are debates at the state and local levels as well.

Not all options involve finance, but many do. The most frequent questions that arise about job creation concern how these many economic development finance tools actually work, where they are appropriate, and what evidence we have that they deliver what is promised. This book attempts to answer all three questions. Some answers are more definitive than others, as the questions are invariably more difficult to answer than they may seem on the surface. But the authors have been asked to contribute to this collection because they are experts in economic development finance and in techniques that attempt to answer the hard questions.

As readers will note, we have divided the book into sections that explore public, private, and combined methods of finance. We increasingly see more activity in the combined arena. More cooperation is occurring because of the realization that no single entity or approach is the answer. Creating jobs requires initiatives from several directions. The world has gotten more complex as the resources available have gotten scarcer. It is our hope that the exploration of finance options in this book will give readers a clear understanding of what is possible and what options are available.

Before launching into the specifics of finance, we would like to thank several individuals. First, we offer our profound thanks to two individuals who have contributed significantly to the field of economic development and economic development finance, Richard (Dick) Bingham and Edward (Ned) Hill. Both were involved as co-editors of the preceding edition of this book.

Dick Bingham had a long and distinguished career as a political scientist, author, editor, and organizer in the field of economic development. He was an inspiration, a driver of the move to apply lessons learned, and a good friend. Dick recently retired and is pursuing other interests. Ned Hill has taken on many administrative duties at Cleveland State University and is using his spare time actually to practice economic development, not just to write about it. Both Ned and Dick have helped to inspire others to seek solutions to economic development quandaries. And both have been a pleasure to work with.

Thanks also are extended to Harry Briggs and M.E. Sharpe for requesting an updated version of this book. Given the changes in the financial world, revisions are needed. We thank Harry for asking us to take on the task of assembling a new version.

We especially thank the many chapter authors who have given a good deal of time to the construction of their chapters. We greatly appreciate their efforts and the timely delivery of their manuscripts.

I (Sammis) would like to thank my wife for her encouragement and understanding, as I disappear for hours into my study on nights and weekends. I (Zenia) would like to give special thanks to John Mullin for his introduction to economic development and our long-term work together to bring economic insights and vitality to communities around the globe.

Sammis B. White
Zenia Z. Kotval

Part I

Introduction

1

Local Economic Development and Its Finance

An Introduction

Stephen Malpezzi

Since the previous edition of this volume, the United States has experienced the end of the longest continuous economic expansion in our history, followed by the "Great Recession" (officially dated December 2007 to June 2009), and, as of this writing, a "recovery" that may be charitably labeled anemic. Of course, by the time you read this chapter, much more will have happened to move the GDP and employment aggregates—we hope, forward. However well or poorly the U.S. aggregate economy performs, it is worth reminding ourselves (especially if we describe ourselves as "macroeconomists") that every economy is, in fact, a summation of the performance of hundreds of local economies. In my classes I like to make the provocative (and only slightly overstated) argument that nobody finds a job in the United States, or buys or sells a car in the United States, or makes a real estate investment there. We find jobs, buy and sell things, and save and invest in Madison or Milwaukee, in Manhattan or Miami, or some such local labor market, retail market, or real estate market.

This book, then, is about understanding this on-the-ground performance of these local economies. In this chapter, we have three specific objectives. First, we briefly discuss what is meant by *economic development*. Second, we provide a short overview of the general role *finance* plays in economic development. Third, we briefly introduce some of the particular ways *local economic development* (LED) is financed in the United States.

What Is Economic Development?

Economic development is surprisingly difficult to define precisely. What is our goal, and how can we measure our progress in reaching it? Is it the number of jobs, income or wages, wealth, an improved distribution of income, educational and health outcomes, structural change, or a better environment? Or is it the "quality of life," measured in some broad way, incorporating noneconomic as well as economic factors? All these elements are valid components of the multidimensional thing we call development. As we will see later in the text, it is fortunate that many positive measures are at least roughly correlated; for example, actions that increase employment also tend to increase wages and income, and even to some extent improve the distribution of income.[1]

If you meet an economist in the street and ask her what the best measure of development is, she'll probably reply, "welfare" or "well-being." Since we can't easily measure welfare directly, at least in a reliable fashion, we can think of things like income and employment as intervening variables that enable one to attain a higher degree of well-being. Generally a person's welfare is greater if their income rises; and generally a person is better off with a job than if unemployed.[2]

The use of measures like income or gross domestic product in evaluating development is hardly surprising; despite criticism, and greater availability of alternatives, these indicators remain the most popular kinds of summary measures of development. Over the long run and in the aggregate, of course, income and gross product or output are closely linked. In the short run and from person-to-person and place-to-place, these can diverge. For example, localities with large numbers of retirees will have a larger gap between output and income than localities with few retirees.

Many local economic development "practitioners" (local politicians, policy wonks, and applied academics) focus on employment as a gauge of development. Employment matters, of course, but income is probably more directly related to well-being, hence making it a better summary measure. If we look at differences from one metropolitan area to another, there is generally positive correlation between employment and income. Consequently, it's not often that development practitioners have to make a choice to improve one at the expense of the other, at least in the long run.

Other development practitioners focus on the value of local real estate. This is particularly true of local government officials concerned with increasing the size of their tax base, especially in states like Wisconsin, New Hampshire, and New Jersey, all of which rely heavily on the taxation of real property.

Malpezzi (2002) presents empirical tests of the relationships between and among seven candidate measures of development, including income, employment, the size of the real estate stock, and the distribution of income. The results of a detailed statistical analysis show that in most respects the most common "usual suspects," namely per capita income or output, and measures of employment, are well correlated with each other and with other potential measures. The most important exception is that income and employment measures are not strongly correlated with a more even distribution of income. However, even in this respect, it appears that faster growing metropolitan areas are usually seeing some improvement in their income distribution. Furthermore, there is even stronger evidence that higher incomes and growth are correlated with lower poverty rates (which is related to, but different from, the distribution of income per se).[3] In the rest of this chapter, we will focus on income and employment, though we'll say a little more about distribution as well.

U.S. Growth and Distribution: A Few Stylized Facts

In order to present some basic underpinnings for the discussion below, we need to present some stylized facts. In this chapter, we will focus on state-level data; more detailed comparisons, including metropolitan-level comparisons, can be found in Malpezzi (2002). Tables 1.1 through 1.3 present some basic data on population, employment, and real income per capita, and these data are for the 50 states, the District of Columbia, and the United States as a whole.[4]

From Table 1.1 we see that U.S. *population* grew more or less steadily over the past 30 years, from about 227 million in 1980 to an estimated 309 million in 2010, or an annual compounded growth rate of about 1.0 percent. The five largest states—California, Texas, New York, Florida, and Illinois—comprise 10 percent of the states but over a third of the U.S. population. Wyoming, on the other hand, barely breaks half a million in population, and there are another half-dozen states with populations under a million. Generally, the Midwest has been growing more slowly than the country as a whole, and a number of states in the South and West, such as Arizona, California, Colorado, Georgia, and Texas, are growing faster. The fastest growing state, Nevada, racked up an average growth rate about four times the national average; Arizona tripled the U.S. rate of growth, and Florida, Utah, Georgia, Alaska, and Texas grew about double the average. At the other extreme, West Virginia shrank slightly, and Pennsylvania, Iowa, North Dakota, Louisiana, and Ohio barely budged.

Table 1.1 also gives a quick look at some other basic demographics. The fifth and sixth columns present the percentage of each state's population under age 16 and age 65 or older, respectively. Unsurprisingly, they are correlated, though not perfectly: states with a lot of older residents tend to have fewer children. Utah, Idaho, Texas, Georgia, and Arizona are among the youngest states, by either measure; Florida, West Virginia, Vermont, and Maine are among the oldest. But perhaps the most impressive variation among the states is in the fraction of their foreign-born population; immigrants comprise over a quarter of California's population, while roughly a fifth of the populations

Table 1.1

State Population

	Population 1980	Population 2010	Annual growth rate of population 1980–2010 (%)	Percent of 2010 population 16 or over (%)	Percent of 2010 population under 16 (%)	Percent of 2010 population 65 or older (%)	Percent of population foreign-born 2009
Alabama	3,900,368	4,779,736	0.7	79.1	20.9	13.8	3.2
Alaska	405,315	710,231	1.9	76.6	23.4	7.7	7.1
Arizona	2,737,774	6,392,017	2.9	77.4	22.6	13.8	14.0
Arkansas	2,288,738	2,915,918	0.8	78.4	21.6	14.4	4.0
California	23,800,800	37,253,956	1.5	78.1	21.9	11.4	26.9
Colorado	2,908,803	5,029,196	1.8	78.3	21.7	10.9	9.8
Connecticut	3,113,174	3,574,097	0.5	80.0	20.0	14.2	13.0
Delaware	594,919	897,934	1.4	79.8	20.2	14.4	8.3
District of Columbia	638,284	601,723	–0.2	85.2	14.8	11.4	12.2
Florida	9,839,835	18,801,310	2.2	81.3	18.7	17.3	18.8
Georgia	5,486,174	9,687,653	1.9	77.2	22.8	10.7	9.4
Hawaii	967,710	1,360,301	1.1	80.2	19.8	14.3	17.1
Idaho	947,983	1,567,582	1.7	75.6	24.4	12.4	6.1
Illinois	11,434,702	12,830,632	0.4	78.5	21.5	12.5	13.4
Indiana	5,490,721	6,483,802	0.6	78.1	21.9	13.0	4.3
Iowa	2,914,018	3,046,355	0.1	78.9	21.1	14.9	3.8
Kansas	2,369,039	2,853,118	0.6	77.3	22.7	13.2	6.4
Kentucky	3,664,221	4,339,367	0.6	79.1	20.9	13.3	2.9
Louisiana	4,223,101	4,533,372	0.2	78.2	21.8	12.3	3.3
Maine	1,126,860	1,328,361	0.5	82.0	18.0	15.9	3.4
Maryland	4,227,643	5,773,552	1.0	79.4	20.6	12.3	12.9
Massachusetts	5,746,075	6,547,629	0.4	81.0	19.0	13.8	14.4
Michigan	9,255,553	9,883,640	0.2	79.2	20.8	13.8	6.1

Minnesota	4,085,017	5,303,925	0.9	78.6	21.4	12.9	6.8
Mississippi	2,525,342	2,967,297	0.5	77.5	22.5	12.8	2.0
Missouri	4,921,966	5,988,927	0.7	79.0	21.0	14.0	3.5
Montana	788,752	989,415	0.8	80.1	19.9	14.8	2.0
Nebraska	1,572,296	1,826,341	0.5	77.6	22.4	13.5	5.7
Nevada	810,215	2,700,551	4.1	78.1	21.9	12.0	19.1
New Hampshire	924,250	1,316,470	1.2	81.0	19.0	13.5	5.4
New Jersey	7,376,330	8,791,894	0.6	79.4	20.6	13.5	20.2
New Mexico	1,309,400	2,059,179	1.5	77.7	22.3	13.2	10.0
New York	17,566,754	19,378,102	0.3	80.4	19.6	13.5	21.3
North Carolina	5,898,980	9,535,483	1.6	78.8	21.2	12.9	7.1
North Dakota	654,380	672,591	0.1	80.3	19.7	14.5	2.7
Ohio	10,800,650	11,536,504	0.2	79.2	20.8	14.1	3.7
Oklahoma	3,040,758	3,751,351	0.7	78.0	22.0	13.5	5.3
Oregon	2,641,218	3,831,074	1.2	80.0	20.0	13.9	9.8
Pennsylvania	11,868,305	12,702,379	0.2	80.8	19.2	15.4	5.3
Rhode Island	948,773	1,052,567	0.3	81.4	18.6	14.4	12.9
South Carolina	3,134,502	4,625,364	1.3	79.3	20.7	13.7	4.6
South Dakota	690,851	814,180	0.5	77.9	22.1	14.3	2.2
Tennessee	4,600,252	6,346,105	1.1	79.1	20.9	13.4	4.2
Texas	14,338,208	25,145,561	1.9	75.7	24.3	10.3	16.1
Utah	1,472,595	2,763,885	2.1	71.6	28.4	9.0	7.8
Vermont	512,524	625,741	0.7	82.0	18.0	14.6	3.4
Virginia	5,368,334	8,001,024	1.3	79.5	20.5	12.2	10.2
Washington	4,154,678	6,724,540	1.6	79.2	20.8	12.3	12.1
West Virginia	1,951,349	1,852,994	–0.2	81.6	18.4	16.0	1.2
Wisconsin	4,712,045	5,686,986	0.6	79.2	20.8	13.7	4.5
Wyoming	474,185	563,626	0.6	78.6	21.4	12.4	2.9
United States	227,224,719	308,745,538	1.0	78.8	21.2	13.0	12.5

Sources: Foreign-born population from Pew Hispanic Center analysis of 2009 American Community Survey. Other data from the 2010 U.S. Census.

of New York, New Jersey, and Nevada are foreign born. At the other extreme, the Dakotas, Mississippi, Montana, and West Virginia have attracted relatively few global migrants compared to the U.S. average of one person in eight.

Table 1.2 shows that U.S. *employment* grew slightly faster than population over the past 30 years, from about 98 million in 1980 to about 137 million, or an annual compounded growth rate of 1.2 percent. If the reader were to compare this result to that reported in the previous edition of this chapter, where we examined the three decades from 1969 to 2000, she would find employment grew at about 2 percent per year, a much stronger performance. The Great Recession and its aftermath is an obvious candidate explanation, but they only explain part of the difference. During the 1960s and much of the 1970s, employment grew about twice as fast as population, as the "baby boom" and "baby boomlet" entered the workforce; at the same time, workforce participation by women increased. However, demographic forecasts tell us this pattern is not likely to hold over the next few decades.[5] The rise in female labor force participation has tapered off, and the baby boom is retiring, while the baby "bustlet" is entering the labor force.

Table 1.2 also presents each state's unemployment rate (annual average for 2010), and the ratio of each state's employment to its population in 2009. Nevada, Michigan, and California are among the states with the highest rates of unemployment, as of this writing; the heartland states of Nebraska and the Dakotas have much lower unemployment than average. The employment-to-population ratio varies from 41 percent (Arizona) to 59 percent (North Dakota); Washington, D.C., is, of course, an anomaly. This employment-to-population ratio is in turn a function of the age structure of the population and the labor force–participation rate of those of working age, as well as unemployment. Notice that states with fast rates of employment growth (Table 1.2) are the states with high rates of population growth (Table 1.1). In fact, the correlation between population growth and employment growth is about 0.93, as strong as any correlation one would observe in such economic variables across states. By itself, this correlation begs the question of causality. Regional economists have long studied the question, do people follow jobs or do jobs follow people? The consensus view after many studies is that both effects can be found, but in the long run, the latter dominates.[6] That is, the effect of an increase in population on future job growth is considerably stronger than the effect of an increase in employment on future population growth.

While population and employment are important, in many respects *income per capita* is an even better summary measure of local economic performance, since it is most closely tied to standards of living.[7] As Table 1.3 shows, in 1980, average income per capita was about $23,260 for the United States as a whole in today's (2010) dollars. Over the next 30 years, U.S. per capita income

Table 1.2

State Employment

	Employment 1980	Employment 2009	Annual growth rate of employment 1980–2009 (%)	Employment to population, 2009 (%)	Unemployment rate 2010 (%)
Alabama	1,487,636	1,977,766	1.0	44	9.5
Alaska	202,746	351,831	1.9	50	8.0
Arizona	1,107,461	2,524,861	2.9	41	10.0
Arkansas	831,250	1,225,849	1.3	44	7.9
California	10,929,384	15,210,538	1.1	44	12.4
Colorado	1,363,980	2,368,847	1.9	49	8.9
Connecticut	1,508,221	1,696,168	0.4	50	9.1
Delaware	280,480	430,936	1.5	51	8.5
District of Columbia	660,575	733,140	0.4	122	9.9
Florida	3,958,429	7,632,084	2.3	44	11.5
Georgia	2,377,591	4,093,208	1.9	44	10.2
Hawaii	498,755	668,081	1.0	54	6.6
Idaho	367,501	652,701	2.0	45	9.3
Illinois	4,938,847	5,861,229	0.6	48	10.3
Indiana	2,232,960	2,875,683	0.9	47	10.2
Iowa	1,195,816	1,542,693	0.9	53	6.1
Kansas	1,045,186	1,428,124	1.1	52	7.0
Kentucky	1,317,072	1,867,126	1.2	45	10.5
Louisiana	1,715,928	2,000,884	0.5	45	7.5
Maine	460,760	616,087	1.0	48	7.9
Maryland	1,844,630	2,642,916	1.2	48	7.5
Massachusetts	2,769,905	3,298,196	0.6	52	8.5
Michigan	3,540,522	3,957,809	0.4	43	12.5
Minnesota	1,865,288	2,721,944	1.3	54	7.3
Mississippi	932,016	1,179,553	0.8	42	10.4
Missouri	2,092,464	2,797,365	1.0	49	9.6

(continued)

Table 1.2 *(continued)*

	Employment 1980	Employment 2009	Annual growth rate of employment 1980–2009 (%)	Employment to population, 2009 (%)	Unemployment rate 2010 (%)
Montana	306,230	451,829	1.4	48	7.2
Nebraska	694,005	973,871	1.2	55	4.7
Nevada	433,255	1,186,108	3.5	49	14.9
New Hampshire	409,799	635,669	1.5	50	6.1
New Jersey	3,207,037	3,959,228	0.7	47	9.5
New Mexico	512,147	848,266	1.8	44	8.4
New York	7,594,121	8,738,853	0.5	46	8.6
North Carolina	2,627,601	4,163,274	1.6	47	10.6
North Dakota	268,236	382,212	1.2	59	3.9
Ohio	4,535,314	5,236,647	0.5	48	10.1
Oklahoma	1,239,282	1,623,263	0.9	46	7.1
Oregon	1,101,896	1,705,717	1.5	47	10.8
Pennsylvania	4,948,699	5,806,286	0.6	48	8.7
Rhode Island	430,213	477,866	0.4	47	11.6
South Carolina	1,336,777	1,910,702	1.2	44	11.2
South Dakota	261,353	422,985	1.7	53	4.8
Tennessee	1,880,376	2,729,432	1.3	46	9.7
Texas	6,345,484	10,800,414	1.9	45	8.2
Utah	582,877	1,247,375	2.7	47	7.7
Vermont	216,215	311,208	1.3	52	6.2
Virginia	2,439,263	3,881,348	1.6	51	6.9
Washington	1,786,364	3,053,450	1.9	48	9.6
West Virginia	674,453	737,621	0.3	42	9.1
Wisconsin	2,059,560	2,801,296	1.1	52	8.3
Wyoming	230,040	295,461	0.9	56	7.0
United States	97,646,000	136,736,000	1.2	47	9.6

Sources: Bureau of Economic Analysis, Bureau of Labor Statistics.

grew at about 1.9 percent to $40,584. Broadly speaking, at the rate of growth over this period, per capita incomes would double every 38 years. While we can find periods as long as a decade where average incomes grew faster (e.g. late 1960s to early 1970s) or slower (a decade centered on one of several recessions, or of course the Great Recession of 2007–9 and its aftermath, to say nothing of the Great Depression of the 1930s), an examination of annual real per capita incomes back to 1929 reveals an average growth rate of 1.9 percent, coincidentally the same as our 30-year period in Table 1.3.

Such performance is quite stunning when we think of it this way. Even with the declines associated with the Great Recession, real per capita incomes in 2010 were double those found in 1975, within the lifetimes of many readers. If we start from the approximate date of the earliest, small urban settlements, it took us about 10,000 years to get from (at best) subsistence level living (Sjoberg 1965), to $20,000 per capita circa 1975. Then it took us only 35 years to double that amount!

So far we have focused on average incomes. What about distributional considerations? Despite the impressive performance of the U.S. economy in the aggregate, Tables 1.2 and 1.3 have already demonstrated there is substantial variation in the economic performance of states. At the most disaggregated level, it is well known that all citizens have not shared in these economic gains equally. After adjusting for inflation, income per capita figures within the five income quintiles of the United States over the past four decades show that median household incomes have grown about 0.5 percent per year for those in the bottom half of the U.S. income distribution.[8] On the other hand, those in the top 20 percent saw a real growth of about 1.3 percent per annum over the period.[9] Even within this top quintile, the real action is at the very top, as analysis of Internal Revenue Service (IRS) data by Thomas Piketty and Emmanuel Saez (2003) has shown. According to their analysis, the all-time peak since IRS data became available in 1917 was in 1928, when the top 1 percent accrued 24 percent of personal income. This fraction fell rapidly over two decades, and through the 1950s until the early 1980s was mainly in the 9–11 percent range. After that, the fraction accruing to the top 1 percent began to grow rapidly, peaking again at near 24 percent in 2007.[10]

Although national data show that in the aggregate the distribution of income is worsening over time while the overall economy has been growing, two important points need to be put on the table. First, a world in which the distribution is becoming more unequal because top incomes are growing fast while the poor's incomes are stagnant or growing slowly is unquestionably cause for concern. However, while such a divergence is, in my view, a bad thing, such an outcome is still a better situation than an alternative world, where an equivalent increase in inequality is driven by modest increases in

Table 1.3

State Income

	Per capita income, in constant 2010$ 1980	Per capita income, in constant 2010$ 2010	Annual growth rate of real per capita income 1980–2010 (%)	Share of household income to bottom income quintile 2007	Share of household income to middle income quintile 2007	Share of household income to top income quintile 2007
Alabama	18,037	33,945	2.1	3.2	14.7	50.2
Alaska	34,518	44,174	0.8	4.2	16.4	44.9
Arizona	21,861	34,999	1.6	3.8	15.1	48.7
Arkansas	17,336	33,150	2.2	3.5	14.8	49.7
California	27,495	43,104	1.5	3.4	14.6	50.5
Colorado	24,696	42,802	1.9	3.6	15.2	48.9
Connecticut	28,401	56,001	2.3	3.3	14.3	51.9
Delaware	24,793	39,962	1.6	3.8	15.6	47.3
District of Columbia	28,163	71,044	3.1	2.1	12.5	56.9
Florida	22,868	39,272	1.8	3.7	14.4	50.8
Georgia	19,381	35,490	2.0	3.4	14.8	50.0
Hawaii	26,264	41,021	1.5	3.9	16.1	46.1
Idaho	19,909	32,257	1.6	4.3	15.3	48.1
Illinois	25,309	43,159	1.8	3.4	14.9	50.1
Indiana	21,559	34,943	1.6	4.0	15.8	46.8
Iowa	22,066	38,281	1.9	4.1	15.9	46.6
Kansas	22,910	39,737	1.9	4.0	15.1	48.4
Kentucky	18,701	33,348	1.9	3.3	14.9	49.7
Louisiana	20,208	38,446	2.2	3.0	14.5	50.7
Maine	19,208	37,300	2.2	3.9	15.5	47.8
Maryland	25,734	49,025	2.2	3.7	15.5	48.0
Massachusetts	24,364	51,552	2.5	3.1	15.1	49.9
Michigan	23,721	35,597	1.4	3.6	15.3	48.4

Minnesota	23,578	42,843	2.0	3.9	15.6	47.6
Mississippi	16,147	31,186	2.2	3.2	14.3	51.2
Missouri	21,451	36,979	1.8	3.7	15.2	48.7
Montana	20,833	35,317	1.8	3.8	15.5	48.0
Nebraska	21,103	39,557	2.1	4.1	15.7	46.9
Nevada	26,921	36,997	1.1	4.2	15.2	48.1
New Hampshire	22,626	44,084	2.2	4.3	16.1	45.9
New Jersey	26,914	50,781	2.1	3.3	14.9	49.9
New Mexico	19,203	33,837	1.9	3.4	14.9	49.3
New York	25,321	48,821	2.2	2.9	13.9	53.2
North Carolina	18,862	35,638	2.1	3.4	14.8	50.1
North Dakota	18,196	40,596	2.7	3.8	15.7	47.6
Ohio	23,101	36,395	1.5	3.5	15.4	48.4
Oklahoma	21,868	36,421	1.7	3.5	14.8	49.8
Oregon	23,249	37,095	1.6	3.8	15.4	48.0
Pennsylvania	23,143	41,152	1.9	3.6	14.9	49.6
Rhode Island	22,232	42,579	2.2	3.2	15.4	48.7
South Carolina	17,832	33,163	2.1	3.4	15.0	49.2
South Dakota	18,565	38,865	2.5	4.2	15.8	46.6
Tennessee	18,964	35,307	2.1	3.4	14.7	50.7
Texas	22,751	39,493	1.9	3.3	14.4	50.9
Utah	19,575	32,595	1.7	4.6	16.0	45.7
Vermont	19,821	40,283	2.4	4.1	15.7	46.9
Virginia	23,297	44,762	2.2	3.5	15.0	49.4
Washington	24,918	43,564	1.9	3.8	15.4	48.2
West Virginia	18,593	32,641	1.9	3.5	15.1	48.6
Wisconsin	23,246	38,432	1.7	4.1	15.9	46.8
Wyoming	26,895	47,851	1.9	4.2	15.4	47.7
United States	23,260	40,584	1.9	3.4	14.7	50.3

Sources: Bureau of Economic Analysis, American Community Survey.

income at the high end and falling incomes at the low end. In other words, if the spread is getting wider, we need to know *why*.

Second, the fact that we happen to have increasing income inequality at the same time our economy is growing does not necessarily imply that one of these factors always accompanies the other. In fact, careful studies of U.S. metropolitan areas, including those conducted by Bartik (1994) and by Madden (2000), show that in a broad range of metropolitan areas (with some exceptions), faster economic growth, as usually measured, improves the economic conditions of the poor even more than it does of the rich.

These distributional considerations are of interest first on their own account, because most American citizens care about the well-being of their neighbors. But they also have implications for state and local fiscal conditions. For example, Gyourko (1998) has estimated a city with a poverty rate one percentage point higher than average spends an extra $2.20 per capita on police services after controlling for other determinants of such spending. And, unsurprisingly, poorer localities have weaker tax bases.

Table 1.3 presents three columns of state-specific distributional data, namely the fraction of household income accruing to the bottom income quintile, the middle quintile, and the top quintile, from the 2007 American Community Survey.[11] If income were equally distributed across quintiles, each fraction would be 20 percent. On average, 3.4 percent of U.S. household income accrues to the bottom quintile; 14.7 percent to the middle quintile; and just over half to the top quintile.

Why Do Regions Grow and Develop?

Our work above suggests that the "usual suspects," especially income, are reasonable summary measures of development. But our results also suggest that there is much to be gained from considering several indicators at once when feasible, notably those related explicitly to income distribution and/ or poverty. But ultimately, of course, the most interesting questions involve *how* to grow and develop. That's the focus of the rest of this volume. For manageability, most of the discussion in this book focuses on a range of programs and policies usually within the purview of local officials charged with economic development, and even more particularly on programs affecting how we finance local development. Topics covered include various tax and subsidy mechanisms, among them tax increment financing (TIFs), enterprise and empowerment zones, and various lending instruments including government loan pools and venture capital as well as "traditional" bank lending. But this is a good place to remind ourselves that successful development requires many other things besides finance, like well-functioning schools, a solid infrastructure, and a high-performance public sector. In addition to the financial capital and public incentives that are the focus of this volume, a partial list of the things that matter most in the long run might include:

- physical capital consisting of equipment as well as real estate (Jorgenson 1998);
- infrastructure (Gramlich 1994; Hulten and Schwab 1995);
- human capital, education, and training (Black and Lynch 1996; Psacharopoulos 1994; Hanushek and Kim 1995);
- trade (Hewings et al. 1997; Dollar 1992);
- economies of scale, especially those from well-functioning cities (Glaeser, Kallal, Scheinkman, and Shleifer 1992; Henderson 1988);
- the structure of our local economy, appropriate to our resources, skill set, and market opportunities (O hUallachain 1992);
- environment, climate, and amenities (Kusmin 1994);
- business management (Baily and Blair 1988);
- culture and entrepreneurial spirit (Saxenian 1994); and
- a well-functioning public sector, including cost-effective delivery of essential public services, and appropriate incentives and a balanced regulatory environment (Malpezzi 2001).

However, no single volume can do justice to all these important topics. The focus of this volume is finance, and it is to that subject that we now turn.

The Special Role of Finance in the Economy

Every modern economy has *real assets* and *financial assets*. Let us remind ourselves of the distinctions between these two terms, their similarities, and how the two sides of the economy fit together. *Real assets* (or capital) are the things we use to make other things. They comprise tangible capital (equipment and machinery, infrastructure, and real estate), and human capital.

Financial assets (or capital) assign claims on the output of the tangible and human capital. The assets of a firm include primarily its real estate, other tangible capital-like equipment, and of course its people and the knowledge they embody. The stocks and bonds of a firm allocate the cash flows from the firm's operations (i.e., from its tangible/human capital) as revenues, and these are used to make loan or bond payments and pay dividends. Analogously, on the household side, household assets—including human capital, furniture, clothing, vehicles, owned real estate and the like—produce income. Most income is used to trade for goods and services, although some household capital produces consumption goods (notably housing) directly.

Financial systems comprise many elements. There are banks, bond and other capital markets, markets for trading equity, and so on. In addition to these public markets, there is a wide range of important private markets, from the corner moneylender to venture capitalists and large institutional investors. Why is financial capital important? Is it *only* about claims, i.e., about how the pie is divided up? No, well-functioning financial markets are also directly productive. Consider a world *without* financial intermediation. The investors must *first* defer sufficient consumption from today's output long enough to save the necessary resources *before* making an investment. This implies that investments will come later than they otherwise would. It also implies that investments will be made only if the same people who have the investment idea or opportunity can save sufficiently to finance the investment.

Thus, in a world *with* a well-developed financial system, it is no longer necessary that the same people who are investors be the savers. No longer is it necessary that savers figure out how to invest each dollar of their savings productively. A well-running financial system does it for them and better than they could on their own.

Writing in late 2011, one need hardly mention that when the financial system does not run well—when underwriting and prudent risk management are neglected, when agency problems that bedevil the management of banks and other financial entities are uncontrolled, and when finance becomes the dog rather than the wagging tail of the economy—finance can drag the real economy down rather than play its normal positive role. Chapter 9 of this volume, written by Robin Newberger and Michael Berry, discusses what we've learned about the role of finance in development in light of the circa 2008 financial crisis.

A large literature notes the central role financial intermediation plays in economic development, at least under normal conditions. Much of this literature is international in character, for example, Fry (1988) and the works cited therein. But it certainly matters within a country and across small units as well. Studies such as those by Brito and Mello (1995), Fazzari, Hubbard, and Petersen (1988), Guiso, Sapienza, and Zingales (2004), and Mayer (1990) illustrate the point using a variety of data sources and methodologies.

Sources and Types of Finance

Before we discuss examples of specific development finance mechanisms, it is useful to discuss some general categories briefly. The first important distinction to make is that between *debt* and *equity*. Debt finance is characterized by an investment of a predetermined amount, either a single up-front loan, as with a typical home's first mortgage, or a line of credit that can be drawn down over some specific period of time. Debt is usually repaid according to some fixed schedule, and these payments have priority over payments to equity investors.[12]

Equity investments, on the other hand, are those that have claims on the residual cash flows, after debt has been serviced. Some equity investments are characterized by a more or less regular payment of dividends, but unlike debt, the size of the payments will usually vary with the fortunes of the firm or project, and the total amount paid out may be left to the discretion of the entity's management. In case of default, equity investors will be repaid only after debt claims are paid. Thus, equity is generally riskier than debt, but of course there is a corresponding upside; if a project goes well, debt holders' returns will be limited to their contracted payments, with equity investors sharing the higher returns.

The second major distinction in types of finance is between *public* and *private*. Confusingly, there are two very different ways in which the terms *public* and *private* are used, and they carry different meanings when used by investment professionals on the one hand, and planners and public policy wonks on the other. To an investment professional, public markets are those offering investments that can be bought and sold freely (more or less) on recognized markets. Offerings of public shares are subject to legal requirements that accounts and certain other information about the enterprise be made public. Private markets, on the other hand, are those in which such information is held more closely by the investors and is not in the public domain. Securities traded on recognized exchanges like the NYSE or Nasdaq are well-known examples of public investments in this sense, while family-held firms or investments in projects by institutional investors or wealthy individuals are considered private.

The other way we use the terms *public* and *private* corresponds more closely to common usage, which is the way we organize the chapters in this book. *Public* in this sense refers to activities of government, and *private* to those of individuals and firms. But in today's world, especially in the context of this volume, the public-private distinction is more of a spectrum. Community development corporations, local business, and social groups are among the forms of nongovernmental organizations (NGOs) relevant to local economic development, and many of them could be characterized as not-for-profit. However, it can be argued that NGOs are better characterized by their objective functions than their profit/nonprofit status: The latter is largely an accounting/tax rule decision, while the former captures whether the entity's objective is to maximize some financial surplus (whether or not that surplus is considered "profit" by the IRS) or achieve some broader set of social aims.

These issues suffuse the rest of the volume. Laura Reese and Gary Sands present an overview of the local economic development (LED) toolkit, along with principles for their evaluation. Randy Crane gives a conceptual overview of the public side of LED finance, and Kelly Robinson explains revolving loan funds. Two important categories of local public finance are examined in the chapters written by Matt Brinkley and Patricia Machemer (transferable development rights) and Vicki Elmer (municipal bonds); two more chapters focus on the uses, namely brownfield redevelopment (Chris De Sousa) and the support of entrepreneurs (Ziona Austrian and Eli Auerbach).

On the private side, chapters by Robin Newberger and Michael Berry discuss bank financing. John Freear and Jeffrey Sohl explain the role played by venture capital and "angel" investors, and Henry Renski and Ryan Wallace examine the financing of a wider range of small firms and entrepreneurs.

Many techniques of LED are not readily classified as purely public or purely private. Two widely used techniques that involve both the public and private sectors are tax increment financing (TIF), and development exactions. Rachel Weber describes and evaluates the former; Michael Peddle and Roger Dahlstrom the latter. Two chapters focus on the uses of funds, namely Robert Baade and Victor Matheson's review of the financing of professional sports facilities, and John Mullin and Zeenat Kotval-K's case study of a mill revitalization. The final chapter, by Sam White, reviews the lessons learned across these 15 individual contributions and from his experiences.

Public Interventions in the Local Economic Development Process

To put development finance—especially targeted financial instruments with implicit or explicit public support—into context, we need to briefly discuss the wider range of public interventions that affect development. To encourage or otherwise influence LED (or, for that matter, any activity), governments may avail themselves of one or more of the following policy instruments. First, and most fundamentally, government plays a central role in defining and enforcing *property rights and security*, and in enforcing contracts. This includes but is not limited to government's central role in providing a legal system. Furthermore, a well-functioning local criminal law enforcement system could improve basic safety and security, which could certainly affect the attractiveness of a location to firms and workers. At a different level, state laws that affect the cost of enforcing contracts (e.g., bankruptcy law) could easily affect business activity. By global standards, virtually all locations in the United States provide basic property rights and a broadly similar and reasonably functioning judicial system; these are essential for the development of a good economic development climate. In general, see, for example, Furubotn and Pejovich (1972), Jaffe and Louziotis (1996), and North (1990).

Malpezzi (2000) presents more discussion of these instruments and, more fundamentally, principles to help decide when activities should be undertaken by the public sector (through these instruments), rather than the private sector. Briefly, these rationales include the existence of significant economies of scale, monopoly or other market power by firms, real costs or benefits that are somehow omitted from market prices, and information or coordination failures.

Another important class of intervention is *direct public provision* of a good or service. Many kinds of infrastructure fit this mold. Roads and other transportation systems are classic examples that also have important LED effects. The classic rationale for direct public provision of roads hinges on the economies of scale in their provision and their resultant character as natural local monopolies. Of course, sometimes the line between public and private provision is blurred, as is often the case with major sports stadia (see Chapter 14 by Robert Baade and Victor Matheson).

The third major category of public intervention is *taxation*. One important reason to tax is, of course, to finance expenditures. At the local level, taxes pay for some fraction of local services, though in the United States most local governments also receive significant transfers from higher-level taxing authorities (state and national governments). In addition to the obvious need to tax in order to finance government's activities, taxation also can be used to shape behavior. Consider a simple example: Suppose a developer is considering building a new subdivision, of some standard size and quality, in a particular location. In simple terms, the developer will consider her costs (land, construction costs, on-site infrastructure, marketing costs, and others, including a sufficient level of profit to make the project worthwhile), and compare this to the expected market value of the units. If value equals or exceeds cost, the developer will go ahead. In a competitive market with many developers, costs and values will generally be in line.

But suppose further that other costs of the proposed subdivision are missing from the developer's calculation. For example, suppose the development requires additional off-site infrastructure, or perhaps the development greatly increases local traffic congestion. Alternately, let's say that the particular development is expected to generate more local service costs than it will generate in revenues. Under any or all of these scenarios, if the additional costs are large enough, we could easily obtain a socially undesirable result. Suppose, for example, that private value exceeded the developer's private costs, and she would proceed with the project even if the full social costs (i.e., private costs plus external costs such as off-site infrastructure, congestion, and fiscal costs) exceeded social benefit (private benefit plus external benefit).

How can we avoid building such socially inefficient projects? If local planners have a good idea of the size of these external costs, and a tax were placed on development of approximately that amount, the tax would have the effect of "internalizing the externality," in economists' felicitous phrasing.

Hence, the newly calculated private costs (initial private costs, plus tax) would roughly equal the true social cost of the project. Only projects where value exceeded social cost—efficient projects—would therefore proceed. Impact fees and other development charges are examples of real-world taxes that, if correctly set, can solve these externality problems.

Of course, there are other externalities that can exist on the benefit side. Studies like Green and White (1997) and Haurin, Parcel, and Haurin (2001) have documented the existence of external benefits to housing as well as costs, but of special interest to readers of this volume are the external benefits (and costs) that occur with the development or expansion of particular business establishments. Such developments could also generate external benefits, among them forward and backward linkages in the local economy that, for instance, cultivate local supplier networks. Other potential external benefits might be fiscal in nature (if the proposed project is expected to add more to local tax revenues than it will require in public services), or contribute to a burgeoning economy by attracting a critical mass of workers with particularly desirable skills. External benefits such as these are the classic rationales for the fourth type of public intervention: *subsidies* to establishment openings or relocations. (Note that analytically a subsidy is the same as a tax, except for the fact that a subsidy gives money to someone and a tax takes it away.)

Some such subsidies make the national news, such as Alabama's 1993 subsidy package granted to a new Mercedes assembly plant (with subsidies reported to cost roughly $150,000 per worker), or Chicago's 2001 wooing of Boeing's corporate headquarters (reported to cost roughly $63 million, for a headquarters employing about 500).[13] In fact, proponents of such large and visible subsidies sometimes argue that their very newsworthiness generates another externality—namely, a signal that their locality is "open for business" and has been judged desirable by a discerning world-class corporation with many locational alternatives.

Others, of course, have argued that the signal offered is quite different, that a locality is ready to tax its existing firms and residents to attract a small number of new jobs that might have arrived anyway. These controversies will be revisited in some detail elsewhere in this volume. Here we merely note that the question is, just how large *are* these external benefits, how much do we pay for them, and who ultimately bears the cost? Several chapters address these questions, but see in particular Chapter 2 on evaluation by Reese and Sands, as well as the classic older study by Bartik (1991).

Our fifth major class of public intervention is *regulation*. Often local governments can achieve a given objective through different instruments; and, in particular, governments often have a choice between taxes, regulations, or subsidies. For example, it is readily shown that if we chose to forgo impact fees (taxes) as a way to solve the external costs of the housing development that we posited above, we could reach the same general outcome (number of units built, housing price, level of external costs borne by society) by simply restricting the number of units built. In a similar fashion, we could subsidize a relocating firm by writing them a check, or by reducing their local tax liability, or by granting them an exemption or forbearance from some environmental or labor regulation. Regulation can even be used to forestall competition for early entrants to a market, as in the "fair trade" regulations restricting retail trade, or the (now defunct) early city charters granting local monopolies to favored cable companies.[14] Sometimes targeted finance is used to ameliorate unintended consequences of regulations, such as the costs environmental regulations impose on real estate development (see Chapter 7 by De Sousa).

A distasteful proverb tells us that there is more than one way to skin a cat, and this problem-solving advice generalizes to the various government interventions that can be adapted to deal with externalities and other kinds of market failure. But while taxes, subsidies, regulations, property-rights assignments, and direct public provision can be interchanged under the right conditions, that does not mean they are identical in all respects. Take our previous example: we can, with sufficient information, reach the same level of external costs either with impact fees (taxes) or with growth management regulations. In the former case, consumers ultimately pay the external cost to the developer who in turn pays a tax to the local government treasury; in the latter case, consumers will pay a higher price to developers (since with fewer units on the market, prices will rise) who will then retain the increase as excess profits.[15] Among the pieces in this volume that address how interventions affect a developer's bottom line, see especially Weber's on tax increment financing (Chapter 12), and Peddle and Dahlstrom's on impact fees and other development exactions (Chapter 13).

Each of these major classes of public intervention plays some role in local economic development finance: Without clear assignment of property rights, including rights to claim repayment, and bankruptcy and foreclosure laws to help manage project risks, there would be little finance of any kind. LED finance often incorporates some significant subsidy, implicit if not explicit. And local governments are often, in effect, direct providers of at least some financial backing for development projects.

Specific Sources of Finances for Local Economic Development: Two Examples

Armed with the general concepts above, next we proceed to describe and categorize several kinds of LED finance commonly used in the United States.

As will become clear, most LED finance techniques are hybrids, not always fitting neatly into the debt/equity or public/private boxes. And once again, we will greatly simplify our discussion of these techniques; more detailed explanations can be found in the chapters on specific techniques elsewhere in this volume. In this chapter, we will briefly discuss two of the most widely discussed mechanisms, *Enterprise/Empowerment Zones*, and *tax increment financing*.

Example 1: Enterprise/Empowerment Zones

Enterprise/Empowerment Zones (EZs) are a complex, highly localized development tool that has been debated and tried in several forms since the early 1980s. While there are certainly earlier precursors to the idea of enterprise zones, this notion of focusing on very small area financing and subsidies has its roots in the United Kingdom, specifically in British policy experiments conducted under the conservative governments and inspired by the writings of the English planner Sir Peter Hall.[16] For reasons that are apparently partly substantive and partly political, in the United States, Republicans tend to put forward specific program proposals under the rubric "Enterprise Zones," while Democrats have more often preferred the term "Empowerment Zones." While there are some substantive differences between the proposals put forward by each party, these differences need not concern us here, and we will simply refer to these programs collectively as EZs.

The basic idea behind an EZ is to select a small area—usually something along the lines of a census tract—and to apply to it a series of localized subsidies, planning initiatives, and other economic development activities. EZs are thus an attempt to respond to an observed, highly localized pattern of economic development—and unfortunately lack of development—discernable in U.S. cities. Not only have central cities tended to fare worse than the suburbs economically in the United States over the past several decades, but even within central cities it is very common to have a more or less vibrant downtown surrounded by some upscale neighborhoods, some doing moderately well, and some deteriorating. The EZ concept is an attempt to focus economic development efforts on the places requiring the most assistance.

The key feature of a typical EZ program, in addition to its attempt to localize its efforts, is its complexity. No two EZ programs are identical, but they generally bring to bear a package of policy changes, including localized finance, tax incentives, regulatory relief, social services, and new infrastructure. For example, the current Empowerment Zone programs begun in 1994 by the U.S. Department of Housing and Urban Development incorporate six major categories of targeted assistance.[17] Title XX Social Service Block

Grants are one integral part of the current EZ program and can be used for education and training, housing, social services, and the like. In addition, these EZs (1) provide employment credits (a tax credit subsidy for the wages of employees drawn from the local area); (2) grant accelerated depreciation of certain business property; and (3) may supply tax-exempt loan financing to subsidize investment in additional commercial real estate. Furthermore, economic development initiative grants can be used for a wide range of local purposes.

The efficacy of EZs is still hotly debated. Carefully evaluating EZs is challenging for a number of reasons, including the most difficult problem usually faced in such program evaluation: knowing what the counterfactual would be—that is, what would happen to this particular localized area in the absence of the program. An EZ that experiences a decline in employment of, say, 10 percent over some period would truly be a success if, in the absence of the program, the observed decline might have reached 25 percent. On the other hand, if the EZ locality grows, it is always tempting to attribute the growth to the EZ itself, though this is difficult to demonstrate rigorously. Another major issue is the difficulty of accurately ascertaining what spillovers, if any, occur in nearby locations: Do EZs simply shuffle economic activity from one locality to another within the larger market? Or are there possibly positive spillovers? Evaluation is complicated even further by the fact that there have been so many different program designs, and also because local implementation varies.[18]

Example 2: Tax Increment Financing

Tax increment financing (TIF) has become increasingly popular as an economic development tool in most U.S. states since the early 1980s. The initial idea behind TIF is a simple one: to use the incremental tax revenue from a revitalized area to finance the infrastructure or other investments that made the revitalization possible; hence the "increment."

Consider a localized "blighted" area—that is, an area where economic activity is low, residents have low incomes, and in particular the value of local real estate (the property tax base) is low. Assume that in the absence of some intervention, this state of affairs would likely continue. The idea behind TIF is to generate finance for infrastructure and possibly other investment in the local area that will not only boost the local economy but also increase the tax base by raising property values. If property values rise due to the provision of, say, new infrastructure, then proponents of TIF argue that it is reasonable to earmark the incremental tax revenues—the revenues generated by the intervention—to finance the intervention.

A basic example will help make this clear (Figure 1.1). Assume for simplicity's sake that tax rates remain identical over some specified period, perhaps a decade. Let us adopt a 30-year overall time horizon and assume our local government has a discount rate of 10 percent. Suppose an area is currently blighted but still has a tax base that generates initial tax revenue of $1 million in property tax revenues every year. Suppose further that if financing were available for provision of improved infrastructure, the tax base would rise steadily at a rate of 3 percent per year.[19] The tax increment financing idea is to earmark this additional revenue to issue bonds; proceeds generated by the sale of the bonds pays for the improvements, and ultimately, the tax increment finances the bond debt. Thus, in a typical TIF district, at least the stylized version, the municipality or other controlling authority issues bonds to be paid off with the increment financing. The general municipal fund and local school districts continue to get the tax revenue as at the initial period ($1 million in our example), but instead of growing with the tax base, this portion of revenue is frozen for the duration of the bonds. The idea is that over the period the bonds are paid off, the schools and general municipal fund are no worse off than before, since their revenues would not have risen in the absence of the TIF financed activity. Furthermore, once the bonds are paid off, the schools and the localities are better off because they are now enjoying the fruits of the higher tax base.

With our assumptions, in the absence of the TIF, revenue rises slowly over time, and is only about $1.3 million per year at the end of 30 years. Under our assumptions with a TIF, revenue grows faster, to almost $2.5 million after 30 years. Thus, municipalities give up some revenue today, in return for the promise of higher revenue in the future. With our particular assumptions—including the municipality's discount rate of 10 percent—the present value of tax receipts is about $11.4 million with no TIF; and the present value of tax receipts with the TIF, after netting out the increment devoted to debt service, is $12.7 million. Thus, in this particular example, the value of the TIF is the $1.3 million difference.

While an extremely ingenious idea in theory, of course, the devil is in the details. For example, what exactly is the counterfactual: would the tax base have risen as slowly as assumed over the period in question in the absence of the TIF financed investment? If we make a change in our example so that no-TIF tax revenues rise by 2.5 percent (closer to the TIF-financed 3 percent), the present value of TIF-enhanced revenues is about $300,000 less than without a TIF. Which areas are to be determined as blighted, or will there be other rationales for the use of TIF financing? Perhaps most important, are the specific investments undertaken with the TIF well-chosen investments of sufficient scale, so that, in fact, the projected increases in tax base are realized?

Figure 1.1 **Stylized Example of TIF Finance**

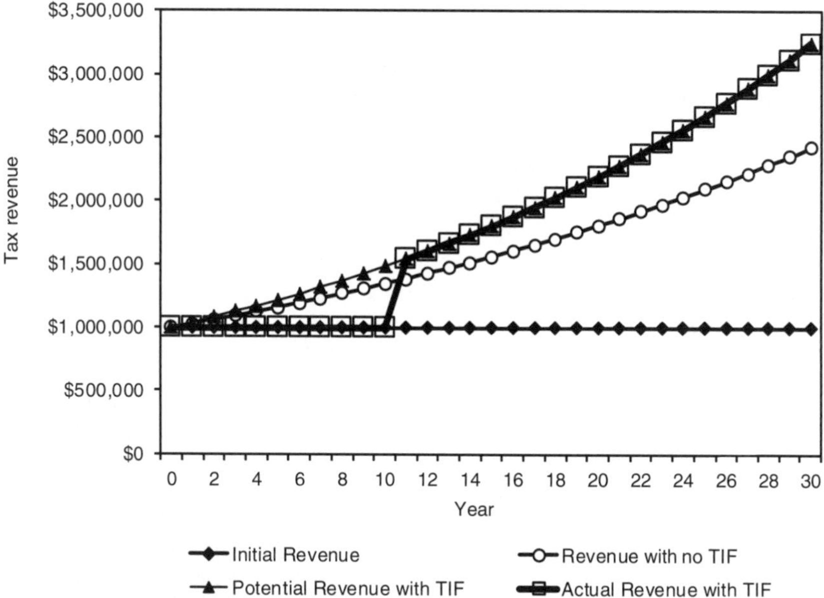

In our simple example, the cash flows from the TIF are sufficient to finance about a $1.3 million bond—hardly a huge investment likely to triple the rate of growth of property prices!

In Chapter 12, by Weber, these issues are investigated in some detail.[20] Here we simply point out that, over time in many states, the eligibility and uses of TIF financing have greatly expanded, often incorporating subsidies to areas that are not blighted. In fact, in some states most TIF financing is undertaken in higher-income locations. Furthermore, the purposes of TIF financing have expanded to include not only basic infrastructure but also other expenditures, including reducing the investment costs of private real estate developers. As TIFs have become more widespread, local school districts and other recipients of property tax funds have begun to take issue with the growth of TIF investments, especially since these local development actors often have little say in whether a TIF is approved, even though they bear part of the cost.

Conclusion

Local economic development is complicated, and it is important. Many elements contribute to an area's development, but little happens without finance. In this chapter we have provided some general discussion of finance and an introduction to two important mechanisms—EZs and TIFs. The following chapters elaborate on these examples but also discuss many other issues, such as venture capital, the role of banks and revolving loan pools, impact fees, and many other approaches to finance and to the public-private partnerships that, if done well, can enhance development. The ultimate objective of this volume is to improve our understanding of some of the special methods by which LED can be strengthened and facilitated.

Notes

1. By an "improved" distribution of income, I mean one in which employment, income, or some other measure of well-being increases as much or more at the bottom end of the distribution as at the top. Such a definition implies a value judgment, but one that I suspect is shared by many readers.

2. The term *generally* is an important qualifier. For example, many students and retired people, among others, are presumably better off not employed, at least for the time being; and many of us have occasionally considered how winning a really big lottery jackpot might ruin our lives.

3. For example, it is possible for one metropolitan area to have an even distribution of income because everyone is poor, while a metro area like Stamford, CT, has little poverty but an unequal distribution of income because of its substantial population of rich households. However, in general, metropolitan areas with a more equal distribution of income tend to have less poverty.

4. Data are from the Bureau of Economic Analysis (BEA) of the U.S. Department of Commerce. Population is self-evident; employment includes public and private, and full and part-time. Per capita incomes are in constant year 2010 dollars, adjusted using the GDP price deflator.

5. These employment figures include both full-time and part-time employment, and another broad pattern from this period was an increase in part-time employment. See the BEA website at www.bea.gov, and see Kruse and Blasi (2000).

6. See Steinnes (1977), Thurston and Yezer (1994), and Mills and Lubuele (1995).

7. Of course, some income is derived from transfers outside the state, not least of which are government transfer payments such as Social Security. Many alternative statistics of income, broadly construed, are available. For example, we could examine GDP per capita, median family income, median household income, or average/median wages. Each measure has its pros and cons. One key advantage of our current measure is that these BEA data are available on a consistent basis for about 80 years for the United States as a whole and for the states, and about 40 years for metro areas and for counties. Also, per capita measures roughly abstract from changes in family/household composition over the period. The flip side is that our measure does not pick up changes in well-being from economies of scale in producing welfare from households of different size and composition (e.g. two one-person households making $20,000 each are equivalent to a two-person household with a total income of $40,000 using our per capita measure; however, the two-person household is probably better off due to economies of scale).

8. See Malpezzi (2011) and especially annual reports on income and poverty

by the U.S. Census Bureau (most recently DeNavas-Walt, Proctor, and Smith 2010) for data and additional discussion. Of course, the set of individuals comprising the bottom 20 percent, or any other quintile, changes from year to year. While there is a well-known "folk theorem" that the United States has one of the more dynamic income distributions in the world, recent research has challenged this assertion; see, for example, Isaacs, Sawhill, and Haskins (2008).

9. Note that the household income growth discussed in these distribution statistics is usually somewhat lower than per capita income growth in Table 1.3, since over time typical household sizes are shrinking.

10. Piketty and Saez (2003) is the canonical reference; they update their data as the IRS releases new information, see http://elsa.berkeley.edu/~saez/.

11. Obviously we've omitted two quintiles to save space; they are readily available at the U.S. Census website or from the author.

12. There are, in turn, often clearly defined priorities for the repayment of different classes of debt. For example, consider the familiar home mortgage. In case of default, the first mortgage must be repaid entirely before claims are paid on second mortgages or equity lines of credit.

13. Details of these and other incentives payments can be found in various issues of *Site Selection*, or at their website, www.siteselection.com/ssinsider/incentive/.

14. In this industry, economies of scale have turned out to be a sufficient natural guarantor of monopoly. Most existing cable companies retain their monopoly position without such sole-source agreements.

15. See Landis (1986) and Malpezzi (1996).

16. See Hall (1981) and Butler (1981).

17. See Hebert et al. (2001).

18. See Busso and Kline (2008), Elvery (2009), Ham, Swenson, Imrohoroglu, and Song (2011), and Neumark and Kolko (2010).

19. In reality, growth rates of revenue may well vary over time. We've assumed two different, constant rates for simplicity. Other, more realistic assumptions could be readily incorporated into our calculations.

20. See also Byrne (2010), Merriman, Skidmore, and Kashian (2011), Smith (2006, 2009), and Weber, Bhatta, and Merriman (2003, 2007).

References

Baily, Martin Neil, and Margaret M. Blair. 1988. Productivity and American management. In *American Living Standards: Threats and Challenges*, ed. Robert E. Litan, Robert Z. Lawrence, and Charles L. Schultze, 178–214. Washington, DC: The Brookings Institution.

Bartik, Timothy J. 1991. *Who Benefits from State and Local Economic Development Policies?* Kalamazoo, MI: W.E. Upjohn Institute for Employment Research.

———. 1994. The effects of metropolitan job growth on the size distribution of family income. *Journal of Regional Science* 34(4): 483–501.

Black, Sandra, and Lisa Lynch. 1996. Human capital investments and productivity. *American Economic Review* 86 (May): 263–8.

Brito, Paulo, and Antonio S. Mello. 1995. Financial constraints and firm post-entry performance. *International Journal of Industrial Organization* 13: 543–65.

Busso, Matias, and Patrick Kline. 2008. *Do Local Economic Development Programs Work? Evidence from the Federal Empowerment Zone Program*. Cowles Foundation Discussion Paper No. 1638, February.

Butler, Stuart. 1981. *Enterprise Zones: Pioneering in the Inner City*. Washington, DC: The Heritage Foundation.

Byrne, Paul F. 2010. Does tax increment financing deliver on its promise of jobs? The impact of tax increment financing on municipal employment growth. *Economic Development Quarterly* 24(1): 13–22.

DeNavas-Walt, C., B.D. Proctor, and J.C. Smith. 2010. *Income, Poverty, and Health Insurance Coverage in the United States: 2009*. U.S. Census Bureau, P60–238, September.

Dollar, David. 1992. Outward-oriented developing economies really do grow more rapidly: Evidence from 95 LDCs, 1976–85. *Economic Development and Cultural Change* 40(3): 523–44.

Elvery, J.A. 2009. The impact of enterprise zones on resident employment. *Economic Development Quarterly* 23(1): 44–59.

Fazzari, Steven M., R. Glenn Hubbard, and Bruce C. Petersen. 1988. *Financing Constraints and Corporate Investment*. Brookings Papers on Economic Activity, no. 1: 141–206.

Fry, Maxwell. 1988. *Money, Interest, and Banking in Economic Development*. Baltimore, MD: Johns Hopkins University Press.

Furubotn, Eirik G., and Svetozar Pejovich. 1972. Property rights and economic theory: A survey of recent literature. *Journal of Economic Literature* 10(4): 1137–62.

Glaeser, Edward L., Hedi D. Kallal, Jose A. Scheinkman, and Andrei Shleifer. 1992. Growth in cities. *Journal of Political Economy* 100(6): 1126–52.

Glaeser, Edward L., Jose A. Scheinkman, and Andrei Shleifer. 1995. Economic growth in a cross section of cities. *Journal of Monetary Economics* 36(1): 117–43.

Gramlich, Edward M. 1994. Infrastructure investment: A review. *Journal of Economic Literature* 32(3): 1176–96.

Green, Richard K., and Michelle J. White. 1997. Measuring the benefits of homeowning: Effects on children. *Journal of Urban Economics* 41: 441–61.

Guiso, Luigi, Paola Sapienza, and Luigi Zingales. 2004. Does local financial development matter? *Quarterly Journal of Economics* 119(3): 929–69.

Gyourko, Joseph. 1998. Regionalism: The feasible options. *Wharton Real Estate Review* 11(2): 7–14.

Ham, J.C., C. Swenson, A. Imrohoroglu, and H. Song. 2011. Government programs can improve local labor markets: Evidence from state enterprise zones, federal empowerment zones, and federal enterprise communities. *Journal of Public Economics* 95(7–8): 779–97.

Hall, Peter. 1981. *The Enterprise Zone Concept: British Origins, American Adaptations*. Working Paper, Institute of Urban and Regional Development, University of California, Berkeley.

Hanushek, Eric A., and Dongwook Kim. 1995. *Schooling, Labor Force Quality, and Economic Growth*. NBER Working Paper No. 5399, December.

Haurin, Donald R., Toby L. Parcel, and R. Jean Haurin. 2001. *The Impact of Home Ownership on Child Outcomes*. Low Income Homeownership Working Paper Series, Joint Center for Housing Studies, Harvard University, Cambridge, MA, October.

Hebert, Scott, Avis Vidal, Greg Mills, Franklin James, and Debbie Gruenstein. 2001. *Interim Assessment of the Empowerment Zones and Enterprise Communities*

(EZ/EC) Program: A Progress Report. Washington, DC: U.S. Department of Housing and Urban Development.

Henderson, J. Vernon. 1988. *Urban Development: Theory, Fact, and Illusion.* New York: Oxford University Press, 1988.

Hewings, Geoffrey J.D., Philip R. Israilevich, Yasuhide Okuyama, Darla K. Anderson, Graham R. Schindler, Matthew Foulkes, and Michael Sonis. 1997. *Returns to Scope, Returns to Trade, and the Structure of Spatial Interaction in the U.S. Midwest.* University of Illinois Regional Economics Applications Laboratory Discussion Paper, October.

Hulten, Charles R., and Robert M. Schwab. 1995. Infrastructure and the economy. In *Readings in Public Policy*, ed. J.M. Pogodzinski. Cambridge, MA: Blackwell.

Isaacs, J.B., I.V. Sawhill, and R. Haskins. 2008. *Getting Ahead or Losing Ground: Economic Mobility in America.* Washington, DC: The Brookings Institution.

Jaffe, Austin J., and Demetrios Louziotis, Jr. 1996. Property rights and economic efficiency: A survey of institutional factors. *Journal of Real Estate Literature* 4(2): 137–59.

Jorgenson, Dale W. 1998. Investment and growth. In *Econometrics and Economic Theory in the 20th Century,* ed. S. Strøm, 234–37. Cambridge, UK: Cambridge University Press.

Kruse, Douglas, and Joseph Blasi. 2000. The new employee-employer relationship. In David T. Ellwood et al., *A Working Nation: Workers, Work and Government in the New Economy*, 42–91. New York: Russell Sage Foundation.

Kusmin, Lorin. 1994. *Factors Associated with the Growth of Local and Regional Economies: A Review of Selected Empirical Literature.* Washington, DC: U.S. Department of Agriculture, Economic Research Service.

Landis, John. 1986. Land regulation and the price of new housing: Lessons from three California cities. *Journal of the American Institute of Planners* 52: 9–21.

Madden, Janice F. 2000. *Changes in Income Inequality Within U.S. Metropolitan Areas.* Kalamazoo, MI: W.E. Upjohn Institute for Employment Research.

Malpezzi, Stephen. 1996. Housing prices, externalities, and regulation in U.S. metropolitan areas. *Journal of Housing Research* 7(2): 209–41.

———. 2000. *What Should State and Local Governments Do? A Few Principles.* Working Paper, Center for Urban Land Economics Research, University of Wisconsin, Madison, July.

———. 2001. *What Do We Know About Economic Development? What Does It Mean for State and Local Governments?* Processed.

———. 2002. *What Is Economic Development?* Working Paper, Center for Urban Land Economics Research, University of Wisconsin, Madison.

———. 2011. *A Primer on Real Estate and the Aggregate Economy, Part 1: Know Your Macro Indicators.* James A. Graaskamp Center for Real Estate, Wisconsin School of Business, University of Wisconsin, Madison.

Mayer, Colin. 1990. Financial systems, corporate finance, and economic development. In *Asymmetric Information, Corporate Finance, and Investment*, ed. R. Glenn Hubbard, 307–332. Chicago: University of Chicago.

Merriman, D.F., M.L. Skidmore, and R.D. Kashian. 2011. Do tax increment finance districts stimulate growth in real estate values? *Real Estate Economics* 39(2): 221–50.

Mills, Edwin S., and Luan Sende Lubuele. 1995. Projecting growth of metropolitan areas. *Journal of Urban Economics* 37(3): 344–60.

Neumark, David, and Jed Kolko. 2010. Do California's enterprise zones create jobs? *Journal of Urban Economics* 68(1): 1–19.

North, Douglass C. 1990. *Institutions, Institutional Change and Economic Performance.* New York: Cambridge University Press.

O hUallachain, Breandan. 1992. Economic structure and growth of metropolitan areas. In *Sources of Metropolitan Growth,* ed. Edwin S. Mills and John F. McDonald. New Brunswick, NJ: Center for Urban Policy Research.

Piketty, Thomas, and Emmanuel Saez. 2003. Income inequality in the United States, 1913–1998. *Quarterly Journal of Economics* 118(1): 1–39.

Psacharopoulos, George. 1994. Returns to investment in education: A global update. *World Development* 22(9): 1325–43.

Saxenian, AnnaLee. 1994. *Regional Advantage: Culture and Competition in Silicon Valley and Route 128.* Cambridge, MA: Harvard University Press.

Sjoberg, G. 1965. The origin and evolution of cities. *Scientific American* 213(3): 55–63.

Smith, Brent C. 2006. The impact of tax increment finance districts on localized real estate: Evidence from Chicago's multifamily markets. *Journal of Housing Economics* 15(1): 21–37.

———. 2009. If you promise to build it, will they come? The interaction between local economic development policy and the real estate market: Evidence from tax increment finance districts. *Real Estate Economics* 37(2): 209–34.

Steinnes, Donald. 1977. Causality and intraurban location. *Journal of Urban Economics* 4(1): 69–79.

Thurston, Lawrence, and Anthony M.J. Yezer. 1994. Causality in the suburbanization of population and employment. *Journal of Urban Economics* 35(1): 105–18.

Weber, R., S.D. Bhatta, and D. Merriman. 2003. Does tax increment financing raise urban industrial property values? *Urban Studies* 40(10): 2001–21.

———. 2007. Spillovers from tax increment financing districts: Implications for housing price appreciation. *Regional Science and Urban Economics* 37(2): 259–81.

2

Evaluation of Economic Development Finance Tools

Laura A. Reese and Gary Sands

The use of economic development strategies, tools, and incentives by state and local governments has a long history. Theories of what causes economic growth have changed over time, as have attendant public policies to encourage it. Several general observations can be made about the field of development policy as a whole; these serve as the frame for this chapter. First, absent a uniform and robust understanding of the dynamics of local growth, economic development policies have largely been driven by fads and fashions as policymakers emulate strategies employed in other communities. Second, a general absence of analysis and evaluation, both before and after the application of economic development tools, has served to trap local officials into these fads because they lack information about which policies should be pursued and which should be stopped or forgone entirely. Third, every state and municipality is different, and there is no one best way to stimulate growth that applies to every case, so reliance on the popular policies of the day and lack of evaluation combine to almost guarantee that economic development tools are not effectively applied to specific local goals and conditions. The result of all of these factors is often a scattershot approach to growth that benefits a handful of recipients at high cost to local communities.

The first section of this chapter considers theoretical concepts, summarizes trends in the last 60 years of development history, and discusses recent policy fads. The next section covers the setting of goals and strategies. We then provide a conceptual framework for assessing specific strategies, and the final section discusses evaluation and assessment methodologies. This organizational structure leads readers from theories to goal setting and only then on to policies. Evaluation is the final step in the policy process that should then feed into future policy decision making.

Theoretical Concepts, Development Trends, and Fads

In many communities, the implicit goal of economic development is growth—more jobs, greater tax base, or higher income. In others, the focus is on preventing deterioration of current economic conditions—preservation of existing jobs and tax base are the primary measures of success. But numbers of jobs created or preserved is not a sufficient indicator of success (Beauregard 1999). More questions must be asked: Are the jobs resulting from economic development incentives a net gain? Are the jobs good ones? That is, do they pay well, provide benefits, and can they be viewed as permanent? Do they provide employment opportunities accessible to local residents, especially those who are under- or unemployed? Economic development success may also be measured in terms of induced investment, which increases the property tax base for the local government. The amount of investment attracted by development activities is generally easier to measure than job creation, but it too is only part of the story.

Economic development initiatives that attract new firms to the local economy tend to garner the most attention. But retaining a firm rather than letting it go out of business or relocate to a different jurisdiction can be just as important, even when little or no new private investment occurs. Ignoring job retention aspects of economic development can seriously understate the scope and value of results.

Economic development should focus on more than job creation and retention and tax base, however. Just as a community must provide adequate physical infrastructure (e.g., roads, sewers) if it is to have a healthy economy, so too must it provide education, public services, and a safe environment: Indeed, those elements are likely even more critical than infrastructure (Reese 2010). These public goods and services are typically provided to meet basic needs rather than as economic development incentives, yet they contribute to general fiscal health, and their economic development role should not be ignored. While some infrastructure investments and services are targeted economic development strategies, investments in general quality of life, cultural and recreation options, and the public schools also serve as important economic development activities.

Assessment Principles

Perhaps the most useful organizing principles for assessing economic development incentives are the classic economic ones of *effectiveness*, *efficiency*, and *equity*. Effectiveness can be measured in terms of whether incentives actually induce firms to move to a given area and create jobs and investment there.

Efficiency measures the costs and benefits of incentives granted against an alternative set of policies that might be expected to have similar results. The principal equity questions are how incentives affect other firms and taxpayers and what type of impact incentive practices in one jurisdiction have on others. The current era of fiscal stress requires that communities be more strategic in their use of incentives. If it is impossible to accede to every request for incentives, the question becomes, which will be the most effective? Evaluation and analysis of development policies, both prospectively and retrospectively, are necessary to answer questions about the efficiency, effectiveness, and equity of tools, incentives, and investments.

History of Local Economic Development Strategies

Local economic development strategies have moved through three phases in the last half of the twentieth century (Eisinger 1988; Tassonyi 2005). These phases are distinctly cumulative rather than evolutionary; once in place, early tools and strategies continue to be used. Businesses come to expect particular incentives once enough states or cities offer them, and the tool becomes locked in place as a standard part of development packages. This is clearly a case of path dependency, where political and economic forces converge to institutionalize the use of tools once they arise on the scene (Reese 2006).

In the first period, lasting until the mid-1980s, the emphasis of economic development was on attracting or retaining businesses through subsidized infrastructure or direct incentives such as tax abatements. Such strategies reflected intense competition among jurisdictions (cities, states) for investment and jobs, resulting in a "race to the bottom" in terms of the generosity of incentive packages (Burstein and Rolnick 1995). For big-ticket items such as an automobile assembly plant, incentive packages and the public cost per job were often well beyond any reasonable expectation of recovery (*Economist* 2003; Ledebur and Woodward 1990).

The second period, beginning in the middle to late 1980s, introduced a new emphasis on financial, technological, and knowledge infrastructure (Tassonyi 2005). During this period, the emphasis shifted from lower-factor costs and real estate development to the establishment of a flexible and supportive context that would foster capacity building, especially for small- and medium-sized enterprises. Technology transfer from universities and public venture capital funds, along with business incubators and job training, became the touchstones of state economic development strategies (Clarke and Gaile 1992).

Since the turn of the twenty-first century, the emphasis has begun to shift to include human capital and quality-of-life enhancement strategies. A logical extension of the shift from highly targeted bricks-and-mortar strategies to more flexible and enabling approaches, the new conventional wisdom assumes that highly mobile capital and talent will flow to locations that offer the richest amenities and highest quality of life. Desirable locations will attract talented individuals who will either become entrepreneurs (Florida 2002) or attract employers that take advantage of the available talent pool.

Fads and Their Consequences

Before local policymakers can select public policies and authorize expenditures to foster economic development, they must understand what actually leads to growth. Their conception of how an urban economy works will influence their selection of goals and policies to achieve those goals, as well as the data required for evaluation. Traditional theories, such as market theory (government should leave the market to operate on its own, thus obviating the necessity of economic development policy), economic or export base theory (localities should determine what products they can export to bring in external revenue and thus enlarge their local pie), comparative advantage theory (based on uneven factor distribution), urban dynamics (a systems approach to identifying likely economic outcomes), and central-place theory (there is a hierarchy of cities, and those on the lower tiers can only move up with difficulty) have given way to newer models (Blakely and Leigh 2010; Malizia and Feser 1999; Sands and Reese 2007). These include development clusters and, more recently, Florida's creative class—a variation of human resource development theories (Glazer and Grimes 2005). The danger of all of these theories is that, as mentioned earlier, there is no single best way to achieve economic growth, and existing theories are often incomplete, not sufficiently supported by robust evaluative research, limited to particular times or spaces, or simply wrongheaded.

Probably one of the most deleterious effects of these fads is that they often promote so-called silver bullets, policies that sound appealing because they have worked in one or a few cities. Even the most effective strategies may not be replicable everywhere with the same level of success. Silver policy bullets have included festival marketplaces, sports stadiums, aquariums, high-tech industrial parks, tax increment financing (TIF) areas, and now, investment in amenities to lure the creative class. The noise of local officials jumping on the bandwagon has been followed by the silence of abandoned festival markets in cities that lack the tourist base to logically sustain them, empty industrial parks in communities too isolated to logically attract new businesses, aquariums in cities that have no geographic connection to a body of water, TIFs that illogically include extremely healthy business districts, and small municipalities developing artist colonies to attract and house the creative class without providing a real rationale for their locating there. Indeed, attempting economic development policies to make a community "cool" and attractive to the creative class is inherently self-defeating, as only a limited number of cities can actually be "cool," which almost by definition is a transient state.

The ultimate purpose of local development policy is to foster a stable economy that is sustainable over the longer term. *Sustainability* has been used in a variety of ways in the urban literature (and probably has as great an array of definitions as economic development), causing some to argue that it is both overused and misunderstood (Roberts and Cohen 2002). Originally, "sustainable development" focused on the relationship between economic values and social and environmental ones, which were often seen as antithetical (Hawken, Lovins, and Lovins 1999). More recently, however, "sustainable development" has come to include explicit consideration of the social and environmental impacts of economic development and a concomitant effort to engage in planning and policy that maximizes success on all three fronts (Innes and Booher 1999). In short, *sustainable economic development means local and regional economic development policies that build social as well as economic capital, enhance quality of life for communities, do not exacerbate stress on the local environment, and lead to more viable and flexible local economies in the future* (Sands and Reese 2005).

Strategic Decision Making

In many communities, decisions related to economic development are reactive. While local economic developers would probably argue that they are aggressive in pursuing development opportunities, they most often respond to external inquiries from firms shopping for a new location (and incentive package) or the internal threat of a business proposing to relocate or close a local facility. When an opportunity (or crisis) is presented, economic developers package available incentives to secure investment or job opportunities. The value of the incentive over what the firm would actually need to relocate profitably is known as the corporate surplus (Jones and Bachelor 1984) and represents a net transfer of public benefits to the private sector.

Rather than pursuing reactive economic development strategies, offering concessions whether or not they are actually necessary, local governments would be better off employing a three-stage economic development strategy. The first stage is largely a political process of setting goals and objectives for local economic development. The second stage is determining how much the community is willing to invest in economic development programs. The final stage is assessing alternative policies in light of community goals and fiscal realities.

Existing research, discussions with local officials, and a variety of consulting experiences, all indicate that the selection of local economic development policies is often a somewhat ad hoc and inverse process. In other words, policies are selected because they are available, used by other communities, familiar to local officials, seemingly low cost, or, most frequently, because they have been used by the municipality in the past. This leads to a situation where policies drive the economic development enterprise rather than the goals the community desires to achieve. Ideally, in rational decision processes, goals promote the selection of policies. Thus, policymakers need to have a general sense of what drives economic growth, identify the challenges and goals of their particular community, and then assess alternative development policies in light of those goals and a consideration of fiscal resources. In short, policy choice should logically be a connection to community goals.

Based on the results of a national survey[1] of U.S. municipalities conducted in 2002, most communities seem to exhibit a traditional and predicable array of economic development goals, focused primarily on business retention and attraction (Figure 2.1). Downtown development and diversification of the economic base are also high on the list of primary goals. These four goals are seen as at least moderately important by over 89 percent of the responding communities. Neighborhood and small-business development are significant as well, with over 64 percent of officials saying that they were at least moderately important. Growth management, minority business development, and social equity rank further behind, with less than half of the communities indicating that they were at least moderately important goals.

An economic development survey conducted by the International City/County Management Association (ICMA) and published in 2009 asked respondents to indicate what they considered significant barriers to economic development. Responses are shown in Figure 2.2.

Based on these responses, one would logically expect that current economic development policies would address the most commonly indicated barriers to growth: cost and availability of land, lack of capital to start and expand businesses, building stock, the pool of workers, and local infrastructure. In particular, it should be noted that taxes are quite low on the list, with only 19 percent of communities indicating that tax rates are a significant barrier to economic growth. Similarly, only 12 percent of respondents indicate that local permitting processes are a barrier, yet efforts to streamline those processes are among the most common of the development incentives employed. Either these efforts are working well or they are addressing problems that aren't really a concern.

The ICMA survey did not include several barriers or issues that recent research indicates are most strongly related to economic prosperity over the long

Figure 2.1 **Local Development Goals**

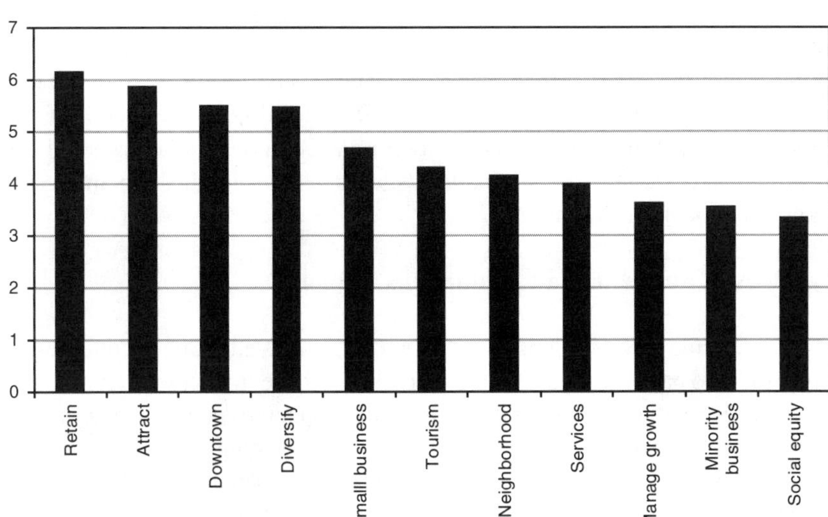

Source: Reese 2002.

Figure 2.2 **Barriers to Local Economic Development**

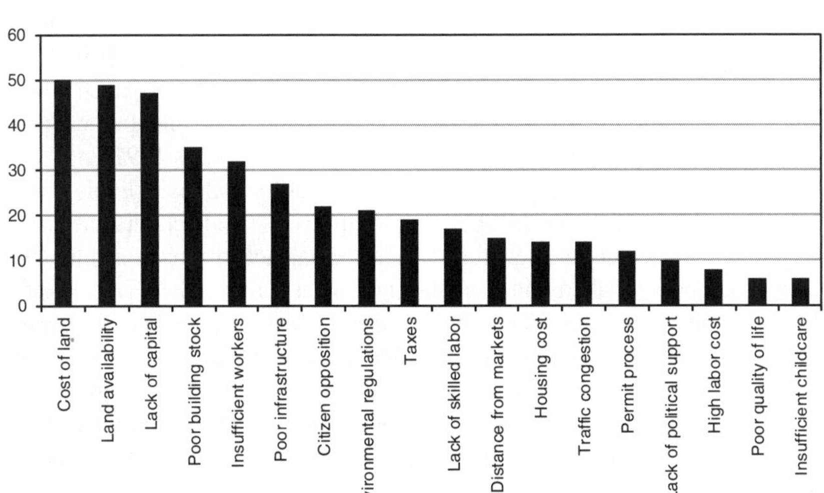

Source: ICMA 2009.

run: public education systems, quality of area universities, and local public services, particularly public safety (Reese 2010). These residential quality-of-life issues are the most strongly and consistently related to economic health in municipalities across the United States and should be considered among the most critical local development goals. Once local goals are identified in light of state-enabling parameters and local revenues, potential policies can be identified and assessed for their likely costs and benefits for different interests and segments of the community.

Typology of Strategies and Evaluations of Tools

Most economic development incentives can be arrayed along a continuum based on who pays for them. At one extreme are those incentives that require the direct expenditure of public funds to achieve specific economic outcomes. At the other extreme are incentives that are self-financing; that is, where the cost burden is borne by the private firm receiving the benefits (see Table 2.1). In between are tools that involve a sharing of costs between the public and private sectors. Economic development policies can also be arrayed along a continuum based on who benefits, with the general citizenry at one end and business interests at the other and most projects falling in between and benefiting some combination of interests. Moreover, there are both indirect costs and indirect benefits to be considered.

Although a detailed quantitative analysis is ideal in theory, in practice the necessary data are extremely difficult to obtain. When an analysis is done, it often includes a mixture of quantitative and qualitative measures. In addition to dollar values for costs and measurable benefits, the analysis will likely include attempts to at least identify the populations that will be affected, even when exact values cannot be assigned to the costs and benefits (Cable, Feiock, and Kim 1993; Clingermayer and Feiock 1990; Sharp and Elkins 1991).

While it is often impossible to attach specific dollar values to likely costs and benefits or to determine the optimal allocation of shared benefits, the exercise of identifying costs and benefits of any potential incentive has considerable value. Local policymakers can think through and assess exactly what costs are likely to be attached to a particular incentive and who is going to bear the greatest direct and indirect burdens. A similar calculus for benefits also helps local officials assess whether a potential policy is relevant for meeting community goals. Because local economic development policymaking is an inherently political process, anticipating likely costs and benefits and the incidence of those realities is not just a financial but a political calculus as well.

The most popular development tools of the decade represented here show significant similarities. Most communities exhibit strong ties between the

Table 2.1

Most Common Incentives over Time

	2009	2004	1999
Used by over 50 percent			
	Partner with chamber Quality of life	Partner with chamber Business calls	Promotional materials Partner with chamber
	Zoning/permitting assistance	Quality of life	Job training
	Online services	Job training	Business calls
	Business calls	CDCs	Online services
	Business surveys		CDCs
	Promotional materials		Infrastructure
	Infrastructure		
	Trade shows		
Used by over 40 percent			
	TIFA	Promotional material	Business surveys
	Partner with local governments	Business surveys	Zoning/permitting assistance
	Affordable housing	Community development loans	Trade shows
	Tax abatements	Business calls	

Source: ICMA.
Note: Activities shown in order of prevalence.

public and private sectors; business leaders are consulted in the policymaking process. Collaboration between local governments and chambers of commerce is a frequent way of engaging business interests in the economic development policy process. Often these linkages are enhanced by the use of business surveys and calls on individual businesses to assess needs among leaders in the private sector. Beyond this, other common activities across time include the delivery of online services and streamlined zoning and permitting processes (two activities that are likely related). Promotional and marketing materials highlighting attributes of the local community are also common.

All of these activities require relatively modest investments of local resources and carry low risks. Consulting local businesses, producing marketing materials, and delivering online services are inexpensive strategies, and generally they benefit a broad array of stakeholders: citizens and business leaders can use online systems, and marketing materials can include attributes of the local housing market, schools, and services while also promoting the municipality as a place for doing business.

There are some important differences over time, however. Consideration of quality of life in the context of economic development was not included on the 1999 survey. Yet, more than 50 percent of communities indicated quality of life as an important attribute of economic development in 2004 and 2009. Two activities prevalent in 1999 and 2004 disappear in 2009: job training and working with community development corporations (CDCs); the latter experienced a particularly precipitous drop.

Not surprisingly, the most common economic development tools increasingly involve business interests rather than residents' interests. By 2009, tax increment financing (TIF) districts and tax abatements had moved up and were among the most commonly used incentives. On the other hand, the provision of affordable housing as an economic development incentive (new to the survey in 2009) was also widely reported, suggesting a growing understanding among policymakers of the ties between a community's economic health and its housing quality. In addition, it appears that more communities are working with each other to pursue economic development and implement development strategies. Partnering with other local governments became more common by 2009, with more than 40 percent of respondents engaging in collaborative activity.

While the foregoing discussion provides a general sense of common policy trends, a more detailed discussion of some representative development policies follows, including discussion of relevant evaluation studies. Examples of a number of different development policy options are organized by the cost incidence spectrum; additional descriptions of economic development policies can be found in Koven and Lyons (2010). By way of summary, Figure 2.3 shows usage patterns for a number of traditional incentives over time.

Strategic Investments

Local governments may make infrastructure investments that have the potential to induce economic development but also have more immediate community benefits. Providing excess capacity in public utilities would fall in this category, as would increases in designated truck route mileage and fiber optic systems. While these investments may result in immediate benefits, having the capacity to accommodate growth can be critical to economic development efforts. Infrastructure investments have relatively high local costs, but they bring with them general community benefits, and these investments represent common local development policies.

Figure 2.3 **Trends in Specific Incentives**

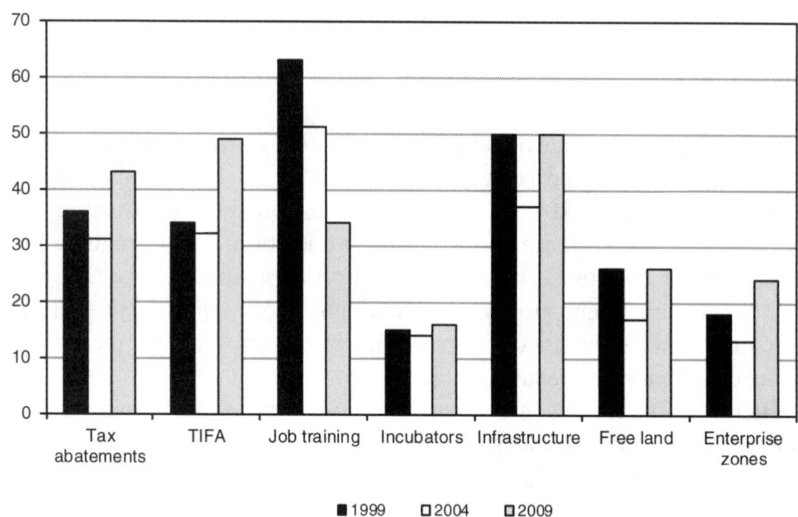

Source: ICMA 2009.

Evaluative studies of infrastructure investment as a driver of economic development have been mixed, largely due to different modeling techniques and levels of analysis. Studies of state-level infrastructure investment have tended to suggest that large projects, particularly those related to highways, do not appear to stimulate growth, partly because highway access is less important to firms over time (Forkenbrock and Foster 1996; Krol 1995). Studies of infrastructure at the county or regional levels, however, have tended to show more positive economic impacts. For example, a number of analyses conducted in the late 1980s and early 1990s pointed to the importance of infrastructure investment in promoting regional economic growth (see, for example, Garcia-Mila and McGuire 1992; Munnell 1990). County-level investment has been shown to have a positive impact, particularly on distressed areas, where infrastructure projects tend to both create and retain jobs (Haughwout 1999). More recent studies of infrastructure investment have focused on the importance of high-technology infrastructure such as broadband access. In general, effects on growth have been positive, particularly in areas close to central cities (Kandilov and Renkow 2010; Kolko 2010). These studies suggest that the economic development effects change over time, with traditional transportation connectivity becoming less important than technology connectivity. It should also be remembered that positive outcomes of infrastructure investment in one community might actually cause negative consequences in others due to increases in traffic and potential shifts in business location (Rietveld 1995).

Public Subsidies

Communities also provide direct subsidies to private firms to reduce costs of operation. Eliminating property and other local taxes falls into this category, as does instituting workforce training programs, on-site infrastructure, and land assembly. All of these can be costly propositions, with funding often dependent on senior levels of government or bonds. Although the assembly of land for development purposes receives a great deal of press, usually relating to the controversial use of eminent domain, the provision of free land for private development is relatively uncommon.

Enterprise Zones (EZs) are a more common public subsidy and are more widespread than other public subsidies at the state level; 39 states had zones as of 2000 (Elvery 2009). EZs are designated districts in which incentives are provided to induce business relocation. Incentives vary but typically include combinations of property and income tax abatements, lenient permitting and regulations, infrastructure improvements, tax credits for job creation, and in some state versions, abatement of property taxes for residents (Peters and Fisher 2002). Much has been written about the effectiveness of EZs (for reviews, see Wilder and Rubin 1996; and Peters and Fisher 2002). Generally, research has suggested that zones tend to (1) move firms around rather than create new enterprises, (2) displace current residents and businesses due to increases in land values, and (3) fall short of creating economic growth commensurate with their inherent tax expenditures. While early assessments tended to find conflicting effects, more recent studies have been consistently less positive. It appears that zones do not create significantly more employment than areas not designated (Greenbaum and Engberg 2000), although firms located in zones may increase employment at a somewhat faster rate (Bondonio and Engberg 2000). In particular, there do not appear to be any significant job benefits for the residents of the zones themselves (Elvery 2009), nor any significant returns either for neighborhoods specifically or for revitalization efforts in general (Lambert and Coomes 2001).

A number of state and local variations on place-based incentive zones have followed the creation of EZs. These have tended to include varying focuses on residents in addition to the traditional business location goals. Research on revitalization zones in Los Angeles found that, even when targeted to more moderately stressed areas, the zones did not stimulate investment (Spencer and Ong 2004). Michigan's Renaissance Zones and Neighborhood Enterprise Zones (NEZs) represent more radical options in terms of forgone revenues

(Sands 2003). Renaissance Zones eliminate virtually all state and local taxes. The exemption from taxes applies to all residents and businesses within the zones that are not delinquent in state and local taxes. The tax benefits apply to both existing and new properties. An early assessment indicated some visible success, although some zones were more successful than others (Sands 2003). While all of the zones reported some development activity, 16 of the 41 subzones had seen little or no private investment in the first three years. The zones appear to have had little effect on statewide revitalization, have had only mixed results in promoting area redevelopment, and have generated virtually no spillover effects.

NEZs reduce property taxes on new residential development (new construction and substantial rehabilitation) for owner occupancy in designated areas of distressed cities. For a period of up to 12 years, the property tax rate is set at half Michigan's statewide average rate. Currently, NEZ-qualified property pays at a rate of about $20 for each $1,000 of assessed valuation. The Homestead NEZ program reduces city and county millage rates by half and exempts improvements from the property tax levy. The city of Detroit, with over 100 NEZs and 16 Homestead NEZs, accounts for most of the statewide NEZ activity. The NEZ program is estimated to cost local governments $19.5 million annually in forgone property tax revenue.

A couple of key issues have been raised concerning NEZs:

- In some communities, NEZ benefits are viewed as something of an entitlement, with no new owner-occupied housing built outside the NEZ.
- The NEZ concept anticipates that public services will improve over time, so that the higher taxes levied on expiration will be viewed as acceptable. If public services do not improve, there may be pressure to extend the life of the NEZ (Sands and Reese 2008).

Shared Costs

Perhaps the best example of a shared-cost incentive program is the granting of partial tax abatement on new investment. A typical cost-sharing arrangement would provide for a 50 percent reduction in property taxes for a fixed period. A recipient firm is still required to pay a portion of the normal tax burden, while the public sector contributes the tax expenditures. The municipality receives some tax revenues in the short run and benefits from the full tax revenues at the end of the abatement period (if the firm is still there). The public investment is justified both by the argument that no revenue would have been received if the abatement had not been granted and by the tax revenues that ultimately will be realized. Often, even the lower tax revenue is sufficient to cover the incremental public costs of serving the new facility (Ladd 1998). Tax abatements and several other common shared-cost programs are assessed in the next sections.

Industrial Property Tax Abatements

Using meta-analysis of tax abatement studies, Peters and Fisher note, "The best case is that incentives work about 10 percent of the time, and are simply a waste of money the other 90 percent" (2004, 32; see also Krugman 1996). More generally, research on property tax abatements has raised concerns that they:

- are only effective at the margins in business location decisions;
- serve to increase the "zero sum" aspect of local development;
- tend to redistribute public-sector revenues to private-sector interests;
- are used primarily by healthy cities that can "afford" to forgo the potential tax revenues;
- tend not to produce jobs and tax base benefits commensurate with the loss of local revenues;
- have not achieved the levels of growth desired and have negative secondary impacts;
- are essentially useless because firms would have remained in place, or even expanded, absent the incentives, thus cities and states "pirate" jobs from each other;
- fail to have an additive impact on overall business activity and have only very short-lived positive effects; and
- are not large enough to counterbalance negative attributes of otherwise high-cost or undesirable locations.

Business Creation

Local government efforts to stimulate the development of new businesses represent another type of shared financing. Lack of capital for the development and expansion of businesses—a common problem for business start-ups—was one of the most common barriers to economic development cited by respondents to the 2009 ICMA survey. Yet, the use of tools that assist in the development of new businesses is relatively modest.

Business incubators have been a well-documented means of local investment in business development (see Augesco 2006; NBIA 2007; and Reese 2008 for reviews of these assessments), but less than one-sixth of the ICMA respondents reported using this tool. Business incubators pair support services and public-sector investment in a facility with entrepreneurial investment in new enterprises. Typically, a small business incubator begins with a facility/building that provides a common location for new firms, offers below-market rents, and includes an array of support services designed to meet the needs of small, start-up firms that are often owned by inexperienced or first-time entrepreneurs. Tangible services may include shared equipment, computing and secretarial services, assistance with business and marketing plans, legal services, joint promotions, and the like. Assistance in gaining start-up capital is also a critical component of incubators. In addition, business owners gain intangible benefits by acting as support systems for each other—and this can turn into tangible benefits in the forms of contracting among incubator tenants. The goal is for new businesses to start in the incubator and then move out when they become too large or stable enough to operate without special benefits.

Research has suggested that incubators have been successful in stabilizing small businesses, generating limited jobs, and increasing sales among incubated firms in return for relatively small investments of public dollars (Sherman and Chappell 1998; Tornatzky et al. 1995). It has been found that the cost per job created for incubated positions is about $6,580, while the cost of other types of firm attraction efforts such as tax abatements range from $11,000 to $50,588 (Markley and McNamara 1995, 277). While evaluations suggest that incubators can indeed be a cost-effective way to increase businesses and jobs, it is also clear that many incubators never graduate a tenant, that many tenants fail once they leave the incubator, and that incubators tend not to be self-sustaining (Fasenfest et al. 2005).

Linkage Programs

Linkage programs or community benefits agreements (CBAs) are other examples of shared-cost programs. Here businesses are offered some type of incentive—tax abatement, infrastructure, or a development agreement—in return for an expenditure or activity by the firm that benefits the larger community or "pays it forward," according to current nomenclature. Linkages or benefits might include, for example, a day care center, job training programs for local residents, provision of a community park, and so on. Assessments of linkage programs indicate that they are successful in generating employment for residents of low-income areas and are particularly effective for racial- and ethnic-minority residents (Molina 1998). Further, such programs do not appear to inhibit developers from locating in the community, as is often feared by local officials; uncertainty is anathema to developers, not local requirements per se (Reese 1998).

Private Financing

Some economic development incentives require little or no public expenditure. The most common example of this is tax increment financing. Once a TIF district has been established, any subsequent growth in aggregate property tax revenues, as a result of new construction or rising values of existing properties, is "captured" by the district and used for investments within the district. The property tax rates are the same within the TIF district as elsewhere in the community; the incentive for being included in the district is that taxes paid result directly in public investments in the district. Firms within the district are likely to have fewer objections to paying property taxes when those taxes are being returned in the form of improved services and infrastructure.

TIF districts can take a number of different forms (Sands, Reese, and Trudeau 2007; Weber 2003). They may provide the basis for bond financing of a specific public improvement, such as a water or sewer line. TIFs also have been used to meet the cost of brownfield site remediation. Downtown development authorities may use revenue from TIF districts for such diverse activities as ongoing operating expenses, infrastructure improvements (e.g., parking decks and street improvements), subsidies to firms, or community events. Virtually all states allow some type of tax increment financing. Michigan law allows half a dozen different types of TIF, the most common of which are for downtown development, local development finance, brownfield redevelopment, and TIF authorities.

TIF is often an attractive option because it allows municipalities to undertake important and costly improvements (particularly when bond financing is required) without levying new taxes. But the use of TIF diverts tax revenues from the general fund to the TIF authority. Thus, there may be substantial opportunity costs. If TIFs capture more than a small amount of total tax base growth, the community will be faced with the choice of reducing services or raising taxes citywide. TIFs are common across the United States, and data from the most recent ICMA survey indicate that the number of municipalities using this financing mechanism has increased significantly over the past five years. The relationship between TIFs and other taxing jurisdictions, such as school or other special districts, is often problematic, raising equity issues as potential revenues are diverted from these entities and from the general revenue fund budget toward what is typically a business district (Weber 2003).

The city of Chicago has made extensive use of TIF districts. About 30 percent of the area of the city (35 percent of total equalized assessed value) is included in some 130 TIF districts. Despite the fact that state law requires a finding of blight for the establishment of a TIF district, most of the downtown loop area is included in a TIF district. In terms of numbers, the majority of Chicago's TIF districts are either mixed use or industrial. Currently, the incremental property tax revenue being generated by the TIF districts is more than $330 million annually. Since most of this tax revenue can be used to fund 23-year municipal revenue bonds, the potential impact in terms of current expenditures is even greater. In many cases, the amount generated exceeds the immediate needs of the TIF district, resulting in accumulating fund balances. Some TIF revenue has been transferred to contiguous TIF districts, bending if not violating the principle that the incremental revenue should be used to benefit the area that produced it.

Studies of TIF districts in Illinois and Missouri suggest that TIFs are subject to abuses through overuse and lack of transparency and accountability (Sands, Reese, and Trudeau 2007). Generally, TIF strategies have raised a number of issues:

- TIF governance can be problematic, if adequate governance structures are not provided or if the district does not provide for a sunset;
- some TIF districts divert funds from other taxing jurisdictions without their consent;
- extensive use of TIF can have a negative impact on the general fund budget (necessitating increases in taxes or reductions in services), while in some cases creating substantial off-budget fund balances; and
- TIF is effective when new development does in fact occur or where property values are increasing (ibid.).

Analyzing the Local Economy and Evaluating Proposals and Outcomes

The current structure and functioning of the local economy establishes the context within which strategies and tools can be applied. As in any planning process, policy consideration must begin with a thorough understanding of the community's current situation before the means of improving it are selected. Analysis of a local economy must recognize that the functional economy is generally not congruent with the boundaries of any one municipality. Consequently, the analysis should include the local labor market, which can be approximated by the larger governmental units (such as counties) or statistical areas such as those defined by the U.S. Census Bureau or state planning agency. In most instances, it is better to adopt a geographic definition that will facilitate data collection.

Within the defined area, a community must assess the availability and current utilization of the basic factors of production: land, labor, and capital. Land (including existing buildings) can be categorized by physical characteristics, by accessibility to road and rail, and by utilities, including telecommunications infrastructure. Similarly, the labor force can be categorized by current employment, age, and skill level. Capital typically draws from a larger market area but is subject to significant market failures.

The issue of geographic incidence of costs and benefits is particularly important for economic development initiatives that involve major investments. A state economic development program that attracts a new oil refinery can create benefits in terms of tax base, jobs, and secure energy supplies that justify the cost to the state. But other costs—for example, pollution, congestion, and potential long-term environmental degradation—may have the greatest impacts on specific localities. Similarly, a local government that undertakes economic development programs to combat a high unemployment rate may incur costs (such as forgone taxes), while the direct benefits of new job creation may go to nonresidents. Analysis at the regional or state level may be positive, but a locality may incur costs that are significantly higher than the benefits received. On the other hand, subsidies or funding from other levels of government (for example, federal community development block grants or highway programs) may substantially lower local costs, making even limited community benefits more attractive. Firms are also likely to consider the level of public services provided as well as their costs (Fisher 1997). If costly economic development incentives result in reduction of critical public services, the net cost to the firm may actually increase as a result of the incentive. Or a general tax increase may be required to maintain services, increasing the burden on the community's other rate payers.

One of the most common tools used to assess the local economy is economic base analysis. Industrial output (measured by employment or value) is divided into export- or local-serving activities. Export industries are given priority because they bring money into the community and support local-serving activities (local retail and service occupations, for example). Export industries are often involved in manufacturing, but may also include services such as higher education or health care. The fortunes of export industries exert a multiplier effect on the economy (see Klosterman 1990).

Shift-share analysis provides a more detailed understanding of the local economy. Not only does it identify leading employment sectors in the local economy, but it also allows comparisons to be made with the regional or national economy or with other firms in the same industry. Frequently, shift-share analysis is used in forecasting local economic trends. Input-output and other econometric models also can be employed to assess impacts of specific changes in the local economy (see, for example, Sands and Reese 2009; Wadley and Smith 2003).

Ideally, a community will have an economic development plan and strategy that can be used to guide decision making. Even when this is not available, other public documents—including the community master plan, capital improvement program, and strategic plan—can help determine whether a proposal is consistent with the community's goals and objectives. Economic development projects that are not consistent may not merit public investment in incentives. The methodology for preparing economic development plans can be found in Blakely and Leigh (2010) or at the website of the U.S. Economic Development Administration, on the page for research and tools (the link titled "Tools of the Trade," www.eda.gov/Research/ToolsOfTrade.xml).

It is also important to evaluate the outcomes of specific development projects and incentives. Most incentives are granted, at least in part, on a speculative basis; that is, there is likely to be some degree of uncertainty with respect to actual investment, employment, and indirect effects on the economy. Evaluating the actual outcomes of the use of incentives will help to ensure that in the future only the most effective are employed (Bartik 2003).

For most communities, there is an expectation that economic development will pay for itself, meaning public investments will attract sufficient private investment to recoup expenses through increased property, income, or sales tax revenues. But many communities are unable to provide an accurate accounting of their expenditures (including tax expenditures) or their return on investment. The seemingly simple and straightforward rule that public investments should be made only when the value of benefits equals or exceeds the costs can in fact be quite difficult to adhere to because measuring costs and benefits can be very tricky. Benefits in particular are difficult to calculate. If the benefit to be derived from, say, granting a property tax abatement is the provision of 100 jobs, what is the value of these jobs to the community? Should they be valued by the wage rate, the taxes generated, direct and indirect (multiplier) expenditures, or perhaps reduction in the unemployment rate? If the new jobs go to nonresidents, should the benefits be calculated differently? If the employment opportunities attract new residents to the community, should the estimated benefits be offset by the costs of providing them with additional services? Research has shown most estimates of investment and job creation to be wildly exaggerated (Sands and Reese 2007).

Even when costs and benefits of economic development measures can be calculated with some precision, numerous other questions remain. Costs and benefits are likely to accrue to different populations in different locations. The issue is not so much whether redistribution occurs but whether the shift is in a desirable direction; this is more a political than a fiscal decision. Moreover, public costs often occur at the beginning of a project, while the benefits are realized over time. Discounting the value of future benefits (and costs) to calculate a net present value provides a better measure of results than simply summing the value of estimated costs and benefits. While the municipality's borrowing costs over the appropriate time period can be used as the discount rate, estimating the timing and value of future benefits is more problematic.

Ultimately, each community must decide for itself the amount of effort it is willing to devote to improving the precision of the estimates of costs and benefits. For large-scale projects, econometric models such as IMPLAN or REMI may be appropriate. For most projects, however, a less rigorous analysis will often suffice. A limit on public investment (or tax expenditure) for each new job can be a useful criterion (Bartik 2003). The boundaries of a new TIF district must be set so as to balance the need to generate required revenues with the need to ensure general fund revenues. New industrial parks or incubator buildings may take longer to show positive results than other projects. In each of these circumstances, ensuring that consideration is given to the project's special factors is at least as important as the quantitative estimates.

Perhaps the best guidance can be derived from evaluation of the outcomes of previously granted incentives. A community should devote at least as much effort to the ex post evaluation of incentives as to their initial assessment. Evaluations should not only identify outcomes but also seek to determine why the projected results were not achieved, if that ends up being the case. Incentives that have had little impact might be discouraged or revised to increase their effectiveness.

Summary

This chapter emphasizes several points about the enterprise of economic development generally and economic development tools and incentives specifically. First, the development policymaking process, although clearly political, should be approached as rationally as possible. This means establishing community goals up front, assessing the nature of the local economy in relation to its surrounding region, and then analyzing the possible array of economic development tools to identify which ones are most likely to meet local goals at acceptable costs given local revenues. Once particular development tools are implemented, post hoc evaluation is necessary to determine, as best as possible given extant data, which incentives have produced desirable outcomes and at what cost to the community.

Evaluations of many common economic development incentives, including tax abatements, TIF, and special development zones, raise significant questions about their continued widespread use. Indeed, recent research following a panel of municipalities over time suggested that the record of local economic development incentives in stimulating growth appears weak (Reese 2010). Financial incentives in particular do not seem to lead to economic growth and actually may make local economies worse. This suggests that local development policies have no effect on economic health at best and are detrimental at worst.

Given this judgment, there seems to be little rationale for continuing to offer many common incentives, particularly those that involve financial benefits for firms and tax losses for municipalities. Since most communities would find forgoing all incentives to be politically impossible, the emphasis should shift to using them more effectively—a task that will require carefully matching anticipated results to clearly articulated community goals and objectives. Clear community objectives are perhaps more important than precisely estimating the dollar value of benefits. It also will require that more effort be devoted to evaluation, in order to identify the relative effectiveness and efficiency of available policies. Finally, officials must be willing to deny incentives in cases where the likely costs exceed expected benefits or when the businesses are not likely to provide jobs that fit with local needs.

What *does* appear to lead to economic growth? Which policies appear to have the greatest promise for achieving sustainable local economies at acceptable costs in terms of forgone revenues or local investment? The answer, based on recent studies, clearly seems to be investments in policies and activities that make the community a better place to live: good local schools, safe streets, parks, libraries, and public buildings and spaces (Reese 2010). These investments have traditionally been the bedrock of local governments. Fads, silver bullets, and efforts to attract particular individuals, be they diverse or creative, are misdirected and can create significant opportunity costs in terms of forgone local revenue. Returning to the basics of good local government—schools, services, and security—appears to promise the greatest return in sustainable economic health. And, if these too prove to be just another fad, the worst that can occur is that the community will, over the long run, be a better place for people to live and for businesses to thrive.

Note

1. More detail on these data is available from the authors. Published research using these data include Reese and Rosenfeld (2012), Reese and Sands (2007), and Reese (2006).

References

Augesco. 2006. Typology of business incubation. www.crupi.biz/augesco/typology.htm (accessed June 22, 2010).

Bartik, T.J. 2003. *Evaluating Local Economic and Employment Development: How to Assess What Works Among Programs and Policies*. Kalamazoo, MI: W.E. Upjohn Institute for Employment Research.

Beauregard, R.A. 1999. The local employment fulcrum: Evaluating local economic performance. *Economic Development Quarterly* 13(l): 23–28.
Blakely, E.J., and N.G. Leigh. 2010. *Planning Local Economic Development*, 4th ed. Thousand Oaks, CA: Sage.
Bondonio, D., and J. Engberg. 2000. Enterprise zones and employment: Evidence from the states' programs. *Regional Science and Urban Economics* 39: 519–49.
Burstein, M.L., and A.J. Rolnick. 1995. Congress should end the bidding war among the states. *Region* 9: 1–13.
Cable, G., R.C. Feiock, and J. Kim. 1993. The consequences of institutionalized access for economic development policymaking in U.S. cities. *Economic Development Quarterly* 7(1): 91–97.
Clarke, S.E., and G.L. Gaile. 1992. The next wave: Postfederal local economic development strategies. *Economic Development Quarterly* 6(2): 187–98.
Clingermayer, J.C., and R.C. Feiock. 1990. The adoption of economic development policies by large cities: A test of economic, interest group, and institutional explanations. *Policy Studies Journal* 18(3): 539–52.
Economist. 2003. The South's imported car factories. November 27.
Eisinger, P.K. 1988. *The Rise of the Entrepreneurial State*. Madison: University of Wisconsin Press.
Elvery, J.A. 2009. The impact of enterprise zones on resident employment: An evaluation of the enterprise zones programs of California and Florida. *Economic Development Quarterly* 23(1): 44–59.
Fasenfest, D., L.A. Reese, R.A. Rosenfeld, and P. Case. 2005. *Evaluation of the Impact of EDA Economic Adjustment Program Investments.* Washington, DC: U.S. Department of Commerce.
Fisher, R.C. 1997. The effects of state and local public services on economic development. *New England Economic Review* (March): 53–67.
Florida, R. 2002. *The Rise of the Creative Class.* New York: Basic Books.
Forkenbrock, D.J., and N.S. Foster. 1996. Highways and business location decisions. *Economic Development Quarterly* 10(3): 239–48.
Garcia-Mila, T., and T. McGuire. 1992. The contribution of publicly provided inputs to state economies. *Regional Science and Urban Economics* 22(2): 229–41.
Glazer, L., and D.R. Grimes. 2005. *A New Path to Prosperity? Manufacturing and Knowledge-Based Industries as Drivers of Economic Growth*. Ann Arbor, MI: Michigan Future.
Greenbaum, R., and J. Engberg. 2000. An evaluation of state enterprise zone policies. *Policy Studies Review* 17(2–3): 30–45.
Haughwout, A.F. 1999. New estimates of the impact of EDA public works program investments on county labor markets. *Economic Development Quarterly* 13(4): 371–82.
Hawken, P., A. Lovins, and L. Lovins. 1999. *Natural Capitalism: Creating the Next Industrial Revolution.* London: Earthscan.
Innes, J.E., and D.E. Booher. 1999. Metropolitan development as a complex system: A new approach to sustainability. *Economic Development Quarterly* 13(2): 141–56.
International City/County Management Association (ICMA). 1988, 1999, 2004, 2009. *Economic Development Surveys*. Washington, DC: ICMA.
Jones, B.D., and L.W. Bachelor. 1984. Local policy discretion and the corporate surplus. In *Urban Economic Development*, ed. Richard Bingham and John Blair, 245–67. Beverly Hills, CA: Sage.

Kandilov, I.T., and M. Renkow. 2010. Infrastructure investment and rural economic development: An evaluation of USDA's broadband loan program. *Growth and Change* 41(2): 165–91.

Klosterman, R.E. 1990. *Community Analysis and Planning Techniques*. Savage, MD: Rowman & Littlefield.

Kolko, J. 2010. *Does Broadband Boost Local Economic Development?* San Francisco: Public Policy Institute of California.

Koven, S.G., and T.S. Lyons. 2010. *Economic Development: Strategies for State and Local Practice*. Washington, DC: ICMA.

Krol, R. 1995. Public infrastructure and state economic development. *Economic Development Quarterly* 9(4): 331–38.

Krugman, P.R. 1996. *Pop Internationalism*. Cambridge, MA: MIT Press.

Ladd, H. 1998. *Local Government Tax and Land Use Policies*. Northampton, MA: Edward Elgar.

Lambert, T.E., and P.A. Coomes. 2001. An evaluation of the effectiveness of Louisville's enterprise zone. *Economic Development Quarterly* 15(2): 168–80.

Ledebur, L.C., and D.P. Woodward. 1990. Adding a stick to the carrot: Location incentives with clawbacks, recisions, and recalibrations. *Economic Development Quarterly* 4(3): 221–37.

Malizia, E.E., and E.J. Feser. 1999. *Understanding Local Economic Development*. New Brunswick, NJ: Center for Urban Policy Research.

Markley, D.M., and K.T. McNamara. 1995. Economic and fiscal impacts of a business incubator. *Economic Development Quarterly* 9(3): 273–78.

Molina, F. 1998. *Making Connections: A Study of Employment Linkage Programs*. Washington, DC: Center for Community Change.

Munnell, A. 1990. How does public infrastructure affect regional economic performance? *New England Economic Review* (September/October): 11–32.

NBIA. 2007. National Business Incubator Association resource library. www.nbia.org/resource_library/ (accessed June 22, 2010).

Peters, A., and P. Fisher. 2002. *State Enterprise Zone Programs: Have They Worked?* Kalamazoo, MI: W.E. Upjohn Institute for Employment Research.

———. 2004. The failures of economic development incentives. *Journal of the American Planning Association* 70(1): 27–37.

Reese, L.A. 1998. Sharing the benefits of economic development: What cities utilize type II policies? *Urban Affairs Review* 33(5): 686–711.

———. 2002. *Survey of Local Economic Development Policies*. East Lansing: Michigan State University Global Urban Studies Program. http://gusp.msu.edu/userdocs/scannedsurve.pdf.

———. 2006. Not just another determinants piece: Alternative hypotheses to explain local tax abatement policy. *Review of Policy Research* 23(2): 491–504.

———. 2008. Small business incubators. In *Municipal Economic Development Toolkit*, ed. S. Loveridge, L. Reese, and D. Nizalov. www.municipaltoolkit.org/ (accessed September 11, 2010).

———. 2010. Creative class or procreative class. Paper presented at the Making Cities Livable Conference, Charleston, SC, October.

Reese, L.A. and R.A. Rosenfeld. 2012. *Comparative Civic Culture*. London: Ashgate.

Reese, L.A., and G. Sands. 2007. Making the least of our differences? Trends in Canadian and U.S. local economic development. *Canadian Public Administration* 50(1): 79–99.

Rietveld, P. 1995. Infrastructure and spatial economic development. *Annals of Regional Science* 29(2): 117–19.

Roberts, B., and M. Cohen. 2002. Enhancing sustainable development by triple value adding to the core business of government. *Economic Development Quarterly* 16(2): 127–37.

Sands, G. 2003. Michigan's Renaissance Zones: Eliminating taxes to attract investment and jobs in distressed communities. *Environment and Planning C: Government and Policy* 21(5): 719–34.

Sands, G., and L.A. Reese. 2005. Sustainability strategies in North American cities. In *Sustainable Development and Planning II*, ed. A.G. Kungolos, C.A. Brebbia, and E. Beriatos, 133–42. Boston: WIT Press.

———. 2006. The equity impacts of municipal tax incentives: Leveling or tilting the playing field? *Review of Policy Research* 23(1): 71–94.

———. 2007. *Public Act 198 Industrial Facilities Tax Abatements.* East Lansing: Michigan State University Land Policy Institute.

———. 2008. Implementing economic development incentives: The case of Grand Rapids, Michigan. In *Building the Local Economy,* ed. D. Watson and J.C. Morris. Atlanta, GA: Carl Vinson Institute of Government.

———. 2009. Michigan's industrial tax abatements: Pyrrhic victories? In *Sustaining Michigan,* ed. R.W. Jelier and G. Sands, 45–62. East Lansing: Michigan State University Press.

Sands, G., L.A. Reese, and K. Trudeau. 2007. Tips for TIFs: Policies for neighborhood tax increment financing districts. *Journal of the Community Development Association* 38(2): 68–86.

Sharp, E., and D. Elkins. 1991. The politics of economic development. *Economic Development Quarterly* 5(2): 126–39.

Sherman, H., and D.S. Chappell. 1998. Methodological challenges in evaluating business incubator outcomes. *Economic Development Quarterly* 12(4): 313–21.

Spencer, J.H., and P. Ong. 2004. An analysis of the Los Angeles revitalization zone: Are place-based investment strategies effective under moderate economic conditions? *Economic Development Quarterly* 18(4): 368–83.

Tassonyi, A.T. 2005. *Local Economic Development: Theory and the Ontario Experience.* ITP Paper No. 0511, Toronto, Ontario, Canada: University of Toronto Rothman School of Management Institute for International Business.

Tornatzky, L., Y. Batts, N. McCrea, M. Lewis, and L. Quittman. 1995. *The Art and Craft of Technology Business Incubation: Best Practices, Strategies, and Tools from 50 Programs*. Athens OH: National Business Incubation Association.

Wadley, D., and P. Smith. 2003. Straightening up shift-share analysis. *Annals of Regional Science* 37(2): 259–61.

Weber, R. 2003. Equity and entrepreneurialism: The impact of tax increment financing on school finance. *Urban Affairs Review* 38(5): 619–44.

Wilder, M.G., and B.M. Rubin. 1996. Rhetoric versus reality: A review of studies on state enterprise zones programs. *Journal of the American Planning Association* 62(4): 473–91.

Part II

Public Finance

3
Public Finance Concepts for Economic Development

Randall Crane

Overview: The Fiscal Implications of Public Regulation

How does money matter for development regulation? Can or should we prepare or compare development plans on fiscal grounds? If so, how?

Clearly, money matters greatly, often playing a central a role in the design, substance, and implementation of both development strategies and associated regulatory practices. The wisdom of this role is a separate issue. One everyday way money dominates economic development is through overt spending and revenue implications for local government budgets. For example, uncomplicated calculations of how land development alternatives rank with respect to associated service demands are often compared to the revenues they are expected to produce. In pure accounting terms, does the project add to or subtract from the municipal bottom line? Although this is only one dimension of how a given project will contribute to or detract from the community's quality of life, it is nonetheless a customary basis for favoring commercial over residential development, and it is often implemented as part of broader "fiscalization of land use" strategies that explicitly frame land-use regulation as a net revenue-enhancing process (Altshuler and Gómez-Ibáñez 1993; Misczynski 1986).

The underlying appeal of this approach to land-use regulation is plain. On a simple level, residential development looks and feels service intensive and thus relatively costly (via the associated demand for schools, parks, and so on), while commercial land uses often appear to generate substantially more revenue per acre—especially such uses as big-box retail and car sales. While some balance is usually considered necessary for additional reasons, city hall debates over alternative proposals for individual sites often turn on these projected public finance impacts, especially when local budgets are under severe pressure.

And yet this strategy has at least two major problems in practice. One, these calculations of spending and revenue impacts are more complicated than usually described. Many analyses of the net fiscal impacts of different land types employ assumptions that, while convenient, are significantly oversimplified and largely ungrounded in actual experience.

Perhaps more seriously, this calculus is only partial; it ignores any number of additional costs and benefits that matter greatly, even if they do not always appear on the local budget balance sheet. For example, elementary fiscal impact calculations do not normally reflect the expected actual *incidence* of taxes, spending, or regulatory burdens—or their associated equity implications. Moreover, they rarely if ever show the *efficiency* costs of various behavioral distortions, such as those brought about by tax, spending, or regulatory policies that unintentionally change behaviors. Neither do budgets show the value of services rendered, especially where these involve providing so-called *public goods* or correcting *externalities*.

All these additional fiscal impacts matter, often substantially, and yet they may not typically be well understood by the regulators who bring them about. This chapter is mainly aimed at addressing that knowledge gap by explaining the concepts in italics in the previous paragraph and their relevance to regulation.

To do so, we profile the public economics of economic development regulation; that is, how spending, revenues, and regulation affect the private economy and general welfare for economic development.

This information is presented in five sections: The economic rationale for economic development regulation, discussions of the fiscal effects of public expenditures, revenues, and regulations, and a closing assessment.

Why? The Public Purpose of Regulation

To understand how public regulation both helps and hurts private economic activity, it is first necessary to explain what we mean by "help" and "hurt." First, let us establish two reference points: what private markets do well, and what they fail to do well. This turns out to provide a fundamental rationale for why we engage in public-sector intervention at all. Although on the surface public regulation often appears to interfere with the economy, a more accurate description is that it is designed to permit private markets to function *better*.

We separate the primary question into two parts: Why have local government at all, and what are the purposes of regulation in those governments?

The Merits of the Private Economy

The most familiar story of what private market economies do well is often called "the invisible hand" theorem, after Adam Smith (1776/2003), but a better name would be "the invisible regulator" theorem. Loosely speaking, it says that an economy of self-serving, uncoordinated, individual buyers and sellers does just as well as an all-knowing central regulator would in determining which goods to make, how much they should cost to make, and then how much they should sell for. Since real regulators know considerably less than all, this is an incredibly fortuitous outcome and a powerful argument for relying on markets rather than public regulators to perform economic functions.

To lay out this argument quickly, we use a highly stylized version of how markets operate—a version close enough to get the key insights across without simplifying so much as to be irrelevant.

This is a story of supply and demand. On the supply side, firms compete against each other for business, bidding prices down to get sales until only the most efficient firms survive to sell only those goods their customers value at those prices. The key requirement here is competition, which leads to low production costs. On the demand side, individuals also compete, in this case against each other to purchase goods, bidding prices right up to the most they are willing to pay, but no more. Here, competition leads to prices that reflect the maximum value of those goods to buyers. Together, supply and demand competition leads to prices that equal both minimum producer costs and maximum consumer value.

As if guided by a really good invisible regulator, goods end up allocated to those who value them most, at the lowest feasible cost. Moreover, firms produce those goods that people value most. If prices are too high relative to demand, firms will accumulate inventory and bid prices down. If prices are too low, there will be shortages and consumers will bid prices up, stimulating producers to produce more. At the so-called market price, therefore, the amount sold is equal to both the amount produced and the amount demanded. It is also equal to both the minimum cost of producing the good and the maximum value to buyers. Goods cannot be made cheaper without firms going out of business. They cannot be priced any higher without going unsold, or any lower without leading to shortages. In this sense, the market outcome is said to be "efficient."[1]

An all-knowing regulator can do no better in this instance. A mortal regulator could indeed do much worse. The key implication of this set of arguments for markets is that you mess with well-functioning markets at your own peril. In many important respects, they do what they do extremely efficiently and are normally self-correcting if left to their own devices. Naive interventions will result in shortages, surpluses, or worse.

This is a potent result. It is also somewhat fanciful in that it requires a good number of critical conditions in order to hold. When any one of these is violated, as they commonly are, the result can be much less neat. Indeed, we say in such cases that the market "fails," by which we mean that it fails to be efficient. (The flip side of this is identifying the conditions required for governments to "not fail," and the implications of those conditions not holding, as in Wolf [1988].)

Moreover, there are many potential sources of market failure. These include a lack of competition (e.g., monopolies), or information problems, or a trilogy of concepts that provide the primary economic rationale for local government and public regulation: *public goods, externalities,* and *equity* concerns. When any of these are present, markets can typically be made efficient only via nonmarket interventions, which is to say, by governments. These are defined and explained in turn below.

Cause of Market Failure: Public Goods

Public goods are things that people value and desire to buy at a store, but which have certain problematic technical properties that tend to keep them out of stores. Before listing those properties, it is worth emphasizing that the word *public* here does not suggest in any respect that such goods are or must be provided by the government. It is no more than a label, used for historical convention, that may suggest, but does not require, government provision. The nature of the good does often mean its provision must involve some group or collective decision making; hence, public goods are sometimes called *collective goods* for the same reason.

Definitions

The two main problematic properties of public goods are usually called *nonrivalness* and *nonexclusiveness.* The problem with nonrival goods is that they can be shared easily—and perhaps even costlessly. Examples would be an empty highway, an empty park, or a housing or zoning code that maintains certain standards for the community as a whole. Once the good or service is available to any one person, the same amount (or nearly so) is also available to others.

This might sound like a good thing. In many respects it is, but private competitive markets choke on such commodities because it is hard to make money from them. Say you make this kind of thing and sell one. If it can be shared, and it is (see next paragraph), why would anyone buy another? Seeing the writing on the wall, private firms will instead go into another line of business.

An often related but distinct property includes goods that you can't keep people from gaining access to or use of. These are called *nonexcludable* because you can't prevent anyone from consuming that good. An example would be unscrambled radio waves or the benefits of living in an area with low crime rates. Once you've lowered the crime rate, or cleaned up the air, or sent out the radio wave, everyone nearby has access.

Note that, as shown in Table 3.1, some nonrival goods are *excludable*. The technical term for these is *club* goods, which makes sense since these are goods that can be both shared and restricted, as in a private club (Buchanan 1965). You can put a fence around a pool or a golf course, or require a certain test score for eligibility, and so on.

Also, some nonexcludable goods are *rival*: these are sometimes called *commons* goods. As in the famous "tragedy of the commons," they can be used up, but are often open to many users or consumers (Hardin 1968). Even free parks or wide-open pastures can eventually get crowded. Since they are nonexcludable, and users may not see the cumulative effect of that use, such commons (such as shared pasture land) are often overused, which is why the "tragedy of the commons" is sometimes considered a primary threat to environmental conservation.

There are few, if any, examples of purely nonrival or nonexcludable goods, but many examples of goods that have some degree of either or both. (Impurely nonrival goods are said to be "congestible." Impurely nonexcludable goods are "partially excludable.")

Problems for the Private Sector

Either characteristic of public goods might cause the private sector huge headaches when trying to supply the good. How do you sell a nonrival good, such as clean air? Once available, everyone can use it, so it isn't as though the next person comes along and says, "I'll take one of those also, please. How much?" And if the good is nonexcludable to boot, you can't even keep them from consuming it. Without the ability to control or monitor use or access, tracking and enforcing sales are real problems. So who and how would you charge to cover costs and stay in business?

Nonexcludability in particular can lead to what is called the "free-rider" problem (Olson 1965). A person cannot consume so-called private goods (rival and excludable) without revealing their desire to do so. This permits suppliers to charge prices and recoup costs. But revealing one's demand for a public good isn't necessary to consume it, since the good is already there, and no one can be kept from consuming it. To return to the clean air example, if I were asked to contribute toward the cost of cleaning the air, I might say that I don't much value clean air at all, or hardly at all, and thus won't help pay for it. There is no market mechanism to force me to reveal whether this is truly how I feel or not. This seems dishonest, particularly the way I phrased

Table 3.1

Kinds of Private/Public Goods

	Excludable	Nonexcludable
Rival	Pure private goods (e.g., a bicycle for one, a grape)	Commons goods, with open access (e.g., aquifers, an air basin, ocean fish, crowded city streets)
Nonrival	Club goods (e.g., concerts, movie theaters, YWCA, toll roads)	Pure public goods (e.g., a large, uncrowded public park, national defense)

the example, but many studies have confirmed the free-rider problem—even if it only describes a small share of users—as a force to be reckoned with. Essentially, it makes paying for nonexcludable goods a voluntary matter.

Indeed, the free-rider problem is probably the main obstacle to the private provision of nonexcludable goods, or at least a sufficient provision. There are various means of minimizing this problem, from education to moral arguments to compulsory consumption, and we see all these in use. Pledge drives to raise funds for public radio or public television, when those are otherwise available without charge on the public airwaves, are another example.

The bottom line is that—through no fault of the goods themselves, their sellers, or their consumers—public goods are difficult to market for gain. This is so even if a large number of people are willing to pay. The goods' purely technical (rather than, say, legal, social, or economic) characteristics keep suppliers from selling them, and monitoring their sales, in the normal way. So they tend not to provide them at all, or they provide less than actual demand would justify. It doesn't pay to supply public goods, and it doesn't pay for individual users to reveal their true demand.

Remedies

The trick, then, is figuring out a way for a group of people to cover the cost of a good they all want and would agree to share. A collective response might work better, where a group gets together and agrees to split the cost of a good they will share among themselves. This is a principal rationale for people forming groups or organizations, often called governments, whether public or private, for providing and then paying for commodities or services.

Imagine a neighborhood organizing a residents' association to maintain common landscaping or a community pool. In fact, there are many such private governments in existence (R.H. Nelson 2005). The key element is that collective, group action and coordination can solve the problem caused by nonrival or nonexcludable features of some valuable good or service. Providing collective, coordinated action is a fundamental explanation for the existence and traditional function of local government (e.g., Musgrave 1959; Stigler 1965).[2]

In particular, group provision avoids the so-called free-rider problem because the group can require payment for the goods from its members. These might be fees or, by another name, taxes. Taxation is coercive precisely to solve the free-rider problem; that is, coercion is one solution to the problem of individuals not having the incentive to reveal their willingness to pay for a nonexcludable good. Public provision is not the only solution, however. Public subsidies to private suppliers would accomplish much the same.[3]

In addition to the easy examples of public parks, public schools, public street lighting, and the streets themselves, briefly consider two others.

Example: Affordable Housing

Is affordable housing a public good, a private good, or something in between? Many quality-of-life elements of a community have public-good elements, especially where they are seen as benefiting residents, or a significant subset of residents, as a whole. If the economic diversity or general cost of living of a city or neighborhood is considered an asset, then it indeed has public-good features. And because it is nonrival within the city (and nonexcludable since people are free to move there), it is unlikely to be voluntarily provided at desirable levels by the private sector.

This remains one of the key rationales for public-housing projects, which are in many cases both constructed and operated by public-housing authorities. Lately such efforts tend to come in the form of regulatory requirements (e.g., inclusionary zoning) or subsidies (e.g., construction or rent subsidies).

Example: Public Health

The strongest arguments for improved housing conditions among lower-income households in the early 1900s centered on the observation that crowded and unsanitary conditions had health consequences that extended beyond individual families, or possibly beyond their neighborhoods. Thus, early zoning, crowding, and infrastructure regulations were based on public goods/externalities reasoning (Fischel 1985).

More recently, there is growing interest in how the physical design of communities affects personal health, by either promoting or discouraging physical activity (e.g., National Research Council 2005). Regulators are asked to promote the mixing of land uses, higher residential densities, and bike- and pedestrian-friendly plans in public spaces, all in the interest of health benefits that will be shared by many.

Cause of Market Failure: Externalities

A related problem for private markets is that of *externalities.* These are goods or actions that impose costs or benefits on others that are not mediated (or negotiated) by markets. They are also called third-party impacts, or spillovers, meaning they impose burdens on persons not party to the transaction. Say I play my car stereo so loud that in addition to making me dizzily happy, as planned, it also wakes babies up as I drive by, which was not planned. Put yet another way, negative externalities are instances in which the private costs of a market transaction are less than the total social costs, whereas positive externalities are instances in which private benefits are less than total social benefits. The former thus tend to be oversupplied and the latter undersupplied.

A textbook example is a new shopping center that, in addition to increasing tax revenues for the town in which it is located, generates additional traffic in the neighboring town. If my retail development dumps traffic into your town and I am not held accountable, the market generally does not acknowledge that your residents suffer the consequences. (Who suffers depends on the time frame, among other details. If it is an unexpected, short-term exposure, residents may not be able to avoid the traffic impacts. Over the longer term, if the damage is well known, then people will refuse to live near those streets—or to pay much for doing so—and it is the owners of impacted land who will absorb much of the traffic cost in the form of depressed land value.)

We tend to have laws to address such coordination problems, and this is exactly why. One party is imposing a cost on others that no market transaction accounts for. We wouldn't need these laws if markets permitted all parties to fairly negotiate an accommodation. In this sense we say that, in the absence of required coordination, such a market fails to operate efficiently. Again, collective action is one way of responding to the underlying difficulty, which is coordinating multiple parties in ways markets fail to do. This can translate into regulations on certain behaviors and not others.

If the developer were held accountable somehow, so that it had to compensate those suffering the consequences of its traffic, it would likely change its behavior. It might well either scale back the project, or relocate, or seek to mitigate the newly generated traffic problems.

The choices of individual drivers, by the way, are another classic cause of another familiar regulation externality, traffic congestion.[4] While we all slow other drivers down when we drive during crowded conditions, we rarely account for this in our own decisions. We choose when and where to drive, or to not take public transportation even if available, based almost exclusively on our own costs and benefits. The greater social consequences of those actions are typically ignored. Thus, we tend to drive more during peak times than we should.

To hold the creator of externalities accountable may, again, require a collective response, since there are rarely market mechanisms to do so. Within a city, zoning is one such response: It recognizes that noncompatible land uses exist and thus should be spatially separated. This approach to the problem is not the only feasible one, but it has served reasonably well over the decades. Other policy tools are taxes for negative externalities (e.g., to cover the social costs of pollution, traffic, etc.) and subsidies for positive externalities (e.g., tax incentives for job creation, tax deductions for home mortgages, subsidized tuition for public education).

Put another way, the private market is not particularly adept at dealing with externalities unless there is a market in pollution, or noise, or whatever the problematic side effect is. When such markets are present, the problem may vanish. The classic example of a market solution to an externality is the farmer adjacent to the beekeeper, each of whom realizes they impose positive externalities on the other (Coase 1960). The farmer benefits from his neighbor's bees, which cross-pollinate the crops. The beekeeper benefits by having blossoms available to feed bees. If they are aware of this, both the farmer and the beekeeper have incentives to account for these positive externalities when negotiating how many bees and flowers to keep. No broader collection action is necessarily required.

Thus, another approach to externalities is to create markets in those external costs or benefits. An example is tradable permits for the right to pollute a certain amount in a given air basin. The regulator determines the absorptive capacity of the basin and the maximum advisable pollution level (also known as the "cap"). It then opens a market for the right to pollute up to that limit. In this instance, firms are forced to recognize the cost they are imposing by paying for the permission to pollute (OECD 1992).

However, many circumstances are less conducive to market negotiations. The problem suggests a broader perspective that can account for both the costs and benefits of some activity and determine the right balance. Hence, this kind of market failure is another candidate for collective action.

Cause of Market Failure: Equity

Equity can also be a source of market failure, in that there are social-equity goals that markets do not ordinarily address. Affordable housing, mentioned above, is one such example, where equity enters as a kind of public good. Another way to look at the problem is to remember that competitive markets in pure private goods represent the uncoordinated interactions of individual sellers and buyers. They do not take into account the comparative social merits of various distributions of resources and opportunities. (Note that Pareto efficiency, the conventional standard by which economists judge market success and failure, is not an equity criterion as such.) As a society, however, we might agree on some objections to the market outcome. We might, for example, agree that people shouldn't starve, or that all children have a right to an education, or that housing should meet certain minimum quality standards.[5]

Without going into the details of the political and educational processes that would determine the standing of these social concerns, it is reasonably clear that if they do have standing, then some manner of collective approach to address them is implied. Local governments often take on that role.

While standards of equity are not absolute, there are public finance conventions for criteria that help to structure any discussion. Two are *vertical* and *horizontal* equity. Horizontal equity concerns how equals are treated. For example, in a town, if similar properties are treated the same in the zoning code, or are taxed at the same rate, this is horizontal equity. That kind of comparison is complicated by the many ways in which "equal" and "the same" can be measured. Moreover, actual policies violate horizontal equity quite regularly. Still, it is a standard by which we can evaluate alternative policies or processes. Vertical equity is a statement of how differently we treat different situations, and is thus more complex still.

In practice, any discussion of the fairness of one regulation decision over another invariably involves the choosing of winners and losers. Opposition to Walmart Supercenters, for example, is often organized by grocery workers' unions, since their wages are expected to be significantly reduced if Walmart gains market share in the grocery sector (Boarnet et al. 2005). This burden is cast as an impact that the community should resist. On the other hand, it is also the case that grocery prices will likely fall for the same reason, thereby benefiting local consumers. Local land authority regulators increasingly find themselves asked to take sides on this issue, though there is no obvious basis for doing so as a general principle.

Then again, many local regulatory decisions are based purely on their distributional consequences—who wins and who loses—rather than on public goods or externality arguments.

How Does Regulation Correct Market Failure?

So why and how do regulators do what they do? A fundamental purpose of land-use regulations is to address externalities and to provide public goods. (In practice, they also have important distributional functions, but since those are less specifically concerned with public finances, I won't focus on them.) Many local amenities have public-good characteristics over which regulators exert substantial influence. To repeat, these include infrastructure, education, transportation, the land-use mix, and the like.

More generally, the kinds of tools and instruments at governments' disposal to address market failure include:

- Public provision
- Regulation of behaviors
- Taxes and subsidies
- Assignment and enforcement of property rights and contracts
- Coordination, mediation, and facilitation

Clearly, governments (or some other collective action) should provide what we are calling public goods if unaided markets will not, when people are willing to pay their cost. Note that the privatization debate in local governments is sometimes about who actually produces the good or service and other times over who makes the decision of how much to provide (Sclar 2001). In this chapter, we do not differentiate between governments whose permanent staff provides plan check services, for example, and those who hire contract regulators for that service. In both cases, it is the city council or equivalent that is making decisions about levels and financing of service.

In addition, government can improve market operations overall if it regulates behavior in the presence of externalities. Zoning is but one example, on which we have more to say in a later section on regulatory issues.

While taxes are generally considered a revenue source, they also have a critically important function as an alternative form of regulation. Taxes change prices, which in turn change behaviors. Taxing pollution will reduce pollution. Subsidizing development near transit stations, on the basis that this will have positive externalities for the community overall, should increase transit-oriented developments (Boarnet and Crane 1998). In economics lingo, we can use taxes and subsidies to "get the prices right."

This may not be necessary if we get the property rights right. In the earlier example of the beekeeper and the farmer, the two parties could use a market transaction to address externalities, because their property rights extended to the external effects (honey and pollination).[6] Essentially, in that example, all affected parties trade in a market for the external effect. Tradable pollution permits (i.e., cap and trade) are another successful example of this approach.

How Much? What Level of Service?

As discussed earlier, markets generally do not provide nonexclusive goods—such as clean air, whose consumption cannot be restricted—because they cannot get people to pay for them. If you do not control access, neither can you generally force payment. In the private sector, firms sell different quantities of goods to people at any given price. Everyone values the good at that price or higher, or they would not buy it. Further, providers of private goods can observe how much people buy at each price. You buy an extra-large coffee; I choose a small.

It is the opposite with public goods: By nonrivalry, one common quantity, such as park size or street capacity, is available to every user. What varies is how much they *value* that quantity, which is not generally observable. So how do governments determine either how much to provide or how much to charge?

Putting public goods out there in the marketplace and seeing how people respond to different prices and qualities will not work. Properly aggregating a group's diverse preferences to select the right quantity of a shared good or service is an obvious challenge. How much open space should be preserved? How good should the elementary schools be? What is the best mix of residential and commercial land use for our city? How often should the buses run? Consensus on such issues, outside of very small communities, is rare.

One way people appear to settle these issues is their choice of which municipality to reside in. Many goods are only nonexcludable and nonrival locally, such as within a city or town. These could be called club goods, but we more often call them *local* public goods. Their importance here is that the free-rider problem is solved if people reveal their demand for such goods by moving to the cities that provide the amount they want at a cost of living they find acceptable—much as we shop car lots looking for the car we want at a price we like.

This way of thinking about the problem is often called the Tiebout hypothesis, after Charles Tiebout, the economist who most clearly characterized it (Tiebout 1956). Tiebout argued that people sort across local jurisdictions according to their preferred level of local public goods. If people shop (and thus compete) for local public goods much as they shop for bread or cars, the problem of providing the right mix and amount of public goods is not so insurmountable. Tiebout called this decision process "voting with their feet."

On the other hand, this argument seems to work best the more alike city residents are, which tends to mean the smaller the jurisdiction is. In larger cities, interests and incomes can be highly mixed, leading to no simple correspondence between the kinds and amounts of public services and residents. Smaller cities have also been accused of using zoning expressly to maintain income or other forms of mixing; this is known as exclusionary zoning (Levine 2005).

Still, Tiebout's insight has been extended in several suitable ways, including using the value of land as a measure of the value of government services, and in evaluating the merits of competition by local jurisdictions for tax base.

How to Pay? Revenues

The nonrivalness of many public goods is similarly unhelpful to public servants trying to pay the bills for those goods. Even if markets did provide such things, they wouldn't price them efficiently because, after the first user, the marginal cost of provision is zero (or varies with congestion). You cannot cover costs by charging zero unless the first user pays everything. People do not tend to volunteer to be the first user in this situation.

This is a complicated issue because revenues have many, often conflicting, goals. They include:

- Adequacy
- Growth
- Equity
- Economic efficiency
- Administrative feasibility
- Political acceptability

The following discussion evaluates each revenue source with respect to each purpose.

Kinds of Revenue

Table 3.2 lists a number of revenue types and their corresponding basis. For example, sales and income taxes are considered broad based, because they apply to broad categories of that tax base. The property tax, by contrast, applies only to property and is thus labeled narrow based.

In addition, revenues may be applied on a unit basis (e.g., 10 cents per gallon of gasoline), on an *ad valorem* basis (e.g., 6 cents per dollar), or on a fee-per-transaction basis (e.g., $1,000 per building plan application). Further, they may be based on a stock of wealth, as with a capital gains tax, or on a flow of resources, as with a wage tax.

Revenues may be intended solely to raise funds, or they may be mainly corrective in nature, as in a tax to correct an externality.

Another common approach to revenue is *ability to pay.* Here, the tax bill is determined by available resources. A tax on income or wealth would be the clearest example. This is the basis for progressive tax systems, where the after-tax base is more equal than the pre-tax base, such as most income taxes with rising marginal rates.

Note, however, that the complexity of tax incidence implies that whether a given tax system is progressive or not is harder to gauge than it may seem.

Table 3.2

Revenue Types

Revenue basis	Corresponding revenue types
Broad based	Sales, VAT, income, trade
Narrow based	Property, sin, resource, hotel
Rate type	Unit, ad valorem, transaction
Wealth/flow basis	Capital gains, income
Revenue or corrective	Income, pollution
Ability to pay	Income and property taxes
Benefits	User charges and property taxes
Other levels of government	Transfers, intergovernmental grants

For example, is the property tax progressive? The so-called new view of the property tax is that it may be, to the extent it is ultimately borne by the owners of mobile capital (Mieszkowski 1972). On the other hand, it has proven harder than expected to demonstrate whether this holds in practice (Zodrow 2006).[7]

Benefit Based

Revenues also may be based on benefits received, known as *willingness to pay.* Note first that this is exactly how we finance private goods. The easiest example is an auction, where you would never pay more than you are willing, and where everyone openly competes on that basis. The winner is the person willing to pay the most.

This may not work for public goods because of the free-rider problem, where there is no auction equivalent. Instead, a group collectively determines how much to provide. Individuals rarely, or at least do not consistently, reveal the value they put on that amount, as there is no market mechanism to help out. In sum, willingness to pay is a terrific way to pay for public goods, if only you could calculate it.

There are reasonable ways to measure the willingness to pay for nonmarketed goods, but they are indirect (Freeman 2003). For example, the price of housing is often said to reflect the value residents place on, among other house attributes, the public services provided in that community. So, good schools may show up in higher home prices. Other studies have measured the value people place on recreational services by how far they are willing to travel to use them, and so on.

Table 3.3 lists examples of benefit-based revenue types, including those based on taxes and on charges. Special assessment districts, tax increment

Table 3.3

Benefit Based

Category	Examples
Tax-based techniques	• Special assessments • Land value increment • Tax increment financing
Development charges	• Plan check fees • Impact fees
User charges/prices	• Consumption measurable (e.g., metered) • Service has no antipoverty purpose

Table 3.4

Property Tax

Advantages	Obstacles
• Locally based revenue • Close linkage to benefits • Taxes wealth (may be progressive) • Can promote efficient land use • Low efficiency costs • Relatively predictable	• Difficult to administer fairly • Difficult to assess • Difficult to enforce • Unpopular • Taxes unrealized income

financing districts, and land value increment schemes are all ways of tying public-service-generated land value improvements to revenue streams.

To better illustrate the complexity of these options, Table 3.4 considers one instrument in more detail: The property tax. As a way of raising funds to support the supply of local public goods, it has several advantages. It is locally based; it has a good linkage to benefits via the private land market; it may tax wealth (and thus capture ability to pay); it is relatively predicable; and it is considered a particularly efficient tax in that it cannot be avoided (George 1879/2009).

On the other hand, the property tax also has disadvantages that limit its utility. It requires the regular assessment of land value, and it is due in regular lump sums in most jurisdictions. It is thus a very visible tax and, since assessment is an imperfect science, a debatable one. For these and other reasons, it is perhaps the most unpopular tax in the United States (and the world).

Table 3.5

Types of Charges

Key distinctions	Examples
• Prices based on usage (user charges) versus bases (such as taxes), or • Prices that reflect costs (cost recovery) versus those that do not (subsidies)	• "Market" prices determined by trade/commerce • Metered water or electricity rates by volume • Passenger or freight fares by trip distance or weight • Entrance or connection fees • Licenses or permit fees

Table 3.6

Priced Services

Types of priced services	Key distinctions
Usually • Water/electricity/utilities • Public transportation • Public housing • Mail delivery/telephone At times • Education • Medical services • Roads and parking • Environmental health	• Services for which usage and benefits are observable versus • Services for which they are not, or which are mainly intended to benefit the poorest people

Fees, Prices, Charges

In some instances, the public sector provides goods and services—trash collection, extracurricular activities at public schools, or a public swimming pool—whose individual benefits are observable. These are best suited for what we call *user charges*, which is just another name for prices of publicly provided goods.

As summarized in Table 3.5, and as for private goods, prices for public services work best as charges for actual use (i.e., for willingness to pay). But this requires that use be easily observable. In addition, sustainable finance generally requires that prices aim to fully recover costs. Targeting price subsidies to only the poor—to address affordability and equity concerns—is very difficult, though "lifeline" rates are a good option.[8] The administrative and political feasibility of full cost-recovery pricing are improving.

Table 3.7

Basis for Setting the Price Level

Basis	Explanation
Cost recovery	To signal scarcity and avoid deficits
To reflect marginal costs	To signal rational choices where fair and feasible
To recover operating costs	These are real costs and should be recovered
Demand management	To deter waste or overuse
Subsidies	Only if use needs to be encouraged for the collective benefit (e.g., disease control), or where the service or good being provided is a basic human need and the poor cannot afford the full cost (e.g., sewage infrastructure)

Table 3.8

Evaluation: Will Pricing Work?

Criterion	Explanation
Adequacy	Should aim to be responsive to population growth and inflation
Equity	Pricing is regressive, but lifeline rates and subsidies to connection fees can address this
Administrative capacity	Pricing can be easy to administer, but it requires technical capacity, the will to impose sanctions for nonpayment, and political integrity
Political acceptability	The role of prices is generally well understood, but their level is a sensitive issue

Why do some governments charge for some goods but not others? In general, it depends on the observability of individual benefits. Table 3.6 distinguishes between services that are often priced and those that may be but often are not; the same table notes the distinction between those for which benefits are observable and those whose benefits are not.

Once the determination is made to charge for a publicly provided good, what should that price be based on? Table 3.7 lists five considerations: Is it to recover costs, to efficiently reflect marginal costs, to recover operating costs only, to manage demand, or to subsidize desirable behavior?

Whether pricing will accomplish a given jurisdiction's objectives requires identifying those objectives clearly. Table 3.8 lays out four objectives: revenue adequacy, equity, administrative capacity, and political acceptability. All matter, but which matters most or how these rank in importance will vary with the individual circumstances of place and time.

As an example, Shoup (2005) extensively reviews the case for charging for parking, if public, or for regulations that encourage the pricing of parking, if private. More often than not, parking is provided freely and oversupplied by regulatory policy. Shoup argues that while individual situations call for different approaches, so-called free parking can in reality involve substantial economic burdens on the community and individual landowners.

Intergovernmental Transfers

The final source of revenues in Table 3.2 are transfers from other levels of government. A very large share of local government revenues is from higher levels. This has two substantial effects on local decisions: it provides more funds, and it encourages or discourages expenditures for some purposes over others. The size of these effects depends not only on the size of the transfer, but its form and whether it is conditional or unconditional.

Transfers come in two general forms: revenue sharing or grants. The former are shared taxes, usually motivated by the relative ease of collecting taxes at higher levels of government. A state sales tax that is partially returned to the local jurisdiction generating it is one example.[9] Alternatively, grants are simply awards of funds.

Both shared revenue and grants can be either conditional or unconditional. Unconditional grants have no strings attached, beyond whatever legal restrictions there are on public spending and accounting practices. These are simply additional funds for legitimate local purposes. Conditional transfers, on the other hand, are restricted to certain purposes and/or may be awarded on a matching basis. They thus tend to have a substantial stimulative effect.

Tables 3.9 and 3.10 summarize the structure, advantages, and disadvantages of each.

Debt

Borrowing is less a revenue source than an alternative way of scheduling long-lasting expenditures. Local governments in the United States are normally only permitted to borrow for capital expenditures—that is, for projects and facilities that will benefit current and future residents. It is hard to tax or charge future residents now, before they become residents, so it is convenient to schedule those revenues for later. Debt is thus an important mechanism for forward-looking regulation.

Table 3.9

Types and Properties of Unconditional Transfers

	Revenue sharing/shared taxes	Grants
	Allocated to each local authority based on some specified share of centrally collected revenues originating in that local authority.	Allocated ad hoc or by formula. The formula is usually either a flat grant per local authority, or based on measures of need and resources, or some combination.
Pros	Revenue sharing returns locally generated revenues that would otherwise be difficult to collect. Usually the smallest administrative burden. Generally predictable and stable revenue source.	Grants redistribute centrally collected revenues according to differences in need and resources across local authorities. Can address different regional circumstances and equalization objectives.
Cons	Revenue sharing requires that the origin of each shared revenue source be documented. Allocates the largest shares to highest-income areas.	Data required for allocation formula must be current. Disbursement procedures somewhat more complicated that revenue sharing.
Example	1 percent of the sales tax collected from Cambridge, MA, would be periodically rebated directly to the general fund of Cambridge, and so on for each local authority.	10 percent of central-government revenues would be allocated to local authorities—10 percent as a flat grant to each local authority and 90 percent on an equal per capita basis.

Table 3.10

Types and Properties of Conditional Transfers

	Revenue sharing/shared taxes	Grants
	Same as above, and in addition, conditioned on specified performance criteria (e.g., staffing levels, acceptable accounts, etc.) and/or restricted to particular purposes (e.g., road maintenance).	Same as above, and in addition, subject to matching local contribution, conditioned on specified performance criteria (e.g., staffing levels, acceptable accounts, etc.) and/or restricted to particular purposes (e.g., road maintenance).
Pros	Same as above, but with additional incentives and/or requirements to enhance local-authority spending and revenue performance.	Same as above, but with additional incentives and/or requirements to enhance local-authority spending and revenue performance.
Cons	Same, but additional monitoring and measurement burdens by center, and reporting burdens on local authorities. May excessively distort local spending choices.	Same, but additional monitoring and measurement burdens by center, and reporting burdens on local authorities. May excessively distort local spending choices.
Example	1 percent of the sales tax collected from Cambridge, MA, would be periodically rebated directly to Cambridge, earmarked for road maintenance expenses, and so on for each local authority.	10 percent of central-government revenues would be allocated to local authorities by a formula that rewards local revenue effort (e.g., percentage increase in rates collections). Another 5 percent of central revenues would be allocated for water projects, where need is demonstrated.

Government borrowing at the local level has become much more complex over the past two or three decades. Where governments used to issue general-purpose bonds (to be repaid from general revenues) or simple revenue bonds (to be repaid from the project being financed), they now rely on literally dozens of different financial instruments (Crane and Green 1989; Vogt 2004). The underlying reasoning remains, however: Borrowing is reserved for capital projects, and repayment should correspond to the flow of benefits from those projects.

Revenue Summary

Successful local governments finance a substantial portion of their expenditures from local sources; otherwise, they are severely limited in their ability to plan for the future and to spend responsibly. A "good" tax mix is a balance of benefit and ability-to-pay revenue types, a balance that depends on the local mix of chargeable services and incomes. "Bad" taxes inadvertently affect behavior and impose large administrative or political costs. Local taxes should also be predictable, stable, equitable, and allow for spending growth.

The Public Finance of Regulatory Goals and Means

Decreased federal funding for municipal operations over the past few decades, combined with the labor-intensive nature of many local services, has led to growing state and municipal fiscal stress throughout the United States. Municipal responses have included service cutbacks on the spending side and increased use of debt (Crane and Green 1989) and impact and application fees aimed at getting development to "pay its own way." Regulators have long incorporated fiscal impact analysis as either a formal or informal element of the development evaluation process (Burchell and Listokin 1980; Wheaton 1959), and both common sense and anecdotal evidence suggest that, if anything, this will continue as fiscal pressures rise.

While public financing of local land regulatory actions was included in the foregoing discussion, this sections looks at two regulatory actions in more detail: the fiscalization of land use and regulation for revenue.

Fiscalization of Land Use

In addition to fee structures aimed at cost recovery, local governments have long made land-use regulation decisions aimed at maximizing revenues and minimizing costs. Budget-conscious officials interested in economic development favor revenue-producing land uses, such as sales-tax-generating commercial/retail, and oppose uses with apparently high costs and low revenues, such as multifamily housing. Cities also compete with one another over development projects based on expected budget impacts.

Together, these practices can distort land-use regulation and development decisions in many ways. Nevertheless, they appear to have dramatically accelerated over the past twenty years, especially in states subject to property tax limits (Misczynski 1986). In California, the propensity to use fiscal zoning was arguably exacerbated after the property tax limitation Proposition 13 passed in 1978. That amendment to the state constitution fixed the typical property tax rate at near 1 percent of assessed value and set assessed property value at the higher of (a) its 1978 market value plus a maximum of 2 percent appreciation per year, or (b) its last sales price since 1978 plus a maximum of 2 percent appreciation per year. (Since the early 1980s, communities have also been permitted an additional property—or "Mello-Roos"—tax of up to 1 percent explicitly for the purpose of financing infrastructure associated with new land developments.)

Proposition 13 had three significant effects on California's local governments that promoted the fiscalization of land-use regulation:

- It changed the relationship between property tax revenues and sales tax revenues, making retail stores more attractive to local governments and other land uses, especially housing, less attractive.
- It placed central control for distribution of local tax revenue with the governor and the legislature, thus reducing city and county budget autonomy and their ability to manage both sides of the land-use/budget equation.
- It made it more difficult for local governments to raise funds for community infrastructure, whether from taxpayers at large or from property owners who benefit from such improvements.

Proposition 13 thus decreased the relative importance of the property tax and increased the relative importance of the sales tax as a local revenue source. (A share of locally generated sales tax collections is rebated by the state back to that jurisdiction.) That said, California communities do not have much direct control over either the property or sales tax rate.[10] Their influence over the fiscal environment is, rather, mainly indirect via their control over the revenue generating ability of alternative land uses.

The broader trends are by no means unique to California. Many communities that do want to accept housing or other land uses that provide relatively little tax revenue will do so only if the budget is balanced through the imposition of large up-front development fees, as discussed below. While such fees do permit needed community infrastructure to be built, they will also drive up the cost of housing. Furthermore, fee revenues fluctuate substantially from year to year, depending on the amount of construction activity, and are therefore not a stable funding source.

Sales tax revenue is one of the few sources of funds over which local governments perceive that they have any control. In California, for example, 1 percent of the 7.25 percent state sales tax is returned to local governments. Thus, for every $100 in retail sales, $1 is returned to the jurisdiction where the transaction took place, no matter where the purchasers actually live. Interjurisdictional competition for and accommodation of auto malls and big-box retailers such as Walmart and Costco may be the most visible example of how regulation can deliver cash cows.

Regulation for Revenue

The phrase "regulation for revenue" refers to the recent but now widespread practice of imposing large impact fees, special assessments, and exactions on new residential and commercial real-estate development (A.C. Nelson 1988). Altshuler and Gómez-Ibáñez (1993) observe that only about 10 percent of American localities imposed exactions before 1960, a fraction that increased to 90 percent by the mid-1980s. They further comment that designing regulatory systems explicitly to produce revenue, as opposed to protecting or supporting a traditional "compelling state interest" like health and safety, shifted power "from the owners of property to government officials" while also shifting more revenue risk to those officials (p. 19).

The use of impact fees and exactions increased substantially in the 1980s, seemingly in tandem with a rise in antitax sentiment and voter-imposed tax limits. In addition to revenue gaps, a popular rationale in development fees was the contention that the public service costs of residential development particularly were greater than new associated tax revenues, though the few studies examining this question are far from clear. Impact fees "do not show up on anyone's tax bill . . . and while they are likely to drive up developer prices they remain imperceptible even to purchasers as a distinct cost item" (Altshuler and Gómez-Ibáñez 1993, p. 126).

In addition, modern impact assessments do more than cover growth-related public works infrastructure. They can also include fees for so-called social infrastructure associated with growth, such as child care, mass transit, and affordable housing.

For all their flaws, property taxes are relatively stable: Property tax revenues generally do not move dramatically up or down in any given year. By contrast, retail sales can rise or fall sharply during an economic boom or a recession, and development fee revenue can fall from millions in a building boom to almost nothing in a real estate bust. Reliance on these tax sources, which fiscalized land-use policies usually seek to attract, makes stable, long-term budgeting that much more difficult for local governments to achieve. Dramatic swings between layoffs and new hires tend to result, possibly helping to erode public confidence in local officials.

Local government finance and land-use regulation will always be bound up with one another. The way land is used inevitably shapes the revenue potential of cities and counties and the cost requirements with which they must contend.

An Example: Transit-Oriented Development

A lively and diverse literature continues to investigate the potential for causal links between rail transit and land-use regulation. This work traditionally concerned the impacts of transit on land use and urban form but a number of recent studies, encouraged in part by policy initiatives such as recent federal transportation reauthorizations, also consider the potential for using land-use regulation to influence transit demand (an extensive review is found in Cervero and Seskin [1995]). Among these, so-called *transit-oriented development* (TOD) research has been particularly visible. TOD advocates more medium- and high-density residential development near commuter rail stations (Bernick and Cervero 1996). The goal is to both increase rail ridership, thus improving rail transit's viability, and reduce traffic congestion. These proposals currently hold great sway in urban design debates and, somewhat more concretely, they appear to have influenced several major cities to incorporate residential development into their transit-oriented land-use plans.

The TOD literature follows on, and in some ways responds to, a large body of research on the land-use impacts of transportation. By the late 1970s, a number of studies examined these impacts, and the majority found that transportation improvements often created relatively small land-use responses (Meyer and Gómez-Ibáñez 1981).

For many years, this was the BART experience in San Francisco. When BART opened in the early 1970s, regulators assumed that the new rail transit stations would become centers for economic development or (more often) redevelopment. The presence of the heavy rail transit system would encourage medium- and high-density development, and presumably some of that development would be residential units offering easy walking access to a BART station.

By the late 1980s, however, it was clear that redevelopment near many BART stations proceeded at a slower pace than expected. Regulators began to conclude that the land market, if left to its own devices, would not fully exploit the development opportunities near stations. Some practitioners and scholars argued that government would have to intervene. Suggested policies included rezoning land near stations for residential uses, offering density bonuses or subsidies, or otherwise facilitating development (especially residential development) near rail transit. This policy activity meshed with academic thought that advocated a return to more dense pedestrian and transit-oriented communities, and TOD was born.

Studies of the barriers to TOD have focused on the behavior of private land markets and individual commuters (Cervero, Bernick, and Gilbert 1994), but recent research suggests that local institutional obstacles to TOD may be a greater problem than generally understood. In an extensive review of land use near more than 200 existing and proposed rail stations in southern California, Boarnet and Crane (1997, 2001) found little evidence of residential TOD in local zoning codes. The overwhelming trend was instead one of commercial and industrial zoning in station areas, a pattern that held across community and commuter rail system characteristics.

One explanation is that while transit-based housing is possibly consistent with *regional* ridership goals, as the TOD literature tends to argue, it may well be at odds with *local* development goals. If conflicts between municipal and regional goals exist, it would seem useful for transit regulation purposes to understand the motives of all the governments with land-use jurisdiction near rail transit lines.

As an example of how public finances influence regulation behaviors, Boarnet and Crane (1998) explored the fiscal motives leading communities to resist residential development near commuter rail stations. One explanation for the limited implementation of TOD is that localities aim, by way of either long-term regulation strategies or incremental zoning decisions, to use rail transit stations as a means to enhance their fiscal position. To the extent that rail transit stations are perceived as opportunities to focus new development or redevelopment, a municipality might choose to emphasize land uses that have the most favorable impact on its tax base—that is, local governments face significant behavioral incentives, often neglected in residential TOD strategies, regarding their economic and fiscal self-interest.

Do localities view rail transit stations with fiscal incentives in mind? It is easy to see why they might. Rail transit stations offer connections to the rest of the regional economy, potentially providing an opportunity to focus development (in the case of stations near open land) or enhance existing land uses (for stations sited in developed areas). Rail transit might thus enhance the capability of existing or future commercial development to generate tax revenue by providing both access for customers and a recognizable landmark that can raise the visibility of nearby development.

To the extent that cities value commercial development, they might prefer that rail transit be sited near existing commercial centers and that commercial land uses near rail stations be expanded. Two points are thus important. First, the fiscal motive to seek commercial land uses might be especially strong near rail transit stations. Second, localities have two ways to act on this motive. They can either encourage commercial development near existing stations or influence regional authorities to site stations near existing commercial developments.

Summary

Public finance is on the one hand a behavioral story of why governments do what they do (or rather what they should do), and on the other a balancing act based on the pros and cons of alternative ways to pay the bills.

Here, we have discussed a bit of both. On the one hand, governments operate largely in order to provide public goods and to correct externalities, which we generally consider to be in the public interest and which private, competitive markets fail to do. On the other hand, the ways in which governments finance their activities can be easily listed and described, but the merits of those options are nuanced, as discussed.

Two examples of trends in how finance drives land-use regulation are the fiscalization of land use, or land regulation toward fiscal ends, and regulation for revenue, or regulation for cost recovery. Whether these trends are good or bad is hard to say, but we can agree that the underlying public finances explain these behaviors and their impacts on our communities.

Many of these new types of fiscally motivated regulation behaviors have not been studied in great detail. This chapter uses transit-oriented development as one example, but there are others. Earlier literatures studied incentives for fiscal zoning and attempts to increase the local tax base, but those typically focused on the property tax (e.g., Mills and Oates 1975). Fiscal competition now is over commercial uses, and the ramification of these new fiscal pressures are not fully understood. Our main purpose is to aid that kind of understanding.

Notes

This chapter benefited from suggestions and questions by the editors, Roz Greenstein, Jack Huddleston, Gregory Ingram, Emil Malizia, and Donald Shoup.

1. Here, economists are specifically referring to a fairly conservative definition of efficiency known as Pareto efficiency. In brief, it refers to a situation that cannot

be improved without someone being made worse off. Put another way, an outcome is efficient if there are no additional mutually beneficial trades to be had.

2. Note that municipal enterprises are often monopolies, another classic source of market failure. Private-sector monopolists charge too much and provide too little of their product, relative to competitive markets. This can and should be avoided in the public sector. Public-sector monopolies can also face the problem of trying to recover costs for declining-cost industries, such as water, sewage, and other utilities. In those cases, pricing at marginal cost will require additional subsidies to cover facility investments. Furthermore, as discussed below, local municipal enterprises can be characterized as competing for customers to the extent they compete with other cities for residents.

3. It is also useful to comment on the superficial difference between ownership and management in the provision of public services. For example, some water agencies own and manage their facilities and operations, while others own the physical infrastructure but subcontract its management, and still others simply regulate private enterprises that provide such goods and services. At the level of detail in this chapter, there is no important distinction between these models. In each case, the test is if collective intervention is necessary to correct market failure. That intervention can take any of these three forms and should lead to the same outcome. In practice, however, the details of governance, administration, and implementation will reveal advantages and disadvantages of each provision model in each case.

4. You will note that congestion was mentioned earlier in the context of public goods. In a general sense, a public good is a type of externality. The availability of public goods to everyone acts much as an externality that provides benefits to others that they do not control. Traffic congestion is a good example of an externality that is also a property of a public good: roads.

5. Housing affordability was raised earlier as a possible public good. It is quite possible and consistent to consider many questions of equity as local public goods especially (Pauly 1973), but for clarity we will stick with the convention of treating equity as a separate example of market failure.

6. The most common obstacle to the applicability of what has come to be known as the Coase Theorem (after Ronald Coase, who was awarded the Nobel Prize in Economics in 1991 in part for his development of this insight; see Coase 1960)—namely, that well-defined property rights can lead to efficient markets in externalities—is generally considered to be transaction costs. On the other hand, such costs are probably best considered a separate potential source of market failure in many contexts, including those involving collective action.

7. An equal tax per person, also called a head tax, is also in broad use. It has the appeal of being easy to calculate and hard to avoid (thus nondistortionary) and is often considered "fair" in some basic sense. On the other hand, it has the drawback of placing the same burden on everyone even if benefits are distributed quite unevenly.

8. So-called lifeline rates refer to lower prices for low-income households for amounts of the good or service below some minimal level, which is considered essential or nondiscretionary. For example, a jurisdiction may charge a very low price for the first 6,000 gallons of water used per month by low-income families. These are most common for electricity and other basic utility services. In practice, the term often refers to any discount offered to low-income users. For example, in San Francisco, a family of four earning less than $30,000 per year was once eligible for a 25 percent discount on trash collection fees.

9. Revenue-sharing transfers can also be, and often are, at least somewhat equalizing in design. That is, they do not merely rebate revenues to their source but can also return more funds to poorer or otherwise deficient jurisdictions.

10. Municipalities can use other tax instruments. There is the local option at the county level in many states to raise the sales tax rate, but in addition to the limited influence that individual municipalities have over the county tax structure, voter support for such increases has lately been limited to funds earmarked for transportation infrastructure. Some localities use special taxes such as business license fees and hotel occupancy taxes, but sales and property taxes are still large revenue sources for most municipalities.

References

Altshuler, A., and J. Gómez-Ibáñez. 1993. *Regulation for Revenue: The Political Economy of Land Use Exactions.* Washington, DC: The Brookings Institution.

Bernick, M., and R. Cervero. 1996. *Transit Villages in the 21st Century.* New York: McGraw-Hill.

Blair, J., and R. Bingham. 2000. Economic analysis. In *The Practice of Local Government Planning,* ed. C. Hoch, L. Dalton, and F. So, 119–40. Washington, DC: ICMA.

Bland, R. 1989. *A Revenue Guide for Local Government.* Washington, DC: ICMA.

Boarnet, M., and R. Crane. 1997. L.A. story: A reality check for transit-based housing. *Journal of the American Planning Association* 63(2): 189–204.

———. 1998. Public finance and transit-oriented planning: Evidence from Southern California. *Journal of Planning Education and Research* 17: 206–19.

———. 2001. *Travel by Design: The Influence of Urban Form on Travel.* New York: Oxford University Press.

Boarnet, M., R. Crane, D. Chatman, and M. Manville. 2005. Emerging planning challenges in retail: The case of Wal-Mart. *Journal of the American Planning Association* 71(4): 433–49.

Buchanan, J.M. 1965. An economic theory of clubs. *Economica* 32(125): 1–14.

Burchell, R., and D. Listokin. 1980. *Practitioner's Guide to Fiscal Impact Analysis.* New Brunswick, NJ: Center for Urban Policy Research at Rutgers University.

Cervero, R., and S. Seskin. 1995. An evaluation of the relationships between transit and urban form. In *Research Results Digest 7.* Washington, DC: Transit Cooperative Research Program.

Cervero, R., M. Bernick, and J. Gilbert. 1994. *Market Opportunities and Barriers to Transit-Based Development in California.* University of California Transportation Center Working Paper No. 223, University of California at Berkeley.

Coase, R. 1960. The problem of social cost. *Journal of Law and Economics* 3 (October): 1–44.

Crane, R., and R. Green. 1989. Debt finance at the municipal level: Decision making during the 1980s. In *The Municipal Yearbook 1989,* 97–106. Washington, DC: ICMA.

Fischel, W. 1985. *The Economics of Zoning Laws: A Property Rights Approach to American Land Use Controls.* Baltimore, MD: Johns Hopkins University Press.

Fisher, R. 2006. *State and Local Public Finance.* 3d ed. Boston: South-Western College Publishing.

Freeman, A.M. 2003. *The Measurements of Environmental and Resource Values: Theory and Methods.* 2nd ed. Washington, DC: Resources for the Future.

Frieden, B., and L. Sagalyn. 1989. *Downtown, Inc.* Cambridge, MA: MIT Press.

George, H. 1879/2009. *Progress and Poverty: An Inquiry into the Cause of Industrial*

Depressions, and of Increase of Want with Increase of Wealth: The Remedy. San Francisco: Wm. M. Hinton & Co. Reprinted, New York: Cambridge University Press.

Hardin, G. 1968. The tragedy of the commons. *Science* 162: 1243–48.

Levine, J. 2005. *Zoned Out*. Washington, DC: Resources for the Future.

Lucy, W., and P. Fisher. 2000. Budgeting and finance. In *The Practice of Local Government Planning*, ed. C. Hoch, L. Dalton, and F. So. Washington, DC: ICMA.

Meyer, J., and A. Gómez-Ibáñez. 1981. *Autos, Transit, and Cities*. Cambridge, MA: Harvard University Press.

Mieszkowski, P. 1972. The property tax: An excise tax or a profits tax? *Journal of Public Economics* 1(1): 73–96.

Mills, E.S., and W.E. Oates, eds. 1975. *Fiscal Zoning and Land Use Controls: The Economic Issues.* Lexington, MA: Lexington Books.

Misczynski, D.J. 1986. The fiscalization of land use. In *California Policy Choices*, vol. 3, ed. J. Kirlin and D.R. Winkler, 73–106. Sacramento: University of Southern California Press.

Musgrave, R.A. 1959. *The Theory of Public Finance*. New York: McGraw Hill.

National Research Council. 2005. *Does the Built Environment Influence Physical Activity? Examining the Evidence.* Transportation Research Board Special Report 282. Washington, DC: Transportation Research Board.

Nelson, A.C., ed. 1988. *Development Impact Fees: Policy Rationale, Practice, Theory, and Issues.* Chicago: Planners Press.

Nelson, R.H. 2005. *Private Neighborhoods and the Transformation of Local Government.* Washington, DC: Urban Institute Press.

Oates, W.E. 1972. *Fiscal Federalism*. New York: Harcourt Brace Jovanovich.

Olson, M. 1965. *The Logic of Collective Action*. Cambridge, MA: Harvard University Press.

Organisation of Economic Co-operation and Development (OECD). 1992. *Climate Change: Designing a Tradable Permit System.* Paris: OECD.

Pauly, M. 1973. Income redistribution as a local public good. *Journal of Public Economics* 2: 35–58.

Sclar, E. 2001. *You Don't Always Get What You Pay For: The Economics of Privatization.* Ithaca, NY: Cornell University Press.

Shoup, D. 2005. *The High Cost of Free Parking*. Chicago: Planners Press.

Smith, A. 1776/2003. *An Inquiry into the Nature and Causes of the Wealth of Nations*. London: printed for W. Strahan and T. Cadell. Reprinted, Bantam Classics Edition. New York: Bantam.

Stigler, G. 1965. The tenable range of functions of local government. In *Private Wants and Public Needs: Issues Surrounding the Size and Scope of Government Expenditure*, ed. E. Phelps. New York: Norton.

Tiebout, C. 1956. A pure theory of public expenditures. *Journal of Political Economy* 64(5): 416–24.

Vogt, A.J. 2004. *Capital Budgeting and Finance: A Guide for Local Governments*. Washington, DC: ICMA.

Wheaton, W.L.C. 1959. Applications of cost-revenue studies to fringe areas. *Journal of the American Institute of Regulators* 25: 170–74.

Wolf, C. 1988. *Markets or Governments: Choosing Between Imperfect Alternatives*. Cambridge, MA: MIT Press.

Zodrow, G. 2006. Who pays the property tax? *Land Lines* 18(2). Cambridge, MA: Lincoln Institute of Land Policy.

4
Revolving Loan Funds

Kelly Robinson

Since their inception in the 1970s, revolving loan funds (RLFs) have become a standard tool for financing economic development. More often than not, funds are controlled at the local level with lending decisions made by people closely tied to the community. The nature of organizations administering these funds is varied, including local governments, quasi-governmental entities such as economic development agencies, and nonprofit organizations. Because these organizations have widely divergent missions, RLFs provide loans for such different purposes as working capital, real estate acquisition, new product development, equipment purchases, and environmental investment.

Not all RLFs are designed to loan to businesses. Some, for instance, are designed to provide infrastructure loans to local government. In this chapter, I will focus on those RLFs that do lend to businesses. In these cases, the role of the RLF in economic development is generally to provide affordable capital to business borrowers who are unable to acquire all of what they need from private banks at affordable rates. Among the borrowers most often targeted by RLFs are women, minorities, and business owners in distressed communities subject to discrimination. They may also include borrowers with few tangible assets to pledge as collateral, start-up firms with uncertain income, and businesses needing loans that are too small to be profitable for private lenders. In addition to providing needed capital, RLFs help borrowers to establish a successful credit history, making them more suitable for subsequent borrowing from for-profit lenders.

Typically, RLFs are organized as public or nonprofit funds capitalized by grants or low-cost loans from governments or foundations. This makes them somewhat different from community development banks or community development credit unions, which are primarily capitalized by deposits from account holders (Williams 1997). Like private-sector banks, RLFs are maintained over the longer run by loan repayments and interest. Unlike private banks, RLFs are largely unregulated by federal authorities. However, state and federal agencies that help to fund RLFs often impose their own regulations on the use of their funds.

The first federally funded RLF was created in 1975, when workers of the South Bend Lathe Company sought help from the Economic Development Administration (EDA) of the U.S. Department of Commerce to buy their plant, which was slated for closure. However, EDA's enabling legislation and regulations did not specifically allow the agency to make grants to employees for investment in a for-profit business. The RLF concept arose when the agency determined it could make a grant to a nonprofit employee organization that, in turn, could make loans to workers to finance an employee stock ownership plan. Soon thereafter, EDA began capitalizing RLFs with grants as a standard procedure. The Department of Housing and Urban Development (HUD) quickly followed suit, vastly expanding the universe of RLFs when it allowed Community Development Block Grants (CDBGs) to be used for RLF capitalization (Dommel 1995).

Because RLFs are largely unregulated, highly localized, and active in many different kinds of lending, there is no single source of statistics for the industry. However, their use has grown rapidly. In 1997, the nonprofit Corporation for Enterprise Development estimated there were in excess of 600 funds supported by federal agencies such as EDA, HUD, and the U.S. Department of Agriculture's Intermediary Relending Program (USDA/IRP) (Levere, Clones, and Marcoux 1997). More recent estimates of the number and value of these funds are shown in Table 4.1.

These numbers almost certainly underestimate the real size of the RLF industry. For one thing, Table 4.1 only includes RLFs funded with federal money.

Why Do We Need RLFs?

The effect of firm size on borrowing is striking. Using 2003 survey data, researchers from the Federal Reserve Board examined borrowing patterns among "small firms"—defined as businesses with fewer than 500 employees.[1] They found that just 59 percent of very small businesses—those with fewer than 20 employees—reported using any sort of credit line, loan, or capital lease. (Mach and Wolken 2006). These very small firms make up the vast majority of firms in the United States. For comparison, among firms with 100 to 499 employees, 94 percent used at least one of these financing methods. While these are still considered small businesses, they are at the upper end of the definition in terms of employee numbers. Firms in the very small category were also far more likely to finance business purchases with personal credit

Table 4.1

The Scale of Revolving Loan Funds (RLFs) in 2010

Agency	Number of funds	Value[1]	Source/Notes
Economic Development Administration	578	$852 million	EDA (2010)
Community Development Financial Institutions	146	$5.5 billion	CDFI Data Project (2008). Excludes CDFI venture capital funds, banks, and credit unions.
USDA, Intermediary Relending Program[2]	1,032	$750 million	USDA (2010)
U.S. Small Business Administration			
504 Program	270	$18 billion (in guarantees)	Brash & Gallagher (2008)
Microloan Program	170	$235 million	Brash (2008). Based on 1997–2005.
Dept. of Housing and Urban Development[2]			Walker et al. (2002)
Community Development Block Grants	511	$1.4 billion	
Section 108	92	$777 million	
Economic Development Initiative (EDI) & Brownfields EDI	11	$16 million	

[1]Throughout this chapter, dollar values are reported in nominal terms unless otherwise stated.
[2]Counts number of grantees rather than number of RLFs. Many RLFs have multiple grants.

cards (48 percent) than were firms at the top end of the small business definition (32 percent).

Even if we ignore the possibility of explicit discrimination, there are many reasons why private, for-profit lending institutions may not lend capital to small businesses to the degree needed—especially in distressed areas. First, these businesses are often risky. As a group, small businesses are much more likely to open and close than larger businesses (Helfand, Sadeghi, and Talan 2007). This instability is further exacerbated for start-ups relative to more established firms, and it can take a business some time to generate enough income to support significant debt repayment.

Even when businesses are financially sound, it can be difficult for lenders to assess the risk of new or nontraditional borrowers. Many first-time business owners have limited credit history. Similarly, small businesses may borrow for very diverse reasons, making it difficult for underwriters to develop reliable risk ratings. When lenders cannot assess risk easily and reliably, they will usually either withhold credit or charge higher interest rates.

Finally, lending to small businesses can be inefficient. The amount borrowed is typically small, so the fixed costs of underwriting and servicing a loan are large relative to the income generated. In addition, to the extent that small firms are less able to afford specialized management personnel, they can require a lot of assistance in applying for and managing their loans. In short, there are many reasons why rational for-profit lenders undersupply capital to small, first-time, and nontraditional borrowers.

How Revolving Loan Funds Work

The primary role of most economic development RLFs is to provide the difference between the amount borrowers need and what they can obtain through private capital markets. In some instances, the RLF will be the primary lender. For example, many RLFs today provide "micro" loans that are too small to be worthwhile for traditional banks (Servon and Doshna 1998). Similarly, RLFs often provide start-up and/or working capital to small borrowers who cannot qualify for credit from traditional lenders. They may also provide venture capital to firms in those sectors and geographic locations neglected by private venture capitalists. Sometimes, RLFs provide "bridge loans" that allow a project to move forward quickly by guaranteeing a short-term supply of capital until longer-term private financing can be arranged.

Most often, an RLF provides a secondary loan to supplement what borrowers can obtain from private credit markets. This "gap loan" is typically structured to ensure that any commercial bank loans are repaid in a timely fashion, with the RLF taking a subordinated position with respect to collateral in the event of repayment difficulties. The RLF may also defer payments until a significant portion of the bank loan has been repaid or until the business is more established and generating enough income to repay its debt. In each case, risk is transferred from private banks to the RLF. In theory, this reduced risk to the bank should be reflected in better terms for the borrower.

Local banks frequently find RLFs to be valuable partners for several reasons. In addition to reducing credit risk to the banks, RLFs often help prepare inexperienced borrowers before they actually approach the bank, making the job of the bank loan officer easier. Second, potential borrowers may not have a viable project without the gap financing provided by an RLF. For instance, the absence of such funding may mean that the scale of a proposed investment is insufficient to generate the income necessary to meet commercial standards for debt servicing. The additional capital provided by an RLF may allow the borrower to proceed with multiple stages of expansion in a more integrated fashion—eliminating financing gaps that can cause inefficient downtime and threaten a project's success. Once RLF borrowers have established a record of successful repayment, most go on to rely on traditional banks for future lending.

Underwriting and Servicing Practices

Whereas private banks base loan eligibility mainly on financial characteristics of borrowers, RLFs also consider issues related to their public mission. Many RLFs lend for very specific purposes, and most RLFs lend only to firms within a limited geographic area. Often, potential borrowers must demonstrate that they have been unable to obtain credit from traditional banks. Eligibility rules also vary significantly, depending on the source of funds used to capitalize the RLF. For example, federally funded RLFs usually are not allowed to support activities that cause businesses to relocate from one area to another (redistributing national wealth rather than adding to it).

As with most banks, RLFs offer a wide variety of terms on their loans, depending on the situation of the borrower. They may include either fixed- or variable-rate loans with a range of maturities. However, in contrast to private banks that structure their loans primarily to protect themselves against loss, RLF loans are routinely underwritten to help the borrower. Historically, many RLFs have offered below-market interest rates. When variable rates are used, RLFs often impose a cap rate to protect borrowers in the event of large increases in market rates. For any given type of loan, RLFs tend to offer longer maturities than their private counterparts do, and RLFs are far more likely than private banks to allow deferred payments. In many cases, RLFs accept types of collateral not allowed by private lenders. This is especially important to young firms that have few tangible assets. RLFs may also allow loans to be undercollateralized and backed by a personal credit pledge. It is also not unusual for an RLF to take a partial equity position.

RLFs also differ from for-profit lenders in how they monitor and service their loans. RLFs typically go to great lengths to avoid foreclosure and will restructure or refinance a loan to avoid default. Most RLFs spend a great deal of effort to prevent borrowers from ever reaching this point. Even before the loan is made, RLFs work closely with their borrowers to prepare their applications and structure a loan package that is realistic.

Many loan funds also provide or act as clearinghouses for technical assistance and services that can help the business succeed (NADO 1999). This is especially common for RLFs associated with business incubators and those that specialize in lending to microenterprises. For young firms, technical assistance is most likely to take the form of business planning and training in how to run a business. For more mature businesses that have established business plans, technical assistance may take the form of specialized financial counseling and help with auditing and tax reporting issues (Servon et al. 2010).

Integration with Broader Economic Development Activities

In order to fulfill its public mission, an RLF must be more than a lender of last resort. It must fund those activities that add the most to local economic development. This is not an easy task. First, there is an inherent tension in RLF lending between trying to protect the RLF's assets and trying to support those businesses most in need of assistance. When an RLF becomes too risk averse, it may end up supporting activities the private sector would have undertaken anyway; when it becomes too aggressive, the RLF may fund investments with little real chance of success. Second, successful economic development depends as much on how different businesses complement one another as on how they perform individually. RLFs are frequently asked to fund businesses that appear viable but fit poorly with the economic goals of the region.

To balance these conflicting demands, RLF managers need a strong sense of their mission. For most RLFs, the first step in developing such a vision is to prepare a lending plan that explains in some detail how the RLF supports the broader economic development goals of the organization in question. Many funders require such a plan. Unfortunately, some funders and RLF managers treat this planning as a bureaucratic exercise and fail to get the most from it. The planning process is best thought of as a tool that provides the RLF operator with day-to-day guidance on how to manage their funds most effectively. The types of issues that should be discussed in the lending plan include, but are not limited to:

- a brief description of the community's economic strengths and challenges, including the particular credit gaps confronting local entrepreneurs;
- a description of how the RLF serves to address these challenges in the short-, medium-, and long-term, including both general goals and specific milestones to be met (and should include references to any other comprehensive economic development plans or strategies in place and how the RLF lending plan relates to those strategies);
- a prioritization of the types of activities and borrowers to support (with descriptions of other nonprofit lending organizations in the area and explanations of how the RLF will avoid competing with those organizations);
- the RLF's relationship to local banks;
- conflict-of-interest policies (especially important in small communities where borrowers may have personal ties to members of the loan committee);
- how much of the RLF's assets should be loaned out at any given time;
- provisions for reserve funds and other forms of protection against loss;
- a description of additional services to be offered by the RLF;
- a plan for longer-term capitalization and growth of the RLF, including alternative loss and financial scenarios;
- policies and criteria for monitoring and evaluating the progress of the RLF in meeting its goals; and
- principles for revisiting the lending plan from time to time.

The lending plan should not be so specific that it robs fund managers of flexibility. On the other hand, it must be specific enough to provide RLF operators with real guidance in how to manage their funds. Obviously, the RLF's lending plan needs to be developed with broad-based local input—including feedback both from borrowers and from individuals with financial expertise. Again, this cannot be treated as a bureaucratic exercise. Aside from being a very practical form of marketing, the involvement of potential borrowers in the process can help prepare them before they go to the RLF for assistance. Participation by local banks and other nonprofit lenders can ensure that the RLF complements their activities and helps to build partnerships for future projects.

Once a lending plan is in place, the RLF is well advised to develop specific guidelines built on that plan. These can cover operational matters such as:

- underwriting practices, including interest rate ranges, types of loans offered, and preference for fixed or variable rates;
- lending policies or terms to be avoided;
- policies and criteria for evaluating loan applications; and
- servicing and foreclosure policies.

RLF activities and policies can often be constrained by regulations of the funding agencies. EDA, for instance, requires that RLFs fund activities only in the specific distressed area where the RLF operates, actually requiring the RLF to recall the loan if the borrower subsequently moves out of the area. One of the more important variables affecting how an RLF operates is whether its funding comes from grants or loans. The U.S. Department of Agriculture (USDA), for instance, capitalizes its RLFs with low-cost loans, whereas EDA gives grants for this purpose. Because the USDA is concerned that the federal government gets repaid, it requires its RLFs to hold 15 percent of their assets as a reserve fund to protect against substantial defaults. EDA, on the other hand, requires its RLFs to loan nearly all of their money and discourages them from maintaining cash reserves.

Evidence on RLF Performance

There is a growing body of evidence regarding RLF performance. Unfortunately, these studies look at a very diverse group of RLFs and often use inconsistent definitions and evaluation methods. Even with these weaknesses, though, studies suggest that loan losses are often comparable for RLFs and private lenders (Table 4.2). For most studies done since 1990, default rates are modest—usually around or under 10 percent. Still, there are wide differences among funds. In an analysis of Ohio RLFs, for instance, the Washington, DC-based Corporation for Enterprise Development (CFED) found default rates ranging from zero percent to 65 percent. Nearly half the funds older than two years had default rates below 6 percent. In examining statistics regarding defaults or problem loans, it is important to differentiate between the percentage of loans in default and the percentage of dollars involved. Most of the studies shown do not calculate true loss rates, because they fail to account for recoveries of collateral. One exception is research by the National Community Capital Association (NCCA).[2] In a survey of 52 certified Community Development Financial Institutions (CDFIs) lending primarily to businesses, NCCA found loss rates averaging between 4 percent and 8 percent (Lipson 2000).[3]

As a group, RLF loss and default rates are higher than those for private banks. This is to be expected, since RLFs are targeting risky borrowers. Indeed, extremely low loss and/or default rates might indicate that RLFs are making loans to borrowers that could qualify for traditional bank loans. RLF losses may be as low as they are precisely because RLFs provide so much hands-on help to borrowers. This is one possible reason why microenterprise funds—which usually involve more direct assistance to borrowers than other types of funds—are often found to have lower loss and default rates than other RLFs (Levere, Clones, and Marcoux 1997; Edgcomb and Klein 2005).

Table 4.2

Past Research on Revolving Loan Fund (RLF) Delinquencies, Defaults, and Losses

Sources[1]	Year	Population studied	Key findings
Mt. Auburn Associates	1987	EDA RLFs. Fixed Asset Loans	Default rate of 9.6%
Levere, Clones, and Marcoux (CFED)	1997	290 federally funded RLFs	Median default rate of 5.7%
		81 Ohio RLFs	Combined delinquency and default rate of 5.1%
Rutgers et al.	1997	304 fully loaned EDA defense adjustment RLFs	Default rate of 13%
		247 partially loaned EDA defense adjustment RLFs	Default rate of 1.9%
NADO	1999	52 rural RLFs	Default rate of 2%; 42% of RLFs had no defaults at all
Lipson (NCCA)	2000	20 business and microenterprise CDFIs with assets under $2 million	Cumulative loss rate of 7.5%
			90-day delinquency rate of 9.4%
		17 business and microenterprise CDFIs with assets between $2 million and $6 million	Cumulative loss rate of 4.7%
			90-day delinquency rate of 2.6%
		15 business and microenterprise CDFIs with assets over $6 million	Cumulative loss rate of 5.7%
Walker et al. (Urban Institute)	2002	224 HUD CDBG-funded RLFs originated between 1996 and 1999	90-day delinquency rate of 6.0%
			23% historical loss rate on closed loans
Aspen Institute/FIELD	2011	28 microenterprise funds. 2009 data. Rates given as percent of loan value outstanding.	Median loan loss rate: 6% Median portfolio at risk: 9% Median restructured loan rate: 9%

[1]See References at end of chapter for full sources.

In the past, there has been little evidence regarding how RLFs perform over the business cycle. Table 4.3 shows the percentage of loans more than 30 days delinquent for 400–800 RLFs serviced by the Community Reinvestment Fund (CRF) between 2005 and 2009. Similar rates are shown for commercial banks as a reference. We show rates for both real estate and commercial and industrial loans for the private banks. In the boom years of 2005 and 2006, the CRF loans actually outperformed the loans of commercial banks, with significantly lower delinquency rate. During the recession years of 2007 through 2009, the CRF loans performed more poorly than private commercial and industry loans, but still outperformed private real estate loans. The CRF loans include approximately 90 percent business loans, but these may include real estate acquisition. Even in the worst year of 2009, the delinquency rate of 6.3 percent was relatively low.

Looking at economic impacts of RLFs, Levere, Clones, and Marcoux (1997) estimated that the 290 RLFs they studied had loaned more than $560 million and created or saved more than 200,000 jobs at a cost of $5,338 per job. Examining EDA RLFs dedicated to helping communities adjust to defense cutbacks, Rutgers et al. (1997) found that every $1 million contributed by EDA created 304 permanent jobs (an EDA cost of $3,312 per job). The total cost per job was significantly higher in the former group because every $1 of EDA funding leveraged an additional $2.50 of private-sector funding. Still, the researchers noted that these funds had been making loans for only a few years. Many of the projects being funded were barely under way, with their greatest impacts yet to come. The NCCA study noted that, as a group, 52 business-oriented RLFs examined (averaging 12 years in age) created more than 42,000 jobs and retained more than 62,000 jobs on a continuing basis. These funds loaned between 83 percent and 93 percent of their funds to for-profit businesses, and between 63 percent and 76 percent of their funds went to firms with fewer than 20 employees (Lipson 2000).

One problem cited frequently in federal audits is that many RLFs fail to relend their funds promptly (USDOC/OIG 2007; USDA/OIG 2010; EPA 2008). This can happen for a variety of reasons. First, RLFs may have trouble finding borrowers who qualify. This is because RLFs routinely impose standards on borrowers designed to manage the risk to the RLF and to ensure that lending advances the strategic mission of the RLF. Second, the willingness of private banks to lend to nontraditional borrowers varies widely over economic cycles. In periods of relatively easy borrowing, RLFs may find themselves competing with private lenders to a much higher degree than in tighter credit markets. Unfortunately, the regulations governing RLFs may not recognize these realities. EDA, for instance, requires that its RLFs lend out 75 percent of their capital at all times. In the mid-1990s, the Department of Commerce Office

Table 4.3

Delinquency Rates Across the Business Cycle

	Percent of Loans Delinquent				
	2005	2006	2007	2008	2009
Community Reinvestment Fund	.44	.45	1.80	3.10	6.30
Commercial Banks					
Real Estate Loans	1.38	1.48	2.27	4.66	8.44
Commercial and Industry Loans	1.51	1.27	1.22	1.89	3.90

Source: Board of Governors of the Federal Reserve System 2011.
Note: Delinquent loans are those 30 days or more past due. Commercial bank data reported as average of quarterly, seasonally adjusted data.

of the Inspector General strongly criticized EDA because roughly one-third of their RLFs examined had excessive cash reserves (USDOC/OIG 2007). What the report fails to account for is that this was the same period during which cash-rich private lenders were expanding into nontraditional markets in very aggressive ways—many of which eventually contributed to the financial market collapse of 2007 (Grossman, Chen, and Chapel 2005).

Ongoing RLF Capitalization

Despite the revolving nature of their loans, RLFs are not necessarily self-sustaining. While typical loan losses from RLFs are small, they still erode the capital base. Also, most funds must pay their operational expenses from their loan income. As already noted, on a per-loan basis, these costs tend to be high due to the close monitoring and training typically provided by RLFs. The ability of RLFs to absorb these operational costs and loan losses depends to a large degree on how much they charge their borrowers. For many years, there has been a debate in the industry regarding the need for subsidized interest rates. Clearly, those funds that offer subsidized rates will have a greater need for ongoing recapitalization (Pollinger et al. 2007). Yet another factor contributing to the need for recapitalization is that many RLFs have moved into new types of lending such as microlending and venture capital.

The demand for RLF loans tends to be highly cyclical, with commercial lending institutions being more or less willing to provide capital to small and nontraditional borrowers depending on wider credit market conditions. At the same time, longer-term deterioration in the fiscal health of federal and state governments has made it increasingly difficult to capitalize new funds and recapitalize existing ones. Rubin (2008) found that for community development loan funds more generally (i.e., not just those making economic development loans), federal funding had declined to less than 10 percent of total capitalization by 2005. Many funders are also hesitant to provide support for RLF recapitalization where funds have been depleted due to loan losses or because loans were made at below-market rates. Faced with these realities, funding agencies and RLF operators have experimented with a variety of new approaches to recapitalizing RLFs by tapping private capital markets.

One of the most straightforward approaches to recapitalization is collateralized borrowing. This refers to borrowing (usually from local banks) using the loans as security. In this approach, the RLF retains control of its loans unless there is difficulty making payment on the recapitalization loan. The main drawback of collateralized borrowing is that participating banks typically insist that a large portion (as much as one-third) of the cash raised be set aside as a reserve against possible defaults (Richardson 1996). Although this reserve ultimately reverts to the RLF and may earn income in the meantime, funds in the reserve pool are not available for immediate lending.

Another approach to recapitalization is to encourage banks to invest in RLFs in return for Community Reinvestment Act (CRA) credit. One example of this approach is the *equity equivalent* (EQ2) investment, pioneered by NCCA and Citibank with support from the Ford Foundation (Park 2000; Stearns 2001). EQ2 investments are loans that have many similarities to an equity investment. First of all, they have a long initial term (typically 10 years). This term is rolling, meaning that it is automatically extended each year unless terminated by the investor. Interest rates on the investment are set independent of the RLF's anticipated cash flows, and no payment on principal is made until the loan is due. Second, the loans are uncollateralized and deeply subordinated. This means, for instance, that the RLF can subsequently pledge its portfolio to back a bond sale. If there were an interruption in repayment, the bondholders would be paid ahead of the EQ2 investors. In return for these very favorable terms to the RLF, the investors (typically banks) receive highly leveraged CRA treatment. Park explains how this works for a hypothetical Community Development Financial Institution:

> Assuming a nonprofit CDFI has "equity" of $2 million—$1 million in the form of permanent capital and $1 million in equity equivalents provided by a commercial bank—the bank's portion of the CDFI's "equity" is 50 percent. Now assume that the CDFI uses this $2 million to borrow $8 million in senior debt. With its $10 million capital under management, the CDFI makes $7 million in community development loans over a two-year period. In this

> example, the bank is entitled to claim its pro rata share of loans originated, 50 percent or $3.5 million. Its $1 million investment results in $3.5 million of lending credit over two years. (Lipson 2002, p. 11)

If there is any weakness to EQ2 investing, it is its complete reliance on the Community Reinvestment Act. Were CRA to be weakened significantly or if other forms of CRA investments came along that allowed investors to earn a greater profit, EQ2 could become less attractive. To date, CRA has survived many challenges and remains a potent tool for promoting investment in distressed areas.

Perhaps the most promising long-term approach to RLF recapitalization is securitization. This refers to using the income stream from an RLF portfolio to back a security sale. Cash from the sale is used to make additional loans, and income from the loans goes to repay investors. Small business loans have been securitized since 1985, when the SBA began to pool and sell the guaranteed portion of their loans. Many other cases of securitization followed. These early models were what were known as "pass-through" securities, in which the loan payments were transferred directly to investors. For any given pool of loans, a single type of security was sold that reflected the risk and income stream characteristics of the entire pool.

One of the largest challenges that the RLF industry had to overcome was that its securities were attractive to very limited types of investors—usually philanthropic investors willing to receive a lower return in order to support economic development. In part, this is because these securities were not rated by credit rating agencies such as Standard & Poor's. The lack of such ratings precluded the purchase of RLF-backed securities by institutional investors such as pension funds, because these types of investors are allowed to buy only those securities rated as "investment grade." RLF-backed securities could be sold to noninstitutional, for-profit investors willing to take on added risk, but only by paying high yields.

Nearly all securities backed by RLF loans have incorporated some form of credit enhancement to lower the interest rates required to attract investors. One of the most common approaches to credit enhancement is overcollateralization. Most often, this involves setting aside the income from additional loans as a reserve pool to safeguard investors. Bond issuers may also obtain insurance to guarantee their payments to investors in the event of large loan losses. Yet another approach is for an issuer to take out a letter of credit from a local bank. The bank then pays the investors. Because the bank's credit rating is likely to be higher than that of the bond issuer, the latter is essentially paying a fee to the bank in return for renting its higher credit rating. The issuer then repays the line of credit from the loan income.

During the 1990s, a more sophisticated form of credit enhancement developed in the form of "structured" securities. These securities have their income flows divided into multiple pools or *tranches.* Investors in the senior tranche are paid first, with any remaining income used to pay junior investors. In return for accepting higher risk, the junior investors typically receive a higher yield. Alternatively, the junior investor might be a philanthropic investor. For example, in 1994 the South Carolina Jobs–Economic Development (JEDA) divided an $11 million pool into two tiers. The first was a $7 million senior security sold to the MacArthur Foundation. The remaining income flowed to JEDA only after the senior investor was paid (Richardson 1996). In principle, there can be any number of tranches, but the basic principle is the same—more subordinated bondholders will usually be more tolerant of risk, but also demand a higher yield.

RLFs considering securitization as a recapitalization strategy need to assess a variety of important factors. First, of course, they need to determine how much cash they can raise by the securitization. In practice, an individual RLF is very unlikely to have sufficient loans to back a bond issue. As a result, they typically sell their loans to an intermediary, which buys a large pool of loans from many different RLFs. To conclude this transaction, the intermediary and the RLF must agree on a market value for each individual loan. This market value is roughly equal to the present value of the payment stream generated by the loan. This, in turn, depends on: (1) current interest rates (usually based on treasury yields), (2) the interest rate on the loan, and (3) the term remaining. Note that, in principle, a loan can actually be sold at more than par if it is earning an interest rate above current treasury yields. This actually occurred for some loans included in a securitization pilot project conducted by EDA during 1999–2001 (Robinson 2001).

In calculating the present value of each loan, the actual interest rate on the loan is usually adjusted downward by some "spread" that reflects the underlying risk to the investor. A loan with greater risk is assigned a larger spread, reflecting its lower expected value to the investor. The types of risk most likely to influence the spread are:

- Credit risk: the risk that the borrower will default (usually measured by a credit score);
- Issuer risk: the risk that the issuer of the security will go bankrupt;
- Prepayment risk: the risk that the borrower will pay the debt off early;
- Interest rate risk: the risk that interest rates will subsequently rise, leaving the investor locked into a low-paying asset; and
- Regulatory risk: the risk that a borrower from a government-funded RLF may fail to comply with some rule or regulation, causing their loan to be recalled.

Other things the RLF will want to consider before undergoing securitization include (1) how the loans are purchased and (2) who services them. Loans are typically purchased either by *forward commitment* or by *warehousing*. In a forward commitment, the intermediary agrees to buy the loans at some future date (when they have obtained enough loans to issue a security) at terms agreed upon in advance. In a warehousing approach, the pool assembler actually pays for the loans in advance, usually with a line of credit. This is the approach used for many years by CRF—the largest and longest operating purchaser of RLF loans. In principle, the main difference in the approaches is who bears the risk that the interest rates will rise between the time an agreement is made and the security is issued. In reality, an intermediary that warehouses loans may build this risk into their spread when pricing the loans.

RLF managers also need to be concerned with who will service the loans after they are sold. As part of their economic development mission, RLFs often have close relationships with their borrowers and do not wish to turn servicing over to a third party. In many instances, intermediaries have allowed RLFs to retain servicing of their loans. One way of protecting both investors and borrowers is to rely on a *recourse* provision. Under this sort of arrangement, if a borrower is severely delinquent or threatens default, the RLF swaps that loan out of the securitized pool for another loan in its portfolio. Of course, this requires the RLF to hold enough loans out of the securitization to honor its recourse obligations.

A number of public policy issues arise in the securitization of RLFs, mainly because so many RLFs are capitalized with public funds. For instance, one frequently asked question is, should federal and/or state governments subordinate the public interest in loans being securitized? If investors are not given first claim to the income from the loans, they are either going to discount the loans on sale or require a higher yield to compensate for the added risk—assuming they do not simply walk away from the deal. Another issue is how cash raised by securitization of publicly funded RLFs should be treated. Is it public money? Virtually all federally funded RLFs have audit requirements that require the tracking of public funds. This gets complicated when the public funds are combined with nonpublic money (such as when there is some matching requirement) in the original loan pool. Credit enhancement, subordination of payments, and other activities that are part of securitization make it even more difficult to track which portion of the funds in any given pool of loans are public. Finally, related issues may stem from how the proceeds from the securitization of publicly funded RLFs can be used. Most federal agencies that fund RLFs specify the types of activities that can be funded and how quickly the money must be loaned out, as well as requiring that borrowers pay prevailing wages under the Davis-Bacon Act.[4] Do these rules apply to money raised from the security sale as well? These are all thorny policy issues with which government agencies wishing to support securitization must grapple.

Since 1990, the market for RLF-backed securities has grown much more slowly than the markets for other types of structured finance. There are many reasons for this. Some RLF operators have been reluctant to offer their loans due to fears that they would have to accept deep discounts or that they would have to sacrifice their mission by accepting standardized underwriting and loss of control over servicing. At the same time, the lack of standardized reporting and underwriting has kept the costs of assembling, rating, and marketing these securities high. Also, the scale of loans offered for sale has generally not been sufficient to support public offerings.

On the positive side, RLFs wishing to securitize their loans have generally been able to do so, albeit not necessarily on the terms they desire. Furthermore, and in stark contrast to other securities markets, there have been very few, if any, instances of investors' losses associated with the purchase of RLF-backed securities.

Conclusion

Thirty-five years after its inception, the revolving loan fund has become one of the standard tools used by economic development professionals. Nationwide, RLFs number in the thousands and have loaned billions of dollars to people lacking ready access to private capital markets. Once dominated by very small, highly generalized, small business lenders, the industry today includes large and highly specialized market segments such as microenterprise lending, environmental remediation, and venture capital.

Although loan losses and delinquencies for RLFs vary widely among funds, there is considerable evidence that loan performance for most RLFs is comparable to that of commercial lenders—especially if we adjust for the nature of the borrowers. At the same time, the solid performance of RLF loans often requires additional costs related to training, technical assistance, and oversight. These costs are recurring, increasing over time, and are often harder to fund than the initial RLF capitalization. This is one reason why it is so critical to continue finding new sources of capital and to increase fund efficiency. Given the severity of state and federal budget deficits in 2010, the prospects for enhanced governmental funding would appear to be poor for many years to come.

Developing reliable funding sources for RLFs will require considerable effort by all parties concerned. In order to preserve any significant governmental funding, RLF operators need to document their community benefits better than they have to date. Moreover, they need to do this in a standardized fashion that allows the industry as a whole to demonstrate its impact on the nation. At the same time, RLF operators must recognize the necessity of attracting private capital. Prior authors have argued that securitization is unlikely to become the main source of fund recapitalization anytime soon (USGAO 2003; Walker et al. 2002). This is probably true, but it could certainly become a much larger contributor than it is today. Fund managers would incur relatively little cost to adopt greater standardization in reporting methods. To be sure, the utility of RLFs would be severely diminished if they lost the flexibility to underwrite loans in ways that suit their wide range of borrowers. Having said that, opportunities remain to adopt underwriting practices that make their loans easier to securitize. In recent years, we have seen many RLFs expand their use of credit scoring and reduce their reliance on below-market interest rates. A logical next step would be for the RLF industry to move toward greater standardization in loan documentation—something that knowledgeable observers have recommended for many years.

Time has shown that the relationship between RLFs and private financial institutions is a complicated one. When capital markets are tight, RLF lending supports private lenders by reducing their risk in lending to new and nontraditional borrowers. However, when credit markets are unusually loose—as they were in the years leading up to the financial crash of 2007—RLFs can end up competing more directly with private banks as the latter move into markets they traditionally avoid (Grossman, Chen, and Chapel 2005). The private sector cannot be counted on to work cooperatively with RLFs simply because there is a need for lending. However, where private firms have a genuine commitment to their communities, or where they are forced to invest locally by regulation, they must understand that working with RLFs is a very effective form of economic development. Whether they buy securitized RLF loans, assist in credit enhancement, or provide capital directly to RLF pools, their help is welcome.

In order to make the most of their severely constrained budgets, federal and state governments are going to use their existing funds more productively. In this respect, it would probably make sense to undertake less direct capitalization of RLF pools, and instead use those same funds to provide additional credit enhancement of existing loans pools. This approach can leverage existing funds by making loans more attractive for securitization.

Aside from the obvious budgetary difficulties, governmental agencies that fund RLFs need to reform their regulations regarding fund use. Utilization requirements that prevent RLFs from retaining cash reserves ignore the tenuous relationship between private banks and RLFs. Providing that they use fair lending practices, it is a good thing when private lenders move into markets traditionally supported by RLFs. However, the current rules force RLFs facing increased competition from private banks either to make riskier loans than they normally would, or to return their funds to the government. In either case, when private lenders pull back, RLFs are inevitably undercapitalized and unable to assist their traditional borrowers during times of greatest need.

This point is key. Deregulation of private capital markets has certainly increased access to capital for many firms, including some smaller firms. However, the ability and willingness of the private market to provide that capital is unreliable at best. The smallest firms and development activities that generate little immediate profit still have difficulty obtaining capital in the best of times. In difficult times, they are the first to be denied capital. In this sense, the role of RLFs remains as important as ever.

Notes

1. More than 99 percent of all firms in the United States fall into this category. Some 96 percent of all firms have fewer than 50 employees (U.S. Census Bureau, 2007).
2. The National Community Capital Association subsequently changed its name to Opportunity Finance Network.
3. The term *community development financial institution* (CDFI) can refer either to a generic form of RLF, or RLFs funded under the U.S. Department of the Treasury program of the same name. The generic term usually refers to RLFs that are organized independent of a governmental organization, although they may receive governmental funds.
4. 29 CFR 1.5.

References

Aspen Institute, FIELD. 2011. FY2009 Program Performance Overview. http://fieldus.org/MicroTest/FY09PerformanceOverview.pdf (accessed April 15, 2011).

Board of Governors of the Federal Reserve System. 2011. *97th Annual Report 2010.* June, www.federalreserve.gov/publications/annual-report/files/2010-annual-report.pdf (accessed June 1, 2012).

Brash, Rachel. 2008. *Public Sector Duplication of Small Business Administration Loan and Investment Programs: An Analysis of Overlap Between Federal, State, and Local Programs Providing Financial Assistance to Small Businesses.* Final report prepared for the U.S. Small Business Administration. Washington, DC: The Urban Institute, January.

Brash, Rachel, and Megan Gallagher. 2008. *A Performance Analysis of SBA's Loan and Investment Programs.* Final report prepared for the U.S. Small Business Administration. Washington, DC: The Urban Institute, January.

Community Development Financial Institution (CDFI) Data Project. 2008. *Providing Capital, Building Communities, Creating Impact.* Washington, DC.

Dommel, Paul. 1995. *Secondary Markets for City-Owned CDBG Loans* (Prepared for the U.S. Department of Housing and Urban Development). Cleveland, OH: Cleveland State University.

Edgcomb, Elaine L., and Joyce A. Klein. 2005. *Opening Opportunities, Building Ownership: Fulfilling the Promise of Microenterprise in the United States*. Washington, DC: The Aspen Institute, February.

Grossman, Patty, Ellen Chen, and Paige Chapel. 2005. *Findings and Recommendations: Supply-Side Scan of Microenterprise Financing*. Washington, DC: The Aspen Institute, October.

Helfand, Jessica, Akbar Sadeghi, and David Talan. 2007. Employment dynamics: Small and large firms over the business cycle. *Monthly Labor Review,* March: 39–50.

Levere, Andrea, Daphne Clones, and Kent Marcoux. 1997. *Counting on Local Capital: A Research Project on Revolving Loan Funds.* Washington, DC: Corporation for Enterprise Development.

Lipson, Beth. 2000. *CDFIs Side by Side: A Comparative Guide,* 2000 edition. Philadelphia, PA: National Community Capital Association.

———. 2002. *Community Investments* (March). www.frbsf.org/publications/community/investments/cra02-2/equity.pdf (accessed February 3, 2012).

Mach, Traci L., and John D. Wolken. 2006. Financial services used by small businesses: Evidence from the 2003 survey of small business finances. *Federal Reserve Bulletin,* October: A167–A195.

Mt. Auburn Associates. 1987. *Factors Influencing the Performance of U.S. Economic Development Administration Sponsored Revolving Loan Funds.* Somerville, MA: Author.

National Association of Development Organizations (NADO). 1999. *The Performance and Impact of Revolving Loan Funds in Rural America.* Washington, DC: NADO Research Foundation.

Park, Kyong Hui. 2000. Information on equity equivalent investments. Memorandum to David Witshci, National Community Capital Association, May 26.

Pollinger, J. Jordan, John Outhwaite, and Hector Cordero-Guzmán. 2007. The question of sustainability for microfinance institutions. *Journal of Small Business Management* 45(1): 23–41.

Richardson, L.B. 1996. *A Strategy to Increase Economic Development by Providing a Source of RLF Recapitalization from the Capital Markets through the Utilization of Private Securitization.* Baltimore, MD: Alex, Brown and Sons, Inc.

Robinson, Kelly. 2001. *Expanding Capital Resources for Economic Development: An RLF Demonstration.* Washington, DC: Economic Development Administration, U.S. Department of Commerce.

Rubin, Julia S. 2008. Adaptation or extinction? Community development loan funds at a crossroads. *Journal of Urban Affairs* 30(2): 191–220.

Rutgers University, New Jersey Institute of Technology, Columbia University, Princeton University, National Association of Regional Councils, and University of Cincinnati. 1997. *Defense Adjustment Program Performance Evaluation.* Final report prepared for the Economic Development Administration, U.S. Department of Commerce. New Brunswick, NJ: Center for Urban Policy Research at Rutgers University.

Servon, Lisa J., and Jeffrey P. Doshna. 1998. *Making Microenterprise Development a Part of the Economic Development Toolkit.* Prepared for the Economic Development Administration, U.S. Department of Commerce. New Brunswick, NJ: Center for Urban Policy Research at Rutgers University.

Servon, Lisa J., Robert W. Fairlie, Blaise Rastello, and Amber Seely. 2010. The five gaps facing small and microbusiness owners: Evidence from New York City. *Economic Development Quarterly* 24(2): 126–142.

Stearns, Kathy. 2001. *EDA Secondary Market Demonstration Project for Revolving Loan Funds in South Dakota.* Prepared for South Dakota Rural Enterprise, Inc. Philadelphia, PA: National Community Capital Association.

U.S. Census Bureau. 2007. Statistics of U.S. Businesses, Washington, DC.

U.S. Department of Agriculture, Office of the Inspector General (USDA/OIG). 2010. *Rural Business Cooperative Service's Intermediary Relending Program.* Audit Report 34601–6-AT, June.

U.S. Department of Commerce, Economic Development Administration (EDA). 2010. About the RLF program: How it works. www.eda.gov/PDF/RLFWorks.pdf (accessed April 15, 2011).

U.S. Department of Commerce, Office of the Inspector General (USDOC/OIG). 2007. *Aggressive EDA Leadership and Oversight Needed to Correct Persistent Problems in RLF Program.* OA-18200, March.

U.S. Environmental Protection Agency (EPA). 2008. *EPA Should Continue Efforts to Reduce Unliquidated Obligations in Brownfields Pilots Grants.* Report No. 08-P-0265, September.

U.S. General Accounting Office (USGAO). 2003. *Community and Economic Development Loans: Securitization Faces Significant Barriers.* Report to Congressional Requesters, GAO-04-21, October 17.

Walker, Christopher, Martin D. Abravanel, Patrick Boxall, Roger C. Kormendi, Kenneth Temkin, and Marsha Tonkovich. 2002. *Public-Sector Loans to Private-Sector Businesses: An Assessment of HUD-Supported Local Economic Development Lending Activities.* Final report. Washington, DC: The Urban Institute, December.

Williams, Marva. 1997. *Credit to the Community: The Role of CDCUs in Community Development.* Chicago: Woodstock Institute.

5

Using Transfer of Development Rights as a Market-Based Approach in Urban Land Use Management

Matt Brinkley and Patricia L. Machemer

Many urban areas contending with land use challenges (e.g., land preservation, habitat fragmentation, historic preservation, affordable housing, and infrastructure planning) are seeking market-based policy solutions (McConnell, Kopits, and Walls 2003). Given the fiscal situations of municipalities and states, solutions that use private funds rather than public funds are attractive (Aoki, Briscoe, and Hovland 2005, Fulton et al. 2004). Land use regulation, takings (restrictions on the use of land), and eminent domain may all be addressed with transfer of development rights (also called transferable development rights, or TDRs). TDR programs offer a potential market-based solution that allows the separation and transfer of the right to develop land in a free-market system of willing sellers and buyers. Feiock, Tavares, and Lubell (2008) support the notion that TDRs improve the actual market allocation of land by reducing transaction costs. However, Fulton et al. (2004) have noted that land-based markets are difficult to manage because it is challenging to predict the number of landowners in the marketplace, the strength of their interest in the development market, and what the time frame for their engagement is likely to be.

Although TDR was developed in the mid-1970s, it continues to interest planners, members of the development and conservation communities, citizens, and scholars. Researchers have reported the existence of 130–181 TDR programs in the United States at the local, county, and regional levels. These programs' stated goals include protecting environmentally sensitive areas, conserving agricultural or historical sites, promoting affordable housing, and rehabilitating urban areas (Fulton et al. 2004; Machemer and

Kaplowitz 2002; Pruetz 2003; Walls and McConnell 2007). Although some describe TDR programs as creative and innovative (Pruetz 2003), many questions concerning their operation and overall effectiveness as a land use tool remain. Walls and McConnell (2004, p. 13) contend that TDRs "have met with only limited success. . . . Only a handful have had active markets with numerous trades of development rights each year and a significant amount of preserved acreage."

TDR Definition and Program Elements

TDR programs involve the option to sell in a free market the development rights—that is, the unused development potential of a parcel of land—to compensate or mitigate the cost of land use restrictions. A program typically offers incentives to landowners to sell TDRs, along with additional incentives to other landowners to purchase them. Usually, rights are sold by landowners in areas where on-site development is limited and purchased by developers who want to build more intensively (build at bonus uses or densities) on other parcels where development is permitted: The development rights from the limited-development area are transferred to the area where development is permitted. The TDR buyer gains bonus density, the seller gains capital through the sale of TDRs, and the community benefits from managed growth and resource preservation, whether it be agricultural lands, open space, historic sites, or environmentally sensitive lands.

The basic elements of a TDR program are a *sending area* (the area to be preserved), a *receiving area* (the area to be developed), severable *development rights,* and a *transfer process* by which rights are conveyed. Most TDR programs work to preserve or protect land or some other spatially defined resource such as historic structures. These resources occupy or are located in a geographic area or zone known as the sending area (or granting area). Landowners in sending areas are limited in their on-site development opportunities but are assigned development rights. Development rights can be removed from sending areas and "sent" to receiving areas, where they can be used. Typically, landowners in sending areas receive a payment in exchange for the sale or transfer of their properties' development rights. After selling their parcel's development rights, landowners may continue permitted land uses on their property (e.g., predevelopment activities such as agriculture or passive recreation), as defined in the easement or deed restrictions. Once development rights to the property in the sending area are sold, those rights can no longer be used in the sending area; the land or building from which they were removed can no longer be developed as it might have been before the transfer.

TDR programs' receiving areas are those regions designated for more intensive growth and development. TDRs usually permit development of a particular type and density beyond those permissible under the receiving area's standard (base) zoning and regulation. For example, the use of TDR may allow for increases in the number of dwelling units per unit area and increases in floor area ratio (FAR). As a result, parcels in TDR receiving areas are often subject to dual zoning regulations—a base zoning regime and a bonus zoning regime for parcels with applicable TDRs. A party interested in developing land in such a region purchases the severed development right(s) from a region where development is limited and uses them to develop at greater density (in the case of residential land uses) or intensity (in the case of commercial land uses) in the target region than would otherwise have been possible given the underlying land use restrictions.

Beyond increased density, other potential incentives exist that encourage receiving-area landowners or developers to purchase TDRs. Changes in parking or impervious surface ratios are among such incentives: Landowners in receiving areas may purchase TDRs for either an increase or decrease in parking requirements. In jurisdictions where the amount of impervious surface is regulated, development rights may be purchased to increase this limit. A landowner in a receiving site may also purchase development rights to substitute for or decrease open space, parkland, or setbacks requirements. If a community requires impact fees, then the purchase of development rights may substitute for that fee. In municipalities that place limits on carbon emissions, carbon credits associated with a development right can offset a development project's carbon emissions or be sold on the open market. In addition, the purchase of development rights may permit a landowner to move through the development submission and approval processes more quickly.

Aside from incentives for individual receiving-area landowners, incentives may also be offered to municipalities that incorporate receiving areas into their master plans. A regional or county program can offer a percentage of the development right value to a city in order to encourage it to accept TDRs.

The components of TDR programs are tied together by the procedures adopted for transferring TDRs from sending-area landowners to receiving-area landowners. TDR transfers may take place (1) between adjacent parcels, (2) within a designated district, as in Chicago's program, (3) from nonurban to urban areas within a jurisdiction (e.g., in Dade County, FL, and Montgomery County, MD), and (4) within a region between jurisdictions (e.g., the New Jersey Pinelands and municipalities within Thurston County, WA; the former under state and federal legislation and the latter under state growth management legislation). While regional and interjurisdictional programs remain relatively rare, they are increasing (Fulton et al. 2004). Transfers between adjacent parcels may involve parcels under the same ownership, as is the case in several townships in York County, PA (American Farmland Trust 1997), or parcels owned by several landowners, as in New York City's program.

TDR Connections to Other Land Use Techniques

TDR programming borrows from accepted growth management techniques such as zoning, purchase of development rights (PDR), mitigation, and cluster development. The process includes preservation (sending areas) and development (receiving areas) districts, thus borrowing from the well-known zoning concept. TDR programming may be tied to increasing density by requiring receiving areas to build at higher densities, rather than simply permitting upzoning and zoning variances. In this way, some of the development potential will be captured for the preservation of other lands. Through this shifting of development, the public can secure some of the windfall profits that accrue to those who now succeed in getting use variances or zoning changes (Moore 1975; Siemon, Larsen, and Marsh 1996; Willis 1975). TDR may be viewed as a type of zoning, one that provides rights as a compensation mechanism to balance the premium in land value that accrues to landowners in the designated growth areas against the corresponding financial wipeout in value experienced by landowners in the preservation areas (Gottsegen 1992).

TDR expands the PDR concept. Once the development rights are severed from one parcel, rather than being retired, they can be sold or transferred to another parcel where the development potential can be realized. A major difference between TDR and PDR is that while the latter relies on public purchases of conservation easements, TDR programming relies on private-market sales of development rights between preservation landowners and developers. Market forces determine which parcels in the preservation area will be protected under easement, whereas with PDR, the administrative body determines which parcels will be protected. Another major difference is that with PDR, development rights never have their development potential realized, whereas with TDR utilization of the development potential is critical to program success.

Fulton et al. (2004) note that the theoretical underpinnings for market-based techniques such as TDR are found in air and water pollution trading. In effect, TDRs are a mitigation program designed to preserve agricultural land, open space, historic buildings and districts, environmentally sensitive lands, or other land that is less suitable for development while still allowing the landowners to recover some financial benefit from their unfulfilled development expectations

(Siemon, Larsen, and Marsh 1996). Like wetlands credits, TDRs mitigate a landowner's unfulfilled development expectations. A TDR thereby moderates the impact of preservation zoning in the sending area (Gottsegen 1992). Looked at another way, TDRs are also mitigation efforts by virtue of the fact that developers are permitted to develop at higher densities if they balance out that increased density through the preservation of other areas.

While cluster development permits a density shift from one portion of a site to another portion of the same site, TDR permits a density shift from one portion of a site to another, noncontiguous site. TDR is a system designed to permit the orderly reallocation of density within a given community in a manner that meets legitimate planning objectives and without placing unfair burdens on property owners (Redman/Johnson Associates 1994). With cluster development, the overall density of the site remains the same; with TDR, the overall density of the program area remains the same.

History of TDR

TDR combines the concepts of separation of development rights and the control of development, neither of which is innovative in itself. European policy has long included such concepts in its land management. For example, Britain nationalized all development rights in 1947 with the passage of its Town and County Planning Act: Now, development rights are created and allocated by society. *Ownership* is simply the right to continue using the land as it is currently utilized. Landowners have no inherent right to develop. The conceptual key to TDR programs is the notion that development rights are one of many sets of rights associated with fee simple (or absolute) land ownership.

In the United States, the TDR concept was first introduced by Lloyd (1961). Chavooshian, Budd, and Nieswand (1973) studied the concept of TDR in environmental planning and open-space preservation. Rose (1975) and Carmichael (1975) examined the legal and economic aspects. Costonis (1975) discussed the use of TDRs as a method of historic landmark preservation that avoided the takings issue.

During the late 1960s and early 1970s, a number of first-generation programs were established. Developers in New York City have undertaken actual transference of the right to development for decades. While they have made use of air rights (vertical development rights) to construct buildings exceeding standard zoning density, it was not until 1968 that a TDR program was developed specifically for landmark buildings. That same year, New York City amended its zoning ordinance to permit a transfer of development rights from a designated landmark building to adjacent lots on the same block, across the street or diagonally (Pruetz 1997, 2003; Roddewig and Inghram 1987). The idea was to protect historic buildings by transferring some or all of the difference between the floor area allowance of the designated landmark building in question and that of the potential new structure that could be developed if the landmark were razed. The TDRs are allocated based on the unused FAR from the landmark building and are transferred to receiving sites on a one-to-one basis. The purpose of this TDR program is twofold: to ensure preservation of historical landmark buildings and to ensure quality development on adjacent sites. New York's TDR program was the first in the country, and it continues to be one of the most successful (Roddewig and Inghram 1987).

TDR was also concerned with agricultural land preservation. In the 1970s, it was considered a mechanism for curbing urban sprawl and protecting farmland and the agricultural community. TDR was also seen as a means to encourage redevelopment and the development or rehabilitation of low-income housing (Kaplowitz, Machemer, and Pruetz 2008; Pruetz 1997, 2003; Roddewig and Inghram 1987; Rory 1975).

Early scholarly examinations of the efficacy of first-generation TDR programs in such locations as New York City, Collier County, FL, and Calvert County, MD, focused on practical aspects of TDR programming and made suggestions for second-generation TDR programs (Barrese 1983; Maabs-Zeno 1981; Pizor 1978, 1986; Roddewig and Inghram 1987; Tustian 1983; Woodbury 1975). A second wave of TDR programs began to be implemented in the 1980s in such places as the New Jersey Pinelands, Denver, CO, and Pittsburgh, PA. TDR use in urbanized areas gained attention in the 1980s for historic preservation in the western American cities of Denver, Seattle, and San Francisco. The literature on these second-generation programs emphasizes the importance of stakeholders and their inclusion in program design and implementation (Heiberg 1991; Johnston and Madison 1997; Pruetz 1997; Redman/Johnson Associates 1994; Walls and McConnell 2007).

That literature, with its emphasis on program participants and incentives, was taken into account by so-called third-generation programs. Walls and McConnell (2007) note that third-generation programs address the challenges and problems with receiving areas identified in the second-generation programs. Third-generation programs include revised versions of earlier TDR programs (e.g., Chesterfield Township, NJ) and completely new TDR programs (e.g., Thurston County, WA).

TDR Case Law Considerations: *Penn Central v. City of New York* (1978)

The most frequently cited case regarding the transference of development potential is *Penn Central Transportation Co. v. City of New York* 38 U.S. 104

(1978). Under the city's Landmarks Law, Penn Central, the owner of the New York landmark Grand Central Terminal, could not build an office tower over the terminal. Penn Central sued the city, claiming that the landmark's regulation was, in effect, a taking. In this case, the New York Court of Appeals and the U.S. Supreme Court upheld New York City's Landmarks Law. The New York Court of Appeals held that there was no taking because there was no physical invasion. The issue was then whether the regulation violated due process by depriving Penn Central of a reasonable return. The court determined that Penn Central did have the capability to earn a return from the parcel, through the availability of transferrable air rights and through the terminal's current use. The court viewed the existence of TDRs as a mitigating factor in determining the validity of the regulation in question. Furthermore, there were several identifiable receiving parcels owned by the plaintiff in the vicinity of the terminal and suitable for the proposed use. "The city's TDR program as it applied to a specific piece of property was important in the decision. New York's highest court approved the development rights concept in theory and developed a standard for determining when the provision of TDRs is constitutionally sufficient to offset any burden imposed on a property owner by regulation or protection of a landmark property" (Roddewig and Inghram 1987, p. 15). While the New York Court of Appeals did not have to view the TDRs as possible "just compensation" because there was no taking, it did comment on the consideration of TDRs:

> If the substitute rights received [the TDRs] provide reasonable compensation for a landowner forced to relinquish development rights on a landmark site, there has been no deprivation of due process. The compensation need not be the "just" compensation required in eminent domain, for there has been no attempt to take property. (366 NE 2d at 1278)

The U.S. Supreme Court affirmed the lower court's finding and commented generally on the TDR concept. The Supreme Court majority opinion agreed that Penn Central was not denied all economic use because rights could be transferred to several parcels. The Court stated:

> While these rights may well not have constituted "just compensation" if a "taking" had occurred, the rights nevertheless undoubtedly mitigate whatever financial burdens the law has imposed on appellants and, for that reason, are to be taken into account in consideration of the impact of regulation. (438 U.S. at 137)

The Supreme Court conceded that, in this takings claim, TDR had value. Aoki, Briscoe, and Hovland (2005) note that this decision seems to classify

TDRs as residual value left in the property after land use regulations are applied. They note that in *Suitum v. Tahoe Regional Planning Agency* 520 U.S. 725 1175 Ct. 1659 (1997), the Supreme Court opinion suggests that a future decision could legally categorize TDRs on the side of just compensation rather than residual value (Aoki, Briscoe, and Hovland 2005).

The U.S. Supreme Court's Justice Antonin Scalia wrote that if a government easement leaves no economic use, a taking has occurred, even if TDRs are allocated. Scalia argued that if TDRs were viewed as residual value, governments could provide only partial compensation for a full taking; furthermore, he stated that TDRs should be evaluated on the "compensation side of the takings analysis"—that is, they should serve as partial or full compensation for a taking, depending on the amount of the taking and the value of the TDRs created (Aoki, Briscoe, and Hovland 2005). In this case, Scalia viewed TDRs as administrative contrivances created to mitigate the impact of government regulations, and thus distinct from the rights inherent in landownership (Renard 2007). Renard supports Scalia's position and argues that TDRs in the United States are a form of compensation offered to landowners for zoning restrictions rather than a tool for developing a market in development rights (2007).

Frequently Cited Advantages and Disadvantages of TDR

The literature on TDR programming from all generations of programs includes claims of the advantages of TDR as a growth management technique as well as recognition of TDR program disadvantages (Aoki, Briscoe, and Hovland 2005; Bateman 1975; Bowers 1995; Pruetz 2003; Siemon, Larsen, and Marsh 1996; Walls and McConnell 2007). What follows is a summary of the frequently cited advantages and disadvantages.

Advantages

- TDRs provide landowners and developers with greater flexibility. For example, preservation landowners retain the underlying property for uses other than on-site development.
- TDRs reduce the "windfalls" and "wipeouts" that frequently accompany governmental use of the police power and zoning to regulate land use. TDR was first developed as a means of avoiding the usually harsh results of downzoning (wipeouts) and the usually beneficial results of upzoning (windfalls) (Siemon, Larsen, and Marsh 1996).
- TDRs balance the advantages and disadvantages of public policy decisions regarding planning and land development (Siemon, Larsen, and Marsh 1996).

- By identifying sending and receiving areas, TDRs make possible appropriate planning of efficient services and infrastructure (Aoki, Briscoe, and Hovland 2005).
- TDRs make possible more effective long-term preservation of environmentally sensitive areas, open space, and agricultural lands. The associated deed restrictions are in perpetuity.
- TDRs make possible unification of plans and programs for development and environmental, historical, and cultural protection.
- Receiving landowners may be eligible for local or state tax deductions.
- Receiving landowners may receive preferential treatment in the development review process.
- TDRs shift a larger share of the total social cost of new development to the developer and ultimate consumer.
- TDRs are market driven, utilizing private funding rather than public funds. They preserve land without spending tax dollars.
- TDRs make it possible to recoup a portion of the private gains created by public investment.

Disadvantages

- TDR is a challenging growth management technique. It is often complicated to design and implement, and it requires continual analysis and management.
- TDRs require planning commitment. The ability to achieve zoning variances and changes would doom TDR programs to failure.
- TDRs require political commitment, municipal leadership, and extensive public education.
- TDRs require developer, builder, and realtor support. These groups have traditionally been opposed to further regulation of land use and development.
- Specific outcomes are uncertain because TDR programs cannot be sure which landowners will participate and how many acres will be preserved or developed.
- Preservation is dependent on the development market. If the real estate market is depressed, the demand for TDRs will be low; consequently, few properties will be protected.
- The purchase of development rights may be viewed as an impact fee or monetary exaction.
- Residents in receiving areas face denser development and concomitant pollution, traffic congestion, and other negative externalities (Bengston, Fletcher, and Nelson 2004).

Overview of TDR Programs with a Focus on Urban Issues

Researchers have conducted case study analysis of TDR programs throughout the United States (Kaplowitz, Machemer, and Pruetz 2008; Fulton et al. 2004; Pruetz 2003). Furthermore, Kruse (2008) notes that TDRs offer a way for politicians, planners, private developers, and cultural interest groups to shape urban policy. TDR programs can be used for specific urban purposes. While many programs were initiated with a primary focus on land preservation, a number of programs include a focus on housing, promotion of affordable housing, downtown revitalization and broader redevelopment, and promotion of urban design goals. Fulton et al. (2004) found 22 (16 percent) of 134 TDR programs had an urban focus. Pruetz (2003) found that 17 (12 percent) of 142 programs were at least partially intended for historic preservation, either alone or as part of a downtown revitalization. Table 5.1 is a summary from Pruetz (2003), showing programs with a focus on urban development and the type of urban focus.

Denver's TDR program encourages rehabilitation and preservation of historic landmarks. Seattle's program seeks to maintain varied building scale, encourage low-scale infill development, retain low-income housing, and preserve and restore historic landmarks. Pasadena's program uses TDRs to compensate property owners whose development potential is reduced due to the city's downtown urban design plan.

Role of TDR in Affordable Housing

If gentrification in an area has created an affordable-housing shortage, a TDR program can be used to designate existing low-income housing as eligible for sending-site status (Aoki, Briscoe, and Hovland 2005). In response to gentrification and loss of housing due to replacement by other land uses, the Seattle TDR program seeks to improve the availability and retention of affordable housing in the downtown. For certain buildings in the downtown area, building densities can increase from a FAR of 10 to a FAR of 14 if affordable housing goals are addressed. Seattle's housing bonus program allows a developer to obtain additional density through moderate-income (up to 80 percent of the median household income) housing contributions. Additional density bonuses can be obtained by transferring development rights created through the construction or preservation of low-income (50 percent or less of the median household income) housing. The city also requires that either 50 percent of the total floor area of the residential building or the floor area of the low-income housing units (whichever is greater) be maintained as low-income for at least 20 years.

TDR programs can address affordable housing goals beyond low-income housing retention on the sending side. On the receiving side, areas may be des-

Table 5.1

Urban TDR Programs and Focus

Program	Focus
Atlanta, GA	Historic
Berthoud, CO	DTC
Dallas, TX	Historic: preservation and rehabilitation
Delray Beach, FL	Historic
Denver, CO	Historic: preservation and rehabilitation
Groton, MA	Affordable housing
Los Angeles, CA	Historic: preservation and rehabilitation, revitalization, urban design
New Orleans, LA	Historic
New York, NY	Historic, historic/cultural
Palm Beach, FL	Affordable housing
Pasadena, CA	Urban design
Pittsburgh, PA	Historical/cultural
Portland, OR	Revitalization of downtowns, affordable housing
San Diego, CA	Historic
San Francisco, CA	Historic
Santa Barbara, CA	Urban design
Scottsdale, AZ	Historic
Seattle, WA	Revitalization of downtowns, affordable housing
Traverse City, MI	Redeveloped areas
Washington, DC	Revitalization of downtowns
West Hollywood, CA	Historic: preservation and rehabilitation

ignated to create affordable housing, community facilities, or reinvest in blighted neighborhoods (Aoki, Briscoe, and Hovland 2005). Receiving areas in Portland's TDR program include sites in the central city district that are designated to preserve low-income housing, open space, and historic buildings. While opponents of TDR have argued that TDR programs make addressing affordable housing issues more challenging, Carroll et al. (2009) found that TDR programs either have no impact or have a positive impact on affordable housing programs.

Urban TDR Case Studies

Two case studies from the state of Washington (King County, Seattle) and one from Washington, DC, further illuminate the use of TDRs in an urban context.

King County, WA

King County, WA, in partnership with county municipalities, has implemented a TDR program to protect rural areas and transfer density and development rights to the blighted or redeveloping areas of its incorporated cities. The 2008

County Comprehensive Plan states that developers can utilize TDRs not only to increase density, but also to capture the benefits that come from reducing greenhouse gases. Such reductions result from restricting development in rural areas and thereby reducing vehicle miles traveled. Furthermore, TDRs can be used to address traffic concurrency requirements in instances where the sending and receiving sites are in the same travelshed. Note, however, that if TDRs are used to meet traffic concurrency requirements, they cannot also be used for increased density.

Each residential development right that originates from a rural sending site is equivalent to two additional units above base density in eligible receiving sites located in unincorporated urban King County. Each residential development right that originates from an urban sending site is equivalent to one additional unit above base density. While development rights are most often bought and sold through private-party transactions, under limited circumstances they may be purchased from the King County TDR bank.

Another potential urban benefit of the King County TDR program is that the TDR executive board can authorize expenditures for amenities in order to facilitate development rights sales. Amenities may include the acquisition, design, or construction of public art, cultural and community facilities, parks, open space, trails, roads, parking, landscaping, sidewalks, other streetscape improvements, transit-related improvements, or other improvements or programs that facilitate increased densities on or near receiving sites. In authorizing amenities expenditures, the county is addressing planning goals that are beyond the primary focus of the TDR program (see Table 5.2).

Seattle

During the early 1980s, development in Seattle threatened the historically residential and commercial downtown. In 1985, the city responded by implementing a TDR and bonus programs. The city linked commercial density to the provision of housing, child care, open space, and other amenities by allowing density to be transferred from one site to another. The 1995 downtown plan for Seattle included the creation of a TDR system that offered public benefits in four areas: retention of low-income housing, preservation of historic landmarks, encouragement of compatible infill development in historic districts, and incentives to vary building scale.

In 2000, an advisory committee recommended that the revised downtown FAR system favor housing. Specifically, the committee advised that 75 percent of incremental floor area above the base FAR allowed outright by the downtown land use code be achieved either through a housing TDR or through a housing–child care bonus. It recommended that the other 25 percent of the FAR

Table 5.2

TDR Market Analysis Summary for King County, WA (2000–2010)

- More than 50 private developers used TDRs
- There were more than 60 private market transactions
- Nearly 500 TDRs were bought and sold
- There were an average of 10 transactions per year
- On average, 108 TDRs were bought and sold annually
- $6.75 million were exchanged between private developers and private landowners
- In the summer of 2009, the sale price of a TDR was $25,000
- 1,090 TDRs were allocated to private sending-site landowners
- Developers redeemed 330 TDRs for increased density in receiving-site projects
- In 2010, there were 809 available TDRs

be earned by providing public benefits unrelated to housing (such as public open space, hillside climb assistance, transit station access, human services, and public restrooms), or through landmark, open-space, or within-block/variable-scale TDRs (Seattle Office of Housing 2010).

Receiving-area developments associated with sending areas that address the four goals of Seattle's downtown plan are eligible to increase their density. While the sending sites are prevalent in most downtown districts, there are some districts from which density cannot be transferred (e.g., the Pike Place Market mixed zone). There are also some districts in which transfers can only take place between sites within the same area (e.g., the downtown retail core).

Sending sites are those that have less than the base zoning's maximal density due to their historic status or because the site provides affordable housing or infill development that is at a scale that is compatible with the surrounding area. If the sending site involves a historic structure, the TDR transfers require that the historic structure(s) be rehabilitated. If historic landmark TDRs are sought, the developer must provide a certificate of approval for the proposed restoration from the Seattle Landmark Preservation Board. The receiving site is given a certificate of occupancy upon the completion of the historic restoration of the sending site. In addition, the sending- and receiving-site landowners must record an agreement (covenant) that guarantees the landmark will be restored and preserved for the life of the receiving-site building/structure. The city gives priority to landmark theaters over other historic structures. Receiving sites are in districts where the maximum density can increase from a FAR of 5 to a FAR of 14, or from a FAR of 4 to a FAR of 10, as a result of TDR and/or density bonuses that come with on-site amenities such as day care, retail, theaters, rooftop gardens, or sculptures. If development rights from low-income housing sites are to be used, the receiving-site project must first generate a FAR of 2 of extra density through on-site amenities or historic landmark TDRs.

Between 1986 and 2009, the average cost per square acre in Seattle's TDR program was $15.41, and the total cost for private TDR transactions was $8,755,142 (Seattle Downtown LUC Reports 2009). The total TDR purchases made by the city between 1992 and 2006 was $6,247,537, with an average square-foot cost of $13.09 (Seattle Downtown LUC Reports 2009). The city's total TDR sales between 1997 and 2007 were $12,257,069, with an average square-foot cost of $15.73 (Seattle Downtown LUC Reports 2009).

The Seattle TDR program addresses housing and affordable housing goals. From 1986 to 2009, 1,034 housing units were regulated by TDR agreements, and 92 percent of those units (948) were at 30 percent, 50 percent, or 80 percent of Seattle's median income. The total TDR sales cost associated with these 1,034 housing units was $8,383,924 (Seattle Downtown LUC Reports 2009). Between 1985 and 2004, commercial developers used 357,104 square feet of housing TDR to build additional floor area in new downtown office and hotel towers. The city also purchased TDRs directly from owners of lots with affordable housing. These TDRs were deposited in a TDR bank and made available for purchase by commercial developers. As of 2009, the TDR and bonus programs had contributed over $52 million in funding for affordable housing projects in downtown Seattle (Seattle Downtown LUC Reports 2009).

Washington, DC

Washington, DC, offers transferable floor area bonuses to downtown developments that incorporate certain features, such as retail or art-related uses or legitimate theater. The groundwork for the TDR program in Washington, DC, was laid in the 1984 Downtown Plan, which provided density bonuses for projects that addressed the planning goals of historic preservation and that provided affordable housing, retail, theaters, and art. Five years later, the city established a special retail overlay district in which all new projects had to include retail, and developers were compensated through TDRs (Pruetz 2003). In 1991, that TDR program was expanded to address planning goals beyond the retail overlay district and to compensate owners of historic property. The main purpose of the downtown development district overlay zone was the creation of a mixed-use downtown area that included retail, hotel, office, residential, centers for arts and entertainment, preservation of historic buildings, a strengthened Chinatown, the retention and expansion of housing, a performing and visual arts corridor, and a concentrated downtown shopping district.

The downtown development district encompasses several subdistricts that have preferred-use requirements in which the TDR program can be implemented. For example, in the downtown shopping district, bonus FAR is available for preferred uses such as department store space, a legitimate theater, an anchor store, a movie theater, performance arts space, or for minority or displaced businesses. In the downtown arts district, bonus density is achieved through the inclusion of arts schools and centers. In the residential and mixed-use districts, bonus density is granted for grocery stores, drugstores, and other retail uses.

The TDR program in Washington, DC, allows two lots within the same preferred-use subarea to be treated as one lot for the purpose of meeting the preferred-use requirements (Pruetz 2003). Perhaps the biggest challenge for the DC program was achieving bonus density within the downtown development district, which was made difficult by the low building height limits. In response, two receiving areas were identified in commercial zones at the edge of downtown: One of them increased density from a base FAR of 6.5 to 9.0 and the other from a base FAR of 6.5 to 10. There are also base and bonus height limits in each of these receiving zones.

Sending-area property landowners establish an agreement with the city and record a standardized TDR covenant. This covenant identifies the sending-site restrictions, renovation schedule (if applicable), land use conversion schedule (if applicable), restrictions on any liens, maintenance provisions, and notification requirements. In addition to the covenant, the city executes and records a TDR certificate that identifies the TDRs sent from the sending property and the owner of those TDRs.

Development rights have been transferred from five historic structures (including St. Patrick's Church, the Calvary Baptist Church, and the Old Masonic Temple), a moderately scaled infill building, a landmark theater (the Warner Theater), and five buildings that provided retail space.

Conclusions

This chapter has sought to introduce the TDR concept, provide an overview of its historical use, and offer brief case studies of its application. TDR is a land-management technique with the potential to address both urban preservation and development goals. This market-based solution has been used in more than 150 communities across the nation with varying degrees of success for over 40 years. Success may be defined by the amount of land preserved, the number of historic structures renovated, the bonus density achieved, or the number of affordable housing units constructed or maintained. Nationally, most TDR programs have focused on the preservation of agricultural or environmentally sensitive lands; however, cities and metropolitan areas are using TDRs to address their urban land use issues, including historic preservation, affordable housing, and the creation of community facilities such as open space and arts centers. Allowing the transference of development rights gives urban property owners greater flexibility in land use. Traditionally, TDRs rely on private funds, but as seen in the case studies presented, there is often a role for the public entity, whether through direct sale or purchase of development rights or through TDR banks. Each community that adopts a TDR program is different, and each program needs to be tailored to meet the community's planning goals and objectives. Nonetheless, TDRs are as flexible as they are complex, offering urban communities facing preservation and development challenges a promising tool for their land use toolbox.

References

American Farmland Trust. 1997. *Saving American Farmland: What Works.* Northampton, MA: American Farmland Trust.

Aoki, K., K. Briscoe, and B. Hovland. 2005. Trading spaces: Measure 37, *MacPherson v. Department of Administrative Services,* and transferable development rights as a path out of deadlock. *Journal of Environmental Law and Litigation* 20(2): 273–328.

Barrese, J.T. 1983. Efficiency and equity considerations in the operation of transfer of development rights plans. *Land Economics* 59(2): 235–41.

Bateman, W. 1975. *The Need for Further Experimentation: Transferable Development Rights.* Planning Advisory Service Report No. 304. Chicago: American Society of Planning Officials.

Bengston, D.N., J.O. Fletcher, and K.C. Nelson. 2004. Public policies for managing urban growth and protecting open space: Policy instruments and lessons learned in the United States. *Landscape and Urban Planning* 69(2–3): 271–86.

Bowers, D. 1995. After 20 years, TDR sees varied levels of activity nationwide. *Farmland Preservation Report,* March.

Carmichael, D.M. 1975. Early American precedents. In *The Transfer of Development Rights: A New Technique of Land Use Regulation,* ed. J.B. Rose. New Brunswick, NJ: Center for Urban Policy Research at Rutgers University.

Carroll, T., N. Bratton, G. Milam, B. Mann, D. Stonington, and D. Newsome. 2009. *Analysis of the Impacts of Transferable Development Rights Programs on Affordable Housing*. Seattle and Tacoma, WA: The Cascade Land Conservancy and the University of Puget Sound.

Chavooshian, B., T.N. Budd, and G.H. Nieswand. 1973. Transfer of development rights: A new concept in land-use management. *Urban Land* 32(11): 11–16.

Costonis, J.J. 1975. *Perspectives for the Future: Transferable Development Rights.* Planning Advisory Service Report No. 304, 57–62. Chicago: American Society of Planning Officials.

Feiock, R., A. Tavares, and M. Lubell. 2008. Policy instrument choices for growth management and land use regulation. *Policy Studies Journal* 36(3): 461–80.

Fulton, W., J. Mazurek, R. Pruetz, and C. Williamson. 2004. *TDRs and Other Market-*

Based Land Mechanisms: How They Work and Their Role in Shaping Metropolitan Growth. A discussion paper prepared for the Brookings Institution Center on Urban and Metropolitan Policy, Washington, DC.

Gottsegen, A. 1992. *Planning for Transfer of Development Rights: A Handbook for New Jersey Municipalities*. West Trenton, NJ: Burlington County Board of Chosen Freeholders.

Heiberg, D.E. 1991. The reality of TDR. *Urban Land* 50(9): 34–35.

Johnston, R.A., and M.E. Madison. 1997. From landmarks to landscapes: A review of current practices in the transfer of development rights. *Journal of the American Planning Association* 63(3): 365–78.

Kaplowitz, M., P. Machemer, and R. Pruetz. 2008. Planners' experiences in managing growth using transferable development rights (TDR) in the United States. *Journal of Land Use Policy* 25(3): 378–87.

Kruse, M. 2008. Constructing the special theater subdistrict: Culture, politics, and economics in the creation of transferable development rights. *Urban Lawyer* 40(1): 95–146.

Lloyd, G. 1961. Transferable density in connection with zoning. *Technical Bulletin 40*. Washington, DC: Urban Land Institute.

Maabs-Zeno, C.C. 1981. Design of programs using transferable development rights to preserve farmland in the Northeast. *Journal of the Northeastern Agricultural Economics Council* 10(2): 57–62.

Machemer, P., and M.D. Kaplowitz. 2002. A framework for evaluating transferable development rights programmes. *Journal of Environmental Planning and Management* 45(6): 773–95.

McConnell, V., E. Kopits, and M. Walls. 2003. *How Well Can Markets for Development Rights Work? Evaluating a Farmland Preservation Program*. Discussion Paper 03–08. Washington DC: Resources for the Future.

Moore, A. 1975. As a primary system of land use regulation: The Fairfax County Virginia proposal. In *The Transfer of Development Rights: A New Technique of Land Use Regulation,* ed. J.G. Rose. New Brunswick, NJ: Center for Urban Policy Research at Rutgers University.

Pizor, P.J. 1978. A review of transfer of development rights. *Appraisal Journal* 46(3): 386–96.

———. 1986. Making TDR work: A study of program implementation. *Journal of the American Planning Association* 52(2): 203–11.

Pruetz, R. 1997. *Saved by Development: Preserving Environmental Areas, Farmland, and Historic Landmarks with Transfer of Development Rights*. Burbank, CA: Arje Press.

———. 2003. *Beyond Takings and Givings: Saving Natural Areas, Farmland, and Historic Landmarks with Transfer of Development Rights and Density Transfer Charges*. Marina Del Rey, CA: Arje Press. Supplements available online at http://smartpreservation.net/.

Redman/Johnson Associates. 1994. *Transfer of Development Rights Feasibility Study for Thurston County, Washington.* Easton, MD: Redman/Johnson Associates Ltd.

Renard, V. 2007. Property rights and the "transfer of development rights": Questions of efficiency and equity. *Town Planning Review* 78(1): 41–60.

Roddewig, R.J., and C. Inghram. 1987. *Transferable Development Rights Programs: TDRs and the Real Estate Marketplace.* ASPO Planning Advisory Service Report No. 401. Chicago: American Planning Association.

Rory, M.J. 1975. Encouraging redevelopment through a TDR system: Georgetown waterfront, Washington, DC. In *Transferable Development Rights,* ed. F.S. Bangs, Jr., and C. Bagne, 40–42. Chicago: American Planning Association.

Rose, J.G. 1975. British and recent American precedents: A proposal for the separation and marketability of development rights as a technique to preserve open space. In *The Transfer of Development Rights: A New Technique of Land Use Regulation,* ed. J.G. Rose, 75–89. New Brunswick, NJ: Center for Urban Policy Research at Rutgers University.

Seattle Downtown LUC Reports. 2009. Data received from the City of Seattle, dated June 22.

Seattle Office of Housing. 2010. *Seattle's Transferable Development Rights (TDR) and Housing Bonus Programs.* Seattle: Office of Housing.

Siemon, Larsen, and Marsh (law offices). 1996. *Transferable Development Rights Report: Analysis of Issues and Opportunities and the Application of Transferable Development Rights Technique*. Prepared for Lexington Fayette Urban County Government. April.

Tustian, R.E. 1983. Preserving farming through transferable development rights: A case study of Montgomery County, Maryland. *American Land Forum* 4: 63–76.

Walls, M., and V. McConnell. 2004. *Incentive-Based Land Use Policies and Water Quality in the Chesapeake Bay.* Discussion Paper 04–20. Washington, DC: Resources for the Future.

———. 2007. *Transfer of Development Rights in U.S. Communities*. Washington, DC: Resources for the Future.

Willis, S. 1975. New Jersey proposal: Preserving essential open space. In *Transferable Development Rights,* ed. F.S. Bangs, Jr., and C. Bagne. Chicago: American Planning Association.

Woodbury, S.R. 1975. Transfer of development rights: A new tool for planners. *Journal of the American Institute of Planners* 41 (1): 3–14.

6

Municipal Bonds and Local Government Borrowing

Vicki Elmer

Municipal bonds are the chief means by which state and local governments obtain capital for large-scale economic development projects. The typical city or county government operating budget does not have $26 million to help start up green businesses, $50 million for a bridge, $200 million for an airport, or $1 billion to upgrade local sewers. Bonds, sold to investors in a public market, are the way that governments borrow money to finance these projects. Therefore, it behooves economic development practitioners to know how the bond process works.

This chapter defines bonds and provides background information on who issues them, who buys them, and the size of the bond market. It then moves to a discussion of different types of bonds: general-obligation bonds, limited liability or "revenue" bonds, lease-based bonds, geographically-based bonds, and taxable bonds. Following a section on the roles of the actors in the process is a section on creditworthiness and defaults. Last, the bond issuance process is outlined and suggestions for more in-depth reading are made.

General Facts About Bonds

A bond is an interest-bearing certificate that an organization issues in order to borrow money. It is actually a loan between the borrower (who is called the issuer), and the lender (investor). A bond is similar to a promissory note—a promise by the issuer to repay the investor the principal of the loan by the end of a fixed period of time, which can be anywhere from one to 40 years, plus interest. Bonds are often contrasted with stocks, which are shares in a company that are sold to the public to raise money. Stockholders are subject to a company's financial ups and downs. In the corporate world, bonds are considered a more secure form of investment than stocks because they must be paid back before stockholders are issued dividends (Mysak 1998).

Bonds can be issued by corporations and by state and local governments, but governments cannot sell shares in the governmental entity to raise money the way a corporation can sell shares in the corporate entity. Instead, governments issue *municipal bonds*, the term used for loans entered into by both local and state governments as well as special districts and authorities. These loans or bonds are repaid with taxes or revenues from user fees, exactions, leases, and, more recently, with intergovernmental grants.

Municipal bonds are also called *tax-exempt bonds*, because the interest received by the investor is not subject to the federal income tax. In some states, the interest is not subject to state or local income taxes either. By contrast, the interest received from corporate bonds is taxable. Recently, a market has emerged for taxable municipal bonds, discussed next.

How Big Is the Bond Market?

The municipal bond market does not have a physical location like the stock exchanges do. Instead, all transactions occur between individual buyers and sellers. This occurs because bonds must be tailored to the specific requirements of the specific project they are financing, as well as to the different state laws and to specific sectors (e.g., health care, public power). There are over 1.5 million different types (GMS Group 2009).

The first debt issuance in what was to become the United States occurred in 1751, in Massachusetts. In the 1800s, as the country expanded west, state and local debt was a major source of financing for canals, roads, and railroads. In the 1900s, as New York, Chicago, San Francisco and other major cities grew, debt financing helped fund transportation, water, sewer, ports, hospitals, and housing (Maco 2010).

The total value of the bonds issued in a year depends upon economic conditions, population pressures, and federal and state policies (GMS Group 2009). In the 1950s, capital spending at the state and local levels was financed primarily by *general-obligation bonds*, paid by taxes. In the 1960s and 1970s, federal grants were added to the mix to fund a variety of local capital projects. In the 1980s and 1990s, in addition to taxes, user fees became an important source of funds for local bonds. The 1984 and 1986 Tax Reform Acts eliminated many tax-exempt activities, leading to a precipitous decline in yearly municipal bond issuances (Temel and the BMA 2001). During the recession of the early 1990s and again in 2008, the total value of new bonds issued annually dropped (see Table 6.1 for the annual dollar volume of municipal bond sales from 1986 through the second half of 2010).

Table 6.1

Dollar Volume of Annual Municipal Bond Sales from 1986 through Q2 2010 Total

Year	Total
1986	$150,697,700
1987	$105,485,500
1988	$119,367,800
1989	$125,568,700
1990	$128,045,800
1991	$173,074,900
1992	$235,486,400
1993	$293,009,000
1994	$165,151,000
1995	$160,309,500
1996	$185,204,900
1997	$220,671,400
1998	$286,655,100
1999	$227,540,600
2000	$200,847,500
2001	$287,729,300
2002	$358,400,400
2003	$383,342,500
2004	$359,747,600
2005	$408,282,800
2006	$388,838,300
2007	$429,893,700
2008	$389,631,800
2009	$409,724,300
2010 (1st half)	$233,370,400

Source: Bond Buyer 2010.

The total amount of bonds outstanding has continued to increase, however. In spite of the Great Recession begun in 2008, by mid-2010 cumulative municipal debt had reached $2.8 trillion (Board of Governors of the Federal Reserve System 2010). Several benchmarks can be used to evaluate the size of municipal debt currently outstanding. One is the amount per capita spent by state and local governments—this figure has risen from 1980 onward, varying regionally (Maco 2010). Another benchmark is debt as a percent of gross national product (GNP). State and local municipal debt fell from about 14 percent of GNP in 1970 to 11 percent in 1980. Throughout the 1980s, the figure stayed between 10 and 12 percent (Petersen and McLoughlin 1991). At the end of the first quarter of 2010, it had risen to 17 percent, primarily due to the slowdown in the growth of gross domestic product (GDP) during 2008–9 (Author's calculation 2010).

Who Issues Municipal Bonds and What Are the Proceeds Used For?

Municipal bonds are issued by state and local governments, nonprofit organizations such as hospitals and universities, and by special authorities and special districts. There are over 55,000 different issuers of municipal bonds in the United States, and they range from very large entities, such as the states of California and Illinois, to very small ones, such as rural school districts deep in the hinterland (Agriss 2008). Generally, authorities have been the largest borrowers, followed by special districts, then cities, and then colleges and universities (U.S. Census Bureau 2002a). In 2008, special districts (including school districts) and authorities issued $262 billion of new bonds, while cities and counties issued $72 billion. States issued only $32 billion (U.S. Census Bureau 2010). At the end of the first quarter of 2010, state and local governments accounted for 83.6 percent of all bonds outstanding, while nonprofits and industrial revenue bond issuers accounted for 9.4 and 7.0 percent respectively (see Table 6.2).

Municipal bonds are issued to fund a wide variety of projects, including noninfrastructure expenditures such as student loans and pollution control, and the more typical education projects, utility facilities, economic and industrial development projects, and health facilities. Although the amounts in each category fluctuate depending upon economic vagaries, the relationships have been roughly the same over time, with education and health (including both hospitals and nursing homes) eliciting the largest amounts of bond funding, followed by transportation, industrial aid, and finally water, sewer, and flood management utilities (U.S. Census Bureau 2002b). Although the majority of projects financed with municipal bonds are public, under certain circumstances (discussed later) the bonds may be used for private purposes associated with industrial development.

Who Buys Bonds?

Tax-exempt municipal bonds have always been attractive to wealthy corporations or individuals in the United States. In 1980, investments by individual households or their proxies accounted for about 34 percent of all investment in municipal bonds, but this figure had doubled by 1999 to almost 75 percent. This growth coincided with the shifting of household investment to mutual funds, which invest in municipal bonds. By contrast, commercial banks were the largest holders of municipals (*munis*) in 1980 at about 37 percent, but this dropped to 7 percent by 1997, since tax reform permitted banks to deduct only 80 percent of interest on tax-exempt securities. At the end of the first quarter of 2010, the household sector and mutual funds held 66.7 percent of munis, while banks and insurance funds accounted for another 23.9 percent (see Table 6.2).

Table 6.2

Municipal Securities and Loans Outstanding as of March 31, 2010, by Type of Issuer and Investor

	$ (billions)	Percent
Issuers		
State and local governments	2,369.80	83.6
Nonprofits	266.10	9.4
Industrial revenue bonds	198.40	7.0
Investors		
Household sector	1,020.10	36.0
Mutual funds	869.40	30.7
Banks and insurance funds	676.40	23.9
Business-commercial	188.60	6.7
Foreign investors	71.90	2.5
State and local governments	7.90	0.3
Total Bonds Outstanding 2010	$2,834.30 billion	

Source: Board of Governors of the Federal Reserve System 2010.

During the first decade of the twenty-first century, foreign holdings increased as a result of global financial turbulence. In 2003, they accounted for only 1 percent of municipal bonds outstanding. This figure rose to 2 percent in 2007 and to 2.5 percent by the end of the first quarter of 2010 (Board of Governors of the Federal Reserve System 2010).

Types of Bonds

Although every bond issue is different, they can be put into some general categories. One author divides bonds into three categories: *general obligation* (GO), *revenue*, and *certificates of participation* (COPs) (Mysak 1998). Another divides tax-based bonds into *general obligation* and *limited liability* (Petersen and McLoughlin 1991). A third notes that *certificates of participation* are just one way of marketing bonds based on *leases* (Vogt 2009). This chapter will use the five categories in the following list. The discussion of these categories draws from Temel and the BMA (2001), Petersen and McLoughlin (1991), and Vogt (2009).

- General-obligation bonds (GO bonds)
- Revenue bonds
- Leases/certificate of participation
- Geographically based bonds
- Taxable bonds (including Build America Bonds)

Tax-Exempt GO Bonds

GO bonds are backed by the full faith and credit of the issuing government. This means that the government is obligated to use its unlimited taxing power to repay the debt. GO bonds are subject to some restrictions. First, local governments in 44 states have constitutional or statutory limits on the amount of GO debt they can incur, while cities in 40 states have limits on the amount of interest they can pay. Second, 42 states require voter approval of GO bond issues. In some states, two-thirds approval is needed at the local level for a bond issue (other areas require only a simple majority). In Oregon, a supermajority is required—more than 50 percent of the registered voters must turn out to vote—and of these, 50 percent must approve the issuance of the bond.

Although GO bonds were the original mechanism local and state agencies used to finance large-scale capital improvements, today these bonds account for only 30 percent of all new issues, having been overtaken by revenue bonds (Bond Buyer 2010). GO bonds generally have a lower interest rate than revenue bonds. If the issue is popular enough for the voter requirement not to be an impediment, GO bonds should be an agency's first choice, since they provide money at the least expensive rate for the taxpayers.

Revenue Bonds

Revenue bonds rely upon user fees or dedicated revenue sources from the proposed capital facility to repay investors. They are also called limited-liability bonds because they do not rely upon the taxing power of an agency for repayment; furthermore, because they are not repaid through taxes, they are not legally part of a government's debt ceiling and do not require voter approval. Sometimes these are referred to as *special-obligation* (SO) bonds. They generally carry a higher interest rate because they are less secure than GO bonds. However, they are still tax-exempt.

Since 1990, limited-liability bonds have been the security of choice for local governments, special districts, and authorities. In 2010, about 70 percent of all new issues for state and local governments were of this type. Revenue bonds are the workhorse of single-purpose special districts formed to build and operate infrastructure such as water and sewage plants or solid-waste facilities. They are also used to pay for convention centers, sports facilities, and parking garages (Provus 2006) (see Box 6.1).

As part of deregulating the energy and telecommunications sector, federal rules were changed to permit certain private companies to issue tax-exempt revenue bonds as well. These are called *private-activity bonds* (PABs).

Box 6.1

Industrial Development Revenue Bonds

In the words of Stan Provus, "industrial revenue bonds are corporate bonds disguised to look like municipal bonds." A state or local government may wish to provide tax-exempt financing to a manufacturing company as an incentive for the firm to locate within the jurisdiction. The net impact for the firm may be savings of up to 30 percent below the prime interest rate. This is also called "conduit" financing.

The first industrial development bond was issued in 1936 by the State of Mississippi, and until 1954, when the IRS officially sanctioned their use, they were sanctioned by the courts. The Tax Reform Act of 1986 curtailed their use, and today they are used for small issues for manufacturing facilities. Localities have to demonstrate the economic benefit to the community through job creation or retention (Provus 2006).

Lease-Financing Bonds (Certificates of Participation)

Lease-financing bonds, sometimes called certificates of participation, are a category of municipal bonds secured with lease payments from the local jurisdiction. Since leases are an obligation on the part of the municipality or special district to make rental payments, not a commitment to service a debt, they are not subject to the limitations placed on debt by state and local laws. This enables the local agency to issue the bonds without voter approval and the large majorities required for GO bonds (Vogt 2009).

Schools, public buildings, hospitals, and even parks and transportation facilities have been built using lease-financing bonds. They can be used to finance prisons, courthouses, convention centers, or similar projects when political support is insufficient for a GO bond. They can also be used to purchase fire trucks, police vehicles, computers, and telecommunications equipment. Any type of city fund can be used to enter into the lease agreement: general funds, gas taxes, sewer funds, or even community development block-grant funds.

The local government usually enters into an agreement with a developer, a nonprofit, or a joint-powers authority to build a facility and then lease it back to them with a long-term lease. Bonds to finance the capital facility are issued at a tax-exempt rate, with the rental stream and interest rate determining the size of the issue, and hence the size of the facility to be built.

The term *certificate of participation* actually refers to the way a capital lease is marketed to investors. Certificates of participation are used for large leases (over $1 million). The capital lease is divided into certificates of participation that are sold publicly. For smaller leases, the debt can be privately placed (Vogt 2009).

The process by which this was done for an airline terminal in Philadelphia is illustrated in Figure 6.1. Encouraged by the Philadelphia Industrial Development Corporation (a nonprofit corporation set up by the city of Philadelphia), the city used a state authority (the Philadelphia Authority for Industrial Development, or PAID) to issue bonds and was able to develop a facility that it needed without having to incur debt. The steps were as follows: PAID issued bonds and transferred the money to an airline. The airline used the money to build a new terminal, which it then transferred back to PAID. PAID then leased the terminal to the city, which then leased it back to the airline (Brown 2004).

Tax-Exempt Bonds for Geographically Defined Areas

The third category of tax-exempt bonds is defined by a specific geographic area. Here, we consider three types: the *special-assessment district*, *redevelopment and tax increment bonds*, and the *business improvement district* (BID). These are another type of limited-liability bond, since they are not secured with the full faith and credit of the taxing power of the jurisdiction. Instead, they are repaid with a tax assessed for the purpose of the project, or taxes projected to be received as a result of the investment.

Special-Assessment Districts

If the benefit of a project can be linked with a particular geographic subsection of the locality, such as curbs and gutters for a specific neighborhood (see, for example, Box 6.2), the local government may consider establishing a special-assessment district to raise the revenue to repay the bond. Unlike the special-district agencies used to issue revenue bonds, assessment districts are not independent of the government that creates them (Leithe and Joseph 1990).

Special assessments are similar to property taxes, since the amount assessed is related to the value or size of the property. The assessment can be a function of the property's value, or its street frontage, or any other mechanism that relates the cost of the capital improvement to the benefit received by the property owner. To determine whether to levy the assessment, all the property owners are polled, and if a majority concur, then the assessment is made mandatory for all properties in the area. Assessment districts have been used by many localities to fund federally required storm water

Figure 6.1 **Certificates of Participation Example**

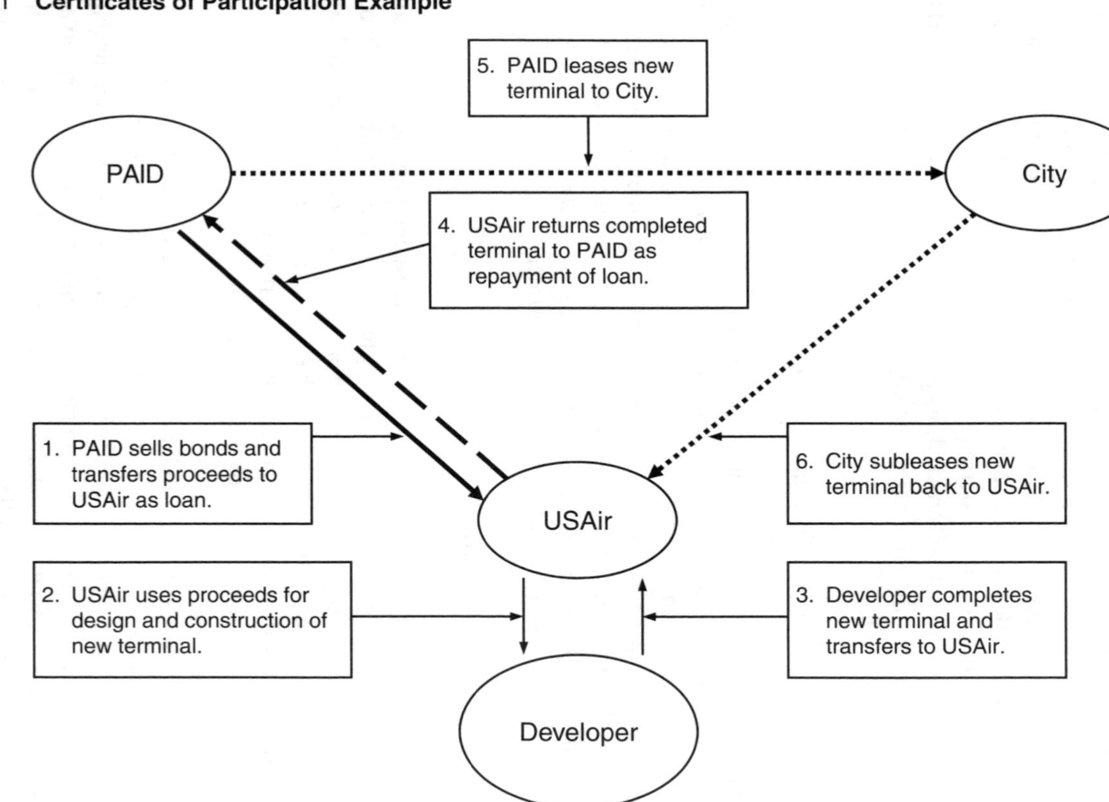

Box 6.2

Street Lighting and Assessment Districts

In California, many localities used to use citywide special assessments to replace property tax revenues lost as a result of Proposition 13 (a 1978 amendment to the California Constitution that lowered property tax rates and made future tax increases more difficult to pass). One of the most popular special-assessment districts was the street lighting and landscape assessment district. Local governments were able to use assessments for capital and maintenance activities for streetlight replacement and tree maintenance in the right of way, as well as for park improvements and maintenance. However, the rise in local expenditures caused by these districts led to the passage of Proposition 218 in 1996. Among other reforms, this initiative required increases in citywide assessments to be put to the voters instead of being adopted legislatively by the local government.

improvements. The cost per parcel might be a function of the amount of its impervious surface.

Redevelopment and Tax Increment Bonds

Redevelopment agencies were originally established to provide financing for "slum clearance" and infrastructure provision for blighted sections of large urban areas. The funds to pay off the bonds they issue come from the difference between the property tax that would have been collected in the area and the increased revenue the area is able to provide thanks to the rising property values attributable to the redevelopment. How this actually works varies from state to state.

Two types of risk are associated with redevelopment districts. First, the assumption that sufficient growth in assessed value will occur in the district if improvements are made may not be warranted. Second, parent jurisdictions may drop their tax rates. The redevelopment district does not control the base rate, which is the purview of the local government.

Business Improvement Districts

The past decade has seen the rise of business improvement districts (BIDs) in older urbanized areas. The impetus often comes from local merchants who are trying to revitalize an area. Since they are voluntarily assessed, usually by a simple majority of area property owners, the funds can be used for whatever was put in the assessment district formation, including operating costs and maintenance items. They are typically used for items like pedestrian lighting, street furniture, curbs, gutters, and paving for a business district. The proceeds can be used to issue a bond or to pay for improvements on a pay-as-you-go plan. In New York City, the proceeds from some BIDs have been used to hire homeless persons to do extra street sweeping in the district.

Taxable Bonds, Including Build America Bonds

The American Recovery and Reinvestment Act of 2009 included a new program for municipal bonds called Build America Bonds, or BABs. This program encourages municipalities to issue taxable bonds by providing a reimbursement of 35 percent of the interest on the bond. The program was enthusiastically received, with BABs accounting for 32 percent of all municipal issuances in the first half of 2010. The U.S. Treasury estimates that interest savings to local governments over tax-exempt issues amounted to $12 billion in 2009 and proposes permanently extending the program at a subsidy rate of 28 percent. Since these are not tax exempts (where the benefit accrues only to U.S. taxpayers), they are attractive to a broader investment base, including foreign investors (SIFMA 2010a) (see Figure 6.2).

The Hiring Incentives to Restore Employment Act was passed in March 2010. This law provides for subsidies of up to 100 percent of the interest for certain school construction bonds and up to 70 percent for renewable energy bonds and energy conservation bonds (SIFMA 2010b).

Taxable bonds have also been used by municipalities in times of low interest rates, where the comparative speed in which a taxable bond can be issued could result in lower total costs over the life of the project.

Actors in the Bond Issuance Process

Actors in the bond issuance process can be divided into two broad groups: government agencies on the one hand and outside experts and professionals on the other, with the latter group comprising bond counsel, financial advisers, underwriters, consulting engineers, polling experts, and rating agencies.

Government Agencies

The major actors in the bond issuance process within the government agency are usually in the finance department or budget office. However, someone from the economic development department, the redevelopment agency, or

Figure 6.2 **Taxable versus Tax-Exempt Issuance, 2004–2010** ($ billions)

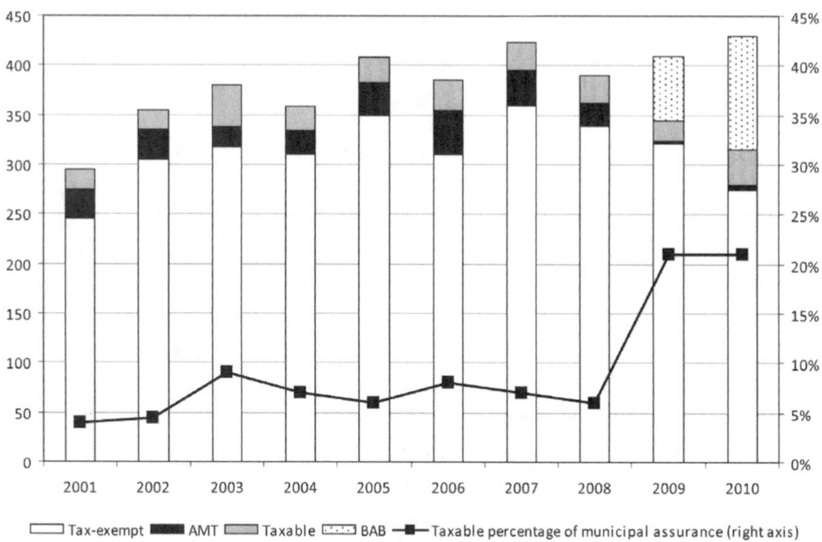

Source: SIFMA.

even the planning department may be the project manager for a large-scale capital project such as a convention center, a downtown revitalization, or a green infrastructure project. He or she will be responsible for convening the team charged with issuing the bond and will work closely with the finance and budget offices on the issuance.

Because of the highly specialized nature of redevelopment law and financial reporting, often the redevelopment staff takes the lead in managing its own bond issuance process. However, even though the redevelopment agency is a different legal entity than the city or county, the bond issue's impact on property taxes affects both entities, so the bond issue needs to be coordinated with the appropriate general-purpose government. This is particularly true for bonds designated for infrastructure development, since although the redevelopment agency may construct the improvements, it will not operate and maintain them (Vogt 2009).

Outside Experts and Professionals

Since issuing a bond is usually a major event for general-purpose governments—and even for special-purpose districts and authorities—a team of outside experts is usually hired or is put on retainer to complement the local staff. Often the finance department has many of these experts already on retainer to assist with other financing activities. The following outlines the roles of the major players. This section relies upon Temel and the BMA (2001), Vogt (2009), and Mysak (1998).

Bond Counsel

Ever since the late nineteenth century, when some issuers of bonds for railroads defaulted on their obligations by asserting that the bonds had not been properly authorized, bond issuers and underwriters have included a bond counsel opinion with the issue that states that all the relevant laws and regulations have been complied with. The bond counsel prepares the bond proceedings, confirms their tax-exempt status, and drafts key financing documents. Today, a bond issue is not marketable without a positive opinion by a bond counsel.

The bond counsel needs to be selected early in the process—sometimes authorizing legislation at the local level is necessary, and this may take some time. Several nationally recognized firms that are commonly used are listed in the so-called *Red Book—The Bond Buyer's Municipal Marketplace*. If pressured to hire a local law firm, co-counsel arrangements can be made whereby the local firm does some of the work, which a national firm then reviews and signs off on. However, this arrangement is usually more expensive. An RFP (request for proposal) process can be used to select the counsel.

Financial Adviser

Local governments that do not routinely issue long-term debt will want to have a financial adviser during the bond issuance process. Even though large issuers often have their own in-house financial staff, they may hire financial advisers to assist in certain aspects of the issuance. The financial adviser helps the local government understand the amount of debt it can afford and decide whether debt is the most appropriate strategy for the desired purposes. When necessary, the financial adviser also develops RFPs to hire the other professionals and helps the locality prepare for the bond rating process. In addition, he or she will advise the local government about whether to accept the bids in a competitive bond sales process and assist in any negotiated sales.

Like the bond consul, the financial adviser should be hired at the beginning of the bond issuance process. A competitive RFP process can and should be used to ensure that the financial adviser has the proper technical qualifications and will be sensitive to local needs. In the past, financial advisers were compensated with a fee based on the size of the bond issue, but this provides an incentive to make the issue larger. Instead, an hourly fee, a flat fee, or a retainer method should be used.

Underwriter

The underwriting firm buys the debt from the issuer and resells it to investors. If the firm is successful, it holds the loan briefly and is able to sell it for more than the original purchase price. The "underwriter's spread" consists of the management fee for helping to plan and structure the debt; the take-down, which is the sales commission to the individual sales staff; expenses; and a fee for the underwriting risk. If the issue is strong and not unusual, the local government can sometimes pressure the underwriter to waive the risk fee. The underwriter can be an investment banker, a securities dealer, or a consortium to help spread the risk.

Consulting Engineer

Revenue bonds usually require the opinion of an outside engineer about the feasibility of the projected revenues. Bonds funded from limited-liability taxes, such as a special-assessment district bond, also require a feasibility study. This study is used to reassure all parties that the revenues will be adequate to cover the debt service as well as operating and maintenance costs.

Polling Expert

To assist in determining the size or focus of a bond issue, a locality may contract with a polling firm to conduct a voter survey. Many firms specialize in polling voter attitudes, and although their primary expertise may be political campaigns, many can quickly and easily provide results on the feasibility of a prospective bond measure.

Rating Agencies

Three national firms rate local government and corporate debt—Standard & Poor's Corporation (S&P), Moody's Investors Service (Moody's), and Fitch IBCA. The local government will pay a fee to one of these firms to rate its debt.

Defaults and Creditworthiness

A default occurs on a bond when a payment is not made on time. Throughout the Great Depression, there were almost 5,000 recorded defaults on municipal bonds; however, by the beginning of the recovery in the early 1940s through the mid-1970s, there were very few defaults. Then, between 1972 and 1984, there were 21 municipal bankruptcies, and from 1981 through 2000, there were

156 filings of Chapter 9 bankruptcy by local governments. These included the 1983 default of the Washington Public Power Supply System on $2 billion of debt for five nuclear power plants, only one of which was built; the Chapter 9 filing of the San Jose (California) School District to void a labor agreement; the 1994 bankruptcy of Orange County, California, due to investment losses; and the bankruptcy of Vallejo, California, in 2008 (Niquette and Selway 2011). Historically, however, most defaulters recover and continue to make debt payments or otherwise satisfy the creditors (Litvak 2007). Recovery rates on defaulted municipal bonds are fairly high at almost 70 percent of par (Public Bonds 2004).

The economic downturn that began in 2008 is expected to result in additional municipal bankruptcies and defaults. In 2007, there were only 31 defaults on a total of $348 million, but this figure rose to 183 and $6.4 billion in 2009. These were what are termed "risky" municipal issues for projects in high-growth states. In 2010, *Fortune* magazine noted that Jefferson County, Alabama, Harrisburg, Pennsylvania, and Detroit, Michigan, were all in critical condition (Behunek 2010). Despite projections by the International City Manager's Association that local governments can expect serious revenue shortfalls through 2012, investment advisers feel that most governments will take drastic measures to avoid default and that widespread defaults are unlikely (Niquette and Selway 2011).

Analyses of municipal defaults conclude that they are most likely to occur in high-growth areas in the downswing of a business cycle and that likelihood of default varies significantly by sectors. A 2003 study that looked at all municipal issues from 1987 to 2002 concluded that there were three categories of default risk. The lowest risk category is traditional tax-backed or revenue bonds, which had a default rate of 0.24 percent (for comparison, triple-A-rated global corporate bonds have a default rate of 0.43 percent). The second category is bonds for essential functions that are not fully protected from the economic cycle or competition, including hospitals, private colleges, airports, and toll roads. Here the study found the default rate to be 0.70 percent (comparable to double-A-rated corporate bonds, which have a default rate of 0.76 percent).

The third risk category of bonds comprises projects that compete against private-sector activities or that have volatile revenue streams. These include industrial development revenue bonds, tribal gaming bonds, local multifamily housing, nursing homes, and retirement communities. Their default rate was 0.65 percent (comparable to triple-B-rated corporate bonds, which have a default rate of 3.97 percent). Specifically, industrial revenue bonds had a cumulative default rate of 14.62 percent; multifamily housing, 5.72 percent; and nonhospital health care facilities, 17.03 percent. These latter three types of bonds accounted for only 8 percent of bonds issued, but for 56 percent of the defaults (Litvak 2007).

These results were echoed in another analysis published in early 2010. Overall municipal bond default rates were between 0.09 percent and 0.33 percent, while corporate default rates were over 11 percent (see Table 6.3.) Recovery rates on defaulted municipal bonds are fairly high at almost 70 percent (Public Bonds 2004).

Bond Ratings

Even though default is a remote possibility, investors want to know whether they are buying bonds from a locality that will repay the loan. Rating agencies are used to establish the rating for a particular bond issue, and this in turn sets the interest rate that the jurisdiction will have to pay on the funds. A bond rating is a significant expense for the issuer. One agency notes in its literature that a rating costs from $1,000 to $350,000. Some issuers may get two ratings to make it easier for the underwriter to sell the bonds, while others may not get one at all. According to one source (Mysak 1998), a third of all newly issued debt was rated, while another found that only between 6 and 13 percent of bonds issued during the 1990s were rated (Temel and the BMA 2001).

The rating firms use letter grades to rate long-term debt. The four highest categories are called "investment grade," because many banks and municipal mutual funds are prohibited from investing in debt that is rated lower. Lower-rated bonds are often called "junk bonds" and are viewed as speculative. Most issuances by local governments are investment grade. In 2010, as a result of pressure from the Securities and Exchange Commission (SEC) and from California politicians, the rating agencies moved to use the same standard for municipal bonds as they do for corporate bonds: the so-called global standard. For several years, state and local governments noted that municipal default rates were lower than comparably rated corporate bonds in each category and that recovery rates were higher. Therefore, governments felt they were paying unnecessarily high interest rates (Foster Pepper 2010).

Factors Considered by Rating Agencies

Rating agencies consider various factors—depending on the type of bond—when assessing risk and assigning it a letter rating. The factors relevant for GO bonds, revenue bonds, lease financing, and geographically based bonds are considered in the following sections. Bonds that are too small to be rated on their own can make use of cooperative bond pools and credit enhancement devices.

Table 6.3

Cumulative Default Rates of Municipal and Corporate Bonds by Bond Rating Category, as of February 2010

Bond Rating		Moody's		S&P	
Moody's	S&P	Municipal (%)	Corporate (%)	Municipal (%)	Corporate (%)
Aaa	AAA	0.00	0.05	0.00	0.65
Aa	AA	0.03	0.54	0.32	1.20
A	A	0.03	2.05	0.25	2.91
Baa	BBB	0.16	4.85	0.37	7.70
Ba	BB	2.80	19.96	2.07	19.33
B	B	12.40	44.38	7.70	33.14
Caa-C	CCC-C	11.60	71.38	41.76	52.93
Investment-grade only		0.06	2.50	0.25	3.76
Noninvestment-grade only		4.55	34.01	6.75	27.82
All		0.09	11.06	0.33	11.38

Source: Moody's, S&P, LPL Financial, as of February 2010.

Note: Moody's data reflect the average 10-year cumulative default rate from 1970 and 2009. S&P municipal data reflect the average cumulative 23-year default rate from 1986 to 2008. S&P corporate data reflect the average cumulative 15-year default rate from 1981 to 2008.

GO (Tax-Backed) Bond Rating Factors

The process for rating general-obligation (GO) bonds evaluates the risk for the debt over the entire life of the issuance. The rating agency typically looks at the political mood of the jurisdiction, existing debt, the condition of the local economy, municipal financial health, and the management capacity of the jurisdiction. The agency may evaluate the jurisdiction's per capita income and its ability to address infrastructure needs. Local educational levels may be used to indicate whether the economic base of the locality will be able to compete in the twenty-first century. In addition, the long-term impact of pension requirements for local governments is scrutinized carefully because of the long-term increases locked in place during the late 1990s, when local governments were flush (Temel and the BMA 2001).

One of the key steps in rating GO bonds is an analysis of the existing local debt supported by the same tax base, whether these tax revenues accrue to the issuing jurisdiction or a superior or subordinate jurisdiction. The level of debt as a percentage of the local government's budget is examined, with 10 percent or more raising questions. Rating agencies also use debt per capita (including the underlying and overlapping debt from other jurisdictions) to assess the ability of local residents to support debt, although that measure does not take into account the positive impact of large corporate presences. Additionally, rating agencies look at local debt as a percentage of real estate market value in the jurisdiction. The average range of total debt as a percentage of market value is 2–5 percent, with above 6 percent considered high and 10 percent viewed as a credit problem (Vogt 2009).

Revenue Bond Rating Factors

In the case of bonds issued by organizations, a rating agency is primarily concerned about whether the enterprise will produce the revenue to repay the loan. It therefore looks at the viability of the overall organization, as well as the specific capital facility that is being financed. The agency wants to know that the organization, if it is fully funded by user fees, will have more than enough funds to repay the loan after considering needs for operating and maintenance. This is called *coverage ratio.* In the past, ratios of net available funds to the debt service of the bond were about 1.5–2 times the debt service. These days, they are about 1.25, lower if the project is strong and higher if it is weak. The rating agency will require, among other information, five years of audited statements, a rate study, an engineering report, and lists of customers by class, along with overall economic information for the area, as above (Vogt 2009).

Rating Factors for Lease Financing (Certificates of Participation)

Since the primary security for repayment in the case of lease financing lies with the facility that is being leased and the creditworthiness of the lessee, the rating agency will look at both these things (much of the information being the same as for the GO bond). Raters look at how essential the facility is to the local government. For example, jails, schools, and water and sewer facilities are deemed to be essential and receive higher ratings, while parks and recreational facilities are thought of as less essential and (unfortunately) receive lower ratings. The rating agencies will also look at whether there was opposition to the project locally and what the local government's attitude is toward debt repayment. Some local governments can pledge additional collateral or establish reserve funds for repayments to mitigate these concerns.

Geographically Based Bonds

For special-assessment district bonds and redevelopment districts, rating agencies look at the wealth in the specific area. The collection practices of the issuers is especially important in the former case, while redevelopment (urban renewal) bonds are evaluated on the history of tax-base growth in the area, the powers of the redevelopment agency, state laws, and the wealth and general credit of the jurisdiction creating the redevelopment area (Vogt 2009).

Use of Cooperative Bond Pools and Credit Enhancement Devices

Sometimes, when the issuance is a small one, or when the locality may not have a competitive bond rating, it may join with another local government that is issuing a bond to take advantage of shared overhead costs. If there is a regional council of government that offers a program for small issuances made by its member jurisdictions, the locality can participate in that. States may do a large bond measure to provide low-cost loans for infrastructure for local jurisdictions. For revenue bonds, the jurisdiction can pledge tax revenues. Bond insurance can also be purchased, although the financial collapse of 2008–9 resulted in all but one of the bond insurance agencies going out of business. Use of credit enhancement devices is currently on the wane: Between 2004 and 2008, 41 percent of new issuances used them, but only 20 percent of the issuances in 2009 and 10 percent of issuances in the first quarter of 2010 had credit enhancement (SIFMA 2010a).

Key Steps in the Bond Issuance Process

Two types of considerations govern whether the locality chooses pay-as-you-go or borrowing. The first concerns values; the second concerns the financial capacity of the agency and the political and economic climate in the jurisdiction.

Who Should Pay?

At the heart of the values question is who should pay. Those in favor of new debt argue that users should pay for the facilities—the pay-as-you-use argument. Since most infrastructure is long lived, borrowing today and paying back the debt over time seems reasonable. On a practical basis, the ability to borrow often makes a large capital project feasible for the local government. On the other hand, some argue that borrowing burdens future generations with debt and infrastructure decisions that may not be appropriate. Paying for a facility out of current revenues means that interest costs can be avoided (Temel and the BMA 2001).

What Can the Jurisdiction Afford?

The second consideration about borrowing is whether or not the locality can afford to issue debt. Essentially, the locality must go through a process similar to that followed by the rating agencies to determine whether and how much debt to incur. Although many localities are subject to state and local debt ceilings, local financial managers use a variety of other measures to help make decisions about the level of debt a city can or should incur. See the city of Lubbock's debt policy indicators (Table 6.4) for an example of how one city decided to address debt (City of Lubbock, TX 2010).

Striking the Right Balance of Debt and Pay-As-You-Go

Most governments rely on both debt and pay-as-you-go to finance capital infrastructure. A fast-growing community with large operating fund balances may be able to finance half of its needs with current revenues, but will likely need to issue debt for the balance. A community without significant fund balances may have to issue debt for three-quarters of its need. Rapid development usually expands the tax base of a jurisdiction, which makes it possible to service the debt. A community with stable population growth may choose to finance 75 percent of its replacement needs with current revenues, with debt used only for large projects. In contrast, communities with shrinking tax

Table 6.4

Debt Affordability Indicators for the City of Lubbock Texas, 2001–2010

Fiscal Year	Population	Net Bonded Debt (Including TIF)	Ratio of Net Bonded Debt to Assessed Value (%)	Net Bonded Debt per Capita	Percent of Debt Service for GO Bonds to Total General Gov't Expenditures (%)
2001	201,097	$51,667,715	0.76	$256.93	8.0
2002	202,000	56,808,301	0.82	281.23	6.9
2003	204,737	67,814,313	0.89	331.23	7.0
2004	206,290	67,580,197	0.83	327.60	6.8
2005	209,130	84,350,929	0.98	403.36	5.7
2006	211,187	103,480,144	1.11	489.99	5.5
2007	212,365	115,083,259	1.15	541.91	6.1
2008	214,847	135,627,224	1.24	631.27	6.3
2009	218,327	139,235,418	1.19	637.74	6.7
2010	219,643	158,962,135	1.31	723.73	6.9

Source: Compiled by author from Tables K and N, City of Lubbock, Texas, 2010.

bases are challenged even to pay for adequate maintenance. Such jurisdictions must try to maintain significant fund balances but also should aggressively apply for grants for capital needs (Vogt 2009).

Sizing the Bond

The size of the bond is one of the most important decisions in the bond issuance process. This determination is often a complicated process, involving a series of triangulations between project needs, funds available for the project from all sources, and the increase required in the revenue source that will be used to pay off the bond. The size is not dictated by the need alone. The size of a GO bond, for example, might be determined by the political feasibility of obtaining a positive vote from the elected body. The size of a revenue bond is determined by the ability of the facility being financed to raise revenues. In addition, very few jurisdictions permit the city or county manager, or CEO of the special district, to proceed without approval from the elected officials during the capital facility process.

Determine the Demand for and Cost of the Project

The first step is to determine what the need or the demand for the project is. Usually, several alternative configurations are developed—high, medium, and low. Quite often, the locality will contract with subject area specialists to help develop the cost and revenue estimates. Depending upon the locality, for streets, street improvements, and public buildings, a public participation process may be used as well as a design competition.

Determine the Impact on the Local Tax Bill

Once agreement on the costs or alternatives has been reached, the budget office, working with the finance department and the financial adviser, identifies the financial impact on the average citizen over time. Every agency with revenues on the property tax bill is contacted to determine if they contemplate issuing bonds or raising their assessments in the near term. This information is analyzed to show the impact of different bond levels over time and often compared with equivalent data from other jurisdictions.

How Will the Issue Be Sold?

By far the most common way to market the bond is through a negotiated sale. In 2005, local and state governments issued $330.4 billion of bonds using this form, or 81 percent by dollar volume, compared with only $76.1 billion through competitive bidding and $1.8 billion by private placement. GO bonds are more likely to be competitively bid than revenue bonds, which are overwhelmingly negotiated. A similar pattern was seen for 2010 (*Bond Buyer* 2010).

Competitive Sale

At a competitive sale, bonds are sold at an auction to the underwriting firm providing the best bid on true interest or net interest cost of the bonds. (This used to be called an advertised sale.) The date, time, and place where the bids for the bonds will be opened are advertised. The bids are then taken, and bonds are awarded to an underwriter, who then sells them to investors. It is the easiest way to sell, but it is more risky for the underwriters, who actually own the bonds until they are turned around. Many state statutes require GO bonds to be sold through a competitive bidding process.

Negotiated Sale

As the municipal bond market has tilted more toward limited-obligation bonds and/or revenue bonds, negotiated sales have become more common. For a negotiated sale, the underwriter is chosen before the sales date of the bonds, usually through an RFP process. The underwriter, using its sales force, then drums up interest in the bond so that buyers will be lined up when the day of the sale arrives. Some believe that with negotiated sales, underwriters are really acting more as brokers than as underwriters (the latter being paid to take risks). Negotiated sales are useful when the issue is quite complex or unusual and needs special explaining. They are also useful when the bond market is unsettled (Mysak 1998).

Private Placement

One alternative to both the competitive and negotiated sale is private placement, where the issuer goes directly to the investors, bypassing the underwriter altogether. Without competition, however, administrative and interest costs may be higher, and the locality may be open to charges of cronyism. To avoid this, several banks or private investors can be approached in a competitive bid process, a common practice in some parts of the country. Another problem is that, unlike publicly sold debt, for which an active secondary market exists, private placement is less liquid. Private investors may buy directly because they intend to hold the debt to maturity, and they may demand higher interest rates (Vogt 2009).

Preparation of the Bond Documents

The SEC requires a preliminary official statement (POS) and an official statement (OS) for public sales of municipal bonds. The POS is used to market the debt and is prepared before the sale, while the OS is prepared after the sale and includes sales results such as the interest rates and prices. For GO bond sales, these documents contain information on the general economic condition of the jurisdiction issuing the bonds, while the OS for a revenue bond also includes information about revenue sources and operating information. The documents for revenue bonds, or nontax sources of revenue, can sometimes run to hundreds of pages. If a capital lease is involved, the POS and OS contain information about the specific property described. They are prepared by the team of technical experts described earlier (Temel and the BMA 2001).

The following items are usually part of the documentation:

- *Loan amount.* The loan amount is also known as the "face amount" or "par value" or "principal" of the loan. It is the amount that the agency promises to pay when the bond becomes due.
- *Interest rate.* The rate of interest is determined by the competitive bond market when the bond is issued. This is also called the "coupon" rate.
- *Schedule of payments.* Debt service payments can be level, declining, or ascending. The latter is useful when improvements paid for by the bond, such as a new water treatment plant, will add customers over time.
- *Maturity structure or term of the bond.* Bonds can be issued as serial bonds, when each individual certificate has its own maturity date, or as term bonds, with a single final date for all the certificates.
- *Security for the loan.* This element outlines the recourse the investor (lender) has if the agency defaults. In the case of a bond that is to be repaid based on revenues instead of taxes, detailed information is included on how the bonds will be disbursed and how the facility's revenues will be applied.
- *Call provisions.* Some bonds can be redeemed, or "called," by the issuer before the maturity date, if there are lower interest rates and the issuer wants to refinance.

Approval of the Issue by the Governing Body

Generally, the agency's elected or governing body must approve the bond documents. Depending on how controversial the capital facility is, hearings may be required before the elected body, which is usually the entity that votes to place a bond issue on the ballot, if required.

Conclusion and Additional Resources

Bonds are the chief mechanism local governments use to borrow funds. Debt repayment may come from a variety of sources, including property taxes and revenue generated by the project itself. Today's bond market is incredibly complex, but it has been an effective tool to mobilize capital for growth and economic development. Although state and local governments' financial woes may continue for several years, municipal bond defaults have been rarer than other sorts of defaults, especially for GO bonds where recovery rates are near par. The local practitioner should therefore consider bonds and borrowing as an important tool for financing improvements needed for economic development.

For more detailed information on the bond market, bonds in general, and how bonds can be used for economic development purposes, see Toby Rittner, *Practitioner's Guide to Economic Development Finance* (Columbus, OH: CDFA, 2009), and Judy Temel for The Bond Market Association's *The Fundamentals of Municipal Bonds* (New York: Wiley and Sons, 2001). *Bond Buyer* (www.bondbuyer.com) is a subscription service that provides excellent daily, weekly, and monthly reports and has a good data archive. The Securities Industry and Financial Markets Association (SIFMA) issues a brief quarterly research report that provides analysis and data—both quite readable (see www.sifma.org).

References

Agriss, T. 2008. *Municipal Bond Market Issues: Recent Developments*. Overland Park, KS: Black & Veatch Corporation, December. www.bv.com/downloads/Resources/Reports/EMSMunibond20081222.pdf (accessed August 2010).

Behunek, S. 2010. American cities at risk of default and bankruptcy. *Fortune*, May 28. http://dailycaller.com/2010/05/31/american-cities-at-risk-of-default-and-bankruptcy/ (accessed November 2010).

Board of Governors of the Federal Reserve System. 2010. *Flow of Funds Accounts of the United States: Flows and Outstandings, First Quarter 2010*. Federal Reserve statistical release, June 10. Washington, DC: Board of Governors of the Federal Reserve System.

Bond Buyer. 2010. Bond Buyer Market Statistics Archives: Annual Municipal Debt Sales, 1989–2010. www.bondbuyer.com/marketstatistics/msa_main.html (accessed August 2010).

Brown, P.H. 2004. Port authorities and urban redevelopment: Politics, organizations, and institutions on a changing waterfront. PhD diss. January 1. Philadelphia: University of Pennsylvania. http://repository.upenn.edu/dissertations/AAI3125792/.

City of Lubbock, Texas. 2010. *Comprehensive Annual Financial Report for the Fiscal Year Ended September 30, 2010*. http://finance.ci.lubbock.tx.us/CAFR.aspx (accessed April 2011).

Foster Pepper. 2010. Municipal bond rating recalibrations are coming soon. April 2. www.foster.com/newsroom.aspx?t=1&nid=485 (accessed April 2011).

GMS Group. 2009. *A History of Capital Preservation and Tax-Exempt Income*. Report, October 1. www.gmsgroup.com/?q=Special-Tax-Exempt-Municipal-Bonds-Income (accessed August 2010).

Leithe, J.L., and J. Joseph. 1990. Financing alternatives. In *Financing Growth: Who Benefits? Who Pays? And How Much?* ed. Susan Robinson, 91–107. Chicago: Government Finance Officers Association.

Litvak, D. 2007. *Default Risk and Recovery Rates on U.S. Municipal Bonds.* Special report. New York: Fitch Ratings. www.fitchratings.com (accessed August 2010).

Maco, P.S. 2010. A country built by bonds: A short history of the U.S. municipal bond market and the building of America's infrastructure. PowerPoint Presentation to China Environment Forum Environmental Financing in China Initiative, Vinson & Elkins LLP. Washington, DC. www.docstoc.com/docs/51927559/A-COUNTRY-BUILT-BY-BONDS-A-SHORT-HISTORY-OF (accessed February 2012).

Mysak, J. 1998. *Handbook for Muni-Bond Issues*. Princeton, NJ: Bloomberg Press.

Niquette, M., and W. Selway. 2011. Risk of widespread municipal bond defaults near 'zero,' Moody's Zandi says. Bloomberg, February 27. http://mobile.bloomberg.com/news/2011-02-27/risk-of-widespread-municipal-bond-defaults-near-zero-moody-s-zandi-says?category= (accessed February 2012).

Petersen, J.E., and T. McLoughlin. 1991. Debt policies and procedures. In *Local Government Finance: Concept and Practices*, ed. J.E. Petersen and D.R. Strachota. Chicago: Government Finance Officers Association.

Provus, S. 2006. CDFA spotlight: The basics of industrial development bonds. Council of Development Finance Agencies, July. www.cdfa.net/cdfa/cdfaweb.nsf/ordredirect.html?open&id=july2006tlc.html (accessed August 27, 2010).

Public Bonds. 2004. Municipal Bonds and Defaults. June. www.publicbonds.org/public_fin/default.htm (accessed April 2011).

Rittner, T. 2009. *Practitioner's Guide to Economic Development Finance*. Columbus, OH: CDFA.

Schroeder, P. 2010. Tax-exempts beat BABs in after-tax yields: Study. *Bond Buyer,* September 1. www.bondbuyer.com/issues/119_417/tax_exempt_best_babs-1016742-1.html (accessed September 2010).

Securities Industry and Financial Markets Association (SIFMA). 2010a. Municipal bond credit report Q1 2010. *Research Report* 5(9). www.sifma.org/research/item.aspx?id=19456 (accessed November 2010).

———. 2010b. Municipal bond credit report Q2 2010. *Research Report* 5(11). www.sifma.org/research/item.aspx?id=19467 (accessed November 2010).

Temel, J.W., and the Bond Market Association 2001. *The Fundamentals of Municipal Bonds*, 5th ed. Hoboken, NJ: John Wiley and Sons.

U.S. Census Bureau. 2002a. *Statistical Abstract of the United States:* Table 502. Washington, DC: U.S. Census Bureau.

———. 2002b. *Statistical Abstract of the United States:* Table 432. Washington, DC: U.S. Census Bureau.

———. 2010. *Statistical Abstract of the United States:* Table 428. Washington, DC: U.S. Census Bureau.

Vogt, A.J., ed. 2009. *Capital Budgeting and Finance: A Guide for Local Governments,* 2d ed. Washington, DC: International City/County Management Association.

7

Publicly Subsidized Brownfields Redevelopment

Christopher A. De Sousa

A common problem the urban planners and economic development officials face in cities throughout the United States is the management of numerous under-used or abandoned brownfield sites. Historically, interest on the part of developers, landowners, and other private-sector stakeholders in putting these sites back into productive use tended to be minimal because of fears of contamination that would make them too expensive, time-consuming, and risky to redevelop profitably. At the same time, these sites are inherently valuable because they are often located in the core sections of metropolitan areas and, as such, are prime candidates for urban development and revitalization. It is for this reason that policymakers at all levels of government have, since the late 1970s, developed and implemented a variety of innovative environmental and economic policies, programs, and tools designed to lessen the costs and risks associated with brownfields redevelopment. This has increasingly allowed local officials to approach brownfield sites as potential spaces of opportunity as opposed to liability.

This chapter provides an overview of the brownfields issue in the United States. We begin by examining what we know about the scale of the problem, the key stakeholders involved in planning and redevelopment, and their motivations. We then look at some of the barriers to the cleanup and redevelopment of brownfields and describe measures for overcoming them, focusing particularly on financing tools. The chapter ends with an overview of the outcomes that support continued government intervention and expenditures in this domain.

Definition and Scope

Efforts to manage the cleanup and redevelopment of contaminated sites in the United States have evolved considerably in scope and character over the last three decades. Initial actions in the late 1970s were spurred by pollution disasters such as the hazardous-waste tragedy at Love Canal in Western New York, which forced government to better understand the risks posed by contaminants and develop suitable methods for efficient site remediation. During this period, the distinction was often made between *known* contaminated sites (those that had been identified through appropriate testing) and *potentially* contaminated sites (those suspected of being contaminated because of their previous land use or some environmentally detrimental event like a spill, leak, or fire).

In their seminal work, Noonan and Vidich (1992, p. 248) provide a table listing different types of properties and their probability of being contaminated based on their former land use. For instance, while vacant rural land and residential property have a low probability of contamination (20 percent), other uses have a much higher probability, among them former coal-gas plants (99 percent), metal-plating plants (90 percent), landfills (90 percent), vehicle-maintenance facilities (82 percent), gas stations (88 percent), dry cleaners (74 percent), and urban vacant/abandoned land (85 percent).

The term *brownfields* became widely adopted in the early 1990s in order to attenuate the negative connotations associated with the label *contaminated*. The most commonly used definition of brownfields was put forward by the U.S. Environmental Protection Agency (EPA) when it formally launched its Brownfields Action Agenda in 1995. The agency defined brownfields as "abandoned, idled, or under-used industrial and commercial facilities where expansion or redevelopment is complicated by real or perceived environmental contamination" (EPA 2011a). Subsequently, the U.S. Small Business Liability Relief and Brownfields Revitalization Act (Public Law 107–118, H.R. 2869, p. 6), signed into law in 2002, changed the definition slightly to: "Real property, the expansion, redevelopment, or reuse of which may be complicated by the presence or potential presence of a hazardous substance, pollutant, or contaminant" (EPA 2011b). A brownfield, therefore, refers to both *known* and *potentially* contaminated property, although direct reference to commercial and industrial land use is no longer implicit in the term. Brownfields land also tends to connote an urban-infill site and provides a semantic counterpart to greenfield—a clean and undeveloped property located in the urban periphery.

In terms of the number of brownfields in the United States, there is no national inventory that allows for accurate accounting. The EPA estimates that there are more than 450,000 brownfields across the country (2011a). Over time, a tiered system has emerged, with different levels of government working in tandem to compile and manage different kinds of brownfields information. The most severe sites containing hazardous materials deemed to pose the greatest risk to human health and the environment are listed on the National Priorities List (NPL) upon completion of a Hazard Ranking System screening. The Comprehensive Environmental Response, Compensation, and Liability Information System (CERCLIS) contains information on hazardous-waste site assessment and remediation from 1983 to the present. Hazardous-waste information related to treatment, storage, and disposal facilities is also catalogued nationally in the Resource Conservation and Recovery Act Information (RCRAInfo) system.

Many state and city governments also maintain brownfields inventories, although there is no standardized approach for identifying the types of sites to be included or the information maintained. The State of Wisconsin, for instance, has developed a database (i.e., Bureau for Remediation and Redevelopment Tracking System) that synthesizes information from an array of data sources and has been a useful tool in governmental efforts to protect public health and safety. The data collected on a particular brownfield reveals whether it requires management (open) or not (closed); the type of brownfield site it is (e.g., one where a spill has occurred, or where a leaking underground storage tank is located, etc.); whether it is considered a high, medium, or low priority; and whether land-use limitations or conditions in place of deed restrictions have been put on the site following cleanup. Many states also maintain extensive records on projects involved in their voluntary cleanup programs (VCPs; discussed in more detail later).

By far the most widely referenced source of information regarding the quantity of urban brownfields in the United States are the U.S. Conference of Mayors' (USCM) brownfields surveys, which have been administered to member local governments since the mid-1990s. In the 2008 USCM survey (2008, p. 9), which had a larger sample size than the most recent survey, 188 of the responding cities estimated that they had more than 24,896 brownfields, with the average site size being approximately 14 acres. One hundred and seventy-six cities had an estimated 83,949 acres of idle or abandoned land, while 150 of those also estimated that 3,282 sites were "mothballed" (meaning the current owner had no intention of redeveloping or selling a site due to environmental impact concerns).

Motivating Factors: Why Brownfields?

For public-, private-, and nonprofit-sector stakeholders, the decision to become involved with or to invest in a brownfields project is influenced by an array of economic, social, and environmental factors. The U.S. Conference of Mayors' 2010 brownfields survey (p. 10), which differs from previous studies by considering progress made on the issue between 1993 and 2010, lists the most important goals associated with brownfields redevelopment from the perspective of local government as (1) neighborhood revitalization (140 cities/80 percent), (2) increasing the city's tax base (139 cities/79 percent), (3) job creation (132 cities/75 percent), and (4) environmental protection (109 cities/62 percent). In addition, public-sector officials at all levels of government emphasize blight elimination, liability reduction, environmental justice, business retention, enhanced property values, improved health, and the catalytic effect that brownfield projects often trigger.

The decision by the for-profit private sector to invest in brownfields redevelopment is motivated largely by economic factors, such as maximizing return on investment, divesting liability risks/costs, acting on the growing popularity of downtown locations, and taking advantage of devalued brownfields property costs. Interviews conducted by the author a few years back with private-sector stakeholders in Milwaukee, WI, and Chicago, IL, indicate that most of the factors attracting them to brownfields for housing relate primarily to location and surrounding amenities, and depend to a lesser extent on attributes associated with brownfield sites (i.e. the low price of land, lot size, availability of buildings for reuse, etc.) (De Sousa 2008, p. 215). Developers and landowners are also motivated by environmental issues that can affect their bottom line, such as the need to conform to environmental regulations and protect the health and safety of those utilizing their projects and residing in surrounding communities.

More and more, community development organizations and nonprofits are interested in working on brownfields in communities with weaker real estate markets. Community-based nonprofits typically seek to rebuild low-income neighborhoods for the benefit of local residents and tend to be more concerned with the social implications of redevelopment projects and how such projects contribute to affordable housing, neighborhood stabilization, and improving quality of life (Dewar and Deitrick 2004, p. 159). These organizations are flexible and can play multiple roles in brownfields redevelopment, including education, outreach, facilitation, and advocacy.

Overcoming the Barriers to Brownfields Redevelopment

Despite the many desirable environmental, economic, and social goals associated with the cleanup and reuse of brownfields, redevelopment is hampered by a series of obstacles that impose real costs and risks to all interested parties. Governments in the United States and elsewhere have spent decades working on ways to overcome these barriers, the most critical of which include addressing character and application of regulations, uncertainties regarding liability, site assessment and remediation, and funding resources.

Regulatory and Legal Innovation

As already mentioned, the initial priority of all levels of government dealing with brownfields remediation is identifying contaminated property and having responsible parties clean it up. The fact that toxic materials were discovered under homes in Love Canal brought to people's attention the grave risks to human health and environmental integrity that contaminated sites can pose. Indeed, the Love Canal incident marked the first time in U.S. history that federal emergency financial aid was approved for something other than a natural disaster. Soon after, Congress passed the Comprehensive Environmental Response, Compensation, and Liabilities Act (CERCLA) in 1980 [Public Law 96-510, H.R. 7020, SEC 104(a)(1)]. Commonly referred to as "Superfund," the law gave the U.S. EPA and other federal agencies the regulatory authority to respond to a release, or threat of a release, of a hazardous substance or "any pollutant or contaminant which may present an immediate and substantial danger to public health or welfare." The legislation enabled the federal government to recover the costs of cleanup actions from responsible parties or to clean up sites at their own expense. It also established a remediation fund financed primarily by a tax on crude oil and certain chemicals, with proceeds going to the EPA for property cleanup. In 1986, the Superfund Amendments and Reauthorization Act (SARA) was passed, broadening the EPA's mandate to include research and remediation activities and to increase state involvement in negotiating with responsible parties.

Beginning in the early 1990s, reaction against the enforcement-oriented Superfund apparatus intensified on the part of local governments and the private sector, both of which felt that it "put a chill" on investing in potentially contaminated land rather than facilitating it. An international study—conducted by The Business Roundtable (1993, p. 1)—compared the approaches of various countries to contamination problems and concluded, "No other country has adopted a program that is as cumbersome, inefficient, slow and costly as the U.S. Superfund program." One of the main concerns with Superfund was that its "strict" and "joint and several" liability provisions made investors leery of becoming involved in any property suspected of possessing contamination. "Strict liability" allows for the assessment of liability for damages without requiring proof of negligence (i.e., responsible parties are financially liable, even if the release of contaminants was legal at the time). Under "joint and several liability," parties who contribute to a site's pollution are each liable as if they alone polluted the site; therefore, the government can recover all costs from any party regardless of its degree of involvement in causing the problem. This means that property owners responsible for contaminating a site would be held liable for the cost of cleanup, and that any *new* property owner or bank would be considered just as responsible as the actual offenders. In addition to minimizing interest in redeveloping such sites, these provisions seemed to encourage lawsuits and countersuits aimed at deciding who should pay for site cleanup.

In the early 1990s, it became clear that limited progress was being made in land remediation efforts. Governmental attempts to order the cleanup of hundreds of thousands of potentially contaminated sites throughout the country proved largely unsuccessful, so the government had to find ways to facilitate the market's ability to address the issue. The EPA and many state and local governments started to address these inefficiencies in specific ways that led to a refocusing on redevelopment. Both policy and the general discourse began to shift from public health and liability under the banner of "contaminated land management" to economic development and urban revitalization under "brownfields redevelopment."

In 1995, the EPA introduced the Brownfields Action Agenda, which aimed to ignite interest in the redevelopment of brownfields. This agenda had four main components: (1) it provided funds for pilot programs to test redevelopment models and to facilitate stakeholder cooperation; (2) it clarified the liability of prospective purchasers, lenders, property owners, and others regarding their association with a site; (3) it fostered partnerships among the different levels of government and community representatives aimed at developing strategies for promoting public participation and community involvement in brownfields decision making; and (4) it incorporated job development and training opportunities into brownfields efforts. In addition, the agenda put into place the administrative structures for linking brownfields redevelopment with other relevant socioeconomic issues at the local level, while allowing the EPA to use CERCLA to focus solely on the management of high-risk contaminated properties.

By June 2000, all 50 states had participated in the federal government's brownfields program. Individual states throughout the country devised voluntary cleanup and voluntary response programs to loosen the prescriptive structures that both federal and state Superfund-style legislation had imposed (Meyer and Lyons 2000). The newer programs offer more flexible cleanup options and afford the private sector more leeway to work on its own terms on marketable projects. At the same time, they provide technical assistance, financial support, and protection from liability (to be discussed further later in this chapter). Nationwide, the Brownfields Action Agenda and the voluntary cleanup program (VCP) approach culminated in the 2002 passage of the federal Small Business Liability Relief and Brownfields Revitalization Act.

Under the VCPs, individual states intervene only to compel parties to clean up a site when it is deemed hazardous to public health and safety. Otherwise, cleanup activity is largely voluntary. The EPA remains involved in the development and operation of state VCPs, negotiating their content with state governments, signing Memoranda of Agreement (MOA) or Memoranda of Understanding (MOU) with states to endorse many of them, and setting out basic criteria to evaluate them. If a cleanup is carried out properly via the state's program, it provides a Certificate of Completion and No-Further Action and/or Covenants Not to Sue Certificate to help prevent future liability litigation. Although many states have powers to "reopen" a cleanup, a study by Simons, Pendergrass, and Winson-Geideman (2003, p. 265) found, through a systematic inventory of VCP administrators in the United States, that the incidence of reopeners was rather low (between 0.1 percent and 0.2 percent). It should be noted, however, that the "joint and several" and "strict" liability approach is still important, because it sends a strong legal signal to those involved in the types of activities that may result in the creation of a future brownfields to be wary of the activities taking place and perform their due diligence.

Site Assessment and Cleanup

Perhaps the most important issue from a health and environmental protection perspective has been ensuring the effectiveness of cleanup and the lowering of cleanup costs. When the contaminated sites problem first surfaced, the approaches to cleanup were as varied as they were largely ineffectual, often requiring urban sites to be assessed and cleaned up to meet "background or pristine conditions" (i.e. soil conditions that are similar to those found in remote locations or park lands) at a cost that was not feasible to investors. Over the years, however, consensus has emerged that a more uniform approach to assessment and cleanup is highly desirable. Consequently, two types of criteria for evaluating the extent of soil pollution and formulating cleanup goals to protect public health and safety are currently employed throughout the country:

1. Generic, numeric, soil-quality criteria: These are numerical indices that can be used for both assessment and cleanup activities derived from (eco)toxicological studies that identify levels according to a tolerable health risk. These indices can also vary according to the risks of contamination based on the land use proposed (e.g., agricultural, residential/parkland, industrial).
2. Risk-based, corrective action: These are procedures for developing soil and groundwater criteria that consider tolerance and risk exposure levels associated with a specific site and/or land use to be implemented as part of the corrective action process to ensure that appropriate and cost-effective remedies are selected.

It is important to note that the improvement over the last two decades in both the understanding of risks posed by contaminants and the ability to manage those risks has made it possible for governments and private-sector stakeholders to pursue remediation and redevelopment with much more certainty. In the United States, generic criteria and methods for risk assessment are more standardized among states because they have to be developed in a manner consistent with U.S. EPA policies and regulations. For example, the Risk-Based Corrective Action approach developed by the American Society for Testing and Materials (ASTM) is used by all states as a framework for developing risk-based cleanup criteria and methods. This is consistent with EPA regulations and can be adapted to state and local legislative and regulatory practices. The review process for non-Superfund brownfields falls under the jurisdiction of state governments. An important element of the Brownfields Act was the creation of the federal enforcement bar, which ensures that when a site goes through a state review program, the state becomes the primary regulator. This means that the federal government cannot use Superfund enforcement authority over that site. Consequently, virtually all state agencies take a more active role in technical assistance and review activities, usually reviewing and approving work plans and remedial objectives put forward by the responsible party at the beginning of the remediation process and then reviewing its cleanup work for adequacy at the end.

Those interested in acquiring, remediating, and redeveloping a brownfield typically embark on the following course of action, most often with oversight and support from state and local government. First, a Phase I environmental site assessment involves a review of historical records to determine ownership of a site and to identify the kinds of chemical processes that were occurring at the site. It also typically includes a site visit and interviews with past and present occupants and owners. It does not include any sampling. If such an assessment identifies concerns, then Phase II and III assessment are necessary. A Phase II environmental site assessment includes tests performed at the site to confirm the location and identity of environmental hazards, along with the preparation of a report that recommends cleanup alternatives. A Phase III environmental site assessment includes the comprehensive characterization, evaluation, and management of contaminated materials from a site, including their potential removal and legal disposal.

As for the remediation of contaminated property, the most common way to categorize available technologies is on the basis of whether contaminated soil and/or groundwater is treated in place (in situ technologies) or removed from the ground for treatment (ex situ technologies). The most common, and typically least costly, ex situ remediation method is "dig-and-dump," wherein contaminated soil is excavated from the site and placed in a suitable landfill facility. Other common ex situ treatment options include:

- bioremediation—microbial digestion of certain organic chemicals;
- vapor extraction—chemicals removed via aeration;
- thermal desorption—temperatures raised to volatize chemicals from the soil for vapor extraction;
- soil washing—contaminants washed from fine soils;
- solidification-stabilization technologies—specially formulated additive is applied to the soil to generate a low-hazard, low-leaching material, usually for on-site reuse;
- pump and treat—pumping contaminated groundwater from wells and treating it in an aboveground water-treatment plant.

In situ techniques are somewhat similar in their basic technological approach (biological, vapor, thermal, solidification, chemical), but are utilized without removing the soil and groundwater from the site. These approaches usually target a greater area and depth, but they take more time to carry out. Another popular in situ approach is phytoremediation, which uses trees and plants (such as willow) to extract heavy metals and other contaminants from the ground over time. States are becoming more amenable to in situ cleanup strategies involving engineering and institutional controls that reduce remediation costs and make brownfields redevelopment projects more efficient and economically viable. These strategies allow more contamination to remain on site, as long as an engineered barrier or a legal/institutional agreement is in place to limit access or actions that will pose a health risk. Soil contaminants, for example, can be fenced in or paved over, while permeable reactive materials can be placed in the subsurface to degrade or absorb dissolved contaminants as the groundwater passes through them. Institutional controls limiting access or site use also may be combined with monitored, natural attenuation to allow natural processes to absorb, dilute, or biodegrade contaminants without human intervention, as long as exposure is limited. The current challenge for state and local governments is to ensure that these controls are maintained over the long term. Closures with residual contamination typically include legal requirements on the property owner to maintain certain safeguards with regard to handling excavated contaminated soil, maintaining a cap, or accessing groundwater from the site.

Financial Tools

Despite greater certainty over legal and cleanup matters, the primary barrier to brownfields redevelopment is cost. The shift from a focus on issues of contamination to issues of economic development led to a flurry of research on the financial impediments that keep private investors away from brownfields. Early research conducted by Bartsch (1996) and others from the Northeast-Midwest Institute, by Simons (1998), and by the former Center for Urban Economic Development (2000) shed important light on the costs involved in brownfields reuse compared with greenfield sites in the urban periphery. These researchers found, largely through case study analysis, that brownfields property redevelopment for any use is hampered by a variety of additional direct costs (e.g., remediation, consulting) and by the prospect of low rental or sale revenues. And while developers have become more comfortable with redeveloping these properties, the profitability issue continues to be problematic, as real estate markets remain weak throughout the country.

The most straightforward way to visualize the financial obstacles associated with redeveloping brownfields is to take a developer's perspective and use a pro forma or development appraisal to see how brownfields costs and risks affect a project's bottom line. In terms of cost, a pro forma includes hard construction costs and various soft costs. Construction costs typically include those related to the process of getting building permits, the construction of building structures and parking facilities, as well as architectural, engineering, and consulting services. These expenses may be higher for a brownfields project, given the need to demolish existing structures and clean up the site for redevelopment. With regard to soft development costs, legal costs associated with brownfield projects are typically higher than for clean sites because of the need for additional legal services to conduct property review, extra consultation with government agencies, and more detailed communication with prospective purchasers. Brownfield projects may also entail higher contingency fees (reflecting the greater risks associated with such projects), higher realty taxes, higher development fees, and higher interest rates. Financing expenses are also typically higher for brownfield projects than for ones on clean sites, because these projects take longer to complete due to the collection, analysis, and review of soil research and remediation plans, as well as for the cleanup process itself.

If a market functions as it should and a high demand exists for a particular parcel and/or product, then the landowner is expected to reduce the cost of that parcel to cover the additional cost associated with managing brownfields issues. Indeed, in interviews I conducted with residential developers operating in Chicago when the market was strong, several noted that the government just needed to "get out of the way" and let the market operate (De Sousa 2008). Many clever developers have also been able to profit by negotiating significant discounts on property based on estimated cleanup costs and then minimizing those costs through the use of innovative technologies or the integration of novel site design and cleanup approaches. In many cases, however, the value of land in a particular location and/or the profit generated from a permitted use is simply not enough to cover brownfields-related costs *and* entice private capital. This is where government agencies, economic development officials, and other stakeholders come in; they have devised and implemented myriad financial tools to make brownfield projects work. Indeed, research by Paull (2008, p. 6) for the Northeast-Midwest Institute estimates that most brownfield projects (between 55 and 80 percent) involve public subsidy. That said, the major goal is to use tools that incur the least public expense but achieve the highest returns in terms of employment and rateables (i.e., property that generates tax income for local governments).

In the 2010 U.S. Conference of Mayors' report, cities identified the most valuable tools for redeveloping brownfield sites as follows: (1) EPA assessment funding, (2) private-sector investment, (3) EPA cleanup funds and state programs (i.e., the state VCPs), (4) redevelopment funds, (5) local incentives, and (6) insurance. In the early 1990s, the Conference of Mayors urged the EPA to change its approach to the issue, with an eye toward enticing brownfields redevelopment by reducing related costs and risks. Clarifying the rules of the game, as described above, has allowed stakeholders to focus more on the financial side of making projects work, which is unfortunately a much more complex issue that varies by project type and location. To assist with economic feasibility, state and local governments offer incentives that the EPA (2007, p. 4) has grouped into three broad categories: offsets to brownfields financing needs, tax incentives, and direct financing.

Offsets to Brownfields Financing Needs

Offsets—such as technical assistance, process facilitation, and project support—are financially indirect measures that have been employed by governments operating in both weak and stronger markets. A basic tool mentioned earlier is the compilation of brownfield inventories—real estate portfolios showing the locations of potential opportunity sites and the tools that can be used to redevelop them. The creation of a one-stop shop for assistance with brownfields also facilitates development by allowing representatives from multiple city and state agencies who oversee different aspects of the development process to work in a coordinated manner. This idea is especially popular among developers because it reduces procedural headaches and costly time delays.

The growing popularity associated with living and working in urban areas, particularly along waterfronts, has raised the value of residential, retail, and office products to a level that can make redeveloping brownfields for these uses potentially feasible without direct financial assistance. Local governments can facilitate this process by rewriting neighborhood plans where brownfields are clustered, as well as targeting capital spending to improve these communities. Parcels can be rezoned from industrial to other more profitable uses to increase land values and allow landowners to sell their properties for enough to cover brownfield costs and make a profit. Combining a brownfields inventory with a market analysis can help identify these potential areas of opportunity.

Tax Incentives

Government tax incentives have been used historically to make investment capital available in weaker market areas and to promote specific types of economic development. Tax incentive programs (i.e., credits, abatements, or forgiveness) can increase a project's profitability by allowing available funds or revenue to be used for brownfields redevelopment as opposed to paying taxes. According to an EPA review of state incentives (2007, p. 4), most tax incentives are used to offset remediation costs or to provide a buffer against increases in property value that may result in higher tax assessments before the site preparation costs are paid off. Federal and state governments can also offer tax incentives to retain or attract business to particular areas of need, as well as to construct low-income housing. The New Markets Tax Credit (NMTC) Program, established in 2000 as part of the Community Renewal Tax Relief Act of 2000, has been used to spur revitalization efforts on brownfields located in low-income and impoverished communities throughout the United States. It provides tax credit incentives to investors for equity investments in certified Community Development Entities that invest in such communities.

Direct Financing

Direct financing of brownfields-related costs through grants, loans, and other means (e.g., revolving, low-interest, forgivable loans; tax increment financing [TIF]; reduced land cost) has a direct impact on the developer's pro forma. These funds can be used to cover front-end costs associated with site assessment, which is often identified as one of the key hurdles developers must clear before entering into a brownfields redevelopment. Funds can also be used for remediation, demolition, and other site-preparation activities needed to ready the property for construction. In addition to helping finance specific components of a project, these tools and other public insurance products can be used to increase the lender's comfort by limiting the risk of potential losses or defaults.

A review of the application of financial incentives to brownfields projects in Milwaukee, WI, between 1990 and 2001 (the research was conducted for an earlier study) reveals how governments employ financial resources from a host of local, county, state, and federal sources. It should be noted, however, that federal funds are often administered through lower levels of government. (De Sousa 2005, p. 319). In Milwaukee, the city's redevelopment authority was involved in supporting more than half of the brownfield projects analyzed because of its ability to consolidate funds from a variety of sources (including EPA funds, federal block grants, Wisconsin Site Assessment Grants, TIFs, and money retained from the sale of city-owned property). Other sources of brownfields funding administered by the city of Milwaukee include Community Development Block Grant funds (through HUD) (12 percent of projects); TIF funds (11 percent of projects); forgiveness of back taxes (7 percent); Land Bank funds (5 percent); funds from the Milwaukee Economic Development Corporation (5 percent); and other general public funds (3 percent). Money from upper levels of government was also employed extensively for redevelopment projects; funding sources included the Wisconsin Department of Natural Resources' Site Assessment Grant (23 percent of projects); the Department of Commerce Brownfields Grant (15 percent); petroleum project funds (10 percent); and county government brownfields grants (4 percent). During the period examined, public funds for brownfields-related costs came from city (48 percent of total funding) and state sources (48 percent of total funding broken down as follows—38 percent from the Department of Commerce, 8 percent from the Petroleum Environmental Cleanup Fund Award [PECFA], and 2 percent from the Department of Natural Resources [DNR]), with the remaining 4 percent from the county (although it should be noted that these public funds are often granted to state and local entities from the EPA).

The ability to bring together numerous sources of financing is particularly important when cities target large brownfield parcels, clusters of parcels, or uses that are less profitable but needed in a particular market (e.g., residential, industrial), and/or they seek to make sites "shovel ready" for investment. Efforts to redevelop a former 140-acre railroad shops property in Milwaukee into an industrial center provide a good example. In 2004, the city established a $16 million dollar Tax Increment Financing District to pay the cost of site remediation, demolition, filling and grading, stormwater utilities, local roadways, and infrastructure. The Milwaukee city government also engaged in aggressive fund raising for remediation and redevelopment activities, winning more than 20 local, state, and federal grants and dozens of private donations totaling $24 million (Misky and Nemke 2010, p. 14). The ultimate goal was to make the site shovel ready and achieve flexible closure for the site so that future property owners were not required to manage environmental closure of their individual parcels.

A smaller project in Milwaukee that provides a more typical example of public finance and facilitation is the Alterra Coffee Headquarters development

(Wisconsin DNR, 2010). Alterra was founded in 1993 by local entrepreneurs with a sincere interest in community and building preservation. One property of particular interest to the city, and eventually Alterra, included three adjacent buildings that once housed a dry cleaner, a car dealer, and a car painting facility, among other uses. In 1998, the Redevelopment Authority of the City of Milwaukee (RACM) acquired the buildings through tax foreclosure and assembled them into a single development site. Site investigation revealed the presence of petroleum and chlorinated solvents. Seven underground storage tanks were removed from the site in 1996, and two hydraulic lifts were taken out in 2001. Remediation involved removing contaminated soil, capping some areas, installing a vapor barrier under the buildings, and establishing a system for groundwater monitoring. The Wisconsin DNR's Remediation and Redevelopment Program provided technical assistance during the cleanup and awarded a Brownfields Site Assessment Grant (SAG) to each of the properties. RACM provided $200,000 in EPA cleanup funds toward the redevelopment, while the Wisconsin Department of Commerce provided $55,000 in Petroleum Environmental Cleanup Fund awards (PECFA). Alterra officials selected the site for their new company headquarters in 2003 and began refurbishing the buildings even though new construction would have been less costly. The site now includes the company's main offices, the headquarters for the Alterra Baking Company, a coffee shop, retail space, and a roasting facility on the site of two of the former properties, with the remaining property developed as parking for the new retail space and coffee shop. The $3.5 million project has created approximately 28 new full-time and 13 part-time jobs and has won several awards for its community integration and green design, particularly in relation to its reuse of salvaged building materials and furnishings (City of Milwaukee, 2010).

Payoffs and Outcomes

The shift from an enforcement-driven approach focusing on soil remediation to a facilitation-oriented one encouraging private-sector investment has definitely improved the development climate in this domain of urban revitalization. Nonetheless, assessing the payoff of such intervention has become increasingly important as government budgets tighten. The most commonly used benchmark of public benefit continues to be measuring the value of redeveloped projects and the employment opportunities they generate. Even the EPA's website (2010) prominently notes that investment in the brownfields program has leveraged more than $14 billion in brownfields cleanup and redevelopment funding from the private and public sectors and created approximately 60,917 jobs. According to a recent study by the U.S.

Conference of Mayors (USCM 2010, p. 10), 50 cities reported that since 1993, $309 million in additional local tax revenue was generated from 654 redeveloped brownfields, while 58 cities estimated that if their brownfields were redeveloped they could collect anywhere from $872 million to $1.3 billion annually. As for employment, the USCM survey notes that 54 cities created 161,880 jobs through the redevelopment of 2,118 sites, with 64,730 jobs in the predevelopment/remediation stage and 97,150 permanent jobs. In all, Paull (2008, p. 6) estimates that public investments in brownfields leverage total investments at a ratio of approximately $1/public investment to $8/total investment.

American cities face increasing pressure for their brownfields policies and programs to serve both economic and environmental needs. In addition to addressing the primary barriers to private investment and generating taxes and jobs, cities are charged with ensuring that redevelopment is connected to broader community goals—goals related to protecting environmental health and safety, combating sprawl, revitalizing neighborhoods, improving quality of life, and promoting sustainability. Needless to say, the primary environmental benefit associated with brownfields redevelopment has been to clean sites and reduce health risks. The EPA's (2009, Appendix A) most recent update of state voluntary response programs reveals that an increasing amount of progress is being made, with over 93,000 sites having already completed a state program and over 52,000 "in the pipeline." The USCM report (2010, p. 10) also notes that most cities responding to its latest survey (84 percent) reported success in redeveloping brownfields since 1993. Of these, 65 cities were able to redevelop 1,010 sites encompassing approximately 7,210 acres; an additional 70 cities reported that 906 sites, comprising 4,683 acres, were in the process of being redeveloped.

Beyond protecting public health, a preliminary goal associated with the redevelopment of vacant or underutilized brownfields in urban areas was combating urban sprawl and the negative consequences associated with it (i.e., inner-city decline, segregation, automobile-generated air pollution). One highly quoted study by Deason, Sherk, and Carrol (2001, Table 4), finds that 4.5 acres of greenfield land are required to accommodate the same development as a single acre of brownfields land. This was further broken down for alternative land uses, with a mean ratio of 1 to 6.24 acres (median = 1.33 acres) for industrial development, 1 to 2.4 acres (median = 1.74 acres) for commercial development, and 1 to 5.57 acres (median = 2.15) for residential development.

Another measure of interest is the impact of brownfields redevelopment on neighboring property values, because it helps gauge the spillover or ripple effect on the surrounding community that is often associated with brownfields reclamation and redevelopment. A study conducted in Milwaukee and Minneapolis of publicly supported brownfield projects completed between 1997 and 2003 found that the redevelopment led to an 11.4 percent net increase in nearby housing prices in Milwaukee and a 2.7 percent net increase in Minneapolis (De Sousa, Wu, and Westphal 2009, p. 105). The geographic scope of influence was also significant (4,000 ft. in Milwaukee and 2,500 ft. in Minneapolis). Interestingly, all types of land uses had a positive influence on surrounding property values, because each helps erase the negative effect imposed by a blighted property. From a policy perspective, it is interesting to note that project size, project cost, and the amount of public investment in brownfields reuse had virtually no impact on the surrounding property effect, which indicates that both small- and large-scale projects are worthy of public support. Also noteworthy is the fact that the mean redevelopment cost and public investment value for the brownfields redevelopment projects in the sample were approximately $6 million and $130,000 respectively for Milwaukee, and $18 million and $8.6 million for Minneapolis. Part of the difference in public investment value between Milwaukee and Minneapolis is due to differences in how they track data, with Milwaukee focusing on brownfields-specific costs tied to site assessment, remediation, and/or preparation (aka "the brownfields premium"), and Minneapolis also including support for infrastructure and construction. Milwaukee has also tended to provide public support for many small projects requiring minor site assessment and cleanup activities, while Minneapolis has supported more than a dozen large megaprojects.

While interest in linking brownfields, sustainability, and quality of life continues to increase, there are very few documented efforts of incorporating quality of life and sustainability into measuring brownfields redevelopment outcomes (Berman et al., 2012). The few studies that do exist find that individual brownfield projects are having a positive impact on specific issues such as vehicle-miles traveled, greenhouse-gas emissions reduction, and recreation. Rating systems such as the U.S. Green Building Council's Leadership in Energy and Environmental Design (LEED), along with benchmarking initiatives such as the Menomonee Valley Benchmarking Initiative in Milwaukee (MVBI; tracks redevelopment on the basis of 57 economic, environmental, and community indicators) point the way to potential approaches for incorporating and tracking a broader array of outcomes. Still, there are many challenges to applying these techniques to the day-to-day operations of private developers and local governments. Without proper tracking of outcomes, however, it is difficult for cities to achieve an efficient allocation of funds, quantify the cost-benefit ratio of public programs, or determine the payoffs of new initiatives to all parties, whether they have an economic, environmental, or social focus.

Conclusion

Although project funding, procedural complications, and the lagging real estate market continue to inhibit the redevelopment of brownfields, there is a growing sense that these projects are not only economically profitable but also bring benefits of an economic, social, and environmental nature to all parties. The evolution of policy in this domain shows the efficacy of refocusing on economic development with support from public finance and policies. Liability protection and the clarification of rules for site assessment and cleanup have been necessary for setting the playing field and allowing investment to take place, while a growing range of public-financing programs have been used effectively to realize projects on the ground. Indeed, the growing number of projects throughout the United States provides a clear indication that such approaches, policies, and financing schemes are achieving success.

As for the kinds of policies that must be created to facilitate further redevelopment, private stakeholders continue to call for accelerated procedures, increased levels of public funding, and more redevelopment assistance, particularly in the early stages of the process. Community stakeholders call for policies and funding mechanisms that better connect brownfields redevelopment to broader community and sustainability objectives. The key objectives for public officials are (1) identifying the barriers to the private sector of delivering brownfield projects that offer a broader array of public benefits, and (2) implementing policies, programs, and funding tools that allow the projects to pay off.

References

Bartsch, Charles. 1996. Paying for our industrial past. *Commentary,* Winter: 14–24.

Berman, Laurel, Christopher De Sousa, Terry Linder, and David Misky. 2012. From blighted brownfields to healthy and sustainable communities: Tracking performance and measuring outcomes. In *Reclaiming Brownfields*, ed. R.C. Hula, L.A. Reese, and C. Jackson-Elmoore, R.C. Hula. London: Ashgate.

City of Milwaukee. 2010. Brownfield redevelopment success: Alterra coffee. http://city.milwaukee.gov/Alterra-Coffee.htm (accessed March 30, 2010).

Council for Urban Economic Development (CUED). 2000. *Brownfields Redevelopment: Performance Evaluation.* Washington, DC: Council for Urban Economic Development.

Deason, J., G.W. Sherk, and G. Carrol. 2001. *Public Policies and Private Decisions Affecting the Redevelopment of Brownfields: An Analysis of Critical Factors, Relative Weights and Areal Differentials.* Project funded by the Office of Solid Waste and Emergency Response and the U.S. EPA. Washington, DC: Environmental and Energy Management Program, The George Washington University.

De Sousa, Christopher. 2005. Policy performance and brownfield redevelopment in Milwaukee, Wisconsin. *The Professional Geographer* 57(2): 312–27.

———. 2008. *Brownfields Redevelopment and the Quest for Sustainability.* London: Elsevier Science/Emerald Group Publishing.

De Sousa, Christopher, Changshan Wu, and Lynne Westphal. 2009. Assessing the effect of publicly supported brownfield redevelopment on surrounding property values. *Economic Development Quarterly* 23(2): 95–110.

Dewar, Margaret, and Sabina Deitrick. 2004. The role of community development corporations in brownfield redevelopment. In *Recycling the City: The Use and Reuse of Urban Land,* ed. R. Greenstein and Y. Sungu-Eryilmaz, 159–74. Cambridge, MA: Lincoln Institute of Land Policy.

Meyer, Peter, and Thomas Lyons. 2000. Lessons from private sector brownfield redevelopers: Planning public support for urban regeneration. *Journal of the American Planning Association* 66(1): 46–57.

Misky, Dave, and Cynthia Nemke. 2010. From blighted to beautiful. *Government Engineering* May-June: 14–16.

Noonan, Frank, and Charles Vidich. 1992. Decision analysis for utilizing hazardous waste site assessments in real estate acquisition. *Risk Analysis* 12(2): 245–51.

Paull, Evans. 2008. *The Environmental and Economic Impacts of Brownfields Redevelopment.* Washington, DC: Northeast-Midwest Institute.

Simons, Robert. 1998. *Turning Brownfields into Greenbacks.* Washington, DC: Urban Land Institute.

Simons, Robert, John Pendergrass, and Kimberly Winson-Geideman. 2003. Quantifying long-term environmental regulatory risk for brownfields: Are reopeners really an issue? *Journal of Environmental Planning and Management* 46(2): 257–69.

Small Business Liability Relief and Brownfields Revitalization Act of 2001. 2002. H.R. 2869, 107th Congress of the United States.

The Business Roundtable. 1993. *The Business Roundtable Comparison of Superfund with Programs in Other Countries.* Washington, DC: The Business Roundtable.

U.S. Conference of Mayors. 2008. *Recycling America's Land: A National Report on Brownfields Redevelopment* 7 (January). Washington, DC: United States Conference of Mayors. http://usmayors.org/brownfields/library/brownfieldSURVEY08.pdf.

———. 2010. *Recycling America's Land: A National Report on Brownfields Redevelopment (1993–2010)* 9 (November). Washington, DC: United States Conference of Mayors. www.usmayors.org/pressreleases/uploads/November2010BFreport.pdf.

U.S. Environmental Protection Agency (EPA). 2007. *Financing Brownfields: State Program Highlights.* Report prepared by ICF International. Washington, DC: U.S. Environmental Protection Agency.

———. 2009. *State Brownfields and Voluntary Response Programs: An Update from the States.* Washington, DC: U.S. Environmental Protection Agency, 2009.

———. 2011a. Basic information: Brownfields and land revitalization. February 28. www.epa.gov/compliance/basics/cleanup.html.

———. 2011b. Brownfields and land revitalization: Brownfields definition. October 4. http://epa.gov/brownfields/overview/glossary.htm.

Wisconsin Department of Natural Resources (DNR). 2010. Alterra Coffee Headquarters. Madison, WI: Wisconsin Department of Natural Resources, Remediation and Redevelopment Program, Case Study PUB-RR-853, February.

8

State Financing of Innovation and Entrepreneurship

Ziona Austrian and Eli Auerbach

Ohio Third Frontier: Historical Overview

For many years, various states have been involved in technology-based economic development: the Ben Franklin Program in Pennsylvania, established in 1983; the Edison Program in Ohio, begun in 1984; and the Centers for Advanced Technology Program in New York, established in 1983. The purpose of these programs was to promote and accelerate technology development and commercialization and create high-paying jobs in their respective states.

The Ohio Edison Program became an early model for technology-based economic development, first by developing greater university-industry-federal collaboration to promote technological innovation within Ohio's existing industrial base, and later by creating business incubators to support the formation of new technology companies.

In fiscal year (FY) 2002, then Ohio governor Robert Taft initiated the Ohio Third Frontier (OTF), which focused on funding innovation and entrepreneurship.[1] OTF is a technology-based economic development (TBED) program that has been housed within the Ohio Department of Development. The program is based on the assumption that a high-performing innovation network creates and sustains high-wage jobs, and that the state must not only expand its innovation potential but also convert these ideas into new products, companies, industries, and jobs. An essential principle of OTF is that successful innovation must occur within an ecosystem.

OTF introduced a "commercialization continuum" (Ohio Third Frontier 2010b) with the following components:

- imagining the innovative commercial opportunity,
- incubating the innovation to prove its feasibility and identify its commercial potential,
- demonstrating the products and processes in a commercial context,
- achieving market entry to realize commercial viability, and
- exhibiting growth and sustainability to generate financial returns and sustain high-quality jobs (State of Ohio 2011a).

The OTF leadership understood that emerging technologies and firms were most at risk during the "imagining" through "demonstrating" phases of the continuum. As a result, a substantial portion of OTF funds have been designated to those critical needs.

Since 2002, the OTF has developed six principles that continue to guide its evolution (Baunach and Cox 2010; Ohio Third Frontier 2010b):

1. Competitive merit-based awards that include an external review
2. Definable technology areas
3. Balanced strategy
4. Responsiveness to the economic environment
5. Clear metrics
6. Mandate for collaboration

The original list recommended by Battelle in 2002 recommended investments in the following technology platforms: Advanced Materials; Biosciences; Information Technology; Instruments, Controls, Electronics and Advanced Manufacturing Technologies (ICE & AMT); and Power & Propulsion (Ohio Business Roundtable 2003). The current list of technology areas was updated in 2008 to include Advanced and Alternative Energy; Advanced Materials; Advanced Propulsion; Biomedical; and Instruments, Controls, Electronics (SRI International 2009).

The OTF focuses its investments on five strategic objectives:

1. Promote excellent research with commercial relevance to Ohio companies.
2. Expand access and availability to investment capital.
3. Provide entrepreneurial assistance through networking and developing entrepreneurial management talent.
4. Promote targeted technology clusters by addressing the technical needs of existing companies that are pursuing new products and production processes.
5. Contribute to the expansion of technologically proficient talent.

When Ohio Third Frontier first began, the majority of funding came from sources that already existed in the state budget. The initial investment of $1.1 billion used four primary sources, each of which came with its own purpose and set of constraints. The first source was the Wright Capital Fund (part of the State Capital Budget), which provided initial financing of $500 million toward capital equipment and research infrastructure at state-supported and state-assisted institutions of higher education. The use of this fund for operating expenditures, however, was prohibited. The second source was the Biomedical Research and Technology Transfer Trust Fund, which provided $350 million and was established with tobacco settlement funds. The majority of these funds were used for research operations purposes, but use of the money was restricted to bioscience projects. The third source of funding was the Technology Action Fund, which made available $150 million. This pool of dollars was to be allocated for general revenue funding and the support of research and development. Finally, there was an additional $100 million in OTF funding derived from state liquor tax profits (SRI International 2009).

As pointed out, much of the $1.1 billion for the Ohio Third Frontier was classified as restricted for capital expenditures, and only a small portion of available dollars was to be used for operating expenses associated with research, technology development, and early-stage investment capital. Consequently, a bond initiative was proposed to help infuse the OTF with operating dollars. In 2003, by a narrow 51–49 percent margin, voters rejected a $500 million, 10-year bond proposal to support the OTF. Two years later, the proposal appeared on the ballot again, but this time it was a part of a larger $2 billion measure, of which $1.5 billion was devoted to public works projects and environmental site cleanup and the remaining $500 million was designated for the OTF. The ballot proposal won voter approval by an 8 percent margin. The successful bond initiative provided the OTF with an infusion of unrestricted operating funds. The total available funding for OTF was raised to $1.6 billion. This resulting funding is set to expire after FY 2012.

The approved bond initiative afforded the OTF appropriation authority. The specific language of the referendum permitted the OTF to spend the funds on general operating expenditures but included maximum spending caps for each fiscal year. Between FY 2006 and FY 2011, OTF was allowed to spend no more than $450 million. However, the OTF is not required to spend all the dollars appropriated. Bonds are issued by the state only according to how much funding is needed to cover current expenses. The OTF estimates funding requirements for a 12- to 18-month period, and bonds are sold to cover these amounts. The OTF is allowed to carry forward remaining funds for subsequent fiscal years.

The 2005 bond legislation called for the institution of a governance structure with a nine-member OTF Commission and a 16-member Advisory Board.[2] The commission includes three state officials who are mandated as members by the legislation—the chancellor of the Ohio Board of Regents, the director of the Ohio Department of Development, and the governor's science and technology adviser. The commission also includes six regional representatives who are appointed by the governor. Current regional representatives include leaders from Business Strategy Associates (Central Region); Cincinnati Business Committee (Southwest Region); Diagnostic HYBRIDS, Inc. (Southeast Region); Eaton Corporation (Northeast Region); TaraData (West Central Region) and Pilkington North America (Northwest Region) (State of Ohio 2011f). The governor selects the chair of the commission from its members.

The commission approves OTF strategy, programming, and all awards; these awards are subsequently appropriated by the General Assembly. All proposals go through an external review, and this extensive review process enables the commission to feel confident about the decisions they make. All commission meetings are public. During these meetings, formal votes are conducted on the programs that will be offered and the dollars that are allocated as grants. Since the OTF Commission's establishment, most of its votes have been unanimous.

In contrast to the commission, the advisory board has no fiduciary responsibility. The members of the board are charged with advising the OTF Commission on strategic planning, general management, and program coordination. The advisory board is composed of citizens from industry, academia, and government (State of Ohio 2011h). Fourteen of the 16 members are appointed by the governor, including nine representatives from business and five from higher education and nonprofit research institutions. Industry representatives from across Ohio are recommended to the governor by regional partners.

Organizations and companies currently represented on the OTF Advisory Board include Case Western Reserve University; Cleveland Clinic Innovations; Ohio State University; Plastic Technologies, Inc.; Procter and Gamble; Team NEO; Triathlon Medical Ventures; University of Cincinnati; University of Toledo; USPrivatecompanies, LLC; and ZIN Technologies (State of Ohio 2011e). In addition, the advisory group includes one member appointed by Ohio's Senate president, and one appointed by the Speaker of the House. In early 2011, the advisory council had multiple vacant seats.

From the beginning, the OTF Commission respected and engaged with the advisory board. The commission considers the board to be advisers, strategic planning partners, and the voice of the constituencies from which they were drawn. The commission and advisory board work jointly to identify and select what they believe are the best programs for the targets and economic conditions within which entrepreneurial companies are working. Any public meeting of the advisory board includes members of the OTF Commission and is called a Joint Advisory Board & Commission meeting; policy matters are discussed in this venue. The advisory board chair conducts the meeting even though the commission chair is present. On occasion, the advisory board casts a formal vote to lend additional credence to a specific recommendation.

The OTF Advisory Board works alongside staff members from the Ohio Department of Development (ODOD). They bring in state and national experts to ensure that the advisory board and commission have enough information to make an informed decision. ODOD staff members also play an important role because they are responsible for the planning and management of individual OTF programs.

Additionally, the ODOD staff manages the entire proposal and review process. All dollars spent by OTF must be supported by an independent competitive review. The ODOD staff arranges for reviews to be conducted, and they assist in the process of bringing recommendations of the evaluators to the OTF Commission. The staff has no role in the evaluation or ranking of the applications, but they do manage the process and keep the commission aware of the budgeted dollars available, past performance of potential grantees, and updates on business conditions of the grantees since the time that their proposals were submitted. On the rare occasions when the commission does not accept the reviewer's recommendation, the commission is required to send a public statement to the governor, Speaker of the House, and president of the Senate explaining why the members did not vote for the recommendation. Once awards are made, ODOD staff transitions into the administration of the grants. This includes the grant agreements, programmatic and financial monitoring systems, and performance metric systems. The staff submits annual reports and performance metrics to the General Assembly.

The original sources of OTF funding did not provide sufficient noncapital operating funds for the awards. Due to state revenue challenges, the use of funds from the 2005 bond initiative proved critical for funding a balanced program of both capital and operating funds. As a result of the OTF successes and the value of flexible bond dollars, a new bond initiative to extend the OTF was planned. In May of 2010, the Ohio electorate was asked once again to vote on additional bonding authority for OTF to support economic development. With its successful passage, an additional $700 million over the next four years was approved. Because the appropriation authority afforded to the commission for the 2010 bond initiative is scheduled to overlap with the initiative from 2005, funding for FY 2012 is increased by $50 million to $225 million, while each subsequent fiscal year is restricted to $175 million (Ohio Ballot Board 2010). Furthermore, dollars that are not spent in any one year may be extended to other years and beyond 2015.

In total, the OTF has $2.3 billion in funding since 2002 to allocate for programs throughout Ohio. This enables the state to further invest in technology and innovation, entrepreneurship, research and development, industrial clusters, and ultimately in job creation.

OTF has proved to be a significant economic development program for Ohio. By the start of FY 2011, OTF was credited with the creation of more than 60,000 direct and indirect jobs. OTF attracted or created nearly 600 new companies with its investments (State of Ohio 2011j). In September of 2009, studies showed that the economic impact of OTF to the state exceeded $6.6 billion (SRI International 2009). This equates to a leverage ratio of six to one.

Awards and Funding Distribution

The OTF allocates funding by different program categories that change over time. Table 8.1 aggregates the number of awards and dollars allocated by the OTF annually since its inception in FY 2002. OTF began with only three programs that awarded funding in FY 2002, allocating $37 million for ten individual award recipients. By the conclusion of FY 2010, there were almost two dozen types of programs that had provided funding awards, and two additional programs had been introduced for FY 2011. At its peak in FY 2008, among all the programs, 74 awards were approved for a total of almost $246 million. In sum, over $1 billion has been invested in 390 approved awards.

Awards by Individual Programs (State of Ohio 2010c)

Table 8.2 outlines the number of awards each program has funded per year since OTF began. As few as three programs issued awards in 2002 and as many as 10 programs were funded in FY 2007 and FY 2010. FY 2008 saw the largest number of awards dispersed (74) followed by 2010 (56). The fewest number of awards were issued during the first two years of OTF; 10 awards were given in FY 2002 and 30 in FY 2003. The Fuel Cell Program has issued the largest number of total awards; since its inclusion in OTF in FY 2003, it has awarded funding every year, providing 60 awards to date. The Ohio Research Commercialization Grant Program distributed 51 total awards between FY 2004 and FY 2009 but was not slated for inclusion in FY 2011.

The fewest awards issued were through the Wright Mega-Centers of Innovation, which issued one award in FY 2007. The Wright Centers of Innovation program has dispersed 14 total awards to date. There are several programs

Table 8.1

Ohio Third Frontier Awards and Dollars Allocated, FY 2002–FY 2011 (to date)

FY year	Total programs provided funding	Number of awards	Total award dollars	Per award ($)
2002	3	10	37,377,164	3,737,716
2003	6	30	85,586,805	2,852,894
2004	7	33	82,493,056	2,499,790
2005	7	45	104,948,335	2,332,185
2006	6	33	112,637,199	3,413,248
2007	10	41	215,751,569	5,262,233
2008	9	74	245,557,590	3,318,346
2009	8	47	87,327,485	1,858,032
2010	10	56	83,517,730	1,491,388
2011 (as of Dec. 2010)	4	21	33,058,676	1,574,223
Total		390	1,088,255,609	2,790,399

Source: Ohio Third Frontier website.
Note: Information accurate as of December 2010.

that have issued only two awards, including Asset-Based Company Attraction, Research and Commercialization Program, and Research and Development Center Attraction Program.

OTF had the largest number of awarding programs (14) in FY 2011. The programs are Advanced Energy Program, Advanced Materials Program, Biomedical Program, Entrepreneurial Signature Program, Fuel Cell Program, Medical Imaging Program, Photovoltaic Program, Pre-Seed Fund Capitalization Program, Research and Development Center Attraction Program, Sensors Program, Targeted Industry Attraction Grant, Wright Center Success Fund, Third Frontier Internship Program, and Wright Projects.

The OTF Internship Program is not included in the table, although it was scheduled to award funding in the spring of 2011. Together with the Ohio Research Scholars Program, categorized in the table as part of Research and Commercialization, it targets funding toward building talent. More specifically, the OTF Internship Program addresses the fifth strategic objective: "Contribute to the expansion of technologically proficient talent." Under this program, funding will be awarded to companies that will hire student interns, and 80 out of Ohio's 88 counties will participate.

To appreciate the impact OTF has had, it is important to understand the number, distribution of awards, and dollars awarded by program. Some programs are funded for only one year, but the dollars allocated are substantial. This may not correlate to a successful investment. Rather, the programs that

Table 8.2

Ohio Third Frontier: Number of Funded Programs by Year, 2002–2010

Program Name	FY 2002	FY 2003	FY 2004	FY 2005	FY 2006	FY 2007	FY 2008	FY 2009	FY 2010	FY 2011	Total awards by program
Cluster Development											
Advanced Energy Program*							17	10	8	7	42
Advanced Materials Program*									3		3
Biomedical Programs*									4		4
Fuel Cell Program*		6	3	6	6	13	12	7	6	1	60
Medical Imaging Program*									8		8
Ohio Research Commercialization Grant Program			12	11	7	7	8	6			51
Photovoltaic Program*									6		6
Sensors Program*									5		5
Targeted Industry Attraction Grant*						2	2	1			5
Entrepreneurial											
Asset-Based Company Attraction						2					2
Entrepreneurial Signature Program*					6	6				4	16
Pre-Seed Fund Initiative	2	3	1	7	4	3					20
Success and Pre-Seed Fund							6	6	8		20
Pre-Seed Fund Capitalization Program*										9	9
Research and Commercialization											
Biomedical Research and Commercialization Program	4	3	3	4	5		6	5			30
Ohio Research Scholars Program							11				11
Product Development Pilot Program				3							3
Research and Commercialization Program						2					2
Research and Commercialization Program-EPS						2	5	4			11
Research and Development Center Attraction Program*									2		2
Third Frontier Action Fund	4	8	9								21
Wright Centers of Innovation		3	3	5		3					14
Wright Mega-Centers of Innovation						1					1
Wright Projects*		7	2	9	5		7	8	6		44
Total awards by year	10	30	33	45	33	41	74	47	56	21	390
Total programs providing funding by year	3	6	7	7	6	10	9	8	10	4	

Source: Data about programs and funding adapted from the Ohio Third Frontier website; *Notes:* FY 2011 data are accurate as of December 2010. Included for FY 2011, but not listed above, Wright Center Success Fund and Third Frontier Internship Program; *Programs slated for inclusion in FY 2011.

Table 8.3

Ohio Third Frontier: Dollars Allocated per Program by Year, 2002–2010

Program name	FY 2002 ($)	FY 2003 ($)	FY 2004 ($)	FY 2005 ($)	FY 2006 ($)	FY 2007 ($)
Cluster Development						
Advanced Energy Program*						
Advanced Materials Program*						
Biomedical Programs*						
Fuel Cell Program*		3,740,163	2,794,439	4,065,362	5,446,838	9,755,893
Medical Imaging Program*						
Ohio Research Commercialization Grant Program			2,091,519	1,905,150	2,347,116	10,094,325
Photovoltaic Program*						
Sensors Program*						
Targeted Industry Attraction Grant*						2,000,000
Entrepreneurial						
Asset-Based Company Attraction						3,000,000
Entrepreneurial Signature Program*					58,812,000	25,988,000
Pre-Seed Fund Initiative	2,150,000	2,401,650	1,162,111	6,000,000	6,585,921	5,000,000
Success and Pre-Seed Fund						
Pre-Seed Fund Capitalization Program*						
Research and Commercialization						
Biomedical Research and Commercialization Program	31,700,000	24,480,147	23,588,444	18,250,000	32,107,924	
Ohio Research Scholars Program						
Product Development Pilot Program				3,953,169		
Research and Commercialization Program						13,446,076
Research and Commercialization Program–EPS						15,992,375
R&D Center Attraction Program*						
Third Frontier Action Fund	3,527,164	5,431,256	8,107,623			
Wright Centers of Innovation		37,920,000	41,748,920	60,231,583		70,475,814
Wright Mega-Centers of Innovation						59,999,086
Wright Projects*		11,613,589	3,000,000	10,543,071	7,337,400	
Total Awards by Year	37,377,164	85,586,805	82,493,056	104,948,335	112,637,199	215,751,569

Cluster Development						
Advanced Energy Program*	12,037,306	9,154,192	9,126,544	5,658,801	35,976,843	3.31
Advanced Materials Program*			2,791,000		2,791,000	0.26
Biomedical Programs*			3,986,373		3,986,373	0.37
Fuel Cell Program*	8,970,370	5,298,393	6,383,022	999,875	47,454,355	4.36
Medical Imaging Program*			8,975,869		8,975,869	0.82
Ohio Research Commercialization Grant Program	2,789,580	2,099,900			21,327,590	1.96
Photovoltaic Program*			6,032,171		6,032,171	0.55
Sensors Program*			4,288,188		4,288,188	0.39
Targeted Industry Attraction Grant*	1,250,000	160,000			3,410,000	0.31
Entrepreneurial						
Asset-Based Company Attraction					3,000,000	0.28
Entrepreneurial Signature Program*				8,400,000	93,200,000	8.56
Pre-Seed Fund Initiative					23,299,682	2.14
Success and Pre-seed Fund	7,500,000	7,975,000	12,252,000		27,727,000	2.55
Pre-Seed Fund Capitalization Program*				18,000,000	18,000,000	1.65
Research and Commercialization						
Biomedical Research and Commercialization Program	22,700,000	20,040,000			172,866,515	15.88
Ohio Research Scholars Program	146,510,334				146,510,334	13.46
Product Development Pilot Program					3,953,169	0.36
Research and Commercialization Program					13,446,076	1.24
Research and Commercialization Program-EPS	24,200,000	18,800,000			58,992,375	5.42
R&D Center Attraction Program*			12,612,500		12,612,500	1.16
Third Frontier Action Fund					17,066,043	1.57
Wright Centers of Innovation					210,376,317	19.33
Wright Mega-Centers of Innovation					59,999,086	5.51
Wright Projects*	19,600,000	23,800,000	17,070,063		92,964,123	8.54
Total Awards by Year	245,557,590	87,327,485	83,517,730	33,058,676	1,088,255,609	

Source: Data about programs and funding adapted from the Ohio Third Frontier website.

Notes: FY 2011 data are accurate as of December 2010. Included for FY 2011, but not listed above, Wright Center Success Fund and Third Frontier Internship Program.

*Programs slated for inclusion in FY 2011.

have been consistently funded over the past decade, with multiple annual awards, best represent the programs with the greatest possible impact.

Table 8.3 outlines the dollar amounts each program has given to award recipients per year since the inception of OTF. The Wright Centers of Innovation Program has dispersed over $210 million, which is almost 20 percent of all dollars allocated and the most of any program. The Biomedical Research and Commercialization Program had the second largest distribution total, with almost $173 million or 16 percent of all awards. The Advanced Materials Program, which began funding in FY 2009, had allocated the smallest amount of funds, with just under $2.8 million. This was followed closely by the Asset-Based Company Attraction Program, with $3 million dispersed. These programs, though, have only issued three and two awards respectively.

Only $33 million of the total monetary awards for FY 2011 had been allocated as of December 2010, the first six months of Ohio's FY 2011. The largest total amount of funds issued in one year was in FY 2008 ($246 million). The average amount of dollars funded each year was over $117 million between FY 2002 and FY 2010. Overall, OTF programs have allocated over $1 billion in total funding.

The Ohio Third Frontier Portfolio of Programs

Program Summary

When the Ohio Third Frontier began in FY 2002, only three programs awarded funds. Throughout the rest of the decade, more than two dozen programs issued awards. In FY 2010, six new programs were introduced that issued awards for the first time: Advanced Materials, Biomedical, Medical Imaging, Photovoltaic, R&D Center Attraction, and Sensors.

In FY 2011, OTF was set to issue funds through 14 different programs, the most in any year since OTF began. Two new programs (Wright Center Success Fund & Third Frontier Internship Program) were added to the list in 2011. These programs fall into four categories: Cluster Development, Entrepreneurial, Talent, and Research and Commercialization.

The OTF Advisory Board and the Ohio Department of Development staff investigate whether the programs are relevant to the target audience and if there have been environmental or economic changes around the state that require programmatic changes. Pertinent information is derived from people involved in the program, as well as from community leadership, constituents interested in technology-based economic development, statewide and regional forums, and state and national trends. Based on this information, programs are either discontinued or extended for another fiscal year.

The programs' funds are directed primarily toward universities and companies, many of them high-tech. Along with the outline of the programs offered by the Ohio Third Frontier are testimonials from several companies that benefited directly from grant funding. The testimonials, based on interviews with company leaders, describe the number of awards and dollar amount the companies received, the specific use of the funds, and why the funding proved so valuable during each firm's development process.

Cluster Development

Advanced Energy Program

The Advanced Energy Program (AEP) seeks to advance the research and development of the Advanced Energy Industry in Ohio. The program invests in firms that will create new products or processes, and commercialize or improve existing manufacturing strategies and technologies. Preference is given to projects that include innovations in wind, biomass, and energy storage (State of Ohio 2011o). AEP helps companies to reach performance standards while reducing costs. Awards are given to firms that project increased employment within a three- to five-year window. Strong candidates for funding have technologies that have earned technical proof or have a possible end user identified. Ideally, dollars are awarded to fund work for two years, but not more than three (State of Ohio, 2010a).

AEP first began allocating these awards in 2008. Since its inception, AEP has distributed 35 awards for over $30 million. This equals almost 3 percent of all dollars allocated through FY 2010. OTF planned to award approximately $7 million in FY 2011 for this program (State of Ohio 2010b).

Advanced Materials Program

The Advanced Materials Program (AMP)[3] supports research and development that addresses the technical and cost barriers to commercialization of advanced materials products in Ohio. AMP focuses on firms that explore near-term marketable objectives. The program gives preference to polymer and carbon nanomaterials, liquid crystals, and biobased materials (State of Ohio 2011o). AMP assists companies in their efforts to increase performance standards while reducing costs. Awards are given to firms that project increased employment within a three- to five-year window. Strong candidates for funding have prototypes constructed and prepared for demonstration or products that are ready to enter the market. Ideally, dollars are awarded to fund work for two years, but not more than three (State of Ohio 2011d).

AMP began awarding funds in FY 2010. Three awards were issued for a total of $2.8 million. In FY 2011, AMP was expected to award an additional $7 million (State of Ohio 2011c).

One of the companies that received OTF funding through the Advanced Materials Program is Imaging Systems Technology (IST), located in Northwest Ohio (Kurtz 2011). Imaging Systems Technology has received two grants from the Ohio Third Frontier totaling over $600,000. The funds received have been directed toward product development, commercialization, and job growth. IST produces Plasma-shells™, which are hollow, gas-encapsulated spheres the size of a pellet. When a current is run through the shells, they glow, making this technology suitable for application in a plasma display. Because the product is not glass, it can be molded into a flexible display.

IST initially engineered the Plasma-shells™ using money from federal grants. However, these grants did not permit the funds to be used for commercialization. OTF funding was essential in order to take the development to the product stage. The dollars allocated were vital for the company to advance marketing and commercialization. Additionally, IST has been able to hire eight new employees due to OTF dollars. The OTF helped position them as a world leader in Plasma-shells™ technology. According to Vicki Kurtz, vice president of Imaging Systems Technology, the company is a small family business and was never interested in pursuing funding from venture capital companies. Therefore, the OTF funds have served as a great monetary bridge for job creation and commercialization. Had they not received funding from the OTF, IST would have kept the course, but development would have been set back by several years. OTF funding has expedited their business goals.

Biomedical Program

The Biomedical Program (BMP) aims to increase development and growth of the Ohio biomedical industry. Financial support is offered to firms capable of producing imminent commercial products and services. The Biomedical Program invests in Ohio-based research and development that addresses the technical and cost barriers to commercialization of biomedical products. Preference is given to firms with projects in cardiovascular, regenerative medicine, and orthopedics (State of Ohio 2011o). The Biomedical Program helps companies reach safety and efficiency standards necessary for end users. Awards are given to firms that project increased employment within a three- to five-year window. Strong candidates for funding should be producing biomedical products that have attained regulatory approval for use or approval for clinical trials on humans. Ideally, dollars are awarded to fund work for two years, but not more than three (State of Ohio 2011b).

The Biomedical Program began awarding funds in FY 2010. Four awards were received for a total of almost $4 million. In FY 2011, the Biomedical Program was expected to award up to $7 million (State of Ohio 2010d).

Fuel Cell Program

Through direct financial support, the Fuel Cell Program (FCP) aids in the development of the Ohio fuel cell industry. It is among the oldest programs still issuing awards. FCP supports Ohio-based research and development that addresses the technical and cost barriers to commercializing fuel cell and other advanced energy components and systems (State of Ohio 2011o). The FCP helps companies reach performance standards while reducing costs. Awards are given to firms that project increased employment within a three- to five-year window. Strong candidates for funding should have prototypes constructed and prepared for demonstration or ready to enter the market. Ideally, dollars are awarded to fund work for two years, but not more than three (State of Ohio 2010e).

The FCP began operations in FY 2003. Through the life of the program, there have been 59 awards made for over $46 million, equaling 4.4 percent of all dollars allocated through FY 2010. At its peak in FY 2007, the program issued nearly $10 million through 13 awards. In FY 2011, FCP was scheduled to award up to $7 million (State of Ohio 2010f).

Mound Technical Solutions, Inc., a company located in West Central Ohio, has received two grants from the Ohio Third Frontier totaling over $1 million (McClelland 2011). The funds received have been directed toward the development of a product line of fuel cell test instrumentation in three formats: a modular format, direct methanol, and reformed methanol from the cell level up to the stack level. Additionally, Mound Technical Solutions product development includes a suite of test equipment involving various software and hardware components and services for environmental testing of fuel cell products (such as shake and vibration), electromagnetic interference (EMI), durability testing, and effluent monitoring. The funding Mound Technical Solutions received has enabled the company to hire 10 additional employees; enhance its technology; successfully apply for patents; develop new product lines, market units, and products; add services; and experience business growth. Doug McClelland, president of Mound Technical Solutions, states that without the funding from the OTF the company would not have been able to advance in the fuel cell arena.

Another fuel cell company that received funding from OTF is Nanotek Instruments, Inc. The company, also located in West Central Ohio, received two grants from the Ohio Third Frontier totaling nearly $1.4 million (Beech 2011). Most of the first award was used to buy equipment essential to making fuel cell batteries. The equipment purchased was critical to the company's goal of moving ahead in the fuel cell field. Without it, the in-house creation and testing of fuel cells at Nanotek Instruments would have been impossible. There are not many places, especially in Ohio, where fuel cell batteries are manufactured. OTF funding gave Nanotek Instruments a substantial competitive advantage, allowed it to expand internationally, and made it eligible for federal grants. Buyers want to know that the products they are purchasing have passed important quality tests. Nanotek can now approach manufacturers with a proven and reliable brand of material. Additionally, OTF funds allowed Nanotek to hire essential personnel—15 employees as of 2011 and even more projected in the future. The second grant, received in 2011, will go toward development, production, and materials evaluation.

Nanotek continues to expand research and development (R&D) and materials testing, which is essential to their battery business. Additionally, the company has been able to offer more and diverse types of fuel cell batteries, while creating new technologies for the batteries themselves. Ron Beech, director of Marketing and Sales for Nanotek, noted that if OTF funding had not been available, the organization would have had to pursue a federal grant. No other viable sources of funding existed. Had federal grants not materialized, progress most certainly would have been delayed.

Medical Imaging Program

The Medical Imaging Program (MIP) aims to develop the Ohio medical imaging industry. Financial assistance is provided to bring new products and processes to the market. MIP supports research and development that addresses the technical and cost barriers to commercialization of biomedical products in Ohio (State of Ohio 2011o). Financial support is offered to firms capable of producing imminent commercial products and services. Preference is given to firms with projects that are part of a medical imaging cluster within Ohio (State of Ohio 2010g).

The MIP began awarding funds in FY 2010. Eight awards were received for a total of almost $9 million. In FY 2011, MIP was expected to award up to $7 million (ibid.).

Photovoltaic Program

The Photovoltaic Program seeks to advance the research and development of the photovoltaic industry in Ohio. The program invests in firms that will create new products or processes, commercialize, or improve existing manufacturing strategies and technology (State of Ohio 2011k). The Photovoltaic Program invests in companies to increase performance standards while reducing costs. Awards are given to firms that project increased employment within a three- to five-year window. Strong candidates for funding should have prototypes constructed and prepared for demonstration or ready to enter the market (State of Ohio 2011l).

The Photovoltaic Program first began funding in FY 2010. It issued six awards for a total of just over $6 million. OTF was scheduled to award up to $7 million in FY 2011 for this program (State of Ohio 2010h).

Sensors Program

The Sensors Program seeks to advance the research and development of the sensors industry in Ohio. The program invests in firms that will create new products or processes, commercialize, or otherwise improve existing manufacturing strategies and technology. Preference is given to projects that include industry specializations—motor vehicles, aerospace/aviation, advanced energy/environment, biosciences/bioproducts, advanced materials, and agriculture/food processing (State of Ohio 2011r). The Sensors Program seeks to assist Ohio firms in increasing performance standards and reducing production costs. Awards are given to firms that project increased employment within a three- to five-year window. Strong candidates for funding should have prototypes constructed and prepared for demonstration or ready to enter the market (State of Ohio 2011s).

The Sensors Program first began funding in FY 2010. It distributed five awards totaling almost $4.3 million. OTF was scheduled to award up to $7 million in FY 2011 for this program (State of Ohio 2011t).

Targeted Industry Attraction Grants

The Targeted Industry Attraction (TIA) grant focuses resources and incentives on the attraction of firms from outside Ohio that can help build critical mass in selected growth industries in Ohio. OTF evaluates companies within the technology focus areas. TIA provides development incentives that are a part of an entire attraction package. Strong candidates will be able to further develop existing supply chains, create partnerships with Ohio research entities, and capitalize on existing state assets. Grants have ranged from $160,000 to $2,000,000. This program is not open to a Request for Proposals (RFP) process (State of Ohio 2010j).

Entrepreneurial

Entrepreneurial Signature Program

The Entrepreneurial Signature Program (ESP) stimulates and supports technology-based entrepreneurial commercialization outcomes within Ohio. ESP focuses assistance and early-stage investment resources on companies possessing strong economic development potential in specific sectors. ESP looks to accelerate growth of early-stage Ohio technology companies in six regions throughout Ohio (State of Ohio 2011g). The ESP program was designed to enable local entrepreneurial organizations to focus resources on those technologies that are critical and have high potential in their regions. For example, one of the recipients was JumpStart, Inc. in Northeast Ohio, which helps provide early stage investment capital, business planning, and other services to entrepreneurs. Investments in these "signature" technologies have been coupled with the requirement to provide universal assistance to entrepreneurial companies regardless of their industry or technology affiliation.

ESP funded awards in FY 2006 and FY 2007. Six awards were distributed each year for a total of almost $85 million, or 8 percent of all the funds distributed by OTF. ESP was slated for inclusion in FY 2011, with plans to allocate up to $10 million. As of December 2010, the ESP program had awarded a total of $18 million (State of Ohio 2010c). The OTF Commission is authorized to exceed the stated cap for any given program if viable requests for other programs do not materialize. In this instance, OTF chose to exceed the cap for the ESP by the midpoint of FY 2011.

Pre-Seed Fund Capitalization Program

The Pre-Seed Fund Capitalization Program (PFCP) seeks to enhance the accessibility of professionally managed capital and connected services to further the growth of early-stage Ohio technology companies. Funding goes toward pre-seed–stage technology-based businesses (State of Ohio 2011m). As one of the founding programs of OTF, PFCP began giving awards in 2002. The most recent award allocated was in FY 2007. In total, the program has given 20 awards for over $23 million, representing over 2 percent of all dollars allocated by OTF.

OTF funding for PFCP is invested in Biomedical, Advanced/Alternative Energy, Instruments-Controls-Electronics, Advanced Materials, and Advanced Propulsion. OTF was expected to award up to $10 million in FY 2011 for this program. Grant applications should be in the range of $500,000 to $2 million (State of Ohio 2010i).

Talent

Third Frontier Internship Program

The Ohio Third Frontier Internship Program, established in FY 2002, helps provide Ohio businesses with technically trained students in targeted areas. These areas include Advanced Manufacturing, Advanced Materials, Bioscience, Information Technology, Instruments-Controls-Electronics, and Power and Propulsion. The internship program offers students the opportunity to explore career paths within Ohio and has placed over 3,000 interns in high-tech positions with more than 700 employers statewide.

The OTF Internship Program reimburses employers for up to 50 percent of the interns' salary or up to $3,000 in a calendar year. Upon completion of the internship, firms have the opportunity to offer full-time positions to their students (State of Ohio 2011x). The program has received funding since FY 2008, beginning with $1.5 million each year through FY 2010, and growing to $3 million in FY 2011. This program is not included in Tables 8.2 and 8.3.

Research and Commercialization

Research and Development Center Attraction Program

The Research and Development Center Attraction Program (RDCAP) works to draw nationally recognized firms to relocate their research and development or laboratory facilities to Ohio. RDCAP offers a lucrative cost sharing or matching dollar component to existing proposals by Ohio organizations (State of Ohio 2011p). Funding distributed by RDCAP is expected to produce new jobs; increase development of technology-based products; and attract or retain technology-based firms throughout Ohio. Activities funded by RDCAP must yield a strong positive economic impact for Ohio while building the state's research and development capacity (State of Ohio 2011q).

RDCAP began awarding funds in FY 2010. Two awards were issued for over $12 million. The program is slated to continue in FY 2011 and expected to allocate up to $23 million (State of Ohio 2011i).

One of the companies that received funding from OTF in the Research and Development Program is Kent Displays, Inc., headquartered in Northeast Ohio (Khan 2011). A creator and manufacturer of devices, Kent Displays received four grants totaling more than $14 million. The funds have been directed toward the development and commercialization of Reflex™ display technology, manufacturing, and product development. Kent Displays are the makers of the Boogie Board™ LCD writing tablet, which was introduced in 2009. The

Boogie Board™ is manufactured in Kent, Ohio, and sold globally via a network of retailers, distributors, and resellers. Other products by Kent Displays include industry-leading, color-changing electronic skins and the flexible yet rugged information displays for smart card applications. The company has grown by leaps and bounds, employing 110 employees to date. According to Dr. Asad Khan, vice president of technology for Kent Displays, a big part of their growth has been due to support from the Ohio Department of Development through the Ohio Third Frontier Program. Enabling partnerships with local and statewide partners is one of the most valuable achievements of OTF funding. The development and commercialization of various flexible display products, as well as support in establishing the world's first fully automated roll-to-roll manufacturing line, is due in a large part to OTF funding.

Wright Projects

Wright Projects aims to develop research capabilities in technology areas among the state's colleges and universities. Support is directed mainly at capital equipment that may, in turn, provide entrepreneurial and commercial benefits for Ohio-based companies. This initiative fosters collaboration among Ohio institutions to bring near-term products to market. Furthermore, the physical assets of each project are utilized to develop a technically proficient workforce (State of Ohio 2011v). Wright Projects supports programs that are commercial-ready within three years of receiving funding. In addition, preference is given to activities that will generate dollars and jobs while furthering research opportunities throughout the state (State of Ohio 2011w).

The Wright Projects program began funding in FY 2003 and remains active. Throughout its history, the program has issued 44 total awards for almost $93 million—nearly 9 percent of all dollars allocated by OTF. The Wright Projects program is slated for inclusion in FY 2011 and estimated to allocate up to $21 million (State of Ohio 2011v).

The Application and Funding Process (State of Ohio 2011n)

OTF implements a competitive application process that focuses on projects with commendable and exemplary scientific and technical content and a strong potential for commercialization in Ohio. The program framework for each of the funded programs for FY 2011 was derived from a strategic plan recommended by the combined OTF Advisory Board and Commission and then approved by the Commission in an open meeting. The combined groups review and discuss strategy each year. The board's recommendations include specific award criteria and a peer review process.

The OTF has an overall budget for each fiscal year, determined by the commission and the state budget in a given year. The ODOD staff creates a program plan that reflects OTF's five main strategies described earlier. Each program is given a funding cap, which represents the expected amount of money that can be invested in all applications for that program. However, exceptions are sometimes made, as was the case in the beginning of FY 2011. Both the Pre-Seed and the ESP programs were scheduled to allocate $10 million each, but after the external evaluators read all the applications, it became apparent that there were more viable opportunities for the Pre-Seed program than allocated funds could cover. Funds were diverted from the ESP program and from carried-over funds from the previous year in the Advanced Energy and Advanced Materials programs. This illustrates the flexibility OTF has in its allocation to individual programs, even though its total budget is fixed annually.

Each program mandates that applicants present a plan for a collaborative effort. This may be a combination of two or more entities from the private sector, higher education, approved nonprofits, and/or governmental research facilities. Each collaborator must be able to contribute to the commercialization process of the product or service.

Table 8.4 outlines the distribution of available funds for FY 2011. Of the 14 programs that issued awards through OTF in FY 2011, seven intend to award up to $7 million (Advanced Energy Program, Advanced Materials Program, Biomedical Program, Fuel Cell Program, Medical Imaging Program, Photovoltaic Program, and Sensors Program). Grants for these programs are issued for up to $1 million apiece. However, applicants may receive an additional $1 million from the Wright Capital fund.

Four other programs were expected to be funded in FY 2011 at higher levels than the standard $7 million. These included the Entrepreneurial Program ($10 million), Pre-Seed Fund Capitalization Program ($10 million), Research and Development Center Attraction Program ($23 million) and Wright Projects ($21 million).

At the time of this writing, there were two programs—Targeted Industry Attraction Grants and the Wright Center Success Fund—that did not have information available on the FY 2011 funding distribution and RFP process.

The length of the project (project term) for most of the programs will be five years. During the first two to three years, the grant will cover active work; the final two or three years of funding will be used to review the research and commercialization efforts of the project. There are differing project terms for the Entrepreneurial Signature Program (one year), Pre-Seed Fund Initiative (three years), Research and Development Center

Table 8.4

OTF Fiscal Year 2011 Program Dollars and Distribution

Program	FY 11 total available $	FY 11 max. $ per award	Additional resources	Project term	Cost-share requirement
Advanced Energy Program	$7 million	$1 million	$1 million WCF	5 years	Min. 1:1
Advanced Materials Program	$7 million	$1 million	$1 million WCF	5 years	Min. 1:1
Biomedical Program	$7 million	$1 million	$1 million WCF	5 years	Min. 1:1
Fuel Cell Program	$7 million	$1 million	$1 million WCF	5 years	Min. 1:1
Entrepreneurial Signature Program	$10 million	N/A	N/A	1 year	Min. 1:1
Medical Imaging Program	$7 million	$1 million	$1 million WCF	5 years	Min. 1:1
Photovoltaic Program	$7 million	$1 million	$1 million WCF	5 years	Min. 1:1
Pre-Seed Fund Initiative	$10 million	$500 k–$2 million	N/A	3 years	Min. 1:1
R&D Center Attraction Program	$23 million	$5 million	N/A	7 years	None
Sensors Program	$7 million	$1 million	$1 million WCF	5 years	Min. 1:1
Wright Projects	$21 million	$1 million–$3 million	N/A	6 years	Min. 1:1
Targeted Industry Attraction Grant*	N/A	N/A	N/A	N/A	N/A
Ohio Third Frontier Internship Program	$3 million	$3,000	N/A	N/A	N/A
Wright Center Success Fund*	N/A	N/A	N/A	N/A	N/A

Source: The State of Ohio 2011u.
Note: WCF = Wright Capital Fund.
*No information was available as of February 2011.

Attraction Program (seven years), and Wright Projects (six years). Furthermore, each program has a cost-share component. For every dollar of state funding received, the applicant must contribute a minimum ratio of 1:1 in the form of cash.

Every submission goes through a rigorous screening process. The first step consists of an administrative review conducted by staff to ensure compliance with all requirements of the RFPs. The review is based on an established written protocol to ensure that the RFPs' objectives and goals are adequately met. Proposals passing the administrative review are submitted to external bodies for technical and commercial review.

There are multiple external reviewing entities. Each has expertise and specialization in the field of the project proposal. For example, Wright Center proposals and Research Scholars funding are reviewed by panels from the National Academies, among them the National Academies of Science, the National Academies of Engineering, the Institute of Medicine, and the National Research Council (NRC 2011). The National Academies review has been part of the OTF since its beginning, but the comprehensiveness of the process makes it quite expensive and time-consuming. As a result, the National Academies review is used primarily for intensive, research-related programs. The OTF selects Ohio reviewers for other programs that do not merit as high a level of scientific review.

In the first phase of the external review, the evaluators decide whether the criteria have been met. If so, the evaluators move to the second phase of the external review process, which includes a face-to-face meeting with the external evaluators or their representative. The external evaluators gather all collected data into a comprehensive report, rank each proposal, and present the findings to the OTF Commission. The commission also utilizes the ODOD staff in providing additional objective information about previous performance of organizations that have submitted proposals.

In a public meeting, the external evaluator presents the proposals he or she recommends for funding. The ODOD staff provides the programmatic information about the goals, funding criteria, and available dollars. Upon the request of the commission, the ODOD staff offers a recommendation. Commission members deliberate on the information provided by the external evaluator and the ODOD staff. Funding for a project proposal requires an affirmative majority vote. All decisions of the commission are final.

Proposals approved by the OTF Commission are submitted to the State Controlling Board, a legislative body that approves state-appropriated funds. Once the funds are sanctioned, a grant agreement is drafted, outlining the proposal, budget, funding decisions, and terms and conditions of the grant.

Summary and Conclusions

In 1984, Ohio's Thomas Edison Program became one of the first technology-based economic development strategies implemented in the United States, and the success and lessons learned from this program helped create the Ohio Third Frontier (OTF). The OTF follows six guidelines: competitive merit-based awards that include an external review, definable technology areas, balanced strategy, responsiveness to the economic environment, clear metrics, and a mandate for collaboration.

Based on these guidelines, the OTF narrows its focus to five distinct investment pillars that include Research and Development, Entrepreneurial Assistance, Financial Capital, Industry Cluster Development, and Talent.

Since 2002, the OTF has been influenced by three external entities: the state budget, the governor, and the general assembly. Based on information and input from these sources and the varied success of its different programs, the OTF Commission and the Advisory Board adopt their strategies for each fiscal year. The vision and determination of the OTF leadership is what makes the programs successful. The OTF implements a rigorous and competitive funding process. The commission maintains a balanced portfolio, with funds that are invested in an array of technology and research areas. Since its inception, OTF has stood by its founding guidelines.

Why has the OTF been successful? The Ohio Third Frontier is a unique, technology-based, economic development funding mechanism. It is funded by a state constitutional amendment that authorizes the electorate to approve bonding authority for purposes other than capital investment. This flexible funding mechanism is a major contributor to the success of OTF. The first bond initiative from 2005 infused OTF with essential operating dollars; the second 2010 bond initiative allowed the Third Frontier to support its programs entirely outside the biennial budget cycle (Ohio Third Frontier 2010a).

A second reason for the program's success is that the OTF has remained entirely bipartisan since it was established: No political motivations are infused in the OTF's operation. It has always been endorsed by both the gubernatorial administration and the General Assembly. Beginning under Robert A. Taft, a Republican governor, OTF was embraced by Ted Strickland, a Democratic governor, and is now continued by the Republican governor John Kasich. Also, the commission chair (a gubernatorial appointment) can present, but not impose, policy ideas to the commission. These ideas have sparked healthy debate and discussion by the advisory council. Another example of its successful bipartisanship is the fact that the state referendum in 2010 captured votes from both parties. Apparently, having to go to the voters to ensure its existence has made the Third Frontier less partisan, and state legislators recognize that this program is not a political football. If the OTF had been a legislative program, it likely would have been a very different program.

A third factor in the program's success is the fact that OTF has led to the formation of a coalition between three major economic groups: government, universities, and business. All three sectors influence the programming direction, and the program would not have been as successful if a way to forge this public-private partnership had not been developed.

A fourth reason for OTF's success is its programmatic flexibility and the balance it keeps along the commercialization continuum from applied research to entrepreneurship.

The fifth element in OTF's success is its focus on investing in specific clusters, including investments in core/driver companies, supply chain companies, research institutions, and talent/workforce development.

Finally, OTF is successful because it incorporates an external review process. The review and selection process is driven in part by market assessment, not political influence. Independent third-party reviewers, sometimes from the private sector, enable the OTF to apply a rigorous and replicable process for each funding application.

A key public policy question for OTF is what role the state should play in the commercialization continuum and where it should invest its dollars. On one side of the continuum are OTF investments in the Wright Centers and Research Scholars program, which strengthen the applied research infrastructure in the state by building collaborations between universities and companies in each of the centers. On the other side of the continuum are OTF investments in entrepreneurial assistance and the infusion of high-risk start-up capital. OTF made a major investment in the Entrepreneurial Signature Program (e.g., JumpStart, Inc. in Northeast Ohio) to help provide early stage investment capital, business planning, and other services to entrepreneurs. The OTF and similar programs should invest in projects that are in the early stages of development, since the closer a project is to commercialization the more likely it is that private entities will invest in it. A state program such as the OTF needs to continually assess the role it should play and where it can exert the most influence for taxpayer dollars.

Notes

This chapter includes information and data that were accurate as of December 2010. Since January of 2011, the state of Ohio has been under a new governorship and political leadership. The Ohio Third Frontier, along with other state programs, is currently under review.

1. The Ohio fiscal year begins July 1 and ends June 30.

2. The OTF Commission Ohio regions include Northeast, Northwest, Southeast, Southwest, West Central, and Central Ohio.

3. One of six programs introduced in FY 2010 and slated for FY 2011 (Advanced Materials, Biomedical, Medical Imaging, Photovoltaic, R&D Center Attraction, and Sensors).

References

Baunach, Dorothy, and Matthew Cox. 2010. Ohio Third Frontier: An Overview for Wisconsin Economic Summit III. PowerPoint presentation, October 5. Accessible at www.wiroundtable.org/summit/summit3.asp.

Beech, Ron. 2011. Author's interview with Beech, director of Marketing and Sales, Nanotek, August 26.

Khan, Asad. 2011. Author's interview with Dr. Khan, vice president of Technology, Kent Displays, August 22.

Kurtz, Vickie. 2011. Author's interview with Kurtz, vice president, Imaging Systems Technology, August 19.

McClelland, Doug. 2011. Author's interview with McClelland, president, Mound Technical Solutions, August 19.

National Research Council (NRC). 2011. Welcome to the National Research Council. The National Academies. www.nationalacademies.org/nrc/.

Ohio Ballot Board. 2010. *Ohio Issues Report: State Issue Ballot Information for the May 4, 2010, Primary Election.* Report, Spring. Columbus: Office of Ohio Secretary of State. www.sos.state.oh.us/sos/upload/publications/election/Issues10_primary.pdf.

Ohio Business Roundtable. 2003. *World Class Ohio: A Prospectus for Achieving Success in the Third Frontier.* Prospectus, June. Columbus: Ohio Business Roundtable.

Ohio Third Frontier. 2010a. Application for Innovations in American Government Awards Program, Harvard University, Kennedy School of Government, Ash Center for Democratic Governance and Innovation, September 8.

———. 2010b. *Historic Strategic Framework.* Report, December 1.

SRI International. 2009. *Making an Impact: Assessing the Benefits of Ohio's Investment in Technology-Based Economic Development Programs.* Report, September. www.development.ohio.gov/ohiothirdfrontier/Documents/RecentPublications/OH_Impact_Rep_SRI_FINAL.pdf.

State of Ohio. 2010a. *Ohio Third Frontier Advanced Energy Program, Fiscal Year 2011: Request for Proposals (RFP).* http://thirdfrontier.com/Documents/OTFAEP-FY11RFPFinal.pdf.

———. 2010b. Ohio Third Frontier: Advanced Energy Program 2011 Bidders' Conference. PowerPoint presentation, August 19. http://thirdfrontier.com/AdvancedEnergyProgram2011BiddersConference.htm.

———. 2010c. Ohio Third Frontier: All awards current through 07/16/10. http://thirdfrontier.com/Documents/RecentPublications/ALL_OTF_Awards_Current_071610_Web.pdf.

———. 2010d. Ohio Third Frontier: Biomedical Program 2011 Bidders' Conference. PowerPoint presentation, November 22. http://thirdfrontier.com/BiomedicalProgram2011BiddersConference.htm.

———. 2010e. *Ohio Third Frontier Fuel Cell Program, Fiscal Year 2011: Request for Proposals (RFP).* http://thirdfrontier.com/Documents/OTFFCPFY11RFPFinal.pdf.

———. 2010f. Ohio Third Frontier: Fuel Cell Program 2011 Bidders' Conference. PowerPoint presentation, August 19. http://thirdfrontier.com/FuelCellProgram-2011BiddersConference.htm.

———. 2010g. Ohio Third Frontier: Medical Imaging Program 2011 Bidders' Conference. PowerPoint presentation, November 22. http://thirdfrontier.com/MedicalImagingProgram2011BiddersConference.htm.

———. 2010h. Ohio Third Frontier: Photovoltaic Program 2011 Bidders' Conference. PowerPoint presentation, August 19. http://thirdfrontier.com/PhotovoltaicProgram-2011BiddersConference.htm.

———. 2010i. Ohio Third Frontier: Pre-Seed Fund Capitalization Program Bidders' Conference. PowerPoint presentation, September 15. http://thirdfrontier.com/PreSeed2011BiddersConference.htm.

———. 2010j. Ohio Third Frontier: Targeted Industry Attraction Grants. http://thirdfrontier.com/TargetedIndustryAttractionGrants.htm (accessed December 16, 2011).

———. 2011a. Commercialization Framework—Filling Functional Gaps. Third Frontier: Innovation Creating Opportunity. http://thirdfrontier.com/CommercializationFramework.htm.

———. 2011b. *Ohio Third Frontier Advanced Energy Program 2011: Request for Proposals (RFP).* http://thirdfrontier.com/Documents/OTFAEPFY11RFPFinal.pdf.

———. 2011c. Ohio Third Frontier: Advanced Materials Program Bidders' Conference. PowerPoint presentation, January 26. http://thirdfrontier.com/OTFAMP-2011BiddersConference.htm.

———. 2011d. *Ohio Third Frontier Advanced Materials Program, Fiscal Year 2011: Request for Proposals (RFP).* http://thirdfrontier.com/Documents/FY2011OT-FAMP-RFPforRelease.pdf.

———. 2011e. Ohio Third Frontier Advisory Board. http://thirdfrontier.com/OhioThirdFrontierAdvisoryBoard.htm.

———. 2011f. Ohio Third Frontier Commission. http://thirdfrontier.com/OhioThirdFrontierCommission.htm.

———. 2011g. Ohio Third Frontier: Entrepreneurial Signature Programs (ESP). http://thirdfrontier.com/EntrepreneurialSignatureProgram.htm.

———. 2011h. Ohio Third Frontier: Governance. http://thirdfrontier.com/Governance.htm.

———. 2011i. Ohio Third Frontier: Industrial Research and Development Center Program. http://thirdfrontier.com/IRDCP.htm.

———. 2011j. Ohio Third Frontier: Performance Metrics. http://thirdfrontier.com/PerformanceMetrics.htm.

———. 2011k. Ohio Third Frontier: Photovoltaic Program. http://thirdfrontier.com/PhotovoltaicProgram.htm.

———. 2011l. *Ohio Third Frontier Photovoltaic Program 2011: Request for Proposals (RFP).* http://thirdfrontier.com/Documents/OTFPVPFY11RFPFinal.pdf.

———. 2011m. Ohio Third Frontier: Pre-Seed Fund Capitalization Program (PFCP). http://thirdfrontier.com/PreSeedFundInitiative.htm.

———. 2011n. Ohio Third Frontier: Program Opportunities. http://thirdfrontier.com/FundingOpportunities.htm.

———. 2011o. Ohio Third Frontier: Programs. http://thirdfrontier.com/ProgramDescriptions.htm.

———. 2011p. Ohio Third Frontier: Research and Development Center Attraction Program. http://thirdfrontier.com/ResearchDevelopmentCenterAttractionProgram.htm.

———. 2011q. *Ohio Third Frontier Research and Development Center Attraction Program 2011: Request for Proposals (RFP).* http://thirdfrontier.com/Documents/RDCAPFY11RFP.pdf.

———. 2011r. Ohio Third Frontier: Sensors Program. http://thirdfrontier.com/SensorsProgram.htm.

———. 2011s. *Ohio Third Frontier Sensors Program 2011: Request for Proposals (RFP).* http://thirdfrontier.com/Documents/FY2011OTFSP-RFPforRelease.pdf.

———. 2011t. Ohio Third Frontier: Sensors Program Bidders' Conference. PowerPoint presentation, January 26. http://thirdfrontier.com/OTFSP2011BiddersConference.htm.

———. 2011u. Ohio Third Frontier: Wright Centers of Innovation. http://thirdfrontier.com/WrightCentersInnovation.htm.

———. 2011v. Ohio Third Frontier: Wright Projects (WP). http://thirdfrontier.com/WrightProjects.htm.

———. 2011w. *Ohio Third Frontier Wright Projects (WP) Program 2011: Request for Proposals (RFP).* http://thirdfrontier.com/Documents/FY2011OTFWPP-RFP.pdf.

———. 2011x. Third Frontier Internship Program. http://thirdfrontierintern.ohio.gov/3fip/index.php.

Part III

Private Finance

9

After the Financial Crisis

The Roles and Responsibilities of Banking Institutions in Financing Community Economic Development

Robin Newberger and Michael V. Berry

Banks and depository institutions arguably comprise one of the most important sources of funding for community development. Community development is a form of economic development in areas with weak, declining, or impaired local economies. Since passage of the Community Reinvestment Act (CRA) of 1977 (see Box 9.1), banks have had increasingly defined and expanded obligations to finance community development. Community development can include things such as low down-payment mortgages, services to consumers and nonprofits, and accounts designed for low-income households. It also includes direct investments in affordable housing and commercial real estate in lower-income and lower-wealth communities, as well as indirect investments. Indirect investments may be made via an intermediary in pre-development financing or through equity-type investments that do not have defined exit strategies or finite financing terms at the outset. In this chapter, we explore whether the problems facing the nation's financial institutions after the mortgage crisis have influenced how banks participate in and plan to support community development finance activities.

Banks' community development activities and obligations vary based on asset size and other factors, such as local market conditions in places where banks have a physical presence. Generally, the larger the bank, the more it is legally required to do in terms of community development. "Large banks" in this chapter, generally institutions of at least $50 billion to $100 billion in assets, address their community development goals through mortgage and small business lending, tax-credit investments and syndications in real estate projects, and partnerships with community development financial institutions (CDFIs) to finance community assets.[1] These activities are carried out through a complex institutional community development infrastructure. Community development-

Box 9.1

The Community Reinvestment Act

The Community Reinvestment Act (CRA) was passed in 1977 to address the issue of access to affordable credit and financial services. The CRA states that regulated financial institutions have a continuing and affirmative obligation to help meet the credit needs of the local communities in which they are chartered to do business, consistent with the safe and sound operation of such institutions. The CRA was originally a response to the banking practice known as "redlining," where bank management would demarcate red lines on a map around areas of the bank's geographic market. The redlined areas were generally lower-income neighborhoods from which the bank would draw deposits, but these same neighborhoods were deemed too risky for lending and investment.

The CRA has been modified over time. A significant change came in the late 1980s, when bank CRA ratings of "substantial noncompliance," "needs to improve," "satisfactory," and "outstanding," became public information, and thereby, to an extent, leverage for community advocates to press banks for community investments. In the mid-1990s, exam criteria were organized more carefully, and "tests" measuring lending, investment, and service were made part of the examination process.

focused banks, both those with and without CDFI certification from the U.S. Department of the Treasury, are generally smaller and less complex banking organizations. They tend to have product niches, such as purchase and rehab financing of small apartment buildings, or other small business and commercial real estate financing. They serve as place-based economic engines in their local communities, often attracting outside resources (i.e., investment) such as large deposits from firms with philanthropic intent and federal grants.[2] Similarly, mainstream community banks also tend to be locally focused, with a relatively predictable product mix based on local market conditions.

The few studies that have examined the relationship between the mortgage crisis and community development finance have found that community financial intermediaries, particularly CDFI loan funds, have been facing tighter credit terms and less available funding since the crisis (Weech 2009). Banks also report inconsistency in the evaluation and weighting of criteria used to reach CRA ratings over time and across regulators. The notion that CRA was a primary reason for the mortgage meltdown persists, despite extensive research and data proving otherwise (Kroszner 2009; Quercia, Ratcliffe, and Stegman 2009; and

Laderman and Reid 2009). These factors have all fueled speculation that bankers will view their community development obligations differently in the future.

The findings of this chapter are based largely on interviews with bank officers and community development experts, including entities of varying sizes and perspectives on community development. To our knowledge, no study has explored the views of bankers about the impact of the financial crisis on their community development strategies. While the environment is not yet stable as of this writing, we attempt to capture the current thinking within banks about the factors affecting their community development strategies. This thinking is likely to influence how and where banks invest in community development in the coming years.

We begin the analysis with an overview of the available data on mortgage lending to low- and moderate-income borrowers, branch location, and lending and investing in community development intermediaries and projects. We then present a synthesis of responses to a series of questions aimed at understanding:

- the most significant changes to the way that banks carry out community development lending and investing;
- risks linked to lending in low- and moderate-income neighborhoods and the degree to which perceptions of these risks have changed; and
- the key lessons from the financial crisis.

We find a mixed outlook for community development finance varying by, primarily, asset size of the institution whose official we interviewed. Large banks, generally, have not changed their community development activities. While some banks report inconsistency in the evaluation and weighting of criteria used to reach CRA ratings over time, the same basic legal and regulatory regimen—guidelines of the Community Reinvestment Act—drives what types of projects receive support and where resources are directed. We find different conditions for smaller depositories and CDFI banks with a mission to offer responsible financial services to lower-wealth areas (see Box 9.2). Smaller institutions that derive their earnings primarily from lending secured with real estate have experienced distress, as property values continue to decrease and regulators apply pressure to preserve capital and avoid undue risks. These banks are on the front lines in a difficult economic environment. They did not necessarily engage in poor underwriting and lending practices but have nonetheless incurred losses as property values have plummeted and local economies collapsed. Their future ability to serve lower-wealth markets is at risk, as many smaller banks and a handful of CDFI banks have failed or been taken over.

Box 9.2

What Is Community Development Finance?

Community development is a broad term defined differently across organizations. Some banks classify it in terms of the activities covered by CRA such as mortgage lending in low- and moderate-income areas and small business lending. Others extend their definition beyond CRA to a mix of profitable loans, investment, or services that also serve a community need.

At larger institutions, community development departments finance (among other things) affordable housing, industrial and retail development, and charter schools. Large banks are often investors in Low Income Housing Tax Credits (LIHTC) and New Markets Tax Credits (NMTC). Some banks finance activities that do not fit within the definition of CRA lending, like environmental and public finance (schools, hospitals, etc). At large banks, financing often takes place through intermediaries that offer various risk-mitigating and value-added services. Banks enter into relatively complex transactions with tools including swap agreements and other interest-rate hedges once reserved for mainline investment and lending.

Community development products at CDFI banks include home mortgages, small business loans, housing rehab (i.e., construction) loans to small developers, and various loans to nonprofit community organizations and community facilities. Community development banks also specialize in consumer banking services, credit counseling, and business planning for low- and moderate-income (LMI) borrowers. While these products are also common to mainstream banks, CDFI banks generally serve a lower-income consumer, and these products comprise a greater proportion of, if not the entirety of, its business lines.

Data Trends: Mortgage, Small Business, and Community Development Lending and Investing

Information on bank support for community development comes from various surveys of credit conditions, home mortgage lending, and access to capital. Some of these surveys are designed to report on general trends in the financial services industry. Others track community development-oriented finance in particular. The Senior Loan Officer Opinion Survey (of large domestic banks and U.S. branches of foreign banks) reports that most banks generally left lending standards unchanged in 2010 and 2011, after having tightened their lending criteria in 2008 (e.g., imposing higher loan-to-value ratios and credit score requirements) (Board of Governors of the Federal Reserve System 2011) (see Figures 9.1 and 9.2). In both January 2010 and 2011, large banks had eased

Figure 9.1 **Commercial Real Estate Lending Policy**

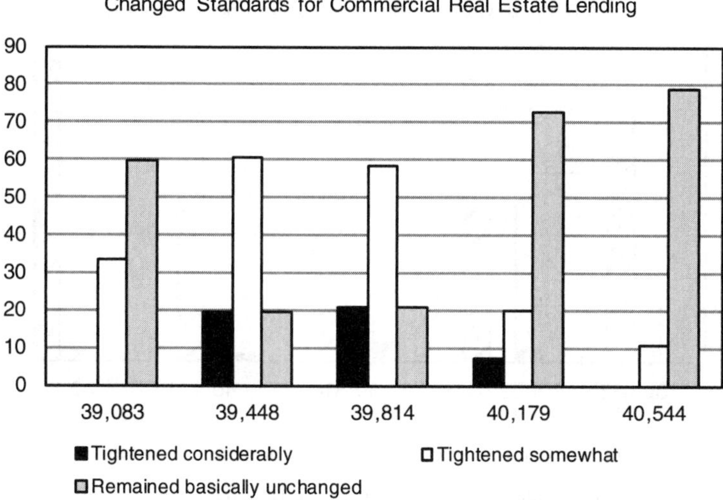

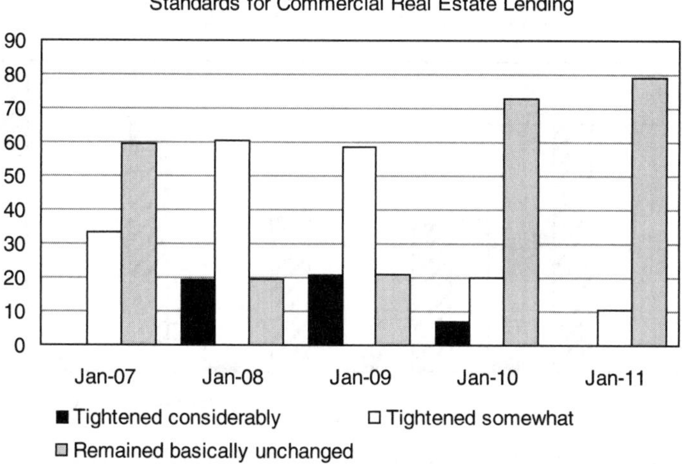

Source: Board of Governors of the Federal Reserve System 2011.

standards for commercial and industrial loans to large- and middle-market firms (with sales above $50 million), although they left standards unchanged for small firms. Banks also reported leaving standards for prime mortgage loans unchanged in 2011, following a tightening in 2008 and 2009; they also left credit score standards unchanged for credit card lending.

Figure 9.2 **Mortgage Lending Policy**

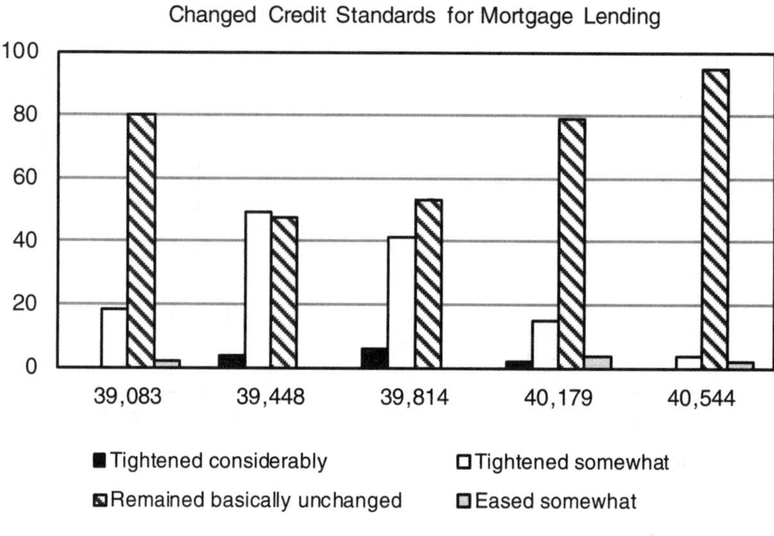

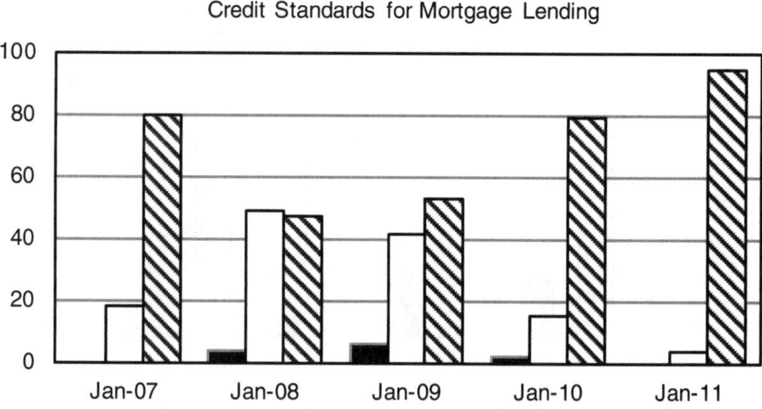

Source: Board of Governors of the Federal Reserve System 2011.

In keeping with these trends, mortgage data collected under the Home Mortgage Disclosure Act (HMDA), and aggregated through the Federal Financial Institutions Examination Council (FFIEC) , shows a substantial drop in the amount of bank-originated mortgages to low- and moderate-income borrowers in 2008 to 2009 compared to previous years (see Figures 9.3, 9.4, and 9.5). (LMI is defined as less than 50 percent and 50 percent to 79 percent of HUD-area median income, respectively). The same pattern is evident for small banks that made or purchased from other institutions fewer than 10,000 loans as for large banks that made or purchased more than 100,000 loans. But the HMDA results also suggest that LMI borrowing declined at a rate somewhat lower than that of other groups. As a proportion of the total dollar value of loans, lending to LMI borrowers trended upward among banks of all sizes.

Business lending data, as defined by the Community Reinvestment Act and aggregated through the FFIEC, collected from 2005 through 2009, show a similar trend in lower-wealth communities. The data show a roughly 11 percent decrease in lending to low- and moderate-income census tracts from 2007 to 2008, with an additional decline from 2008 to 2009 of almost 30 percent (covering loans of $1 million or less). Further, loans to small businesses in these neighborhoods, those with less than $1 million in revenue, declined by 20 percent from 2007 to 2008 and by 34 percent from 2008 to 2009 (see Figure 9.6).[3] However, lending in LMI neighborhoods declined at a rate commensurate with that of small business lending in middle- and upper-income neighborhoods. The decline was proportional to small business lending in higher-income tracts, despite dramatic lending decreases in LMI-tract lending, year over year.

A summary of loan data from the FDIC (1995–2010) also shows a decline in small business lending in the postcrisis period. The dollar value of commercial and industrial loans from FDIC-insured institutions fell in 2009 and 2010, and the value of nonfarm/nonresidential loans fell in 2010 (see Figure 9.7.) In the FDIC dataset, however, small business lending—defined as loans under $1 million—fared worse than business lending overall. The dollar share of small business loans (either commercial and industrial loans or nonfarm/nonresidential loans) as a percentage of all business loans declined in the aftermath of the financial crisis, from about half of all business loans to about one-third. Loans of less than $250,000 saw the biggest decline. The decline in nonfarm, nonresidential lending had begun before the financial crisis.

The National Community Investment Fund (NCIF), a trade/policy organization and certified CDFI that also invests in and advises CDFI banks, produces another set of metrics to evaluate the level of bank support to LMI borrowers and neighborhoods. NCIF's Social Performance Metrics include a *development lending intensity* (DLI-HMDA) score that measures the ratio of home mortgage lending in LMI communities to total mortgage lending. For the largest banks, the development lending intensity score fell in 2009 compared to the ratios in the three years prior, meaning mortgage lending to lower-income borrowers

Figure 9.3 **Lending to LMI Borrowers: Low Origination Count**

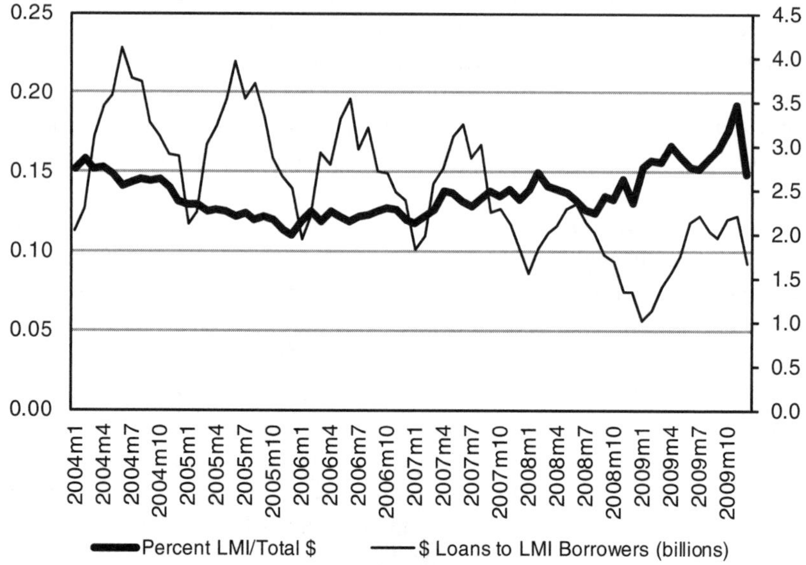

Percent LMI/Total $ — $ Loans to LMI Borrowers (billions)

Source: FFIEC 2011, years 2004–2009.
Note: The number of loans is less than 100,000.

Figure 9.4 **Lending to LMI Borrowers: Mid-Origination Count**

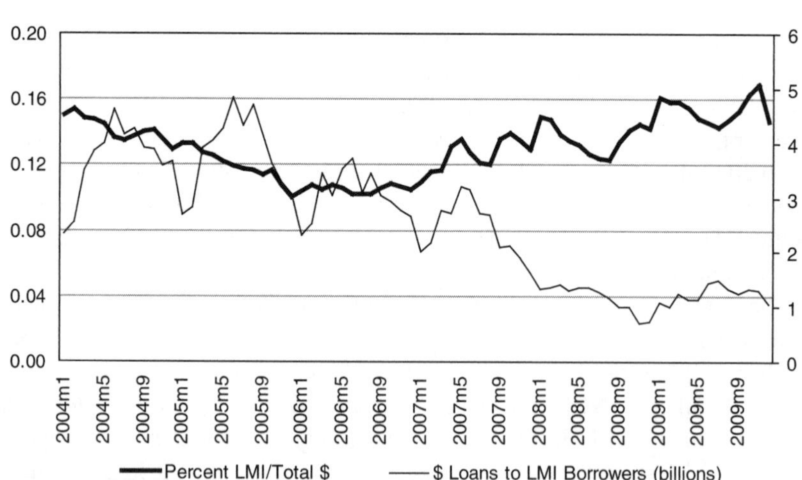

Source: FFIEC 2011, years 2004–2009.
Note: 10,000 < Number of loans < 100,000.

Figure 9.5 **Lending to LMI Borrowers: High Origination Count**

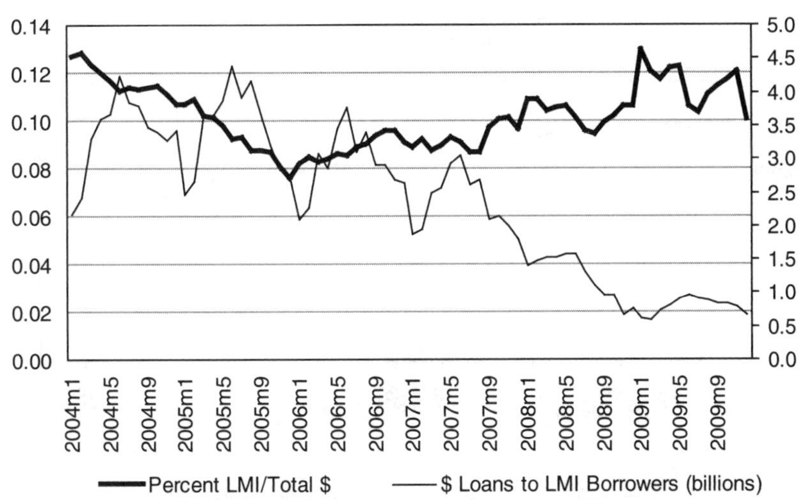

Source: FFIEC 2011, years 2004–2009.
Note: The number of loans > 100,000.

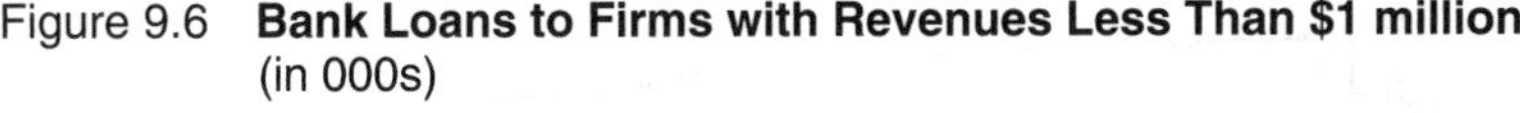
Figure 9.6 **Bank Loans to Firms with Revenues Less Than $1 million** (in 000s)

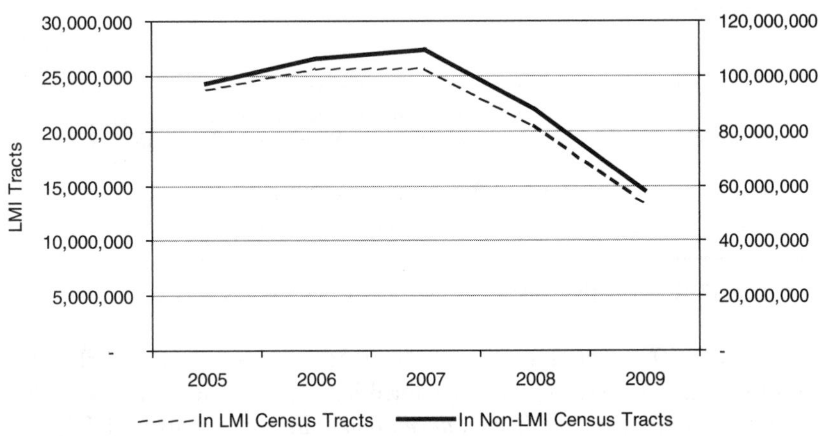

Source: CRA National Aggregate Data 2005–2009.

Figure 9.7 **Small Business Loans**

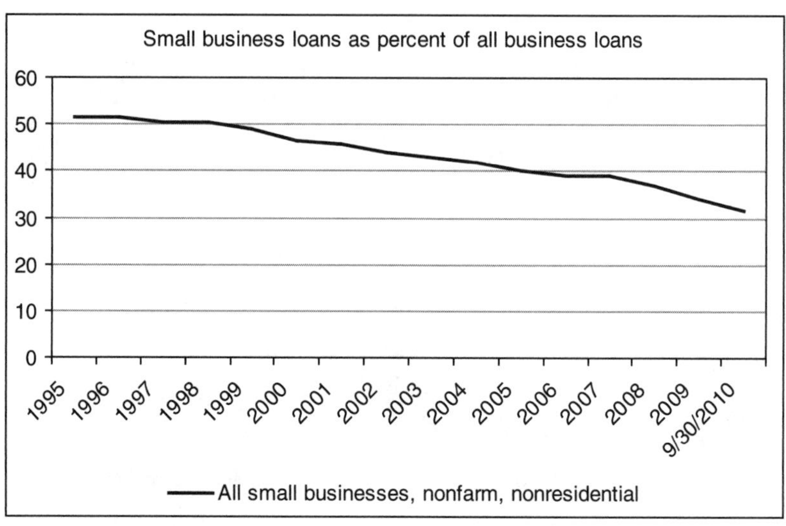

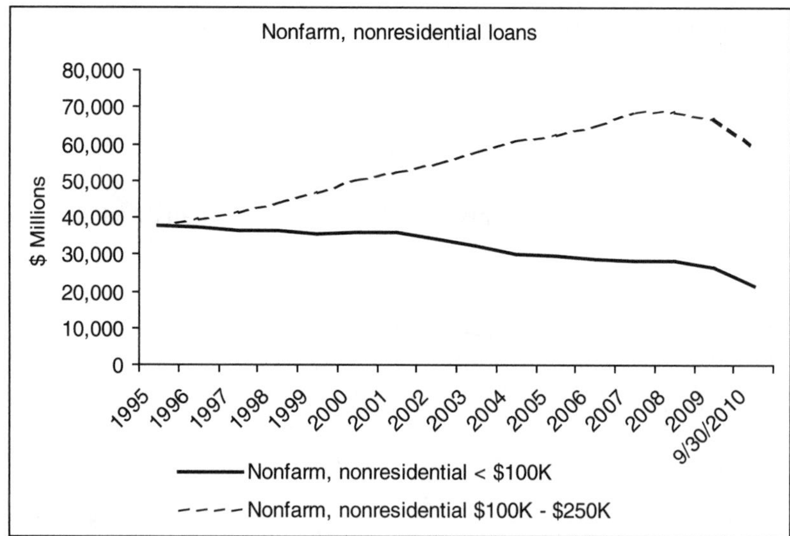

Source: FDIC Quarterly Banking Profile Time Series Spreadsheets.

was lower in 2009 than in previous years (see Table 9.1).[4] For CDFI banks and other small banks, the ratio remained largely consistent between 2006 and 2009. NCIF also calculates a *development deposit intensity* (DDI) that shows the percentage of an institution's physical branch locations situated in low- and moderate-income census tracts. The development deposit intensity

Table 9.1

Development Lending Intensity Summary, 2005–2009 (in percent)

DLI Summary	2005	2006	2007	2008	2009
CDFIs (12/31/2010)	60	52	51	53	53
MDIs (6/30/2010)	50	46	43	45	47
Banks with assets ≤ $2B	21	21	21	21	24
Top ten banks	18	21	21	24	15
All banks	21	21	21	21	24

Source: National Community Investment Fund.

score showed an uptick in branches for the largest banks in 2009, possibly due in part to bank consolidations and acquisitions of failed community banks by larger institutions, and a stable trend for the smallest banks, CDFI banks, and minority-owned banks (see Table 9.2). The implication is that banks did not close branches in lower-income neighborhoods in the aftermath of the crisis, at least as of 2009.

The Opportunity Finance Network (OFN), a trade group and policy research organization for all types of CDFIs, including loan funds, credit unions, venture capital organizations, and banks, shows CDFI loan funds generally turning the corner in terms of capital access in 2010, but confronting weak loan applicant quality and a decrease in loan originations. OFN began conducting its own survey of lending and investment in community development intermediaries in October 2008 to understand the impact of the economic downturn on the community development finance industry (Opportunity Finance Network 2010).[5] In the third quarter of 2010, most CDFIs reported that they were not capital constrained. Only about one-quarter of survey respondents (the majority of which were loan funds) reported lacking access to either investments or debt, compared to about half of respondents who reported capital constraints in previous years. (CDFI investors tend to be larger regional or national banks). On the issue of capital costs, a small but growing share noted that the average cost of capital had risen from the previous quarter. Loan funds were not, on balance, increasing originations compared to the previous years. More CDFIs experienced a decrease in originations, given a tightening of their own lending criteria. For the first time since the beginning of the survey, more CDFIs reported a decrease in the number of loan originations over the year than reported an increase.

Finally, data collected on investments in Low Income Housing Tax Credits and New Markets Tax Credits (NMTC) give an additional perspective on the response of banks to the financial crisis. LIHTCs are the leading source of subsidy for the construction and rehabilitation of affordable housing for

Table 9.2

Development Deposit Intensity Summary, 2005–2009 (in percent)

DDI Summary	2005	2006	2007	2008	2009
CDFIs (12/31/2010)	68	66	62	68	67
MDIs (6/30/2010)	56	53	54	56	54
Banks with assets ≤ $2B	27	27	25	27	27
Top ten banks	32	31	26	34	40
All banks	28	27	25	28	27

Source: National Community Investment Fund.

lower-income households. The NMTC tax credits are awarded for investments in community development entities that provide debt and equity capital to businesses or organizations in low-income communities. According to an Ernst and Young survey conducted in the wake of the financial crisis, investments in LIHTC fell to about $4 billion in 2008; they had exceeded $8 billion in 2006 (Ernst & Young 2009) (see Figure 9.8). However, LIHTC investments returned to a level of about $7.5 billion in 2010 (*Tax Credit Advisor* 2011). The demand for the NMTC credits remained strong in the aftermath of the crisis, with demand exceeding the available allocation by at least 4.5 times in each allocation round (U.S. GAO 2010) (see Figure 9.9). The level of interest that banks show in tax-credit vehicles is significant, because tax-motivated investments exceed the dollar value of community development lending at many large banks.

Overall, the postcrisis environment has been one of less home mortgage and small business lending flowing to low- and moderate-income neighborhoods, but the decline has not been disproportionate to the decline in lending overall. Equity investments in residential real estate projects were halved in the aftermath of the crisis, though this market has lately been returning to precrisis levels. Banks of all sizes initially tightened lending standards for most types of loans—commercial and industrial, residential mortgages, consumer loans, etc.—but held these (more restrictive) standards unchanged in 2010 and 2011. Community development loan funds have also slowed their pace of originations, given tighter lending criteria and weaker applications. Lending data collected by the FDIC show a decline in the dollar value of small business loans (loans under $1 million) in 2009 and 2010, as well as a decline in small business loans as a fraction of all commercial loans. Data collected for CRA purposes also show a decline in the amount of lending to low- and moderate-income census tracts postcrisis (loans to businesses with less than $1 million in revenue), but again, the drop in this sector is not disproportionate to the

Figure 9.8 **Estimated Overall LIHTC Market Volume** (in billions $)

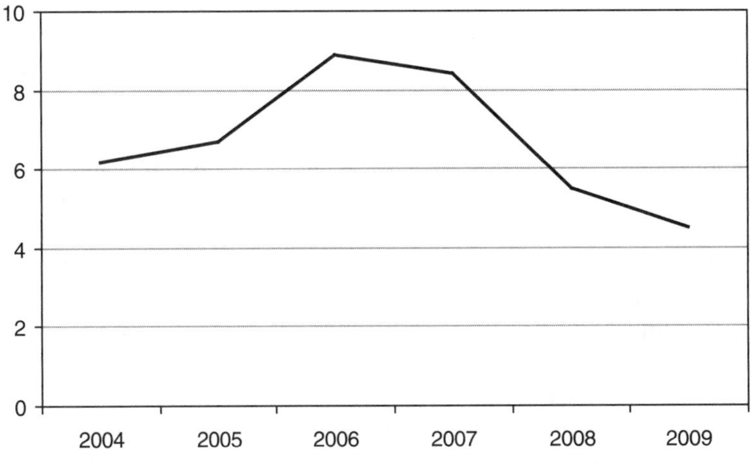

Source: Ernst & Young 2009.

Figure 9.9 **Dollar Value of NMTC Qualified Investment/Lending**

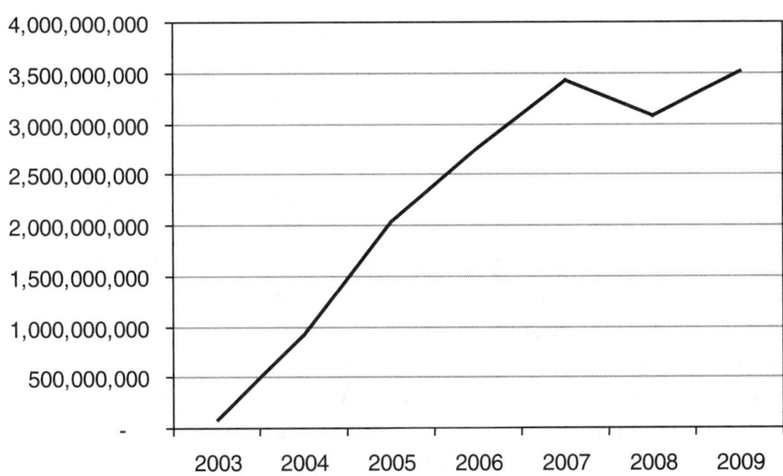

Source: U.S. Department of the Treasury 2010b.

drop in lending overall. In terms of community development tax-motivated investments, the demand for Low Income Housing Tax Credit investments began to rebound in 2010 and 2011, as the banking industry generally returned to modest profitability. Other than banks, insurance companies and other large corporations have fueled demand for tax credits.

Perspectives from the Community Development Finance Field

Using the survey results and other data as a basis to dig deeper into the question of bank support for community development, we interviewed bankers, community development experts, and Federal Reserve field and supervisory examiners. We sought their perspectives on the trends, lessons, and other contextual factors influencing bank lending and investing in LMI areas and to LMI people in the postcrisis period. This is not a representative sample; however, we included multinational and large national banks, regional banks, community banks, and CDFI-certified banks in our interview group. Our findings emphasize two types of institutions in particular: large national institutions and CDFI (mission-oriented) depositories, although we include the perspectives of all bankers and community development experts in developing the five essential findings below. These themes cover qualitative as well as more measurable aspects, and they distinguish between the experiences of large and small institutions where their postcrisis perspectives diverge substantially.

1. In large banks, the basic structure of community development departments has generally remained the same in the aftermath of the mortgage crisis. To the extent that change has occurred, some entities have suspended certain lines of community development lending/investment and reorganized/reduced staff with expertise in community development.

The consistency of the CRA framework throughout the financial crisis is an important reason why many of the largest banks have continued to support the same types of community development activities as before the crisis. To be sure, a good deal of lending that qualifies as "CRA lending" for examination purposes—mortgage and small business loans that happen to fall within low- and moderate-income census tracts—occurs in the normal course of business at many banks and is not influenced by CRA directives. But for a great many banks, their community development agenda is largely based on the guidelines of CRA. The types of activities that banks support are determined by what gets counted toward the rating (Outstanding, Satisfactory, Needs to Improve, or Substantial Noncompliance), namely affordable housing and lending and investments that revitalize or stabilize LMI and lower-wealth geographies. Banks also target lending and investments to the areas from which they draw deposits, even though large banks in particular often draw deposits via online banking from a much broader area. As long as the framework of CRA remains constant and the rules essentially unchanged, bankers contend that their community development finance methods will not change. Large institutions view

CRA as a business line and expect community development departments to meet their return hurdles just as they did prior to the financial crisis.

To the extent that banks have made institutional changes as a result of the crisis, they have suspended less profitable community development-related businesses. Some banks have disbanded their multifamily lending departments in certain regions, and are now determining how they want to position themselves in the real estate market. (They still make loans to good customers, but from other bank lending divisions.) As real estate values continue to fall, some have stopped financing for-sale development (affordable or otherwise), but continue to finance affordable rental housing, which is a growth area as many former homeowners now seek apartments. Some have curtailed their affordable housing activities and switched over to New Markets Tax Credits as their primary community development investment. Some banks with little or no taxable income have constrained all types of tax credit investing, while others have withdrawn from activity related to commercial real estate investment. Stemming from a variety of factors, including concerns about the overall economy, some banks have also pulled back from small-business loans secured with commercial real estate (CRE). Banks report that regulator concerns around the current and even future potential loss of value of commercial real estate, even in cases where the business is relatively sound or loans have credit enhancements such as a third-party guarantor, have led some institutions not to renew existing lines of credit or to curtail CRE lending.[6]

Changes have also been made to the size and staffing of community development departments. Consolidations at some banks have led to the merger of lending and equity platforms into a single office. Bank consolidations have also expanded the scope and goals of community development departments. These higher production goals have given some banks the incentive to pursue larger projects (where the average deal size is roughly $500,000) or work with larger intermediaries that can redistribute the funds across a wide area. Consolidations and cost-cutting at some banks have also led to a decline in the number of employees with the technical expertise necessary to do complicated transactions and a firm understanding of the sometimes idiosyncratic risks in community development deals. In particular, some large banks have eliminated the "corner office executive"—the person who could look broadly across their own institutions' product suite (SBA lending, FHA mortgages, etc.) and collaborate in a holistic manner to help community development. The people in charge of community development are now, in many cases, not in a position to make a commitment to a community development deal. These managers must now make the case to their own credit officers, who in turn have the decision-making authority to choose the organizations in which they will ultimately invest. As the power centers of the largest banks have moved further away from local needs, the most senior executives tend to have weaker ties to a given community and not the same sense of urgency to take a leadership role. This makes it more difficult for banks to develop comprehensive strategies for communities that tap the range of products that banks have to offer. This is not a completely new phenomenon, but economic conditions have exacerbated the trend of cost-cutting within banks.

2. Community development lending on the part of mission-driven depositories has decreased because of bank failures and capital constraints.

Bank failures nationwide occurred at a rate of more than 13 per month in 2010, and most of these were banks with less than $1 billion in assets, i.e., community banks. While there have been few failures among CDFI banks, only about 90 banks nationwide identify themselves as CDFI banks (and more than one-third of these received CDFI certification for the first time in 2010). Three CDFI-certified banks failed in 2011 (one of which had been a certified CDFI for less than one year). In 2010, four others failed (one of which had also been certified as a CDFI for less than one year). The failure of Chicago's Shorebank, the nation's oldest and largest CDFI depository, was the most noteworthy event in the community development finance field in many years. As of this writing, it is clear that Shorebank was harmed by the same environmental realities that have impacted most community banks with heavy commercial or residential real estate exposure. Shorebank's primary lending product—purchase/rehab loans for older multifamily buildings—exposed the institution to decreases in property values, which have been precipitous in Chicago and which continue to decline.

Beyond the actual closures, the most widespread effect of the crisis has been the reduction in lending capacity at community development depositories. Since 2008, many CDFI banks have not necessarily come under formal regulatory action, but according to some respondents for this article, they have been restricted in how much loan volume they are permitted to originate. Lending capacity has been curtailed by falling real estate prices and high unemployment, felt most acutely in lower-income neighborhoods where CDFI depositories focus their activities. Community-bank and CDFI balance sheets have concentrated assets in concentrated geographies. As banks mark-to-market their portfolios, the write-down in assets has caused capital shortages among community and CDFI banks.[7]

These problems have set the stage for community development banks to rethink their commercial lending strategies. The area where these banks have gotten hit harder than many others is commercial real estate exposure. CRE lending refers to loans secured by commercial real estate whose repayment typically comes from rental income or the sale/refinancing of the property. CDFI as well as minority-owned banks in particular tend to focus on lending for community facilities—for churches, nonprofits, and multifamily housing. Going forward, regulators may discourage these banks from holding 50 to 80 percent of their portfolios in CRE. Instead, these banks are likely to have to get into other types of lending with which they have less experience, like commercial and industrial lending, which is shorter term and secured with receivables, equipment, or other assets as opposed to real estate. This transformation will take time. Banks will have to hire and/or train staff and outsource cash management services tailored to small businesses in order to compete with larger banks.

Capital shortfalls have also put CDFI depositories more in survival than growth mode. Absent shareholders or other investors with sufficient resources and a community development agenda, there are few sources of capital for small banks in the current environment. Some community banks facing capital shortfalls have opted to shrink their assets—intentionally offering fewer housing and small business loans in the communities they serve in order to improve their capital ratios. Small banks have faced pressure for many years to grow their capital base—pressures resulting from regulatory, compliance, and technology costs that force institutions to grow in order to reach sufficient economies of scale. These trends began before the mortgage crisis, but the downturn has revealed how vulnerable smaller banks can be.

Some CDFIs have looked to the federal government as a potential source of capital. The community and CDFI banks have sought to layer federal money on top of their existing capital in order to give regulators the confidence that they are doing everything right in terms of their risk and asset quality. Indeed, the Treasury Department's CDFI Fund, which has an expanded budget under the current administration, has been a highly valued resource for CDFI banks through various restricted and unrestricted grants, as well as New Markets Tax Credit allocations. The CDFI Fund under the current director has raised the visibility of community development banking, streamlined the process for banks to gain CDFI certification, and decreased the span of time from grant application to approval. In addition, the Capital Purchase Program under TARP allowed small banks to apply for capital by issuing preferred stock, which the U.S. Treasury purchases from a qualifying bank.[8] The Treasury also created the Community Development Capital Initiative (CDCI) to provide additional and lower-cost capital for CDFI-certified banks and credit unions.[9] The availability of CDCI funds were the incentive for many of the newly certified banks to seek CDFI certification, since these banks were already targeting the majority of their lending to underserved communities. For some banks, these programs represent the difference between survival and failure.

By October 2010, when the Treasury Department closed the initiative, CDCI funds had been disbursed to 40 banks or bank-holding companies, but 28 of these (70 percent) included an exchange of TARP funds for CDCI funds (U.S. Dept. of the Treasury 2010a). The difficulty of obtaining these funds has underscored a tension between regulators and community advocates and intermediaries. Bank regulatory oversight, from the standpoint of safety and soundness, is following a more conservative approach in estimating the potential for repayment of underlying debt. If nonperforming loans move above certain benchmarks in the present environment, regulators have been quick to intercede, review lending practices and internal controls, and ultimately slow down lending. Bankers perceive this as a conundrum, as they must, particularly in the absence of outside investment (capital), earn their way back to better financial standing and profitability. Earnings also feed their capital base, which they must have to cover nonperforming loans. For community banks in particular, lending, which generates fees and profit margins, is the principal source of earnings. Banks, like any business, must cover overhead costs, and they cannot stand still waiting for local economies to turn around.

3. Lending standards have been tightened across all product lines, but bankers do not single out community development intermediaries or low- and moderate-income borrowers as being riskier prospects since the financial crisis.

Bankers say that their perceptions of risk of community development lending/investing and of low- and moderate-income borrowers have not changed because of the crisis. First, the crisis fundamentally changed the way that people view a "distressed market," as some of the most unlikely places in America became distressed markets in a matter of months. In addition, after 10 years or more of community development lending, the risk-management teams at even the largest institutions have learned that the track record of community development loans is comparable, and sometimes superior, to risk levels and performance of other loans.

Bankers nonetheless acknowledge that the industry is in transition. Even the lenders whose banks were never close to failure are wary of regulators' perceptions. Secondary market players such as Fannie Mae and Freddie Mac have reinforced this caution with tighter scrutiny (for loans they purchase and securitize) of originating lender underwriting processes and close adherence to their published standards. The atmosphere of caution means that post-crisis, mainstream banks are less likely to make unsecured or longer-term loans to nondepository CDFIs, and when they do, they more frequently expect CDFI borrowers to adopt credit standards similar to the banks' versus their own criteria. Lending to borrowers who depend on state government cash flows has also slowed considerably, as regulators frequently require banks to charge off any of these loans and investments in states where the government has delayed payments, regardless of how the loans are performing. Banks may even avoid places where too little public money has been allocated to infrastructure—such as to police and firefighter protection or to maintenance of roads. According to CDFI industry experts, the (remaining) banks that supported CDFIs before the financial crisis continue to support CDFIs after the crisis, but they now spend more time ensuring that their credit files contain the necessary documentation. They assert that these more restrictive criteria and an increased focus on documentation have little to do with concerns about the financial capacities of community development intermediaries themselves, but have to do with internal bank policy and the regulatory environment.

Perhaps surprisingly, both large banks and mission-driven depositories have generally heralded many aspects of this "new normal" as a welcome change. Many of the CDFI banks have raised prices and credit standards for their own borrowers. The general sentiment is that it should be more difficult to qualify for credit secured by property when property values are in decline. Even the most community-oriented bankers acknowledge that more conventional underwriting has allowed their institutions to build portfolios, business they would have lost to other banks if they were using the same standards as before the crisis. Some bankers and community development experts express concern, however, that the current attention paid to the principles of credit quality and the focus on the value of local assets will not continue with the same intensity once the economy improves. They will want to get back to the less costly, algorithmic systems of evaluating credit risk and will have missed the opportunity to make positive, permanent changes to credit evaluation and risk assessment.

4. The financial crisis has reduced the number of organizations in the community development delivery system, creating new opportunities for the remaining (well-capitalized) lenders and investors.

Community development professionals note that some traditional lenders and developers have left certain neighborhoods. In addition to many banks rethinking their affordable housing investments, a handful of banks that were active in the affordable housing tax credit market have been folded into other institutions. Many smaller developers have been driven out of business by market conditions, and more established developers have limited their activity due to questions about the reliability of state funding. Foundation endowments and pension-fund support for these types of investments have also declined.

In certain places, bankers anticipate that new construction of multifamily, affordable housing will be stalled for the next decade due to the confluence of financial and economic factors.

These challenges notwithstanding, the erosion of competition has brought new opportunities for banks and well-capitalized CDFIs in certain credit markets. For example, some bankers see a new opportunity for community development banks to originate home mortgages. Many of the community banks that recently sought CDFI certification specialize in residential mortgage lending, as well as lending to small businesses and nonprofits. CDFI banks generally did a minimal amount of single-family lending before the crisis. It was difficult for them to compete with the convenience of storefront mortgage brokers, and/or some of the nondepository lenders engaged in unscrupulous practices that undermined both borrowers and neighborhoods. Now that these predatory entities are largely gone, CDFI and community banks with capital and lending capacity can make sound mortgage loans based on what people can afford and that suits their needs and goals. Banks, including CDFI banks, have applied in droves to qualify as FHA lenders in the past two years. Considered pedestrian prior to 2007 in contrast to fast-turnaround, low-documentation lending that led to the foreclosure crisis, FHA certification has taken on new appeal, as it facilitates mortgage lending with principal (mostly) insured against default.

In certain markets, opportunities also exist in the multifamily affordable housing arena. Financial institutions that could barely compete with bank lenders before the mortgage crisis now have more opportunities, as other institutions have retrenched or gone out of business. With a number of large financial institutions lacking taxable income, the negotiating leverage has shifted in favor of the remaining bank lenders and investors in Low Income Housing Tax Credits (LIHTC). (Investments from Fannie Mae and Freddie Mac used to account for 40 percent of this market.) Bankers have been able to exact repayment and operating guarantees from developers that had not been possible in the preceding years. Investing through proprietary funds, versus multi-investor funds, has also made LIHTC deals more profitable for large banks, allowing the banks to dictate more of the terms and time the investments better on a per-transaction basis relative to when the tax credits take effect. While competition in the most-crowded markets like New York and San Francisco has since driven up the price of tax credits postcrisis, in other markets, institutions with CRA and community development obligations have been able to cherry-pick the highest-yielding deals. With assistance from Federal Home Loan Banks and other intermediaries, banks with smaller portfolios and limited staff capacity have also been able to participate through loan pools.

Opportunities for established CDFI loan funds stem from (1) larger banks with obligations to facilitate community development loans and investments under CRA, (2) banks with TARP money that seek to demonstrate their civic commitment to LMI communities, (3) banks looking to better manage their risk, and (4) banks that pay close attention to the cost of delivery. Banks with a broader national footprint, which have rapidly increased in size as a result of recent mergers, face the highest CRA goals that they have ever had. Bankers need knowledge and expertise for community development. They want to work with institutions familiar with and able to manage the associated risks and that are already making an impact. Some mainstream banks consider CDFI banks competition and do not invest in them. The opportunities for relationships with big banks are greatest for larger and more established CDFI loan funds that understand their markets, have transparent financial statements, and provide sound and useful information about their organizations, markets, relationships, etc. to banks. These trends point to a greater dependence on CDFI loan fund intermediation than before the crisis.

5. Despite a weak economy and much concern about preserving core capital, bankers perceive renewed diligence in fair lending and CRA examinations stemming from environmental changes.[10]

Some bankers say that one of the most perceptible changes in the community development environment postcrisis relates to fair lending and CRA examinations. Regarding fair lending, a number of bankers felt that the 2008 multibillion dollar settlement stemming from the charge that Countrywide Home Mortgage had been engaged in predatory lending aimed at lower-income households and racial minorities had raised the profile of fair lending enforcement. Some bank respondents likened the current degree of scrutiny among regulators to the 1990s, when other landmark fair lending cases made headlines. In addition, under the financial reform legislation passed in August 2010, new mortgage lending rules relating to sound underwriting are to be applied to all mortgage lenders and originators. Even though banks argued they did not engage in discriminatory practices or poor mortgage underwriting on any significant level (and, in fact, claimed that they had been at a competitive disadvantage for many years to mortgage brokers and other originators with questionable lending and underwriting practices), ultimately it was lower-wealth and minority communities that were impacted to a greater degree than other borrowers by foreclosures stemming from improvident lending. For regulators, stepped up scrutiny on fair lending is also part of an effort to understand the causes of the foreclosure crisis from all aspects and help prevent future crises.

The CRA did not change under the recently passed financial reform package, but was the subject of bank regulator–organized information-gathering hearings around the country in the summer of 2010, as the regulatory agencies considered updating CRA rules. While there have been no changes to the regulation as of early 2012, the state of the economy postcrisis has required CRA examiners to reconsider benchmarks and standards that would have applied relatively recently, as lending risk exposure is a major concern. For many banks across the asset size spectrum, the challenges to delivering credit and capital include lower loan demand (even among borrowers qualified under tighter standards), falling real estate values, and small businesses impacted by low employment and consumer malaise. With respect to mortgage lending, secondary market standards are more restrictive postcrisis, and with the trend toward "old fashioned, common sense banking," there are fewer loan products available. The new context—a slow economy, high unemployment, and much fallout from foreclosures in LMI areas, among other conditions—requires examiners and banks to be sensitive to needs of a different nature than in the past and also to what is possible and practical to achieve.

Banks face sometimes conflicting challenges related to financial risk and the need (and desire) to serve struggling communities. The difficulty for many banks is how to balance their fiduciary responsibilities with the quantitative output that drives CRA evaluations. This conflict is sometimes revealed in exam findings where, on the one hand, safety and soundness examiners feel that the bank is taking too much lending risk and, on the other hand, CRA and fair-lending examiners determine the bank is not working creatively enough to meet the needs of lower-wealth areas or qualified minority borrowers, respectively. This conflict is more acute in the current environment, given the number of institutions in tenuous or borderline capital situations and with performing loans that may yet default.

Larger banks with more resources are among the more vocal proponents of updating the CRA. Bankers at larger institutions observe that they sometimes compete for the same community development business—usually high-impact investments including multifamily affordable housing, grocery stores, or other large projects—and thereby drive pricing down.[11] The CRA, they contend, should include rules that reward large institutions for meeting needs where the needs exist, sometimes far from their branch locations, as opposed to layering investments in markets that are served adequately or do not have the most acute need. They also contend that major investments in LMI communities, where risks are already greater than in established markets, should not be subject to undue scrutiny.

Conclusion

The need for community development finance has never been greater. Lower-income people and places are disproportionately affected by hard economic times. They suffer worse and recover more slowly than the mainstream population, yet the financial crisis reduced the flow of money to the community development field. There is less mortgage and small-business lending taking place at small and large banks. Lower earnings, at least temporarily, at banking and financial institutions have also led to lower demand for Low Income Housing Tax Credits, as the primary motivation for investing in tax credits is reduced taxes. The withdrawal of LIHTC-investing institutions has left some cities and towns with substantially less investment in affordable multifamily housing than needed and has left some developers unable to find investors to purchase their tax credits for a price that makes their projects viable. This is particularly true where foreclosures have been widespread among investment properties and multifamily rental buildings, and where there is less competition among investors. The flipside has been higher yields for investors with a tax credit appetite.

Mainstream banks remain key players in community development finance, as businesses look for capital, families apply for mortgages, and communities seek funding partners for redevelopment. The community development departments of some of the largest banks report that they are profitable and more active than ever. Some types of investments will likely continue to work through CDFI loans funds, which are not subject to the same risk restrictions as banks or mandated examinations. Although loan funds have begun to model the behavior of banks in maintaining more capital and reserves, they can use greater creativity in meeting community needs in partnership with banks and government. For other types of community development activities, banks will lend or invest with less reliance on tax credit syndicators or other intermediaries.

For large and small banks, the challenge to delivering credit to LMI areas relates to the need to preserve capital. Larger banks also explain the challenge in terms of their need to realize a more direct business benefit from their sizable investments in community development activities, particularly during periods of significant cost cutting. While different banks have sometimes very different cultures and approaches to community development, the general sense is that it is more efficient and effective to assimilate community development activities into the strategic goals of the institution (with, for example, cross-selling of services similar to what occurs with other bank customers and relationships), rather than to treat community development as a discrete area with discrete goals. Banks also want to receive CRA credit for lending and investing outside of delineated areas. Banks want regulators to evaluate performance based on whether bona fide needs are being met, not based on the location of bank branches. Many believe this change would have broad implications for the nature and scope of community development investments.

As of this writing, the hearings that took place in August 2010 have not led to fundamental changes or even more moderate adjustments to the CRA.

Community development banks also face opportunities and challenges in lending and investing in LMI communities. In some cases, CDFI depositories are the only financial institutions in distressed neighborhoods other than so-called fringe providers, including payday lenders and check cashers. CDFI banks are the principal actors creating, innovating, and collaborating to address the many problems facing lower-wealth communities, which include high rates of vacancy and abandonment, still decreasing property values, and foreclosure fraud. Community-based banks have a broader array of tools and services than community development loan funds; they have a relatively reliable funding source, at least in more stable economic times (deposits); and they often serve as economic anchors to their local neighborhoods. Community-based banks provide depository, counseling, and consumer credit services essential to local commerce that other development finance institutions do not offer. But to be successful in the future, CDFI depositories need to focus on asset quality and risk management, along with technological expertise, efficient cost structures, and good governance.

Access to low-cost deposits and inexpensive capital is another major hurdle. At a time when small business lending is needed most, the incentive for community banks is to protect existing capital and improve their capital ratios, not to provide credit to their communities. Federal programs to bolster bank capital have been important to help small CDFI banks raise capital. The wave of community banks seeking CDFI certification in 2010 in response to the CDCI program is testament to the attractiveness of government funds. But, ultimately, many CDFIs are limited in their impact due to high qualifying standards. Going forward, the inability of CDFI depositories to raise more capital, including government money, may undermine more CDFI-certified and other smaller banking institutions that work to assist underserved communities. Failure of these institutions may also undermine the public's faith in the banking system to meet the financial needs of nonprofit organizations, small businesses, and affordable housing developers, among others.

Our interviews with bankers and community development experts reveal some tension in the community development field in the wake of the financial crisis. Even though bankers do not see community development intermediaries or deals as inherently more risky than in the past, bank credit standards have tightened, leading to the same net effect of reduced amounts of capital entering lower-wealth communities. Falling property values are another factor keeping banks from lending more, as well as a reason why banks have diverted more resources to loan restructuring and foreclosure prevention than to making new deals. Regulators want capital to flow to these communities and banks to fulfill their CRA obligations, but they are also more concerned than in the past—given economic conditions—that banks have adequate capital reserves, and do not assume lending or investment risks, or sustain losses, that would reduce reserves below an acceptable level. Community development practitioners realize that some banks embrace their social, civic, and public responsibilities. But other banking institutions are less inclined to do so, particularly in difficult economic times. On the horizon are potential changes to the CRA that may have an impact on both perspectives. With no changes in policy, the community development field will continue to wrestle with meeting goals, as a key set of financial partners, now reduced in number, works toward establishing a more stable financial footing.

Notes

1. Community development financial institutions provide financial services and products to low- and moderate-income people and communities. For more information on certified CDFIs, see U.S. Department of the Treasury, 2011.

2. "Community development deposits" refers to funds of corporations, foundations, or wealthy individuals, who leave these amounts on deposit for extended periods, often at below-market rates, to increase the lending capacity and liquidity of mission-focused financial institutions.

3. The Federal Financial Institutions Examination Council (FFIEC) defines small business lending as loans to businesses with annual revenue of less than $1 million. The FFIEC prescribes examination principles, standards, and report forms for bank, thrift, and credit union regulatory agencies.

4. The data available from NCIF are based on 2009 HMDA data and the 2009 FDIC summary of deposits database.

5. One hundred and five CDFIs responded to the first quarter 2010 survey. Most respondents (86 percent) were loan funds, 10 percent were credit unions. Banks and venture capital funds each comprised 2 percent.

6. The U.S. Small Business Administration insures portions of loans to small businesses and is an exception. An SBA guarantee is considered sound and the SBA has made public statements, in the hopes of encouraging more SBA insured lending, that the insured portions of SBA loans are generally not classified as higher-risk assets in the course of bank exams.

7. Credit unions are also struggling in the wake of the mortgage crisis. A number of credit unions are slowly going out of business or being acquired by others.

8. In October 2008, the U.S. Treasury announced the TARP Capital Purchase Program to encourage U.S. financial institutions to build capital and thereby increase the flow of credit to U.S. businesses and consumers. The bank must pay a dividend of 5 percent for the first five years stepping up to 9 percent after five years. Treasury-certified CDFI banks were given more favorable terms in light of their mission focus; the preferred shares did not dilute the value of existing common shares. For more information, please see U.S. Dept. of the Treasury, 2010c.

9. The Community Development Capital Initiative (CDCI) is a program of the U.S. Department of the Treasury. Using returned funds from the Troubled Assets

Relief Program (TARP) to support the continued viability, growth, and expansion of CDFI-certified depository institutions, CDCI makes low-interest secondary capital deposits in CDFI-certified community development credit unions and community development banks. Under this program, certified CDFI banks and thrifts—subject to approval by their federal banking regulators—can apply for capital up to $1 billion at a 2 percent rate for up to eight years. After eight years, the rate steps up to 9 percent to encourage repayment. The CDCI program ended in 2010.

10. Fair lending examinations primarily assess compliance with the Equal Credit Opportunity Act (ECOA) and Fair Housing Act (FHAct). For more information on examination procedures, please see Office of the Comptroller of the Currency et al., 2009.

11. This is a view that is not shared universally by community development practitioners.

References

Board of Governors of the Federal Reserve System. 2011. *The January 2011 Senior Loan Officer Opinion Survey on Bank Landing Practices.* Report, January. www.federalreserve.gov/boarddocs/snloansurvey/201102/fullreport.pdf.

Ernst & Young. 2009. *Low-Income Housing Tax Credit Investment Survey.* Study prepared for Enterprise Community Partners, Local Initiatives Support Corporation, October. www.lisc.org/files/17728_file_ey_lihtc_study.pdf.

Federal Deposit Insurance Corporation (FDIC). 1995–2010. *FDIC Quarterly Banking Profile* Time Series Spreadsheets. www2.fdic.gov/qbp/ (accessed July 14, 2011).

Federal Financial Institutions Examination Council (FFIEC). 2011. Home Mortgage Disclosure Act. www.ffiec.gov/hmda/default.htm.

Kroszner, Randall. 2009. The CRA and the recent mortgage crisis. In *Revisiting the CRA: Perspectives on the Future of the Community Reinvestment Act,* ed. P. Chakrabarti, D. Erickson, R. Essene, I. Galloway, and J. Olson. The Federal Reserve Banks of Boston and San Francisco, February. www.frbsf.org/publications/community/cra/revisiting_cra.pdf.

Laderman, Elizabeth, and Carolina Reid. 2009. CRA lending during the subprime meltdown. In *Revisiting the CRA: Perspectives on the Future of the Community Reinvestment Act,* ed. P. Chakrabarti, D. Erickson, R. Essene, I. Galloway, and J. Olson. The Federal Reserve Banks of Boston and San Francisco, February. www.frbsf.org/publications/community/cra/revisiting_cra.pdf.

National Community Investment Fund. 2012. Development Lending Intensity Study, 2005–2009. www.ncif.org/index.php/services/spm/ (accessed June 6, 2012).

Office of the Comptroller of the Currency et al. 2009. *Interagency Fair Lending Examination Procedures.* Report, August. www.ffiec.gov/PDF/fairlend.pdf.

Opportunity Finance Network. 2011. *CDFI Market Conditions, Third Quarter 2010: Report II–Detailed Tables.* Report, January. Philadelphia: Opportunity Finance Network. www.opportunityfinance.net/store/downloads/CDFI_Market_Conditions_Q310_Report_II.pdf (accessed December 7, 2011).

Quercia, Roberto, Janneke Ratcliffe, and Michael A. Stegman. 2009. The CRA: Outstanding, and needs to improve. In *Revisiting the CRA: Perspectives on the Future of the Community Reinvestment Act,* ed. P. Chakrabarti, D. Erickson, R. Essene, I. Galloway, and J. Olson. The Federal Reserve Banks of Boston and San Francisco, February. www.frbsf.org/publications/community/cra/revisiting_cra.pdf.

Tax Credit Advisor. 2011. LIHTC gets its mojo back—Industry savors recovery but nervous about 2011. *Tax Credit Advisor* 23(2): 14–20. www.housingonline.com/Documents/TCA%20Issues/TCAFEb2011.pdf (accessed December 7, 2011).

U.S. Department of the Treasury. 2010a. *Transactions Report for Period Ending September 30, 2010: Capital Purchase Program*. Report, Office of Financial Stability, September. www.treasury.gov/initiatives/financial-stability/briefing-room/reports/tarp-transactions/DocumentsTARPTransactions/10-1-10%20Transactions%20Report%20as%20of%209-29-10.pdf (accessed December 7, 2011).

———. 2010b. Community Development Financial Institutions Fund: NMTC Program Projects Financed Through 2009. September 21. www.cdfifund.gov/what_we_do/nmtc/NMTC-Program-Projects-Financed-Through-2009.asp.

———. 2010c. Treasury announces TARP capital purchase program description. Press release, October 14. HP-1207. www.treasury.gov/press-center/press-releases/Pages/hp1207.aspx.

———. 2011. Community Development Financial Institutions Fund. www.cdfifund.gov/.

U.S. Government Accountability Office (U.S. GAO). 2010. *New Markets Tax Credit: The Credit Helps Fund a Variety of Projects in Low-Income Communities, but Could Be Simplified*. Report to Congressional Committees, GAO-10-334, January. Washington, DC: GAO. www.gao.gov/new.items/d10334.pdf.

Weech, Paul. 2009. Observations on the effects of the financial crisis and economic downturn on the community development finance sector. In *The Economic Crisis and Community Development Finance: An Industry Assessment*, ed. B. Bernanke et al. Community Development Investment Center Working Paper 2009-05, June. San Francisco, CA: Federal Reserve Bank of San Francisco. www.frbsf.org/publications/community/wpapers/2009/wp2009-05.pdf.

10

Angles on Angels and Venture Capital

Financing Entrepreneurial Ventures

John Freear and Jeffrey E. Sohl

Who are the angels and venture capitalists and what role do they play in the financing of entrepreneurial ventures? How important is private equity to the U.S. economy? These and many other more specific questions relating to private equity financing are addressed in this chapter.

The private equity finance market comprises investors seeking investment opportunities (the suppliers of capital) and smaller, privately owned business ventures seeking investors (the demand side of the equation). Investors fall into two categories: formally organized investment institutions, known as venture capital firms, which manage one or more venture capital funds, and individual investors who invest alone or in concert with other individual investors and are variously known as "informal investors," "business angels," or simply "angels."[1] In exchange for their investment, both groups will become part owners of the equity in the venture.

This chapter focuses on the angel, the venture capital fund, and the entrepreneurial venture. Entrepreneurial ventures, like most small businesses, begin with little capital. They differ from most small businesses in that they are created, as the name implies, by one or more entrepreneurs—people who perceive a business opportunity and create a venture to pursue it energetically with the aim of achieving rapid growth.

Small Firms and Entrepreneurial Ventures

Approximately three-quarters of all U.S. business firms have no payroll. Most of these are self-employed persons operating unincorporated businesses, and they may or may not be the owner's principal source of income (U.S. Census Bureau 2008). In 2004, 19,523,741 U.S. firms (77 percent) had no payroll, out of a total of 25,409,525 firms in the economy. Of the 5,885,784 firms with a payroll, about 86 percent had fewer than 1,000 employees (U.S. Census Bureau 2008, Table 2a). These small firms have an important role in the U.S. economy: They employ 56 percent of U.S. private-sector workers (ibid.).[2]

Small firms fall into three general categories: lifestyle firms, middle-market firms, and entrepreneurial ventures (Bygrave 1994). Lifestyle firms are the classic small firms that account, at any one time, for around 90 percent of all start-ups. They tend to be small and to stay small, with five-year projected revenues of up to $10 million, and are perceived by investors as having little prospect of very high future returns or capital gains.

Of the remaining 10 percent of start-ups, some 9 percent are middle-market firms—firms with a five-year projected annual revenue growth of up to about $50 million. Such firms may exhibit characteristics similar to the smaller lifestyle firms or may demonstrate sufficient growth potential to be counted as entrepreneurial ventures. If a deal is properly structured, these middle-market firms can be attractive investment opportunities for private investors.

Firms with high potential growth constitute the remaining 1 percent of start-ups. These are the entrepreneurial ventures that offer the prospect of long-term capital gains large enough to reward the entrepreneur and investor for their acceptance of high risk, low liquidity, low or zero short-term financial rewards, and of course their patience. Entrepreneurial ventures have projected revenue in excess of $50 million, and they anticipate annual growth rates from 20 percent to more than 50 percent.

The Private Equity Market

The public equity finance market in the United States is easily recognizable. Companies may raise cash directly through an initial public offering (IPO) of stock. Exchanges, notably the New York Stock Exchange (NYSE) and Nasdaq, provide secondary markets by listing and trading public company and government securities in the form of stocks (equity) and long-term debt (bonds).[3] The secondary markets enable investors to buy and sell securities, including those purchased in an IPO, thus avoiding the liquidity problems associated with being locked into an investment.

Privately held companies may be unable to gain access to the public markets because they cannot afford to, are too small, are not financially secure, or are unwilling to go public. The private equity finance market is an umbrella market that includes both organized (venture capital funds) and informal (angel) investors. The private equity market began to acquire a relatively clear definition from about 1980 onward. By the mid-1990s, private equity finance had become a "recognized and accepted investment plan asset category for institutional investors such as public and private pension funds, corporate partnerships, insurance companies and endowment funds" (Brophy 1997, p. 11).

Angels are the primary source of external private equity financing in the earlier stages of an entrepreneurial venture's existence (Freear, Sohl, and Wetzel 1995a, 1997; Freear and Wetzel 1989, 1990; Gaston and Bell 1988; Wetzel 1987). Venture capital firms, although they have a presence in early-stage financing, tend to concentrate their managed funds on the later financing stages, making larger dollar investments and having a shorter exit horizon—in the five- to seven-year range. They have more resources, more capital, are more organized, and are more visible and easier to find than angels (Meyer et al. 1995; Pratt's Guide 2009; Timmons and Bygrave 1997; Timmons and Sapienza 1992). Angels, on the other hand, tend to be less visible and harder to find, typically invest in smaller dollar amounts, and are likely to have a longer exit horizon.

In 2009, some 1,188 venture capital funds (managed by 794 venture capital firms) had $179 billion under management (NVCA 2010). As noted in Figure 10.1, between 2002 and 2009, venture capital funds invested annually within the $18 billion to $31 billion range in entrepreneurial ventures (PWC/Moneytree 2010). At the peak of the economic boom in 2000, venture capital funds invested over $100 billion, a figure unequaled before or since. The best estimates for angel investments are that between 200,000 and 300,000 angels invested $15 billion to $26 billion in entrepreneurial ventures annually in the years 2002 to 2009 (Figure 10.1), amounts similar to those invested by venture capital funds during the same period (CVR 2002–2009).

It appears that angels and venture capital funds play complementary rather than competing roles, at least in the financing of new technology-based ventures (Freear and Wetzel 1992). A UK study found five types of complementarity: "co-investing in deals; sequential investing in ventures; business angels as investors in venture capital funds; deal referring; and fund raising by business angels for ventures in which they have invested," (Harrison and Mason 2000, p. 290). Venture capital funds have invested between 2 and 9 percent of their annual investment at the seed and start-up stage of entrepreneurial ventures (see Figure 10.2, for more detail), but the majority of their investing is done at the later stages of financing that involve much larger dollar amounts than angels are typically able or willing to supply. Angels, however, have a more significant impact at the seed and start-up stage, although they do invest at the early or expansion stage and the later growth or established stage.

The combined seed and start-up financing stage covers the inception of the venture, product or service development, and business development. Sometimes a pre-seed stage is identified as the period during which there is an idea for a product or service and preliminary exploration of its commercial feasi-

Figure 10.1 **Angel and Venture Capital Fund Annual Investment**

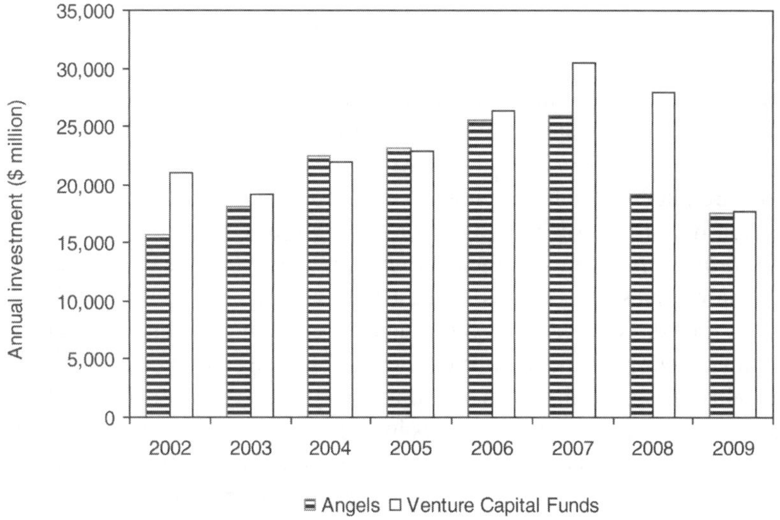

Source: CVR 2002–2009; PWC/Moneytree 2010.

bility. From a financing viewpoint, the pre-seed stage would involve mainly internal financing sources such as capital supplied by entrepreneur-founders, family and friends, bootstrapping, and possibly business alliances.[4]

At the early growth or expansion stage, the venture is likely to have exhausted its internal sources of financing, although business alliances will probably continue to be an option. It may also be close to exhausting any earlier angel financing. At this point, it may need additional angel or venture capital fund financing, or both. With the financing, the venture will be in a position to establish a full-scale manufacturing, marketing, and sales presence. As the venture expands, it may still be incurring losses and lacking adequate working capital and therefore need multiple rounds of private equity financing.

By the later growth or established stage, the venture is likely to be at or above the break-even point,[5] with established customers and suppliers and increasing sales. In order to support continued growth, it will probably need additional working capital and capital to finance manufacturing expansion, product improvements, and distribution channels. If the venture is able to develop to this point, it will have established a successful track record and an asset base such that banks may be more interested in granting loans. Nevertheless, it is probable that from now on the major external private financing source will be the venture capital fund. Acquisition or an IPO may follow.

Angel Profiles

Angels tend to be high-net-worth individuals, male, affluent, self-made, in their forties or older, with graduate degrees, who invest their own money—often in the industry in which they made their money (Freear, Sohl, and Wetzel 2002; Freear and Wetzel 1989; Gaston and Bell 1988; Haar, Starr, and MacMillan 1988). Not all high-net-worth investors become angels; some do, some are interested but have not yet invested, and others have no interest in venture investing. Angels range from successful, cashed-out entrepreneurs with venture investing experience to individuals with little or no experience in venture investing. Studies suggest that while angels invest for financial return, they are motivated also by such factors as the fun and excitement of helping a young business, the creation of jobs, the economic development of a locality, and assisting women and minority entrepreneurs. They expect to be involved actively in the ventures in which they invest, either as members of the board of directors or by formal or informal consulting. To the extent that they are motivated by such factors, they will tend to invest in ventures that are located within a day's drive of their principal residence. Often, they will invest with other angels, one of whom might be the lead investor on a particular deal (Erlich et al. 1994; Freear, Sohl, and Wetzel 1990, 1993).

A 2009 survey of angel groups conducted by the Center for Venture Research found that angel groups invested an average of $308,205 per deal, with an average of between four and five individual angels in each investment, each investing an average of $68,000 (CVR 2002–2009). The data distinguished between new and follow-on deals. For new deals, the angel group received, per deal, a median of 14 percent and an average of 19.5 percent of the venture's equity. For follow-on deals, the median was 5 percent and the average 5.8 percent. A median of 59 percent and an average of 54 percent of angels in the group made no investment during the survey year, perhaps because of a lack of interest in the opportunities, or because their investment funds were already committed.

In the last few years, researchers have begun to look more closely at the role of race and gender in angel financing. Gai and Minniti (2009) reported that self-employed African Americans represent 3.8 percent of the working population, whereas self-employed whites represent 11.6 percent. The study examined some 2,399 single-owner start-ups between 2005 and 2007. Race was found not to be a statistically significant factor in a start-up's survival, but age and education were.

The number of women-owned firms in the United States increased between 1997 and 2004 by over 17 percent, at a time when the growth rate for all firms was only 9 percent (Sohl and Hill 2007). The implications for angel financing are significant. Angels often are cashed-out entrepreneurs; as the number of female cashed-out entrepreneurs increases, it is reasonable to suppose that there will be an increasing number of female angels. Sohl and Hill (2007) reported that female angel groups were active and were attracting more women-owned ventures than were male angel groups: the percentage of female entrepreneurs seeking capital from female angel groups was more than double the percentage that sought capital from male-dominated angel groups (see also Becker-Blease and Sohl 2007). Nevertheless, female angels may still miss investment opportunities because they are not part of traditional male angel groups. This trend is likely to decrease over time as barriers and perhaps even prejudices break down. Becker-Blease and Sohl (2007) discerned no significant difference between the rates at which women-owned ventures are funded (13.33 percent) compared with men-owned ventures (14.79 percent), suggesting a comparable investment quality.

Similar research on female angel groups (Becker-Blease and Sohl 2011) provides support for efforts to encourage greater participation of female investors in the angel market, especially in the form of predominantly female or all-female groups. The benefit of these groups is not that they will favor women entrepreneurs' proposals; the evidence suggests that they will not. However, if women entrepreneurs, due to homophily,[6] are more likely to know about and seek funding from groups with more women, and if these groups invest at rates similar to groups that receive high proportions of proposals from men (and Becker-Blease and Sohl's research indicates that this is the case), then predominantly or entirely female angel groups will help to improve women entrepreneurs' access to vital early-stage capital.

Venture Capitalist Profiles

In contrast with angels, venture capitalists are organized formally in general partnerships of professional managers who (1) raise funds from limited partners such as insurance companies, pension funds, individuals, and corporations; (2) invest those funds in entrepreneurial ventures; and (3) manage those investments on behalf of the investors.[7] A fund usually runs for 10 years or until none of its venture investments requires further financing. In return, the professional managers take a share in any capital gains (or losses) and receive an annual management fee of 2 to 3 percent of the value of the managed portfolio of venture investments.

A survey in 2008 (NVCA/Dow Jones VentureWire 2008) found that the managers, or general partners, and their associates are likely to be male and to hold graduate degrees (63 percent). Ninety-six percent have moved to venture capital firms from related professional fields, notably entrepreneurial and start-up ventures (22 percent), middle-market ventures (20 percent), a different venture capital firm (20 percent), and the law, consulting, and investment banking professions (19 percent). Van Osnabrugge and Robinson (2000) noted that profile studies conducted mostly in the 1990s identified other characteristics of venture capitalists: They undertake a more comprehensive due diligence and investment contractual agreement (although angels are moving closer in this regard); they are less concerned with the location of the venture, but more concerned with exit strategies and financial returns; and they tend to adopt a broader strategic approach to post-investment monitoring of the investment, whereas angels are likely to be more regularly involved in the details of running the business.

Market Inefficiency

The private equity market, particularly the angel market, is inefficient because information flows are poor, barriers to entry are high (the high net worth needed to be an angel is an effective barrier to entry), deal transaction costs are high, and although there are many market participants, they often are unaware of each other.

Angel-entrepreneur matching services have existed since the 1980s, and many have migrated to the web (Harrison and Mason 1996; Wetzel and Freear 1996). Many angels seek anonymity but also want an adequate flow of prospective investments. In the absence of a developed and organized market, the two are not easily reconciled. The quandary has been eased to a degree by the creation of informal groups of angels. These are often local or regional and are able to make their presence known to the local business community while protecting the anonymity of individual angels in order to shield them from finance-hungry entrepreneurs. The same is true of formal angel groups (angel alliances) and of the forums at which entrepreneurs are given time to present their financing case to potentially interested angels.

Other inefficiencies include delays, usually of several months, between the entrepreneur's decision to seek financing and angels supplying it. These delays stem from the entrepreneur's need to protect product and other business confidentiality, and from the need on the part of angels to conduct due diligence (Freear and Sohl 2001; Freear, Sohl, and Wetzel 1994a). Freear, Sohl, and Wetzel (1994a) found that, on average, it took longer to arrange a meeting with a venture capitalist (about seven weeks, assuming it could be done at all) than with a business angel (about four weeks). Angels were, on average, also quicker to sign the check after the first meeting (about 10 weeks; half the respondents took about one month or less) compared with about 18 weeks for venture capitalists. The total time from first looking for an investor to receiving a check was about 14 weeks for angels and more than 26 weeks for venture capitalists. The difference may be explained in part by the fact that venture capitalists tend to undertake more exhaustive due diligence.

A later study (Sohl 2003) confirms the general picture, although the angel due diligence time appears to have increased from 10 weeks to about 17 weeks. This increase in thoroughness may have been brought on by the angel market contraction in 2001 that followed the market expansion in 2000. Of course, there remain other problems with both angels (finding them in the first place) and venture capitalists (actually succeeding in arranging a meeting).

Angel Groups and Alliances

In the last few years, angels have increasingly moved toward informal groups or formal groups (alliances). There are now about 170 angel alliances across the United States. These alliances often have formal voting on an investment opportunity, more explicit and perhaps stringent terms and conditions on the investment, and a minimum dollar investment activity requirement for individual angels. In other words, in many cases, these formal angel alliances are beginning to look like venture capital funds in terms of organizational structure, term sheets, a preference for later-stage investing, and their investment criteria. The alliances have higher visibility than individual angels or informal angel groups and account for perhaps 10 percent of the angel deals and dollars invested. They also increase the chances that a venture may receive successive rounds of angel financing beyond what would have been available from individual investors or informal groups, thus reducing the need for later-stage venture capital funding (Amatucci and Sohl 2006). This increased institutionalization does not necessarily imply an increased level of sophistication or effectiveness. Amatucci and Sohl (2006) expressed reservations about the growth of angel alliances:

> The potential institutionalization of the business angel market . . . could present a significant impediment to the viability of the business angel investor as the major provider of seed capital to entrepreneurial ventures. In contrast, angel groups that provide a venue for reviewing business plans, work on generating quality deal flow, maintain individual decision making among members and provide a venue for informal syndication on a per deal basis, are providing a valuable service to the angel community. (p. 103)

Acceptance Rates

Acceptance, or yield, rates are defined as the percentage of investment opportunities that are brought to the attention of investors and that result in an investment. From 2002 to 2009, angel acceptance rates varied widely, between

7.1 percent in 2002 and 23 percent in 2005. Since 2007, the acceptance rate has settled back into the 10 to 15 percent range (CVR 2002–2009). In contrast, as noted earlier, the NVCA (2010) reported an acceptance rate of only one percent for those who come to a venture capital fund for funding.[8] The swings in acceptance rates from year to year may be explained in part by changes in angels' degree of caution as a reaction to the changing economic climate. It also may reflect variations in the quality of deal flow from year to year and the extent to which angels are fully invested at a particular point in time.

Angels and venture capital funds have similar acceptance criteria, although the weights and acceptability level afforded to each may differ. The criteria include the quality of the venture's management team, an assessment of the venture's target market, the stage of development of the venture, a technical and commercial evaluation of the venture's product or service, and the venture's financial potential. Petty and Gruber (2009) found that ventures sometimes failed to obtain venture capital fund financing partly because of the particular stage in the life cycle of the fund itself. As the fund ages, more venture capitalist time is taken up with managing the portfolio of existing investments, thus leaving less time for deal selection. Further, some 10 percent of the deals that failed to materialize were the consequence of the venture itself not responding to requests from venture capital funds for specific additional information.

Investor Exits and Beyond

The founders of entrepreneurial ventures often aspire to see their venture acquired by another firm or become publicly traded. These outcomes, known as "cashing out" or "harvesting," enable entrepreneurs to sell some or all of their equity in the venture and thereby to reap the rewards for their patience, innovation, and risk taking. Even for those relatively few ventures that are successful in being acquired or that make a successful IPO, the process may be long (often 10 years or more), difficult, and expensive.

What happens after the IPO, however, may be very rewarding. The NVCA (2010, p. 8) noted that "far from being a destination, the IPO process provides needed growth capital for growing companies." It goes on to say that 90 percent of the jobs created by venture-backed public companies were created after they went public, and that, therefore, at the time of going public, these companies were only 10 percent of their mature size. It cites as extreme examples: Microsoft, with 1,153 employees at the IPO stage (1986) compared to 91,000 in 2007; Intel with 460 employees at the IPO stage (1971) and 86,300 in 2007; and Home Depot, with 650 employees at the IPO stage (1981) and 331,000 in 2007.

Data for all U.S. IPOs from 2001 to 2005 (Johnson and Sohl 2008) reveal that angel-financed companies are significant participants in the IPO market.

Specifically, 33 percent of the firms going public from 2001 to 2005 were backed by venture capitalists, 13 percent were angel backed, and 16 percent had both venture capital and angel capital. Thus, close to a third of the IPOs had received angel financing. Angel-backed firms tend to be older than those with venture capital financing, are more geographically dispersed, are in low burn-rate industries (industries with low ratios of R&D to assets), and in industries that have high leverage and an ability to borrow funds.

Angels were "more inclined to leave the method of liquidation undefined at the time of investment than were venture capital funds" (Freear, Sohl, and Wetzel 1990, p. 227). It appears that angels were more concerned with making the investment a success than with how to exit. This attitude is confirmed by later studies in other countries (Sohl 2007) and by the manager of a matching service, quoted in Van Osnabrugge and Robinson (2000, p. 200): "I never get asked by angels about exits. But venture capitalists are different because that's the basis of their business: get in, get out." There is evidence, however, that in some instances, angels—especially those in angel alliances—have started to pay greater attention to terms, conditions, and exits (Amatucci and Sohl 2006).

Angel and Venture Capital Fund Investments

Venture capital funds tend to invest in ventures at the later stages of growth and in larger amounts than do angels, in preparation for an IPO or an acquisition within a five-to-seven-year period. Further, many of the ventures in which venture capital funds invest at any one time are already in their portfolio of investments (Sohl 2003); that is, they make repeat, or follow-on, investments in the same ventures through the early and later financing stages.

Sector Investment

Table 10.1 illustrates the importance of technology-based ventures[9] in the annual investments of angels and venture capital funds. Angels committed from 55 to 88 percent to technology-based ventures from 2004 to 2009.[10] Venture capital funds committed between 71 and 86 percent to technology-based ventures over the same period. The proportions invested by angels and venture capital funds in the identified sectors fluctuated over the period, as shown in Table 10.1.

Deal Size

Typically, since 2002, venture capital funds have invested an average (and a median) of around $6.9 million in each venture deal. Angels, by contrast, have an average annual investment in each venture deal of about $430,000 and a

Table 10.1

Angels (BA) and Venture Capital Funds (VC): Principal Sector Annual Investment (percentages of total annual investment)

	2004		2005		2006		2007		2008		2009	
	BA	VC	BA	VC	BA	VC	BA	VC	BA	VC	BA	VC
Software	22	24	18	21	18	19	27	18	13	18	19	18
Biotech	10	19	12	18	18	18	12	17	11	16	8	21
Health	16	10	20	11	21	12	19	13	16	13	17	15
Other Technology	21	33	20	34	10	32	13	28	15	25	15	22
Total Technology	69	86	70	84	67	80	71	76	55	71	59	76

Source: CVR 2002–2009; NVCA 2010.

median of about $450,000. Angel investment fell back in 2008 and 2009, as did venture capital fund investment, though by a smaller percentage. In recent years, the total annual amounts invested by angels have been very similar to the total amounts invested by venture capital funds. Figure 10.1, above, shows that between 2002 and 2009, the total of annual investment deals by venture capital funds[11] varied from about $18 billion to about $31 billion. In over half of the years between 2002 and 2009, the angel total annual investment was similar in size to that of venture capital funds (CVR 2002–2009; PWC/MoneyTree 2010).

The big discrepancy between the average amounts invested in a venture by angels and venture capital funds and the similarity of the total amounts invested (Figure 10.1) is explained by the number of ventures financed or deals concluded by each investor category. Between 2002 and 2009, venture capital funds financed between 2,795 and 4,027 firms, whereas the number of angel-financed deals has grown fairly steadily from 36,000 in 2002 to over 57,000 in 2009 (CVR 2002–2009; PWC/MoneyTree 2010).

Financing Stage

In recent years, venture capital funds have gradually increased their average investment in seed and start-up financing from 2 to 9 percent of their total annual investment (Figure 10.2). Contrast these percentages with those of annual angel investments at the seed and start-up stages: From 2002 through 2006, between 43 and 55 percent of total annual angel investments were at the seed and start-up stage. From 2007 to 2009, however, the angel percentages dropped into the 35 to 45 percent range (Figure 10.2), possibly reflecting the uncertain state of the U.S. economy and the need to provide additional rounds of financing to their previous investments. The venture capitalist, who invests mostly other people's money, has more to invest, but also has a greater incentive to mitigate risk through investing in later-stage, more established ventures.

Financing Gaps

It might seem from the discussion of financing stages that there is a smooth, seamless progression from one stage to the next, culminating in an acquisition or an IPO. Rarely do things move that smoothly, however. The NVCA (2010) reported that a venture financed by a venture capital fund has a 47 percent chance of ending in an acquisition or IPO, and even that will often take one or even two decades to accomplish. Fifty-three percent of the 11,686 ventures in the study were either known to have failed (18 percent) or were

Figure 10.2 **Angel and Venture Capital Funds: Percentage of Annual Investment at Seed/Start-up Stage**

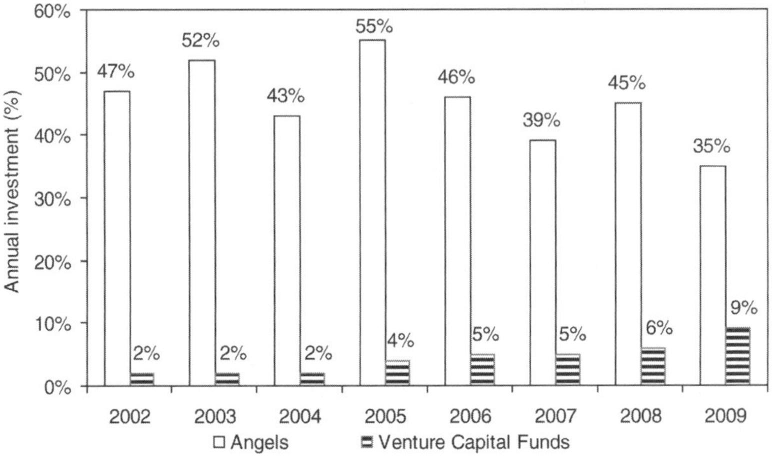

Source: CVR 2002–2009; PWC/MoneyTree 2010.

still privately held but are assumed for the most part to have "quietly failed" (35 percent).

Financing gaps are symptoms of inefficiency in the private equity market (Freear, Sohl, and Wetzel 1994b; Wetzel 1983). There are two gaps, both of which affect financing opportunities: one is caused by poor information about the market—the information gap—and one caused by the investing policies of the suppliers of capital—the financing gap. The information gap may arise in the $100,000 to $2 million range, usually at the seed and start-up stage. The resources supplied by founders, family, friends, bootstrapping, and perhaps business alliances become exhausted or are no longer able to support the growth rate of the venture. The venture now needs external private equity financing to continue its growth and development. Given the stage of development and amount of financing needed, angels are the most likely financing source, but while the entrepreneur struggles to find angels, angels are struggling to find an adequate flow of quality investment opportunities. Poor information on both sides may lead to missed financing opportunities. This gap may be closing with the advent of matching services, informal angel groups, and angel alliances.

The second gap, the financing gap, may arise at some point in the early or expansion financing stage, as the venture's resource needs begin to outstrip the availability of additional angel funds, yet the funds required are too small to interest venture capital funds. The gap tends to occur in the $2 million to $5 million range. The venture capital funds have gradually moved to larger and later-stage financing, raising the lower dollar limit to around $5 million for their financing, partly as a response to market conditions and risk-mitigation strategies and partly because of the high fixed costs of due diligence, negotiation, and subsequent monitoring of the investment. Angels have tended to move in the direction of a higher upper limit, around $2 million. Informal angel groups, smaller venture capital funds, angel alliances, and joint financing rounds with venture capital funds are likely, however, to further reduce the gap between the angel upper limit of $2 million and the venture capital fund lower limit of $5 million.

Public Policy and Economic Development

Venture capital funds are concentrated in two states, California and Massachusetts, and in other financial centers. Forty-seven percent or more of their deals have been made in three regions: Silicon Valley, which has continued to have the largest percentage of deals since at least 1980, New England, and the New York metropolitan region (see Figure 10.3). The Midwest, LA/Orange County, the Southeast, San Diego, Texas, and the Northwest rank among the remaining more active regions. Angels are geographically more dispersed and are less likely to invest in ventures that are beyond a day's drive of their principal residence. California and Massachusetts are also major angel locations, and angels are to be found in increasing numbers in North Carolina, Colorado, the Northwest, Texas, and Utah (Sohl 1999).

For several decades, economic development policy has aimed to promote entrepreneurship and technology-based activity (Gittell, Sohl, and Tebaldi 2010). Some 30 states have state-supported venture capital funds, the first having been established in Massachusetts in 1979 (NASVF 2008). As of 2008, the funds had about $2.4 billion in investment funds, a very small amount (1.3 percent) compared with the $179.4 billion under management at private venture capital funds (NVCA 2010). The state-supported funds invest mostly in the seed and early stages, but some have made investments at later stages. From the late 1980s onward, economic development organizations have encouraged local venture start-ups by means of business assistance programs, technical assistance, subsidized incubators, and tax breaks. A study of 394 regions in the United States identified entrepreneurship and innovation as drivers of the development of regional economies (Camp 2005). Angels and venture capital funds are very active in the financing of technology-based ventures, each group having committed a substantial majority of its funds to technology-based industries, especially health, biotechnology, and software (see Table 10.1).

Figure 10.3 **Venture Capital Investment: The Three Largest Regions**

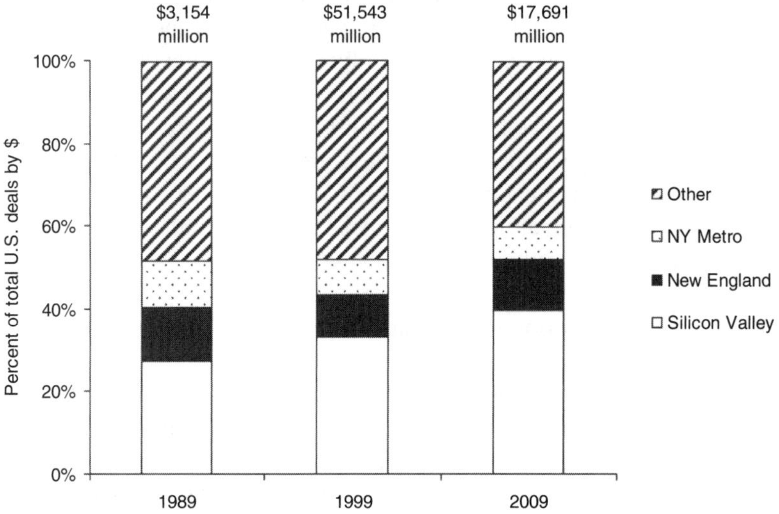

Source: NVCA 2010, Figure 3.08.

A study by Gittell, Sohl, and Tebaldi (2010) concluded, first, that over the last business cycle, 1991–2007, entrepreneurship had a powerful positive impact on employment growth during all stages of the cycle. There is evidence to suggest that while levels of technology concentration were negatively correlated with employment growth, the growth in technology concentration encouraged employment growth in Metropolitan Statistical Areas (MSAs). Expansion in technology concentration rather than its size creates the conditions favorable to job growth.

Second, the study found that there exists a strong link between entrepreneurship and technology-based activities supported by a highly qualified work force (and through the financing by angels and venture capital funds; see Table 10.1). MSAs with growing technology-based activities and above-average entrepreneurship levels can be expected to add jobs more quickly than other MSAs. These results suggest that technology-based entrepreneurship is a more powerful job creator than entrepreneurship on its own, and especially than the generality of small businesses. Plummer and Headd (2009, p. 593) found that there was little difference between the birth and death rates of ventures in rural areas and those in urban areas and concluded that "it would appear that rural counties are just as 'entrepreneurial' as urban areas." If this is the case, and if the entrepreneurship is technology based, then it might be reasonable to extend the conclusions in Gittell, Sohl, and Tebaldi (2010) to areas other than MSAs.

Such studies suggest that public policy encouraging economic development should be directed to the promotion and encouragement of technology-based and innovative entrepreneurial ventures. Evidence suggests that 30 to 50 percent of prospective entrepreneurs who take at least two real steps toward starting a venture actually do so and are helped by business assistance programs (White and Reynolds 1994). A diverse portfolio, based on varied technologies, might further strengthen the impact of these ventures and provide a greater degree of stability in growth patterns over time. Infrastructure support for technology and innovation through incubators, technology parks, local universities, and other institutions might further strengthen growth (Gittell, Sohl, and Tebaldi 2004). Underlying these policy tools are the more traditional ones of benign local and state taxing policies, favorable housing costs, a well-educated workforce, and the provision of social and cultural amenities.

There is another necessary set of supports: adequate sources of finance at the right time and in the most appropriate form. Entrepreneurial ventures, whether technology-based or not, will often require external private equity capital financing during their development. As noted earlier, venture capital firms tend to be based in California, Massachusetts, and other financial centers rather than spread out in smaller communities across the country (Muzyka et al. 1993; Sapienza, Manigart, and Herron 1992; Sapienza, Manigart, and Vermeir 1996; Sapienza and Timmons 1989). Angels tend to be more geographically dispersed, and many angels prefer to invest in ventures that are geographically close in order to be involved in a hands-on manner and perhaps also because they wish to foster economic development in their home area (see, for example, Aram 1989; Freear, Sohl, and Wetzel 1993; Landstrom 1992; Mason 1996; Postma and Sullivan 1990; Short and Riding 1989; Wetzel and Seymour 1981). Angels are not, however, spread evenly across the country and are not always where they might be particularly needed. They tend instead to cluster where entrepreneurial and technological innovation is intense. Angels need entrepreneurs and entrepreneurs need angels. This circularity is a challenge for local and regional economic development, which would benefit from seeking greater input and involvement from angels and venture capitalists as means of supporting local entrepreneurial initiatives.

Summary, Conclusions, and the Future

Entrepreneurial ventures, a small but very significant subset of the small-firm sector, are a major propellant to GDP growth in the United States. In 2008, ventures backed by venture capital funds accounted for about 21 percent of the U.S. GDP and 11 percent of U.S. private sector employment (NVCA 2009, p. 2). Entrepreneurs create new companies, some of which become household names, often with help from the private equity market. Even if they do not reach that eminence, many will still contribute substantially to GDP growth and employment.

Private equity is unlikely to be attracted to firms that are expected to grow at a slow rate or not at all, but it is an important source of external financing for those ventures that appear to have strong growth prospects. Angels have been more willing than venture capital funds to invest at the earlier seed and start-up stage, whereas venture capital funds have tended to invest at the later financing stages. There is a complementary relationship between the two groups, and there is overlap in their investing preferences. Angels may continue to hold their investment during subsequent venture capital financing rounds or to invest in later financing rounds with venture capital funds. Venture capital funds, for their part, sometimes offer financing at the seed and start-up stage. Both will tend to add more value than just their money: Venture capital funds will supply expertise through a seat on the board; angels likewise may seek a seat on the board and may provide consulting and other help on a formal or informal basis.

The private equity market has been, and remains, inefficient and male-dominated, although the information and financing gaps are narrowing, and women are experiencing an increasing presence as entrepreneurs and investors. Finding angels and gaining access to venture capitalists can be difficult. Investors are locked into their investment until the venture is bought out or otherwise liquidated. Structuring deals, performing due diligence, monitoring performance, and negotiating an exit are time consuming and require expertise.

The federal government, states, and other public entities encourage technology-based entrepreneurial activity through such measures as business assistance programs, tax breaks, technical assistance, loans, loan guarantees, and even some very limited amount of equity financing. They have been less likely to recognize the role of private equity in enabling and encouraging entrepreneurial ventures to grow or to incorporate private equity into economic development policy.

Notes

1. The term *angel* originated in theater, where it refers to backers or investors in theatrical productions. It is used in place of the term *accredited investor,* a term defined in Regulation D of the Securities Act of 1933.

2. The series excludes data on nonemployer businesses, private households, railroads, agricultural production, and most government entities (U.S. Census Bureau 2008).

3. Nasdaq stands for National Association of Securities Dealers Automated Quo-

tation. Public companies are able to trade stocks on these secondary markets because they have already raised money by issuing new stock or selling existing stocks through placements or through public offerings.

4. *Bootstrapping* is an attempt to minimize expenses and limit the need for capital by such techniques as seeking customer funding for research and development and building up personal credit card debt. Business alliances are cooperative agreements with other, more established businesses to use complementary resources, for example, to gain access to sales and marketing channels and to improve market penetration. See Freear, Sohl, and Wetzel 1995b.

5. *Breakeven* is defined as the point at which total revenues equal total expenses, i.e., where net income is zero.

6. *Homophily,* a sociological term coined in the 1950s, means the tendency of individuals to associate with others who are of the same gender, or who, for example, are similar in age or organizational role.

7. This may raise agency questions that are much less apparent in the case of angels, who invest on their own account, although note the increasing number of angel alliances.

8. Hall (1989; quoted in Petty and Gruber 2009) suggests 1 to 3 percent.

9. While it may be argued that most products and services today have a strong technology component, included in "technology-based" are businesses that employ a significant proportion of their labor force in R&D-related occupations.

10. The angel figures for 2002 and 2003 were categorized differently, and so it is not possible to identify the percentage for health; any health-related investment is in the "Other Technology" category for those years. From 2004 onwards, the data categories used are the same as are used by the NVCA, 2010.

11. The figure includes any angel investment made as part of the venture capital fund deal. Consequently, the venture capital fund investment is overstated.

References

Amatucci, F.M., and J.E. Sohl. 2006. Business angels: Investment processes, outcomes and current trends. In *Entrepreneurship: The Engine of Growth*, Volume II: *The Process*, ed. A. Zacharakis and S. Spinelli, 87–107. Westport, CT: Praeger Perspectives.

Aram, J.D. 1989. Attitudes and behaviors of informal investors toward early-stage investments, technology-based ventures and coinvestors. *Journal of Business Venturing* 4(5): 333–47.

Becker-Blease, J.R., and J.E. Sohl. 2007. Do women-owned businesses have equal access to angel capital? *Journal of Business Venturing* 22(4): 503–21.

———. 2011. The effect of gender diversity on angel group investment. *Entrepreneurship Theory and Practice* 35(4): 709–33.

Brophy, D.J. 1997. Financing the growth of entrepreneurial firms. In *Entrepreneurship 2000*, ed. D.L. Sexton and R.W. Smilor, 5–28. Chicago: Upstart.

Bygrave, W.D. 1994. *The Portable MBA in Entrepreneurship*. New York: Wiley.

Camp, M. 2005. The innovation-entrepreneurship NEXUS: A national assessment of entrepreneurship and regional economic growth and development. *Small Business Advocacy Research Summary,* no. 256. www.sba.gov/advo/research/rs256.pdf (accessed June 2010).

Center for Venture Research (CVR). 2002–2009. CVR analysis reports. Center for Venture Research, Whittemore School of Business and Economics, University of New Hampshire. http://wsbe.unh.edu/cvr-analysis-reports (accessed June 2010).

Erlich, S.A., A.F. De Noble, T. Moore, and R.R. Weaver. 1994. After the cash arrives: A comparative study of venture capital and private investor involvement in entrepreneurial firms. *Journal of Business Venturing* 9(1): 67–82.

Freear, J., and J.E. Sohl. 2001. The characteristics and value-added contributions of private investors to entrepreneurial software ventures. *Journal of Entrepreneurial Finance* 6(1): 84–103.

Freear, J., J.E. Sohl, and W.E. Wetzel, Jr. 1990. Raising venture capital: Entrepreneurs' views of the process. *Frontiers of Entrepreneurship Research*, 1990 edition, 223–37. Wellesley, MA: Babson College. http://fusionmx.babson.edu/entrep/fer/front_90.html.

———. 1993. Summary: Angel profiles—A longitudinal study. *Frontiers of Entrepreneurship Research,* 1993 edition, 557–58. Wellesley, MA: Babson College. http://fusionmx.babson.edu/entrep/fer/front_93.html.

———. 1994a. Angels and non-angels: Are there differences? *Journal of Business Venturing* 9(2): 109–23.

———. 1994b. The private investor market for venture capital. *Financier* 1(2): 7–15.

———. 1995a. Angels: Personal investors in the venture capital market. *Entrepreneurship and Regional Development* 7(1): 85–94.

———. 1995b. Who bankrolls software entrepreneurs? *Frontiers of Entrepreneurship Research,* 1995 edition, 394–406. Wellesley, MA: Babson College. http://fusionmx.babson.edu/entrep/fer/papers95/index.html.

———. 1997. The informal venture capital market: Milestones passed and the road ahead. In *Entrepreneurship 2000,* ed. D.L. Sexton and R.W. Smilor, 47–69. Chicago: Upstart.

———. 2002. Angles on angels: Financing technology-based ventures—A historical perspective. *Venture Capital* 4(4): 275–87.

Freear, J., and W.E. Wetzel, Jr. 1989. Equity capital for entrepreneurs. *Frontiers of Entrepreneurship Research*, 1989 edition, 230–44. Wellesley, MA: Babson College. http://fusionmx.babson.edu/entrep/fer/front_89.html.

———. 1990. Who bankrolls high-tech entrepreneurs? *Journal of Business Venturing* 5(2): 77–89.

———. 1992. The informal venture capital market in the 1990s. In *State of the Art of Entrepreneurship,* ed. D.L. Sexton and J.D. Kasarda, 462–86. Boston: PWS-Kent.

Gai, Y., and M. Minniti. 2009. Survival and financing of black owned start-ups in the U.S. Interactive paper. *Frontiers of Entrepreneurship Research*, 29(9), Article 5. Wellesley, MA: Babson College. http://digitalknowledge.babson.edu/fer/vol29/iss9/5 (accessed June 2010).

Gaston, R.J., and S.E. Bell. 1988. *The Informal Supply of Capital*. Washington, DC: Office of Economic Research, U.S. Small Business Administration.

Gittell, R., J.E. Sohl, and E. Tebaldi. 2004. Factors influencing the long-term sustainability of entrepreneurial tech centers. *Frontiers of Entrepreneurship Research*, 2004 edition, 192. Wellesley, MA: Babson College. http://fusionmx.babson.edu/entrep/fer/FER_2004/web-content/Section%20VII/S11/VII-S11.html.

———. 2010. Is there a sweet spot for U.S. metropolitan areas? *Frontiers of Entrepreneurship Research,* 30(15), Article 13. Wellesley, MA: Babson College. http://digitalknowledge.babson.edu/fer/vol30/iss15/13/.

Haar, N.E., J. Starr, and I.C. MacMillan. 1988. Informal risk capital investors: Investment patterns on the east coast of the USA. *Journal of Business Venturing* 3(1): 11–29.

Hall, J. 1989. *Venture Capitalists' Decision Making and the Entrepreneur: An Exploratory Investigation.* PhD diss. University of Georgia. Quoted in Petty and Gruber 2009.

Harrison, R.T., and C.M. Mason, eds. 1996. *Informal Venture Capital: Evaluating the Impact of Business Introduction Services.* Hemel Hempstead, UK: Prentice-Hall/Woodhead-Faulkner.

———. 2000. Venture capital complementarities: The links between business angels and venture capital funds. Summary. *Frontiers of Entrepreneurship Research,* 2000 edition, 290. Wellesley, MA: Babson College.

Johnson, W.C., and J.E. Sohl. 2008. Angel investors in initial public offerings. *Frontiers of Entrepreneurship Research,* 28(2), Article 5. Wellesley, MA: Babson College. http://digitalknowledge.babson.edu/fer/vol28/iss2/5 (accessed June 2010).

Landstrom, H. 1992. The relationship between private investors and small firms: An agency theory approach. *Entrepreneurship and Regional Development* 4(3): 199–223.

Mason, C.M. 1996. Informal venture capital: Is policy running ahead of knowledge? *International Journal of Entrepreneurial Behaviour and Research* 2(1): 4–14.

Meyer, R.T., M. David, J.G. Butler, E. Carayannis, and R. Radosevich. 1995. *The 1995 National Census of Early-Stage Capital Financing.* Albuquerque, NM: Orion Technical Associates, Inc. www.oriontechnical.com/95report.html.

Muzyka, D., S. Birley, B. Leleux, G. Rossell, and F. Bendixen. 1993. Financial structure and decisions of venture capital firms: A pan-European study. *Frontiers of Entrepreneurship Research,* 1993 edition, 538–52. Wellesley, MA: Babson College. http://fusionmx.babson.edu/entrep/fer/front_93.html.

National Association of Seed and Venture Capital Funds (NASVF). 2008. *2008 State Funds Chart.* Philadelphia: National Association of Seed and Venture Capital Funds. www.nasvf.org/pdfs/VCFundsReport.pdf (accessed June 2010).

National Venture Capital Association (NVCA). 2009. *Venture Impact,* 5th ed. Arlington, VA: National Venture Capital Association. www.nvca.org (accessed June 2010).

———. 2010. *National Venture Capital Association Yearbook 2010.* New York: Thomson Reuters. www.nvca.org (accessed June 2010).

NVCA/Dow Jones VentureWire. 2008. *Venture Census, 2008.* Arlington, VA: National Venture Capital Association. www.nvca.org (accessed June 2010).

Petty, J.S., and M. Gruber. 2009. "This deal is dead!" A longitudinal study of VC decision-making. *Frontiers of Entrepreneurship Research,* 29(3), Article 1. Wellesley, MA: Babson College. http://digitalknowledge.babson.edu/fer/vol29/iss3/1 (accessed June 2010).

Plummer, L.A., and B. Headd. 2009. Rural and urban establishment births and deaths using the U.S. Census Bureau's business information tracking series. Summary. *Frontiers of Entrepreneurship Research,* 29(16), Article 6. Wellesley, MA: Babson College. http://digitalknowledge.babson.edu/fer/vol29/iss16/6 (accessed June 2010).

Postma, P.D., and M.K. Sullivan. 1990. Informal risk capital in the Knoxville region. Unpublished report. University of Tennessee.

Pratt's Guide. 2009. *Pratt's Guide to Private Equity and Venture Capital Sources, 2009.* New York: Thomson Reuters.

PWC/MoneyTree. 2010. *PricewaterhouseCoopers/Moneytree Report.* London: PricewaterhouseCoopers. www.pwcmoneytree.com (accessed June 2010).

Sapienza, H.J., S. Manigart, and L. Herron. 1992. Venture capitalist involvement in portfolio companies: A study of 221 portfolio companies in four countries. Summary. *Frontiers of Entrepreneurship Research*, 1992 edition, 368–69. Wellesley, MA: Babson College. http://fusionmx.babson.edu/entrep/fer/front_92.html.

Sapienza, H.J., S. Manigart, and W. Vermeir. 1996. Venture capitalist governance and value-added in four countries. *Journal of Business Venturing* 11(6): 439–69.

Sapienza, H.J., and J.A. Timmons. 1989. The roles of venture capitalists in new ventures: What determines their importance? In *Academy of Management Best Papers Proceedings,* ed. F. Hoy, 74–78. Briarcliff Manor, NY: Academy of Management.

Short, D.M., and A.L. Riding. 1989. Informal investors in the Ottawa-Carleton region: Experiences and expectations. *Entrepreneurship and Regional Development* 1(1): 99–112.

Sohl, J.E. 1999. The early-stage equity market in the USA. *Venture Capital* 1(2): 101–20.

———. 2003. The private equity market in the USA: Lessons from volatility. *Venture Capital* 5(1): 29–46.

———. 2007. The organization of the informal venture capital market. In *Handbook of Research on Venture Capital,* ed. H. Landstrom, 347–70. Cheltenham, UK: Edward Elgar.

Sohl, J.E., and L. Hill. 2007. Women business angels: Insights from angel groups. *Venture Capital* 9(3): 207–22.

Timmons, J.A., and W.D. Bygrave. 1997. Venture capital: Reflections and projections. In *Entrepreneurship 2000*, ed. D.L. Sexton and R.W. Smilor, 29–46. Chicago: Upstart.

Timmons, J.A., and H.J. Sapienza. 1992. Venture capital: The decade ahead. In *The State of the Art of Entrepreneurship,* ed. D.L. Sexton and R.W. Smilor, 402–37. Boston: PWS-Kent.

U.S. Census Bureau. 2008. Statistics about business size (including small business). www.census.gov/econ/smallbus.html (accessed June 2010).

Van Osnabrugge, M., and R.J. Robinson. 2000. *Angel Investing*. San Francisco: Jossey-Bass.

Wetzel, W.E., Jr. 1983. Angels and informal risk capital. *Sloan Management Review* 24(4): 23–34.

———. 1987. The informal venture capital market: Aspects of scale and efficiency. *Journal of Business Venturing* 2(4): 299–313.

Wetzel, W.E., Jr., and J. Freear. 1996. Promoting informal venture capital in the United States: Reflections on the history of the venture capital network. In *Informal Venture Capital: Evaluating the Impact of Business Introduction Services,* ed. R.T. Harrison and C.M. Mason, 61–74. Hemel Hempstead, UK: Prentice-Hall/Woodhead-Faulkner.

Wetzel, W.E., Jr., and C.R. Seymour. 1981. *Informal Risk Capital in New England.* Washington DC: Office of Advocacy, U.S. Small Business Administration.

White, S.B., and P.D. Reynolds. 1994. What can the public sector do to increase new business starts? *Frontiers of Entrepreneurship Research*, 1994 edition, 1–15. Wellesley, MA: Babson College. http://fusionmx.babson.edu/entrep/fer/papers94/index.html.

11

Entrepreneurship in Rural America

Henry Renski and Ryan Wallace

Historically, rural economies have been most closely associated with farming, agriculture, and raw materials processing. While farming is still important, the rural dependence on it has dropped substantially in the past few decades. For example, between 1972 and 2000, agriculture went from being a leading source of income in 25 percent of U.S. rural counties to 10 percent (Drabenstott 2003; Quigley 2002). As of 1999, 90 percent of rural workers held nonfarm jobs, and only 6.3 percent of the rural population lived on farms (Drabenstott 2003). In part, the decline of agriculture has been the consequence of the long-term consolidation of the farming industry and tremendous gains in productivity that have allowed American commodities to remain competitive in global markets. The downside of these productivity gains is the need for fewer agricultural workers, precipitating out-migration and the long-term population loss that has turned many once-thriving rural communities into near ghost towns.

Similar trends have occurred in rural manufacturing, which expanded dramatically from World War II until the 1970s (Roth 2000). The expansion of rural manufacturing was a direct consequence of the aggressive recruitment strategies of southeastern states, which came largely at the direct expense of the industrial centers in the Northeast and Midwest (Hanson 1993). Technology and growing cost pressures further enabled this rural migration as the expansion of assembly line branch plants greatly favored single-story greenfield sites with access to cheap, semiskilled labor (Quigley 2002). Despite a slight resurgence in the 1990s, rural manufacturing employment share has continued to decline in recent decades amid tightening global cost pressures and a domestic shift to more technologically advanced and flexible modes of production (Wilkerson 2001). Rural America has fallen in line with the national shift toward a service-based economy. But even within services, rural areas tend to specialize in industries that primarily target local populations rather than in the high-growth, high-wage advanced and professional services (Drabenstott 2003).

Rural policy makers have struggled to find an economic base to replace agriculture and manufacturing; they have called for a new course of action for rural economic development policy (Markley 2001). Beginning in earnest with the 1972 Rural Development Act, the federal rural agenda has historically been characterized by agribusiness subsidies that overwhelmingly benefit large-scale farms and by programs to expand power and basic infrastructure in remote areas to encourage industrial development (Freshwater 2001). Little effort was devoted to enterprise development or to building the institutions needed to assist new and small businesses and counter the adverse effects of global competition (Robinson, Dassie, and Christy 2004). State rural initiatives are still focused largely on recruiting mobile branch plants. Yet, the decline of large-scale domestic manufacturing has limited the prospects for business recruitment and retention (Stauber 2001). In response, states have resorted to offering larger and larger incentives and subsidies to lure those few footloose branch plants that remain.

Despite their continued dominance in federal and state policy, neither agricultural subsidies nor branch plant recruitment efforts reflect rural communities' current economic reality. Entrepreneurship offers an alternative way to promote endogenous development in rural places (Corporation for Enterprise Development 2003; Dabson 2001; Drabenstott and Henderson 2006; Henderson 2002; Markley 2009). Some see entrepreneurship as inherently more sustainable and cost-effective than traditional approaches to attracting businesses, which often resign a considerable portion of the local tax base, leaving few resources for poor communities to invest in infrastructure and education (Robinson, Dassie, and Christy 2004). The excitement over entrepreneurship also follows a number of influential studies and reports showing that start-ups yield the bulk of new jobs in the economy and that such new business formation is strongly correlated with regional economic growth (Acs and Armington 2006; Advanced Research Technologies 2005; Audretsch, Keilbach, and Lehmann 2006). Entrepreneurship in the form of microenterprise development is also closely associated with community development initiatives that empower residents to become more self-sufficient and reduce rural communities' dependence on a small number of dominant employers.

But is entrepreneurship really the savior for rural areas, or is it merely offered in lieu of any better options? Regional development theory generally views entrepreneurship as inherently favored in a metropolitan climate. More specifically, the urban-incubator hypothesis holds that new firms emerge to fill niches created by new technologies and changing consumer preferences (Hoover and Vernon 1959; Leone and Struyk 1976; Renski 2009). Firms competing in the emergent phases of the product life cycle are particularly sensitive to the local economic ecology and less sensitive to physical space and cost constraints found in mature industries, where production methods and markets are stable.

The research community's ability to answer this challenging question has been stymied by the fact that we know little about rural entrepreneurs, and, in particular, how they differ from their urban counterparts. Empirical research on entrepreneurship is itself in somewhat of an embryonic stage, and few have examined entrepreneurship explicitly from the perspective of rural-urban differences. Doing so requires fairly large and representative data sets that are difficult to come by.

This chapter uses data from a newly released longitudinal survey conducted by the Kauffman Foundation (2009) to investigate the start-up conditions of new firms in rural areas compared to those in urban areas. It seeks to offer insights on a number of critical questions, such as:

- Do new rural firms differ from urban start-ups, and if so, how?
- Are rural start-ups more or less likely to survive than urban start-ups? Among the eventual survivors, are rural start-ups more or less likely to grow and hire additional workers?
- Within rural areas, what are the start-up conditions that distinguish eventual survivors from nonsurvivors? Are these the same conditions that explain survival rates in urban areas, or are there specific rural advantages and disadvantages?

The remainder of this chapter begins with a primer on the major challenges facing rural entrepreneurship to set the stage for examining rural-urban differences. It then moves to our analysis of the Kauffman Firm Survey (KFS), beginning with a discussion of the survey and its sample frame. After that, we examine a variety of factors that have been associated with entrepreneurial survival and growth in previous studies, focusing on six general areas: (1) firm characteristics such as legal form, number of owners, and size; (2) industry technological intensity and innovation; (3) owner experience and education; (4) markets orientation and sales; (5) revenues, profits, and losses; and, finally, (6) start-up finance. We pay particular attention to issues of start-up finance, given the relative importance of this topic to rural policy and research. The chapter concludes with a summary of our primary findings, identifies possible areas for future research, and comments on policy options for building a strong rural entrepreneurial climate.

Challenges to Rural Entrepreneurship

In advocating for the direction of more resources to rural entrepreneurship, one must first ask why entrepreneurship should succeed in rural areas when other development strategies there have failed. Answering this question requires an honest assessment of the challenges facing rural areas.

The Liabilities of Size and Distance

Rural regions are, at their root, defined by their low population density and distance from urban centers. These two structural conditions also constitute the primary challenges to successful entrepreneurial development (Corporation for Enterprise Development 2003; Dabson 2001; Quigley 2002). Small markets limit possibilities for specialization and growth. The larger markets and the typically more affluent populations found in metropolitan areas provide opportunities for emergent firms to fill specialized niches, whether in new technologies, high-end consumer goods, or advanced business and professional services. Rural start-ups often end up serving more general needs of the local population, leaving little room for growth that does not erode the market share of incumbents. A limited market also leaves less scope for achieving greater productivity through internal scale economies. The result is often higher prices for goods and services that leave small rural "Main Street" retailers highly vulnerable to competition from large discount retailers that are able to leverage their massive purchasing power (Dabson 2001).

The limited extent of the market also has important supply-side ramifications, namely in the form of external economies (Krugman 1991; Marshall 1890/1920). Concentrations of small firms in similar and complementary industries benefit from having access to a greater number and variety of specialized intermediate-goods suppliers that allow the small firm to focus on its core competencies. Because of their relative distance from urban areas, rural firms' transaction costs are often higher, as are costs associated with lending, transporting goods, and interacting with customers and strategic partners. The remoteness of rural areas also means that they have poorer access to everyday business services that are commonplace in urban centers, such as shipping, options for Internet services, and critical support services such as lawyers and financial advisers (Dabson 2001). Likewise, larger areas typically have a greater supply of skilled labor. The deeper labor pools in metropolitan areas allow firms to find more appropriately suited workers than are available in remote locations. Metropolitan areas also offer more vocational options for workers, which is particularly pertinent to an economy increasingly composed of dual-earner households with professional spouses (Costa and Kahn 2000).

Furthermore, rural places are not as likely to reap the benefits of knowledge spillovers enjoyed in dense urban areas, where face-to-face contact is high (Acs and Malecki 2003; Quigley 2002). This has serious implications for innovative activity in the increasingly knowledge-driven economy. While innovation is not essential for entrepreneurship, many of today's growth industries are concentrated in highly innovative fields—industries largely absent in rural areas (Henderson 2002). The deficiency of high-growth and innovation-based industries conditions long-term development prospects, as most entrepreneurs start new businesses close to home and build upon their prior work experience when starting a new business (Renski 2010; Stam 2007). As a result, rural entrepreneurs largely mirror the prevailing industry mix in their areas, with an abundance of microenterprises and small businesses serving established markets, but few innovation-based entrepreneurs with high-growth potential (Henderson 2002).

Remoteness and low population density mean that appropriate infrastructure and the costs associated with its efficient provision are also challenging. Most basic infrastructure and public services, including schools, require large initial outlays and then have diminishing marginal costs. In rural areas, the inability to spread these costs over a large population places a particularly high tax burden on those who remain, who tend to be older and less well educated as a consequence of selective out-migration—the well-known brain drain phenomena. Rural areas, especially those farthest from urban centers, lack easy and inexpensive access to air travel and the interstate highway system, which limits the types of businesses that can operate in those areas (Dabson 2001). Access to high-speed Internet is also lagging in many remote areas, as service providers are often reluctant to establish a presence with small economies of scale (Feser 2007).

Demographic Conditions and Cultural Factors

Demographic and cultural factors present additional challenges for rural development. Poverty rates are higher and educational attainment levels are often lower in rural areas (Corporation for Enterprise Development 2003; Quigley 2002; Stauber 2001), both of which are negatively associated with the likelihood of starting a new business and its eventual success (Bates 1993; Reynolds and White 1997; Shane 2008). This problem is further exacerbated by brain drain, which erodes not only the size of the local market and the future workforce, but also the supply of potential entrepreneurs with the greatest capacity for success.

Rural cultural attitudes and social networks create both barriers and opportunities for enterprise development. Although rural residents are often more independent minded and attracted to the autonomy of self-employment, many remote rural areas lack the type of enterprise culture that rewards risk-taking behavior (Kulawczuk 1998). In some places, the legacy of large manufacturing branch plants' dominance makes it difficult to transition dislocated factory workers into self-employment. The strict division of labor and task specialization that typically characterize large assembly plants does not provide workers the opportunity to develop the range of technical, marketing, and administrative skills needed to launch a successful new enterprise (O'Farrell and Hitchens 1988). The strength of internal network associations may be higher in rural areas due to shared values, familial ties, and personal kinships (Ring, Peredo, and Christman 2010), but the localized nature of these networks may hinder access to distant markets and connection to critical financial resources such as equity investors.

Barriers in Rural Entrepreneurial Finance

One of the most significant challenges facing rural entrepreneurs is lack of access to start-up capital (Barkley 2003; Barkley and Markley 2001; Drabenstott, Novack, and Abraham 2003; Markley 2001; Rubin 2010). Both debt and equity financing are critical to the long-term survival of new enterprises, because in some industries start-up costs are high and it can take several years before a new business shows profits. In rural regions, commercial banks and Farm Credit System (FCS) intermediaries typically provide debt capital. However, changes in the banking industry during the 1990s resulted in the merger and acquisition of smaller independent banks with and by larger institutions, greatly reducing the number of hometown lenders. The Economic Research Service (1997) of the U.S. Department of Agriculture (USDA) estimated that by mid-decade, roughly 27 percent of rural counties were served by two or fewer banks threatening healthy competition. Although large institutions have greater ability to complete complex transactions and to provide the greater allocations of capital needed by some businesses, they are less apt to do "relationship lending" and more likely to engage in pro forma transactions based on financial reports and credit scores (Cole, Goldberg, and White 1999).

Despite a reduction in the number of local lenders, commercial banks remain an important source of start-up funds for many rural entrepreneurs. In part, this is because private lenders are supplemented by a number of government loan guarantee programs operated by the USDA, Small Business Administration (SBA), and Farm Service Agency—all of which target rural small businesses that would otherwise be denied credit. Rural microenterprise lending programs are also gaining in popularity amid growing support from the U.S. Treasury, Community Development Financial Institutions (CDFI) and the SBA's Microloan Program.

Banks and other lending institutions provide funding for less risky ventures that have ensured sustainable cash flows. Equity investments, by contrast, tend to be more "patient" than commercial loans regarding returns and thus are of particular importance to firms that focus on research and development (R&D), and consequently need time to develop prototypes and marketable products. However, venture and other sources of external equity capital are rare in rural areas (Barkley 2003; Barkley and Markley 2001; Rubin 2010).

There are several impediments that keep rural venture capital markets from developing. First, venture capitalists concentrate their investments heavily in technology sectors that have a meager presence in rural places. According to data from Thomson Financial, from the start of 2008 through the second quarter of 2010, over 63 percent of U.S. venture capital investments were concentrated in just four sectors: biotechnology, software, medical devices and equipment, and industrial/energy, with most of the remainder concentrated in other high-growth tech sectors (PricewaterhouseCoopers/National Venture Capital Association MoneyTree™ Report based on data from Thomson Reuters 2010). Even within this limited range of industries, less than 7 percent of venture capital investments are directed at start-up ventures, resulting in a huge gap in seed financing. Second, many of the types of businesses that exist in rural America are family owned and generationally continued, which runs contrary to the favored exit strategy of many venture capitalists, who explicitly target companies ripe for public offerings or likely to be targets for corporate acquisition (Markley 2001). Third, the venture capital industry is highly geographically concentrated, with nearly half of all transactions occurring in the top three regions (Silicon Valley, Boston/Route 128, and LA/Orange County). Venture investors have a strong preference for making investments close by, which reduces the transactions costs associated with overseeing distance ventures and capitalizes on the investors' known support networks of legal, technical, and financial advisers (Florida and Kenney 1988). It is not uncommon for venture capitalists to require those few businesses that receive venture funding to relocate as a condition of investment.

Despite these barriers, rural areas are not at a complete disadvantage. Costs of doing business, such as higher land rents, permitting processes, crime, pollution, and congestion, are typically lower in rural areas (Atkinson 2004; Quigley 2002; Renski 2009). Rural areas have become more adept at using place-based assets to their advantage in attracting professionals and visitors seeking a small-town quality of life or natural amenities (Drabenstott 2003; McDaniel 2000). And although rural firms are less likely to introduce new product innovations, rural firms adopt new productivity-enhancing technologies at rates similar to their urban counterparts (Roth 2000). There are also possible opportunities in the production and distribution of niche market goods, particularly those that leverage rural traditions of quality, craftsmanship, and a connection to place and culture (Dabson 2001), which clearly may be aided by the continued expansion of rural telecommunications and broadband infrastructure. Shifts to renewable energy sources may also shift wealth back to some rural areas, as would a new domestic "on-shoring" of manufacturing facilities in the wake of volatile transportation costs and growing environmental concerns. Finally, and most important, just because high-growth rural entrepreneurs are rare does not mean they are nonexistent: there are many examples of successful entrepreneurs and companies with their roots in rural areas (Corporation for Enterprise Development 2003). The upside of low population is that even modest employment gains, such as those stemming from the expansion of a small business to a medium-size business, can have a noticeable positive impact.

Differences in Rural and Urban Entrepreneurs

The success of any entrepreneurial development strategy ultimately rests upon the collective fortunes of individual businesses. But as mentioned before, there is scant empirical evidence on whether and how rural start-ups differ from their urban counterparts in ways that pertain to development outcomes.

This study makes extensive use of the recently developed Kauffman Firm Survey (KFS)—a representative sample of roughly 5,000 independent companies and sole proprietorships that began operations in 2004.[1] The target population for the KFS is all new businesses in the United States, excluding branches and subsidiaries owned by an existing business or a business inherited from somebody else. The sample frame for the survey was originally based upon new company entries in the Dun & Bradstreet database, which were heavily screened to ensure their status as independent start-up companies. The initial respondents to the 2004 survey were repeatedly surveyed for each of the four subsequent years—distinguishing those that continued operations (survivors) from those ceasing operations (nonsurvivors).

We use the public-access file of the KFS (accessed in the summer of 2010), which contains data corresponding to the first-year survey and the first four follow-up panels. The detailed questionnaire covers topics including firm characteristics, owner characteristics, sources of start-up capital, and performance. The KFS generally does not ask respondents about their perceptions and preferences, thus we can only examine what sources of start-up capital respondents used and not whether they believe there were barriers that prevented them from accessing other sources.

In order to protect the confidentiality of individual respondents in the public-access file, the KFS suppresses certain personal characteristics of owners and firms and reports most continuous variables, such as numbers of employees and investment levels, in ordinal ranges. As such, our analysis is largely descriptive. The KFS public-use data set also does not include detailed geographic information, but it does distinguish metropolitan from nonmetropolitan respondents.[2] We define rural entrants as those founded in nonmetropolitan counties, and urban entrants as all others. While nonmetropolitan is a common proxy for rural, it fails to distinguish different types of rural areas (such as those abutting metropolitan regions), which may be associated with differences in observed rates of survival, growth, and formation (Renski 2011).

Sample Properties and Survival Rates

Our analysis consists mainly of a comparison of the start-year characteristics of rural and urban entrepreneurs. For each characteristic, we also calculate rural and urban survival rates to help discern whether differences in start-up conditions correspond with differences in their eventual success. We define success as survival through all four annual follow-up survey panels. Although the KFS goes to considerable lengths to contact all respondents for follow-up interviews, there is some attrition from year to year. Only companies that were explicitly verified as having gone out of business or remaining in business are included as nonsurvivors or survivors, respectively. Firms that could not be contacted or that refused to participate in later panels are not included. While it is likely that many, if not most, of the firms that could not be contacted went out of business, without verification there is no way to be certain. Thus, while it is likely that we culled some legitimate failures from our sample, leading to higher-than-expected survival rates, we have much greater confidence in the legitimacy of those that remain.

Table 11.1 presents some basic statistics on the sample properties and survival rates of participants in the KFS. The KFS uses a random stratified sample that oversamples start-ups in technologically intensive industries (Hecker 1999). With tech-intensive industries heavily concentrated in metropolitan areas, analysis based on the raw survey data would likely misrepresent true rural-urban differences. We use sampling weights (based on the inverse probability of selection) to adjust for oversampling and sample attrition and to ensure the representativeness of the results.

There were 627 rural start-ups in our sample for 2004, 16 percent of the total sample of 3,876. However, because of the probability sampling weighting, these 627 represent just 15 percent of all start-ups. Of the total of 3,876 entrants in 2004, 2,471 survived through the four panels to yield an overall weighted four-year survival rate of 61 percent. This is generally higher than

Table 11.1

Sample Properties, Kauffman Firm Survey

	Start-ups (2004)			Survivors (2008)		
	Number	Unweighted share %	Weighted share %	Number	Unweighted survival rate %	Weighted survival rate %
Rural	627	16	15	415	66	65
Urban	3,249	84	85	2,056	63	60
Total	3,876	100	100	2,471	64	61

survival rates found in other data sources, although differences in coverage confound direct comparison. For instance, using Bureau of Labor Statistics unemployment insurance files, Knaup (2005) found that only 44 percent of new employer firms (which excludes sole proprietors) survived beyond four full years. An earlier study of self-employed persons by Evans and Leighton (1989) found that within four years of becoming self-employed, 61.5 percent had returned to working for someone else. The KFS attributes its notable higher survival rates to the timing of its sampling procedures that may cause it to miss new ventures that were established in 2004 but failed prior to entry in the Dun & Bradstreet database or the initial KFS screening interview.

There is a general perception that new-firm failure rates are higher in rural areas because of the many aforementioned challenges. Yet there is no solid evidence to back such claims. In fact, among the few studies examining this issue, most have found only negligible differences in rural-urban survival rates (Buss and Lin 1990; Forsyth 2005; Renski 2009; Reynolds and White 1997). In the KFS sample, rural survival rates actually exceed urban survival rates—65 percent to 60 percent, respectively. This may be an anomalous finding resulting from the 2008 recession, although from 2008 through 2009 rural job losses have largely kept pace with the rates seen in metropolitan America (Henderson 2010). We also found that even when stratified by other characteristics, rural and urban survival rates tend to hover around their respective means. To see whether there are relative urban or rural advantages specifically associated with each characteristic, we calculate a survival ratio by dividing each characteristic-specific survival rate by its respective rural or urban mean.

Firm Characteristics: Legal Form, Number of Owners, Size, and Growth

Table 11.2 summarizes our analysis of firm characteristics. Rural start-ups are more likely to be sole proprietorships and less likely to take on more established legal forms, such as limited-liability corporations (LLCs), subchapter S, or C-Corporations. This is not surprising, considering that sole proprietorships are easy to establish and avoid corporate tax reporting requirements. However, they also put the owner at much greater personal liability, as there is little legal protection for the personal assets of the owner if the business fails with outstanding debt obligations.

Conventional wisdom holds that sole proprietorships are more likely to fail than incorporated start-ups. As noted by Shane (2008), incorporated start-ups tend to outperform sole proprietorships in nearly every indicator of success, including survival. Surprisingly, among KFS respondents, sole proprietorships

Table 11.2

Firm Characteristics

	All start-ups		Survival rate		Survival ratio	
	Rural (%)	Urban (%)	Rural (%)	Urban (%)	Rural	Urban
Legal status						
Sole proprietorship	47	34	67	64	1.03	1.06
Limited liability corporation	26	31	66	60	1.02	0.99
Corporation (Subchapter S and C)	19	29	62	58	0.95	0.96
Partnerships (general and limited)	8	5	59	52	0.90	0.86
Number of owners						
One	67	65	67	62	1.02	1.02
Two	25	26	62	58	0.95	0.95
Three or more	8	9	64	58	0.98	0.97
Number of employees						
None	62	58	64	61	0.98	1.01
1 to 2	20	24	66	62	1.01	1.02
3 to 5	10	10	61	56	0.94	0.93
More than 5	8	7	74	57	1.14	0.94

are associated with slightly higher survival rates than incorporated start-ups and partnerships. It may be that sole proprietorships require little investment in terms of either time or monetary resources, and, given an economic downturn, are more likely to persist in a reduced state when a more established business would be forced to close. The added personal liability may also dissuade early departure. The differences in the urban-rural survival ratios are fairly minor—rural entrants do not show a particular advantage for any type of legal status relative to urban entrants, or vice versa. Each differs from their respective rural or urban mean survival rates by similar amounts.

Closely related to legal form is the issue of ownership. Multiple owners spread the risks of failure and can bring a greater range of experience and resources to a new firm. However, this sometimes comes at the cost of autonomy, and for many new firms, secondary owners are not an option. Urban and rural start-ups are nearly identical in this respect; multiple-owner start-ups are quite rare regardless of location. Start-ups with a single owner are also more likely to survive than start-ups with multiple owners, with no measurable differences between rural and urban entrants. Again, this is somewhat contrary to the conventional wisdom, but it corresponds with previous findings on legal form.

Firm size at start-up has also been positively associated with survival (Audretsch and Mahmood 1995; Dunne and Hughes 1994; Renski 2011; Shane 2008). The conventional wisdom is that size (measured by number of workers) entails the benefits of internal scale economies and the ability of the business to access resources that may sustain the company through the rough-and-tumble years of early life. The commitment of resources also sends an important signal to potential investors about the stability of the new venture.

Rural firms do not appear to suffer from a major size disadvantage compared to their urban counterparts. Most new firms start small, regardless of location. Less than 8 percent have five or more employees in their first year, with less than 2 percent having 20 or more employees. Nonemployer firms constitute a slightly larger share of rural start-ups, but there is also a slightly higher share of rural start-ups with five or more employees, leading to a near equivalence in average size. The KFS results support a positive relationship between size and survival, but it is not strictly monotonic. Nor is it consistent across urban and rural firms. Keeping in mind the relatively small sample size of large entrants, rural start-ups with more than five workers have a considerably high survival rate of 74 percent. This pattern does not hold for urban start-ups, where firms with more than three employees have below-average survival prospects. It is likely that the size range of KFS respondents is too limited to show the type of consistent size-survival relationships found by studies using larger databases that contained more instances of large start-ups.

Our final firm characteristic is employment growth. To investigate whether rural areas are deficient in growth-oriented entrepreneurs, we restrict our sample to only those start-ups that survived through the fourth follow-up panel, measuring growth as the difference between the number of workers in 2008 and 2004. Even within the limited time span covered by the KFS, the data support previous findings that new firms in rural areas create fewer jobs (Henderson 2002; Renski 2009). Although few start-ups added large numbers of new workers between 2004 and 2008, rural entrants were much more likely to have remained the same size, lost workers, or added relatively few workers (Figure 11.1). Likewise, urban entrants were more highly represented among those entrants adding six or more workers.

Industry, Technological Intensity, and Innovation

One possible explanation for lagging employment growth is that rural areas lack entrepreneurs in emerging industries offering the greatest growth potential. Instead they tend to form in industries with relatively low entry barriers, resulting in fairly high rural entry rates but steep competition in shrinking local markets with fewer opportunities for expansion.

Industrial aggregation in the public-use KFS confounds a finely detailed comparison of the industry mix of rural and urban start-ups. Many broad industry sectors contain both high- and low-growth industries. But even within these constraints, the KFS data show some revealing differences (Table 11.3). There is a notably higher propensity for rural entrepreneurs to start businesses in retail, and, to a somewhat lesser extent, agriculture, construction, and other services. There are relatively fewer rural start-ups in higher value-added services, such as professional, scientific, and technical services/information, administrative support and waste management services, and finance and insurance. These types of industries are highly sensitive to the existence of external economies and the location preferences of the highly educated workers who tend to favor urban cultural and lifestyle amenities.

We see some distinct rural-urban variations in survival rates by industry that cannot be explained purely by differences in rural-urban means. However, the small numbers of rural survivors in many sectors cautions against drawing strong conclusions. Overall, rural start-ups have above-average survival rates in agriculture, construction, professional and scientific services, administrative and support services, as well as in the combined arts, entertainment, recreation, accommodations, and food services sector. Rural start-ups in manufacturing, wholesale, retail, transportation and warehousing, and health care, social assistance/educational services have below-average survival rates. Comparing the rural-to-urban survival ratios, we see possible relative rural

Figure 11.1 **Histogram of Net Employment Change Among Rural and Urban Start-ups**

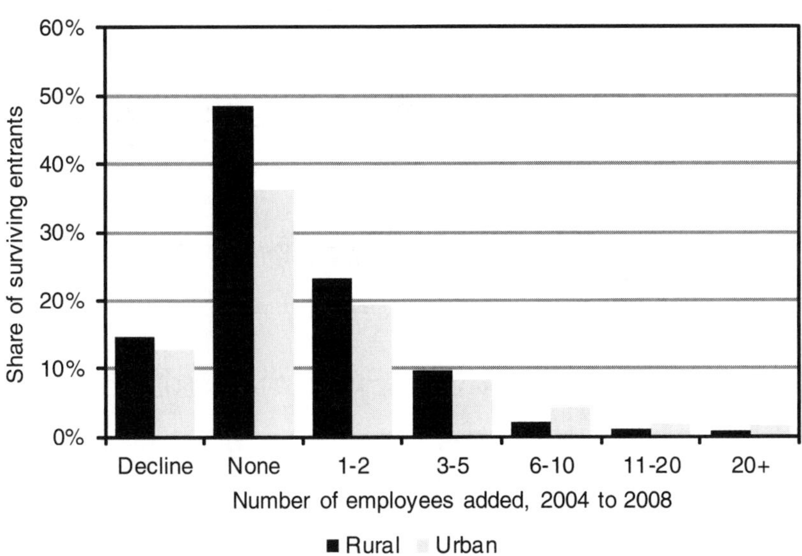

survival advantages in agriculture; retail; finance, insurance and real estate (FIRE) services; administrative, support, and waste management services; and arts, entertainment, recreation, accommodations, and food services—the later reflecting the successful development of recreational and heritage-based tourism. Rural entrants may be at greater risk than their urban counterparts in wholesale trade, transportation and warehousing, health care, and in other sectors that are particularly sensitive to market size and access.

Technological intensity and innovation is another area in which we see clear differences between rural and urban start-ups. The KFS includes several different potential indicators of innovation. The first classifies firms by the technological intensity of their primary industry, based on the classification developed by Hecker (1999). Only 3 percent of rural firms were classified as operating in tech-intensive industries, compared to 6 percent of urban start-ups. And despite the higher risk associated with emerging technologies, tech-intensive start-ups have higher survival rates than other start-ups, whether rural or urban.

Primary industry codes may over- or understate the innovativeness of individual firms. A firm may be innovative even if operating in a low-tech industry, or, conversely, may be at the low-tech end of a high-tech industry. Another indicator of innovation is the establishment of intellectual property rights through patenting and copyrighting. New firms can also acquire ac-

Table 11.3

Industry, Technological Intensity, and Innovation

	All start-ups		Survival rate		Survival ratio	
	Rural (%)	Urban (%)	Rural (%)	Urban (%)	Rural	Urban
Primary industry sector						
Agriculture, forestry, fishing and hunting	3	1	90	69	1.38	1.13
Construction	12	10	71	62	1.08	1.03
Manufacturing	5	6	57	66	0.88	1.08
Wholesale trade	5	5	44	58	0.68	0.96
Retail trade	21	14	61	52	0.93	0.85
Transportation and warehousing	4	3	49	56	0.75	0.93
Finance, insurance and real estate	7	12	67	58	1.02	0.95
Professional, scientific and tech. services/information	13	20	72	67	1.10	1.11
Administrative support and waste mgt. services	7	10	74	61	1.13	1.01
Health care, social assistance and educational services	3	4	61	64	0.93	1.06
Arts, entertainment, accommodations and food	6	5	71	49	1.09	0.81
Other services (ex. public administration)	12	10	65	64	1.00	1.06
Technological intensity and innovation						
Technology-intensive industry	3	6	73	68	1.11	1.13
Have patent(s)	1	2	69	63	1.06	1.03
Have copyright(s)	6	9	68	65	1.05	1.08
License in patent(s)	2	2	34	51	0.52	0.85
License in copyright(s)	3	4	67	63	1.03	1.04
R&D expenditures	13	19	70	62	1.08	1.02

cess to cutting-edge ideas by licensing-in patents and copyrights developed by others. Of course not all firms patent or copyright their ideas and inventions, but these indicators do provide a general barometer of innovation. Few start-ups hold patents or copyrights in their first year, though urban firms are more likely to protect their intellectual property through both legal avenues. Licensing-in is also rare, with only small differences between urban and rural start-ups. Start-ups with patents and copyrights have slightly higher-than-average survival rates, while the survival rates for firms licensing in patents are considerably below average. However, the small number of respondents reporting patenting or copyrighting activity makes interpretation of survival rates and ratios difficult.

Our final measure of firm-level innovation is company expenditures on R&D. The KFS measures R&D by a simple binary indicator of whether the start-up had any (or no) R&D expenditures rather than by the amount of R&D expenditures. Thirteen percent of rural start-ups had first-year R&D expenditures, compared to 19 percent of urban start-ups. And, while fewer in number, rural start-ups with R&D expenditures had above-average survival rates and slightly higher survival ratios compared to their urban counterparts.

In summary, while no single indicator provides a unitary barometer of innovation, the triangulation of multiple metrics all point to the same conclusion—rural start-ups are less innovation and technologically oriented than their urban counterparts. However, although innovation is fairly rare, innovative activity is generally associated with above-average rural start-up survival rates.

Owner Experience and Education

The life experience of the start-up's founder(s) also affects the start-up's prospects for survival and growth (Reynolds 2007; Reynolds and White 1997; Shane 2003, 2008). There are several types of experience that bear on entrepreneurial outcomes: age of the founder, prior industry experience, prior experience starting a new business, and education (Table 11.4).

Age reflects the general life experience, maturity, and potential asset base of the founder. Despite common perceptions that entrepreneurship is a young person's game, the peak age for starting one's own company is close to 40 (Bonte, Falck, and Heblich 2009). Founders of typical rural start-ups are slightly older than their urban counterparts, corresponding with the older demographic profile of rural America. In rural areas, the median owner is between 44 and 54 years old, while the median owner of an urban start-up is between 35 and 44 years old. However, even in urban areas, very few firms are founded by persons under the age of 25 (less than 2 percent). The cor-

Table 11.4

Owner Experience and Education

	All start-ups		Survival rate		Survival ratio	
	Rural (%)	Urban (%)	Rural (%)	Urban (%)	Rural	Urban
Age						
Under 35 years	18	19	60	55	0.92	0.91
35–44 years	30	34	65	61	1.00	1.00
45–54 years	31	29	67	63	1.02	1.04
55–64 years	16	16	74	61	1.14	1.02
65+ years	5	3	63	58	0.96	0.96
Years of industry experience						
None	14	12	67	53	1.03	0.87
1 to 4	27	23	63	57	0.97	0.94
5 to 9	14	17	61	56	0.94	0.93
10 to 19	23	24	66	62	1.02	1.03
20 to 24	8	9	73	68	1.13	1.13
25 or more	13	15	65	69	1.00	1.13
Number of other business start-ups						
None	58	59	68	59	1.04	0.98
1 to 2	31	31	64	63	0.98	1.04
3 to 4	8	7	70	60	1.07	1.00
5 or more	3	3	46	59	0.71	0.98
Educational attainment						
No high school diploma	4	2	67	43	1.03	0.71
High school graduate (diploma or equivalent)	19	12	57	62	0.87	1.03
Some college, but no degree	23	22	65	55	1.00	0.92
Associates, technical, trade or vocational degree	17	14	69	60	1.06	1.00
Bachelor's degree	25	31	68	63	1.04	1.04
Master's degree or higher	12	18	72	63	1.10	1.05

respondence between owner age and firm survival follows a U-shaped pattern. Owners younger than 35 years have the lowest survival rates. Founders above the age of 65 also have below-average survival rates, possibly due to the increased likelihood of the owner's retiring during the five-year study period. Survival rates peak at a slightly older age for rural owners. Owners between the ages of 55 and 64 years old have the highest survival rates in rural areas. In urban areas, the highest rates are for owners between 45 and 54 years old.

The founder's depth of experience in the industry also corresponds with likelihood of success. With experience comes greater insight into market conditions and stronger relationships with important suppliers, potential clients, and potential financers. Few businesses are started in industries in which the founder has no prior experience. Instead, entrepreneurs draw upon their past work histories when starting their new ventures (Renski 2010; Sorenson and Audia 2000; Stam 2007). More than 88 percent of KFS founders reported having some prior experience in the same industry as their current start-up. Despite being slightly older, the typical rural entrepreneur had fewer years of same-industry experience than urban founders (a median of eight years for rural, 10 years for urban). For urban founders, those with the least experience have the lowest survival rates and those with the most experience have the highest. The pattern is more erratic for rural founders. Survival rates of rural founders with no experience are above average rural averages, dip for experience between one and 10 years, and peak with experience between 20 to 24 years.

Beneficial experience may also come from having previously gone through the process of starting a business. Starting a new business is fraught with uncertainty and judgment calls, and the process entails considerable learning by doing (Pakes and Ericson 1998). Rural and urban entrepreneurs are roughly equivalent in this regard—most have never tried to start a business before. However, among those that have, a higher share of urban entrepreneurs (41 percent compared to 33 percent for rural) have experience starting another business in the same industry as their current enterprise. The data also suggest limits to the benefits of prior start-up experience. Rural founders with no experience starting a business have slightly higher survival rates than those founding one or two other businesses, but slightly less than those forming three or four. Among urban start-ups, survival rates are highest among those having started one or two other firms.

The final indicator of experience is that earned through formal education. Several studies show a positive relationship between the owner's education and the likelihood of starting a new business and survival (Bates 1990; Brüderl, Preisendörfer, and Ziegler 1992; Reynolds and White 1997). Rural entrepreneurs tend to have less formal education, mirroring lower rural educational levels overall. Thirty-eight percent of rural entrepreneurs have bachelor's degrees or higher, far below the 49 percent of urban entrepreneurs. Likewise, rural areas also have higher shares of entrepreneurs with no postsecondary education. The KFS data show a generally positive association between educational attainment and survival. The unexpectedly high survival rates of rural founders without high school diplomas is based on very few sample points and should probably be disregarded. More generally, those with a bachelor's degree or higher have higher survival rates. Entrepreneurs with graduate degrees appear to do particularly well in rural areas, with survival rates well above rural averages. There also seems to be a higher level of relative success among rural entrepreneurs with an associate's or technical degree.

Market Orientation and Sales

During their first year, most firms earn revenues through the sale of goods or services (Table 11.5). Rural firms are especially likely to sell a product or service (88 percent) compared to urban start-ups (81 percent). On the one hand, sales are an important source of revenue and send a positive market signal of the future viability of the venture, as signified by above-average survival rates. On the other hand, the higher share of companies with sales also reflects the concentration of rural businesses in retail and personal services and the underrepresentation of R&D-oriented businesses, which may need years before bringing new goods to market.

Among those with sales, urban firms are far more likely to be suppliers to other businesses, while rural firms are more likely to sell to individual consumers, and, to a lesser extent, to the government. On average, sales to other businesses make up only 29 percent of the market for rural start-ups, compared to 36 percent of first-year sales for urban start-ups. Thirty-seven percent of urban start-ups with sales view other businesses as their primary (50 percent or more) market, compared to only 29 percent of rural start-ups. For rural firms, sales to individuals account for roughly 67 percent of sales, compared to 61 percent for urban start-ups. Few firms view the government as their primary market, although rural firms are more likely to make at least some sales to government clients.

Market orientation also affects survival prospects. Rural firms with a high (50 percent or more) dependency on business sales actually have lower survival rates than those with little or no sales to other businesses. The opposite holds for urban start-ups—a higher share of business sales corresponds with higher survival rates. Rural firms that are predominantly focused on sales to individuals had higher survival rates than other rural establishments. By

Table 11.5

Market Orientation and Sales

	All start-ups		Survival rate		Survival ratio	
	Rural (%)	Urban (%)	Rural (%)	Urban (%)	Rural	Urban
Company has sales?	88	81	67	62	1.03	1.03
Percentage of sales to other businesses						
None	36	37	71	58	1.09	0.95
1 to 24	28	20	66	58	1.01	0.96
25 to 49	7	7	75	63	1.15	1.04
50 to 74	7	8	61	63	0.94	1.05
75 or more	21	29	62	71	0.95	1.18
Percentage of sales to government						
None	78	85	67	61	1.03	1.01
1 to 24	16	8	64	71	0.99	1.17
25 to 49	2	3	62	63	0.95	1.04
50 to 74	1	1	100	70	1.53	1.16
75 or more	3	2	73	67	1.12	1.10
Percentage of sales to individuals						
None	12	21	63	69	0.96	1.15
1 to 24	11	11	64	72	0.99	1.19
25 to 49	6	5	55	65	0.85	1.08
50 to 74	8	7	74	61	1.13	1.01
75 or more	63	56	68	57	1.04	0.95

contrast, urban start-ups seemed to do relatively better when they were less dependent on sales to individuals. The impact of the 2008 recession may explain these divergent patterns, with urban retailers and service providers that focus on specialty and niche markets especially hurt by curtailed discretionary purchases. High shares of sales to the government are associated with a higher likelihood of survival, particularly for rural firms, although the small numbers of respondents with sizeable sales to the government make these survival rate calculations unreliable.

Revenues, Profits, and Losses

To succeed in the long term, nearly all private enterprises must make a profit. Yet, roughly half of all new firms do not show profits during their first year (Table 11.6). Nor are first-year profits a clear indicator of eventual survival, particularly for rural start-ups: the survival rates of rural start-ups with first-year profits are on par with those with first-year losses.

Having revenues during the start-year of operations is a better predictor of rural survival than profits, strictly speaking. Rural start-ups are far more likely to have revenues during the start-year than urban start-ups, but they have a near-equal likelihood of showing first-year profits. This may reflect the industry mix of rural entrants, which favors sectors such as retail, personal services, and construction, where early revenues are more common. The median rural start-up has modest first-year revenues, falling within a range between $10, 000 and $25,000. This is slightly higher than the median urban start-up's revenues of between $5,000 and $10,000, primarily due to the higher number of urban starts without first-year revenues. If one only considers firms with some first-year revenues, the median range for both rural and urban start-ups is between $25,000 and $100,000. Very few start-ups (less than 2 percent) have first-year revenues in excess of $1 million, regardless of location. First-year revenues also correspond to above-average survival rates for both rural and urban start-ups. However, rural firms seem capable of getting by with a lower level of revenues (less than $1,000)—presumably due to lower business costs. The situation is reversed at the high end: urban start-ups with revenues in excess of $25,000 have a higher relative likelihood of survival.

First-year profits are more important to the survival of urban start-ups. Rural entrants with first-year profits are just as likely to fail as those without first-year profits. As found with revenues, rural start-ups with lower levels seem capable of surviving at a lower level of profitability. Urban start-ups, by contrast, have higher-than-average survival rates for all levels of first-year profitability. Commensurate with the evidence on revenues and profits, rural start-ups also appear to be able to weather small first-year losses (less than $3,000) without negative

Table 11.6

First-Year Revenues, Profits, and Losses

	All start-ups		Survival rate		Survival ratio	
	Rural (%)	Urban (%)	Rural (%)	Urban (%)	Rural	Urban
Revenues	**73**	**65**	**67**	**62**	**1.02**	**1.03**
Amount of revenues (of those with revenues)						
$1,000 or less	7	7	71	57	1.08	0.95
$1,001 to $5,000	11	12	74	63	1.14	1.03
$5,001 to $10,000	11	9	66	57	1.01	0.95
$10,001 to $25,000	16	16	73	64	1.13	1.06
$25,001 to $100,000	26	29	59	63	0.90	1.04
More than $100,000	28	27	66	65	1.02	1.08
Profits	**48**	**46**	**65**	**65**	**1.00**	**1.08**
Profit level (of those reporting profits)						
Less than $1,000	13	12	74	67	1.13	1.10
$1,001 to $3,000	13	12	67	68	1.03	1.12
$3,001 to $5,000	10	9	70	72	1.07	1.18
$5,001 to $10,000	13	16	65	69	0.99	1.14
$10,001 to $25,000	27	20	64	69	0.98	1.15
More than $25,000	24	32	63	66	0.97	1.09
Losses	**52**	**54**	**66**	**57**	**1.01**	**0.94**
Amount of loss (of those reporting losses)						
Less than $1,000	13	13	76	56	1.16	0.93
$1,001 to $3,000	17	15	70	55	1.07	0.90
$3,001 to $5,000	9	14	55	61	0.85	1.00
$5,001 to $10,000	21	18	58	62	0.90	1.02
$10,001 to $25,000	22	18	67	59	1.02	0.97
More than $25,000	18	23	61	53	0.94	0.87

effects on five-year survival prospects. The same does not hold for urban start-ups, which face reduced survival prospects across a broader range of losses. Both rural and urban firms with sizable first-year losses (greater than $25,000) face diminished survival prospects, although the heavy first-year losses appear relatively more hazardous for urban start-ups.

Start-up Financing

Entrepreneurship policy and research emphasize that acquiring adequate start-up capital is a key to success, particularly in the years before profitability. There are three general sources of start-up funds for new businesses: equity investment; personal debt taken out in the name of, or against the personal assets of, the owner; and debt taken out against the assets of the business (business debt). All sources of financing are also characterized by whether they are sourced internally by the owners of the company or from external investors or lenders.

Equity

Of the three primary sources of start-up capital, equity is by far the most common (Table 11.7). Roughly 83 percent of start-ups receive some type of equity investment in their first year. However, most of this comes from the personal savings of owners, and in relatively small amounts. Eighty-one percent of all start-ups receive equity investment from their owners in their first year. For roughly 78 percent, the primary owner is the only equity investor in the company.

It is commonly argued that rural communities are underserved by external equity markets, and that this lack of external equity funding represents a major barrier to new firm formation and growth (Barkley 2003; Barkley and Markley 2001; Markley 2001; Rubin 2010). We found no appreciable differences between rural and urban start-ups in this regard. The simple truth is that obtaining outside equity in your first year is rare, whether you start your business in a rural or urban setting. Roughly 9 percent of urban starts-up received outsider equity investment compared to 8 percent of rural start-ups, with relatives making up the largest share (5 percent). Examination of the detailed sources of external equity provides some evidence of a rural-urban venture financing gap, with near-zero percent of rural firms receiving venture financing during the first year, compared to 1 percent of urban firms. Government-sponsored equity slightly favors rural start-ups, 2 percent rural versus 1 percent urban. However, the small numbers of KFS firms reporting first-year outside equity calls for extreme caution in interpreting these relative shares.

While the vast majority of start-ups receive equity investment from some source, the amounts tend to be modest (Figure 11.2). Among those with first-

Table 11.7

Sources of Start-up Financing

	All start-ups		Survival rate		Survival ratio	
	Rural (%)	Urban (%)	Rural (%)	Urban (%)	Rural	Urban
Equity (any source)	**83**	**83**	**64**	**60**	**0.99**	**1.00**
Owner(s)	81	81	65	61	0.99	1.00
Relatives	5	5	63	52	0.97	0.86
Angels (nonrelative individuals)	2	3	58	59	0.89	0.97
Other external (incl. govt., venture, and other)	2	2	79	62	1.21	1.02
Personal debt (any source)	**53**	**50**	**62**	**58**	**0.96**	**0.95**
Credit cards	50	49	67	61	1.03	1.01
Bank loans	24	18	61	59	0.93	0.97
Business credit cards (in name of owner[s])	25	30	69	62	1.06	1.02
Loan from family	10	11	60	52	0.93	0.86
Other personal debt or loan	3	3	62	59	0.95	0.98
Business debt (any source)	**27**	**25**	**68**	**60**	**1.04**	**0.99**
Business credit card	19	26	75	65	1.15	1.07
Credit line	13	8	65	64	1.00	1.06
Loan from commercial bank	13	6	65	59	0.99	0.98
Business loan, family	2	3	57	53	0.88	0.87
Business loan, government	1	1	81	80	1.24	1.32
Loan from nonbank financial institution	2	2	76	58	1.16	0.96
Other business debt	2	3	53	55	0.81	0.91

Figure 11.2 **Share of First-year Financing by Amount and Source (Energy, Personal Debt, or Business Debt) Among Start-ups with at Least Some Support Within the Respective Source Type**

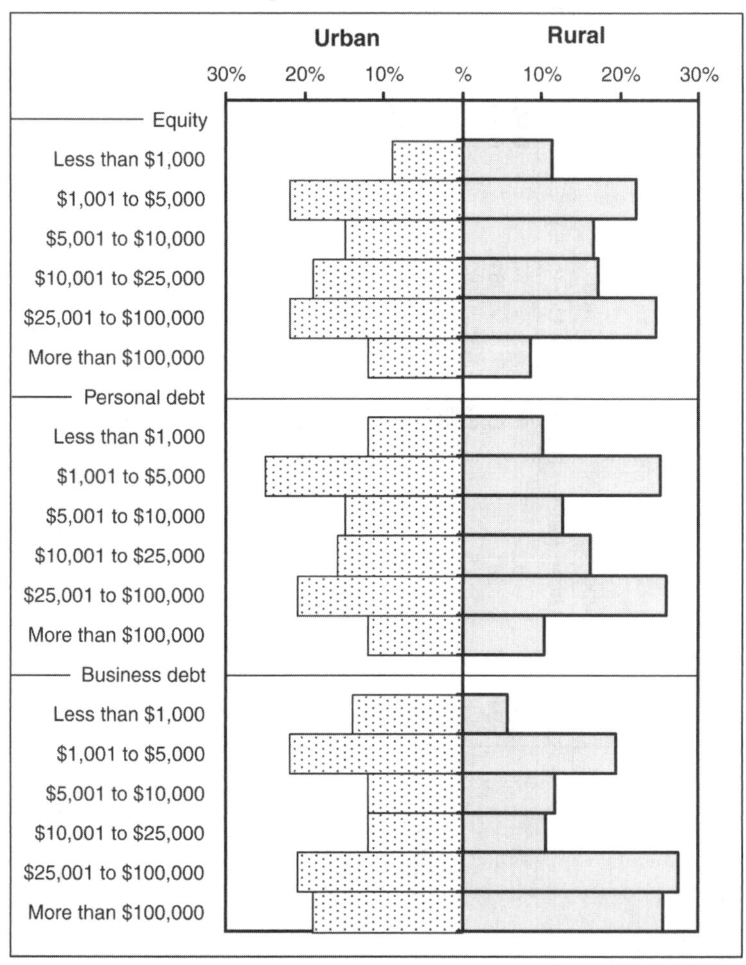

year equity financing, the median falls within the range of $10,000 to $25,000 for both rural and urban start-ups. Slightly higher shares of rural firms have low-level equity investment (less than $1,000), with urban start-ups a bit more likely to take on equity in excess of $100,000. Despite its rarity, outside equity is more important for start-ups requiring larger amounts of capital. Among those firms with at least some equity financing, outsider equity is more prevalent among start-ups receiving first-year equity injections of $100,000 or more (Figure 11.3). Forty-two percent of urban firms and 37 percent of rural

Figure 11.3 **Share of Companies with First-year Equity Investments by Amount: Entrants with Outside Equity Compared to Those Without**

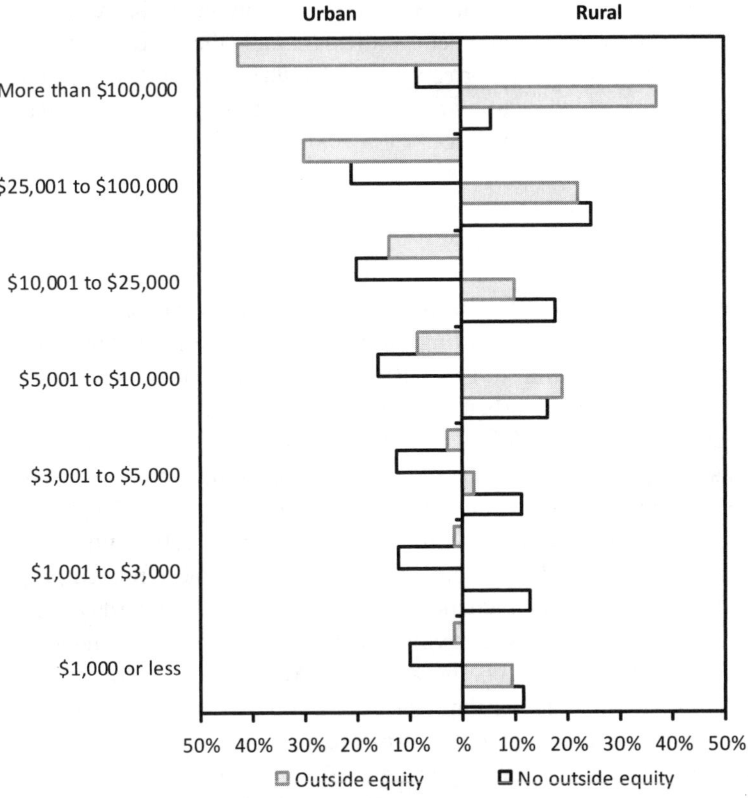

firms with outside equity investment had total first-year equity in excess of $100,000, compared to only 8 percent and 6 percent of firms without outside capital, respectively. There is also a larger share of rural start-ups (9 percent) with external equity investments in very small amounts (less than $1,000) compared to urban start-ups.

The source of first-year equity investment seems to have some relationship to survival, but due to the small numbers of start-ups with external equity, the data are somewhat erratic, and further verification is needed. Start-ups receiving owner equity fall close to their respective averages in both rural and urban areas, with no corresponding difference in the survival rates of start-ups where the owner did or did not invest their own personal savings. Investments from relatives correspond with below-average survival rates, particularly in urban areas where only 52 percent survived five years or beyond. It may be that family investment in urban areas conveys difficulty securing other forms of investment. Investment from angel investors is associated with below-average survival rates for rural firms, although the small numbers of rural respondents with angel funding warns that these estimates may be highly unstable. On the upside, investment from other outsiders (namely the government) in rural start-ups, while just as rare, corresponds with high survival rates—presumably due to both the added scrutiny and the added technical assistance that may accompany the capital infusion.

Personal Debt

Personal debt is the second-most-common source of start-up investment capital. Roughly one-half of respondents had taken on some personal debt on behalf of their business during the first year of operations, with slightly higher rates among rural start-ups. Rural start-ups are more likely to take on more personal debt than urban start-ups, with median personal debt levels of between $10,001 and $25,000 for rural start-ups and $5,001 to $10,000 for urban start-ups. Overall, the relative shares of personal debt used to finance first operations are roughly similar to those found for personal equity.

Credit cards are the most common form of personal debt, with 50 percent of owners having used a personal credit card for business-related purposes and 30 percent carrying a balance on their personal credit cards at the time of the survey. Among those carrying balances, debt levels were modest, with a median credit card balance between $3,000 and $5,000. Business credit cards issued in the name of the owner are also fairly common—used by 25 percent of rural and 30 percent of urban respondents. Because most owners keep their balances low, simply using personal credit cards does not have a negative impact on survival prospects. Rural and urban survival rates for those using personal credit cards or business credit cards in the owner's name are both slightly higher than their respective averages.

Personal bank loans are a particularly important source of start-up capital for rural businesses. Twenty-four percent of rural businesses used a personal bank loan to help start their business, compared to only 18 percent of urban businesses. Personal bank loans often take the form of an additional home mortgage or other equity-backed loan—in which case the higher rural usage rate may reflect greater access to collateral and assets, such as owning one's home or land. Taking on a personal loan to help support the business is associated with modestly lower survival rates—but only for rural firms. Personal loans from family members were found among roughly 10 percent of the respondents—twice as common as equity investment from relatives—with only marginal differences between rural and urban start-ups. And like commercial sources of debt, loans from family also correspond with below-average survival rates, particularly in urban areas.

Business Debt

New businesses use personal debt with much higher frequency than they use business debt to finance their start-up operations. Personal debt is typically easier to access, especially in cases where the start-up has no or few business assets to start with. Slightly more than a quarter of KFS respondents took on debt in the name of the business during the first year, with rural shares two percentage points higher than urban shares. Business debt also is relatively more important for financing investments in excess of $100,000, particularly so for rural entrants. Rural start-ups that secured business debt also had higher survival rates than those taking on personal debt or equity, as well as higher survival ratios relative to urban start-ups with business debt. This may be because urban firms are much more likely to use business credit cards, while rural firms are more likely to secure business lines of credit and commercial bank loans—the latter two financing methods typically requiring a higher standard of financial solvency. As found for equity, government loans correspond with very high survival rates. And, as found for personal debt, business loans from family had relatively low survival rates. However, the sample size for respondents with government or family business loans is small and the survival rates may not be representative.

Summary and Conclusions

This chapter uses data from the Kauffman Firm Survey to profile entrepreneurship in rural America, with a particular focus on how rural entrants differ from urban entrants in their start-year characteristics. To our knowledge, this chapter represents the first comprehensive empirical comparison of rural and urban entrepreneurs based on a data set covering both employer and nonemployer firms.

This study confirms many of the commonly perceived challenges to entrepreneurship as a paradigm for rural development. Relatively more rural entrepreneurs start life as sole proprietors and they are less likely to add workers within the subsequent four years. Part of the problem may be that rural start-ups are overrepresented in low-growth and less tech-oriented sectors such as retail and personal services. They are also less likely to invest in R&D or to seek intellectual-property protections. The owners of rural start-ups are slightly older than urban entrepreneurs, but have fewer years of same-industry experience and formal education. Rural start-ups are more likely to have first-year sales and to focus more of their sales efforts on individual consumers; they are less likely to have other businesses as major clients.

Other results challenge some of the common assumptions about the differences between rural and urban entrepreneurs. For the bulk of characteristics examined, the differences between rural and urban entrepreneurs were modest or negligible. This was particularly true in our examination of the sources of start-up capital. Rural and urban firms use equity, personal debt, and business debt in roughly proportionate shares. The primary sources of start-up capital for rural and urban start-ups alike are personal savings of the owner and credit cards. Rural start-ups are more likely to rely on bank loans and business lines of credit, while urban firms are more likely to utilize business credits cards, but both are similarly reliant on equity investments or loans from relatives. External equity investments from nonrelatives (such as venture capital and angel investors) are exceedingly rare in all cases. Most new businesses start with modest levels of capitalization, although bank loans and external equity are more common for larger levels of capitalization.

Another major finding is that rural entrepreneurs have higher survival rates than urban firms, whereas most previous studies found no significant differences. There were also relatively few characteristics that clearly showed survival advantages specific to either rural or urban areas. While survival rates often differ by start-up characteristics, firms with a given characteristic are likely to have a similar relation to the overall urban or rural survival average. There were exceptions—cases in which urban and rural survival ratios were very different—but in many of these, reliable interpretation of the differences was confounded by the exceedingly small number of rural survivors in the sample. Further investigation is needed.

More work is required to disentangle the root causes of the variation in rural and urban survival rates. Differences in the rural-urban industry mix are one likely source. New firm survival and employment growth rates are known to vary substantially and systematically by industry (Geroski 1995). These industry-specific differences are also likely to transcend other start-up characteristics, such as legal form, R&D intensity, capitalization requirements, and first-year sales and profitability. A multivariate model specification can help tease out the separate contributions of these influences, but such an analysis is beyond this chapter's goal, which is simply to provide a preliminary investigation over a broad spectrum of measures.

So what does our analysis suggest for rural development policy? First, it suggests that if entrepreneurship is to be advanced as a strategy for creating jobs and wealth in rural areas, emphasis must be placed on overcoming the barriers of limited internal markets through exports, import replacement, and market development. The small and declining local population base of many rural areas does not leave much room for growth in nonbasic sectors such as retail and personal services. Because rural areas have limited external networks, economic developers can also play an important role as liaisons between rural entrepreneurs and the larger world by helping businesses identify potential customers and distributors, brand and market their goods, and take part in trade promotion by, for example, including regional businesses in selected trade shows or sponsoring business website development. Expansion of broadband infrastructure is essential to such efforts. While it is overly optimistic to think that high-speed Internet access will lead to droves of lone-eagle professionals and technology companies repopulating the American frontier, it does make it possible for potential niche and craft-based rural business to access distant markets at a fairly low cost.

Considerable effort must also be made to diversify the industry mix of rural entrants, preferably into emerging markets. Given that most entrepreneurs tend to stay close to home and start their businesses in markets in which they have previous experience, the fact that there are few entrepreneurs in high-growth markets indicates that there are few rural incumbent firms in those markets. There is no simple fix for this problem, as the forces of agglomeration and innovation heavily favor the concentration of knowledge-intensive industries in metropolitan areas. However, that is not to say that entrepreneurs in high-growth markets cannot emerge in rural areas. Federal, state, and regional economic developers must be prepared to assist them when they arise by offering a portfolio of flexible finance options and technical assistance services. Workforce development and continuing education in management, sales, business planning, marketing, and technology are also important, as rural factory and farm workers rarely receive the kind of varied on-the-job experience necessary for successfully running a small business.

Government policy is particularly important in supporting the financial structures needed for rural entrepreneurial development. Commercial lending institutions are critical to rural start-ups' financing, and the recent wave of bank failures and the continued consolidation of the banking industry does not bode well for a competitive rural lending market or the continued existence of the relational transactions that have historically characterized hometown banking. Federal and state regulatory policy must ensure that rural credit markets remain competitive and committed to local investment and local investment targets such as those encouraged through the Community Reinvestment Act.

Government must also be prepared to take a lead role as a rural small business financer through the expansion of lending guarantee programs and low-interest loans, as a direct provider of seed and technology development grants, and by providing the initial capitalization for nontraditional venture and equity funds. Private venture capital plays almost no role in the rural economy, and given insufficient deal flow, information asymmetries, and higher transactions costs, it is doubtful that private equity markets will move into rural areas any time soon (Rubin 2010). Publicly supported nontraditional venture and development funds play an important role in helping to fill this void, although few are targeted to investments in rural areas (Barkley 2003; Barkley and Markley 2001; Rubin 2010). There are many different models for such funds, but most operate on a "double-bottom" basis, accepting lower returns in exchange for social and economic benefits. The best of these programs also tend to bundle financial with technical support in key areas such as management, business planning, and market development to overcome the liabilities of size, distance, and the limited education or experience of rural small-business owners. Unfortunately, such funds tend to be woefully undercapitalized, and given current state and federal budgets, they are unlikely to be expanded in the near future.

Disclaimer

Certain data included herein are derived from the Kauffman Firm Survey release 4.1 public-use data file. Any opinions, findings, and conclusions or recommendations expressed in this material are those of the author(s) and do not necessarily reflect the views of the Ewing Marion Kauffman Foundation.

Notes

1. More information on the Kauffman Firm Survey, including its sampling methods and copies of the questionnaire, is available at www.kauffman.org/kfs/.
2. The metro-nonmetro designation was added to the public-use KFS file at the special request of the authors.

References

Acs, Z.J., and C. Armington. 2006. *Entrepreneurship, Geography, and American Economic Growth.* Cambridge, MA: Cambridge University Press.

Acs, Z.J., and E.J. Malecki. 2003. Entrepreneurship in rural America: The big picture. In *Main Streets of Tomorrow: Growing and Financing Rural Entrepreneurs,* ed. M. Drabenstott, 21–29. Kansas City, MO: Center for the Study of Rural America, Federal Reserve Bank of Kansas City.

Advanced Research Technologies. 2005. *The Innovation-Entrepreneurship Nexus.* Powell, OH, Small Business Administration Office of Advocacy.

Atkinson, R.D. 2004. *Reversing Rural America's Economic Decline: The Case for a National Balanced Growth Strategy.* Policy report, February. Washington, DC: Progressive Policy Institute.

Audretsch, D.B., M.C. Keilbach, and E.E. Lehmann. 2006. *Entrepreneurship and Economic Growth.* New York: Oxford University Press.

Audretsch, D.B., and T. Mahmood. 1995. New firm survival: New results using a hazard function. *Review of Economics and Statistics* 77(1): 97–103.

Barkley, D.L. 2003. Policy options for equity financing for rural entrepreneurs. In *Main Streets of Tomorrow: Growing and Financing Rural Entrepreneurs,* ed. M. Drabenstott, 97–105. Kansas City, MO: Center for the Study of Rural America, Federal Reserve Bank of Kansas City.

Barkley, D.L., and D.M. Markley. 2001. Nontraditional sources of venture capital for rural America. *Rural America* 16(1): 19–26.

Bates, T. 1990. Entrepreneurial human capital inputs and small business longevity. *Review of Economics and Statistics* 72(4): 551–59.

———. 1993. Theories of entrepreneurship. In *Theories of Local Economic Development: Perspectives from Across the Disciplines,* ed. R.D. Bingham and R. Mier, ch. 12. Newbury Park, CA: Sage.

Bonte, W., O. Falck, and S. Heblich. 2009. The impact of regional age structure on entrepreneurship. *Economic Geography* 85(3): 269–87.

Brüderl, J., P. Preisendörfer, and R. Ziegler. 1992. Survival chances of newly founded business organizations. *American Sociological Review* 57(2): 227–42.

Buss, T.F., and X. Lin. 1990. Business survival in rural America: A three-state study. *Growth and Change* 21(3): 1–8.

Cole, R., L.G. Goldberg, and L. White. 1999. Cookie-cutter versus character: The micro-structure of small business lending by large and small banks. *The Journal of Financial and Quantitative Analysis* 39(2): 227–51.

Corporation for Enterprise Development. 2003. *Mapping Rural Entrepreneurship.* Battle Creek, MI: W.E. Kellogg Foundation.

Costa, D., and M. Kahn. 2000. Power couples: Changes in the locational choice of the college educated, 1940–1990. *Quarterly Journal of Economics* 115(4): 1287–315.

Dabson, B. 2001. *Supporting Rural Entrepreneurship: Exploring Policy Options for a New Rural America.* Kansas City, MO: Center for the Study of Rural America, Federal Reserve Bank of Kansas City.

Drabenstott, M. 2003. A new era for rural policy. *Economic Review* 88(4): 81–98.

Drabenstott, M., and J. Henderson. 2006. A new rural economy: A new role for public policy. *Main Street Economist* 1(4): 1–6.

Drabenstott, M., N. Novack, and B. Abraham. 2003. Main streets of tomorrow: Growing and financing rural entrepreneurs—a conference summary. *Economic Review* 88(3): 73–84.

Dunne, P., and A. Hughes. 1994. Age, size, growth and survival: UK companies in the 1980s. *Journal of Industrial Economics* 42(2): 115–40.

Economic Research Service, Rural Economy Division. 1997. *Credit in Rural America.* Agricultural Economic Report No. 749. Washington, DC: United States Department of Agriculture.

Evans, D.S., and L.S. Leighton. 1989. Some empirical aspects of entrepreneurship. *American Economic Review* 79(3): 519–35.

Feser, E.J. 2007. Encouraging broadband deployment from the bottom up. *Journal of Regional Analysis and Policy* 37(1): 69–72.

Florida, R., and M. Kenney. 1988. Venture capital and high technology entrepreneurship. *Journal of Business Venturing* 3(4): 301–19.

Forsyth, G.D. 2005. A note on small business survival rates in rural areas: The case of Washington State. *Growth and Change* 36(3): 428–40.

Freshwater, D. 2001. Evolution of rural policy and agricultural policy in North America. In *The Challenges of Rural Development in the EU Accession Countries,* ed. C. Csaski and Z. Lerman, 11–29. Washington, DC: The World Bank.
Geroski, P.A. 1995. What do we know about entry? *International Journal of Industrial Organization* 13(4): 421–40.
Hanson, R. 1993. Bidding for business: A second war between the states. *Economic Development Quarterly* 7(2): 183–98.
Hecker, D. 1999. High-tech employment: A broader view. *Monthly Labor Review* 111(6): 18–28.
Henderson, J. 2002. Building the rural economy with high-growth entrepreneurs. *Economic Review* 87(3): 45–70.
———. 2010. Will the rural economy rebound in 2010? *Economic Review* 95(1): 95–119.
Hoover, E. M., and R. Vernon. 1959. *Anatomy of a Metropolis; The Changing Distribution of People and Jobs Within the New York Metropolitan Region.* Cambridge, MA: Harvard University Press.
Kauffman Foundation. 2009. *Kauffman Firm Survey Fourth Follow-up, Public Use Dataset* [Data file]. Kansas City, MO. www.kauffman.org/kfs/ (accessed December 2010).
Knaup, A.E. 2005. Survival and longevity in the business employment dynamics data. *Monthly Labor Review* 128(5): 2–8.
Krugman, P. 1991. *Geography and Trade.* Cambridge, MA: MIT Press.
Kulawczuk, P. 1998. The development of entrepreneurship in rural areas. In *The Transfer of Power: Decentralization in Central and Eastern Europe,* ed. J.D. Kimball, 97–106. Budapest, Hungary: The Local Government and Service Form Initiative.
Leone, R.A., and R. Struyk. 1976. The incubator hypothesis: Evidence from 5 SMSAs. *Urban Studies* 13(3): 325–31.
Markley, D.M. 2001. Financing the new rural economy. In *Exploring Policy Options for a New Rural America,* ed. B. Dabson, 69–80. Kansas City, MO: Center for the Study of Rural America, Federal Reserve Bank of Kansas City.
———. 2009. Written statement for the record before the U.S. House of Representatives Committee on Agriculture, Subcommittee on Rural Development, Biotechnology, Special Crops, and Forest Agriculture. Washington, DC.
Marshall, A. 1890/1920. *Principles of Economics,* 8th ed. London: Macmillan & Co.
McDaniel, K. 2000. Can scenic amenities offer rural gain without pain? *Main Street Economist,* September. www.kansascityfed.org/Publicat/mse/MSE_0900.pdf (accessed December 2010.
O'Farrell, P.N., and D.M.W.N. Hitchens. 1988. Alternative theories of small-firm growth: A critical review. *Environment and Planning A* 20(10): 1365–83.
Pakes, A., and R. Ericson. 1998. Empirical implications of alternative models of firm dynamics. *Journal of Economic Theory* 79 (1): 1–45.
PricewaterhouseCoopers/National Venture Capital Association MoneyTree™. 2010. MoneyTree™ report based on data from Thomas Reuters. www.pwcmoneytree.com/MTPublic/ns/index.jspon (accessed July 2010).
Quigley, J.M. 2002. Rural policy and the new regional economics: Implications for rural America. In *The New Power of Regions: A Policy Focus for Rural America,* ed. M. Drabenstott and K. Sheaff, 7–34. Kansas City, MO: Center for the Study of Rural America, Federal Reserve Bank of Kansas City.

Renski, H. 2009. New firm entry, survival, and growth in the United States: A comparison of urban, suburban, and rural areas. *Journal of the American Planning Association* 75(1): 60–77.

———. 2010. The influence of industry mix on regional new firm formation in the United States. Unpublished manuscript.

———. 2011. External economies of localization, urbanization, and industrial diversity and new firm survival. *Papers in Regional Science* 90(3): 473–502.

Reynolds, P.D. 2007. *Entrepreneurship in the United States: The Future Is Now*. New York: Springer.

Reynolds, P.D., and S.B. White. 1997. *The Entrepreneurial Process: Economic Growth, Men, Women, and Minorities.* Westport, CT: Quorum Books.

Ring, J.K., A.M. Peredo, and J.J. Christman. 2010. Business networks and economic development in rural communities in the United States. *Entrepreneurship Theory and Practice* 34(1): 171–95.

Robinson, K.L., W. Dassie, and R.D. Christy. 2004. Entrepreneurship and small business development as a rural development strategy. *Southern Rural Sociology* 20(2): 1–23.

Roth, D. 2000. Thinking about rural manufacturing: A brief history. *Rural America* 15(1): 12–19.

Rubin, J.S. 2010. Venture capital and underserved communities. *Urban Affairs Review* 45(6): 821–35.

Shane, S. 2003. *A General Theory of Entrepreneurship: The Individual-Opportunity Nexus.* Cheltenham, U.K. and Northampton, MA: Edward Elgar.

———. 2008. *The Illusions of Entrepreneurship: The Costly Myths that Entrepreneurs, Investors, and Policy Makers Live By.* New Haven, CT: Yale University Press.

Sorenson, O., and P.G. Audia. 2000. The social structure of entrepreneurial activity: Geographic concentration of footwear production in the United States, 1940 to 1989. *American Journal of Sociology* 106(2): 424–62.

Stam, E. 2007. Why butterflies don't leave: Locational behavior of entrepreneurial firms. *Economic Geography* 83(1): 27–50.

Stauber, K.N. 2001. Why invest in rural America—and how? A critical public policy question for the 21st century. In *Exploring Policy Options for a New Rural America,* ed. B. Dabson, 9–29. Kansas City, MO: Center for the Study of Rural America, Federal Reserve Bank of Kansas City.

Wilkerson, C. (2001) Trends in rural manufacturing. *Main Street Economist,* December. www.kansascityfed.org/publicat/mse/MSE_1201.pdf (accessed December 2010).

Part IV

Partnerships

12

Tax Increment Financing in Theory and Practice

Rachel Weber

If the past quarter of a century is any indication, tax increment financing (TIF) is likely to remain one of the most popular forms of finance for local economic development in the United States. TIF is neither a new tax nor a tax abatement in the conventional sense. Rather, it is a reallocation of property tax revenues from the municipality's general fund to a smaller enclave of contiguous properties: a TIF district. TIF allows a municipality or redevelopment authority to designate an area for improvement and then earmark any future growth in ad valorem property tax revenues from the district to pay for the initial and ongoing economic development expenditures there.

The popularity of TIF can be explained in part by the rapidly changing fiscal and political context in which municipalities operate. The flow of federal funds for redevelopment activities has been stemmed by a series of deep cuts, restrictions on tax-exempt bonds, and the administrative devolution of urban policy to lower levels of government (Briffault 1997; Clarke and Gaile 1998; Eisinger 1988). States, responding to threats of taxpayer revolt, have imposed caps on municipal property tax collections and limits on the amount and nature of municipal expenditures. A scarcity of local revenues increases municipal agencies' competition for them. At the same time, heightened public concerns about "corporate welfare" have made it more difficult for local governments to indiscriminately provide tax breaks to select private firms.

In response, local officials have adopted redevelopment strategies that do not rely heavily on federal funds, circumvent state-imposed revenue and expenditure limits, and, at least on the surface, do not resemble the giveaways of yore. TIF addresses each of these concerns. Its funding is derived from a local source: the municipality's property tax revenues. When changes were made to the federal tax code in the 1980s prohibiting the use of tax-exempt status for bonds that funded certain kinds of private development, municipalities turned to TIF as a means of circumventing the restrictions. TIF funds have also evaded state debt limits, which typically restrict borrowing to a percentage of the municipality's assessed property base. Municipalities prefer TIF because it provides the public redevelopment agency with its own budget, funded with earmarked funds for economic development; it does not have to compete with other city departments at budget time. Because the subsidized firm's future property taxes are used as leverage to pay for the initial costs of the development, TIF is often perceived as a "self-financing" form of subsidy and therefore less of a drain on public resources.

But as TIF's popularity has grown, so has scrutiny of its operations and effects. Substantial abuses, public costs, and inequities have been unearthed in localities around the country. Public scrutiny makes it imperative that planners and policymakers fully understand how the mechanism operates in practice as well as TIF's larger implications for the fiscal health of municipalities. This chapter describes the mechanics of using TIF to finance redevelopment projects, the situations in which its use is appropriate, and those in which the benefits of using TIF, as opposed to other combinations of public and private capital, are not as evident. The chapter ends with a summary of the criticisms that have been leveled at TIF, a review of the empirical evaluations of TIF's effectiveness, and suggestions for policy reform.

The Mechanics of Tax Increment Financing

State legislation defines two key legal parameters for TIF designation. First, in most states, TIF can only be used to redevelop areas where a sufficient number of the properties are considered "blighted." In Indiana, for example, the authorizing statute defines a "blighted area" as one in which "normal development and occupancy are undesirable or impossible" due to "lack of development, cessation of growth, deterioration of improvements, age or obsolescence of the area, character of occupancy, substandard buildings," or presence of "other factors that impair values or prevent a normal use or development of property" (Indiana Code § 36–7–1–3). The municipality, in concert with developers and consultants, will write up an eligibility study to demonstrate that the area in question meets the state's definition of blight, documenting the deterioration, the age of the building stock, zoning and land use designations, vacancies, and changing property values.

In some states, nonblighted areas may be designated as TIF districts so long as they serve other legislated goals, such as industrial job creation or military base conversion. In Michigan, for example, the original TIF legislation limited funds to roads, sewers, and other "pure public good" infrastructure expenses until the statute was amended in 2000 to include land acquisition and improvements for private businesses and incubators (Wisniewski 2000).

Second, states require the municipality to demonstrate that the area in question could not be redeveloped "but for" the use of TIF. This provision requires municipal officials to attest to the fact that (a) the redevelopment would not occur without incentives and that (b) other available sources of incentive, such as a combination of bonds, abatements, and tax revenues, would not be sufficient to attract private investment. There is no definitive case law or statutory authority on the "but for" condition (Peddle 1997; Redfield 1995), an absence that is somewhat understandable given the methodological hurdles one would need to traverse in order to prove the counterfactual ex ante (Bartik 1991; Persky, Felsenstein, and Wiewel 1997). If these conditions are met, however, a TIF district may be formed by municipal ordinance after notice is given and a public hearing is held to discuss the redevelopment plan.

State legislation may also set out requirements for the physical boundaries of the proposed redevelopment area. In Illinois, the project area must be at least 1.5 acres in size, must be contiguous, and must contain only properties that will be "substantially benefited" by the proposed TIF plan (Weber and Goddeeris 2007). A review of the shape and size of TIF districts in any state would reveal that boundaries are often highly irregular, and areas covered are quite varied. Parcels that have already reached what may be considered the pinnacle of their property value growth, residential areas, and institutional buildings (that pay no property taxes) are often excluded from TIF districts. Political gerrymandering may also have an impact on the ultimate form of the district as council members demand that boundaries be drawn to reflect their respective interests.

Once an area is approved as a TIF district, the initial assessed property valuation for all of the property in the district is held constant for a designated period (often 20-plus years in most states). The sum of the initial assessed values of the properties in the district forms the base against which growth will be measured. The municipality or authority then makes expenditures in the district, some of which are for infrastructure and some of which are for developer incentives. Developers may be attracted because the municipality has used its powers of site clearance and street repair to improve the district. They may be attracted because the municipality pays for land assembly and sale. They may be attracted because the municipality offers subsidized financing, which lowers the project's financial risk and makes it more financially viable. They may be attracted because of the inherent desirability of the location. The "but for" requirement is intended to guard against this last scenario, as it is the TIF-funded public incentives that are supposed to be the draw. Regardless of the motivation, private investment is expected to be attracted to the area, causing the assessed property value and concomitant tax value to rise. Taxes on the difference between the base value and new assessed value are called the "*tax increment*" (see Figure 12.1).

Figure 12.1 **The Allocation of Assessed Value (AV) in a TIF District**

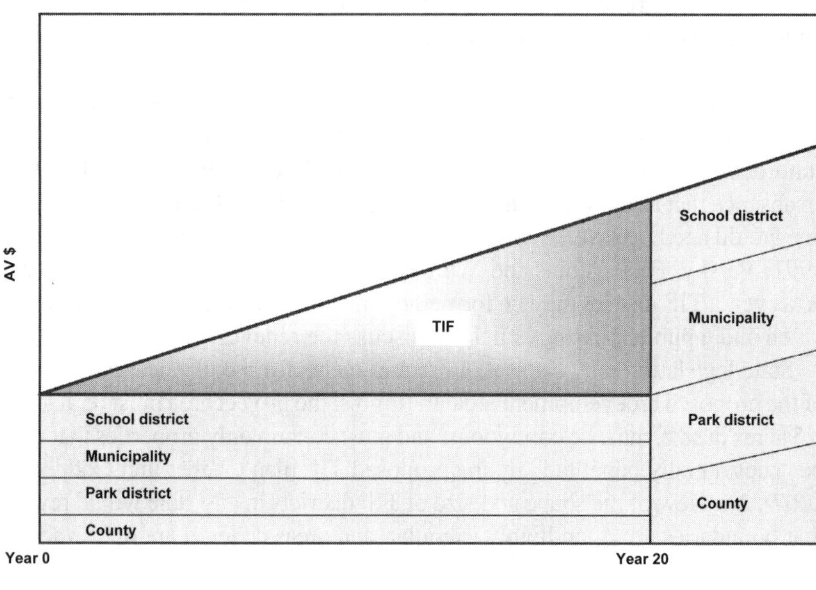

Instead of channeling the increments to the municipality's general fund and to other taxing bodies with jurisdiction over the area (such as school and park districts), they are diverted to the TIF authority and used to finance any debt the authority accumulated when making improvements. In other words, any taxes on the increase in assessed property values of the district over the next 20-plus years will pay for TIF activities, while taxes on the base value of the properties will remain the same and will continue to be paid to the local taxing bodies. Without TIF, each overlapping jurisdiction would levy its individual tax rate on the assessed value available in its district, and the municipality would be but one of several that receives tax revenues.

In order to realize an increase in property values and produce the coveted TIF increment, the municipality must find ways of paying for the up-front costs of those improvements that will make the TIF district attractive to new development. TIF districts do not generate funds for incentives or infrastructure immediately; instead, tax increments trickle in over the lifespan of the district. TIF increments, therefore, are committed *before* they are generated. Tax revenues and expenses flow in and out at different times, even though the municipality must meet all obligations as they come due. Thus, TIF is, in essence, a means of smoothing cash flows in a development project because most expenses come up front while tax revenues and corporate profits come in further down the road.

Municipalities rely on three primary methods of *front funding* expenditures from the expected increments, most of which provide the municipality with the legal means and security to borrow against the future property tax revenues for current spending. Under the first method, the municipality floats revenue bonds for the total amount of the redevelopment, dedicating the expected tax increments to service the debt. Revenue bonds allow municipalities to circumvent constitutional and statutory debt limitations as well as voter referenda. Some TIF bonds, however, do carry a general obligation or general fund pledge and are tax-exempt, allowing investors to earn a slightly higher than normal return. In Colorado, TIF bonds can also be secured by a captured sales tax pledge or a blended structure of property and sales tax increment. For many years, TIF debt comprised a small, unrated, and obscure segment of the bond market, but as the mechanism's popularity has grown, so too has the amount of bonded debt (Johnson 1999; Weber 2010). Once a municipality develops a track record of development that generates incremental tax revenues, it can secure insurance, higher ratings, and, therefore, cheaper debt.

Instead of committing to long-term, low-interest bond issuances, municipalities may issue short-term, higher-interest debt securities in anticipation of future property tax increments—the second method for front funding TIF projects. Such products are referred to as tax anticipation notes, and municipal governments use them to provide immediate funding for capital expenditures. A municipality may provide these notes to the developer, who is then responsible for monetizing (i.e., selling) them to the highest bidder (often through a third-party intermediary). Banks and institutional investors frequently purchase the notes, taking on the project completion risk and the risk that the tax increments will not materialize in return for promises to be paid back with interest. Proceeds from the sale pay the developer's TIF-eligible expenses.

The third method of front funding—commonly known as "pay as you go"—requires the private developer to pay for the up-front costs of the project. The municipality then reimburses the developer annually as it receives the incremental property taxes. Because developers require initial sums of money larger in amount than the increments trickling in, they often turn to banks to fill their financing gaps and pay for TIF-eligible costs such as land acquisition. Lenders require some assurance that the municipality will assist the borrower in servicing the debt.

When Is Tax Increment Financing Used?

The short answer is all the time. Each municipality, however, has its own political process for designating TIF districts, distributing the increment generated within the district, and determining the eligibility of expenditures. Before a TIF designation has been made, the local redevelopment authority or planning department must draft a redevelopment plan. In general, the initial TIF redevelopment plan provides planners with loose guidelines for financing specific development and infrastructure projects. In some municipalities, the plans are mere formalities. In Illinois, for example, some plans are no more than vague and open-ended wish lists of projects that the municipalities would like to see funded with increment. In Wisconsin, on the other hand, project expenditures must be specifically identified, and municipalities must define how much can be recovered by tax increments. In other locales, development plans include strategies to meet redevelopment goals, specific site plans, detailed financial analysis, and fiscal impact assessments for the overlapping jurisdictions.

After the development plan has been approved and the boundaries designated, individual developers must apply and be approved for an allocation of increment by the local administration and city council. In most municipalities, the applicant must describe the particular project in detail, providing specific figures for total development costs, sources, uses of funds, and expected job creation impact. If the authority or city council decides that the project will further TIF objectives and has sufficient front funding from other sources, it will enter into a redevelopment agreement with the developer or business tenant that spells out the details of the subsidy for a specific project.

Unlike the federally funded categorical programs that preceded it, TIF can be used for most kinds of projects that demonstrate financial feasibility and promise increases in property value. In general, the only significant restrictions imposed by state statutes are those directing TIF to certain redevelopment areas, defining "blight," and limiting the project term (Paetsch and Dahlstrom 1990). Because of its flexibility, this tool has enabled municipalities to channel funds to infrastructure improvement, industrial expansion, downtown redevelopment, historic preservation, firm-specific relocation subsidies, and military base conversion.

States can also delimit the eligible private costs that the TIF increment can subsidize. These typically include the cost of demolition, parcel assembly, land preparation, construction, planning studies, and, occasionally, workforce development and training. Most TIF legislation also allows municipalities to offer subsidized, below-market rate financing from the increment. By providing financing for the total development costs, TIF reduces the amount of equity investment required of the project developer. Lower mortgage payments lower the project's total leverage and financial risk, therefore making it appear more viable. Indeed, reducing the up-front costs of development (primarily those costs related to land development) can make an immediate and substantial impact on a developer's bottom line. In this sense, TIF can be more attractive to the developer (but also more costly to the local government) than conventional abatements that reduce a developer's tax burden over time.

The Public Investment Decision

In theory, the municipality decides to allocate the increment when it is persuaded that the subsidized project will create substantial increases in the value of the property. After all, it is the difference between the value of the undeveloped property and the value of the same property after it has been redeveloped (i.e., the increment or "rent gap") that is the basis for the operation of this mechanism. Property owners and developers seeking increments must demonstrate that their investments will equal or exceed the sum of discounted future increases in property tax revenues from the project.

The following example illustrates the type of calculation cities and developers employ to determine how much money can be allocated for a particular project. The owner of a manufacturing plant wants to build a new 100,000-square-foot warehouse on a parking lot in a new TIF district. It applies to the city for assistance to purchase the parking lot and assemble the land for the warehouse. The desired site generated $40,000 in annual property taxes in the base year (i.e., the year the TIF was designated). Both the city and the applicant must estimate how much property tax revenue they think the site would generate if the proposed warehouse were constructed and became fully operational (see Table 12.1). In this case, the difference between the taxes generated as a parking lot and those potentially generated as a warehouse would amount to $238,510 in the first year. In theory, this increment would be available to use for economic development expenditures in the TIF district.

Although it provides a good snapshot, this calculation does not take into account the estimated lifetime of the TIF or the time value of money. If TIF districts are designated for a period of 23 years in this state (as they are in the state of Illinois, for example), the municipality will make assumptions about the rate at which it can reasonably expect property tax revenues to increase if the facility were built. Looking at comparable warehouses, it might assume a 12 percent increase every three years (assuming property taxes are reassessed every three years).

Moreover, the city will take into account the various risks, opportunity costs, and contingencies that arise when relying on any kind of payment or income that is generated in the future. As such, it will discount the future increments by an amount roughly equivalent to the cost of capital, inflation rate, and the perception of future risks. If the city relies on an 8 percent dis-

Table 12.1

Tax Increment for Proposed Warehouse Construction in Year One

Cost per square foot	$50.00
Proposed size (sq. ft.)	100,000
Total cost	$5,000,000
Cost discount factor*	80%
Fair market value	$4,000,000
Assessment rate	36%
Assessed value	$1,440,000
Equalizing multiplier	2.149
Equalized assessed value (EAV)	$3,094,560
Occupancy rate	100%
Total EAV	$3,094,560
Tax millage rate	9.00%
Estimate property tax revenue	$278,510
Property tax revenue as warehouse	$278,510
Property tax revenue as parking lot	($40,000)
Tax increment in Year One	$238,510

*The assessor might apply this factor to new construction to bring the assessments more in line with comparable buildings.

count rate, the present value of the increment would total approximately $3.2 million over 23 years (see Table 12.2).[1]

For the rational local official, this figure represents the upper limit of assistance available to the manufacturer to build the warehouse. If the city planned to go to the bond market for the front funding (an unlikely event, given the small size of the issuance), it would subtract the cost of debt service and other transaction fees from the stream of increments to get a better estimate of the upper limit of assistance.

This example highlights several issues about TIF. The first concerns the number of redevelopment projects in the TIF district. In our example, there is only one proposed redevelopment project in the TIF district, and it needs all the incentives and generates all the increment. In reality, however, after the initial designation occurs, a queue of projects seeking assistance will form. Some may be part of the original redevelopment plan; those are typically given priority. Second, tax increments are generated by all properties in the district that appreciate in value over time. Any property appreciation within the TIF district can be used to fund other, unrelated projects as long as they fall within the designated boundaries. In our case, the city could use a portion of the increment generated by the warehouse to pay the demolition costs for, say, a strip mall sited down the street. In Chicago, the increments

Table 12.2

Present Value of Future Property Tax Increments

Year	Increment
1	$238,510
2	$238,510
3	$238,510
4	$267,131
5	$267,131
6	$267,131
7	$299,187
8	$299,187
9	$299,187
10	$335,089
11	$335,089
12	$335,089
13	$375,300
14	$375,300
15	$375,300
16	$420,336
17	$420,336
18	$420,336
19	$470,777
20	$470,777
21	$470,777
22	$527,270
23	$527,270
Total proceeds	$8,273,530
Present value @ 8.00%	$3,294,998

are not infinitely portable across the city; they must be used in the district in which they were generated or in an adjacent TIF district. In Milwaukee and other cities, the increment can be used to pay down costs incurred in any TIF district in the city.

Third, it is likely that the future tax incremental revenues in the TIF district (the $3.2 million from our example) will include, in no small part, property appreciation that was not in any way induced by the initial TIF-subsidized investments (e.g., appreciation caused by normal inflationary pressures). Many critics have argued that TIF has the potential to "capture" increment to which the municipality has no singular claim (Hissong 2001; Jolin, Legenza, and McDermott 1998).

Fourth, although this example assumes that local governments make allocation decisions in a technically rational manner, in most cases, municipalities apply other, more informal rules of thumb. For example, they may use an informal method that allows them to commit to financing only a set percentage of the developer's total costs. These percentages vary depending on the total development cost of the project, the extent to which the municipality is counting on the project to spur ancillary development, and judgments about the degree to which the subsidy is really necessary for the project to go forward. The city of Chicago, at one point, sought to fund no more than 10 percent of developer-specific total development costs (not including infrastructure that would benefit a wider public) (Meck and Friedman 2005). If the public sector includes infrastructure and site assembly costs, the public share may rise to 20 to 30 percent of total development costs.

In other cases, municipalities may ignore these informal decision rules all together and engage in a process of deal making in which all the financial details of the deal are open to negotiation and depend heavily on the political cachet of the parties involved (Molotch 1990; Reese 1991; Rubin 1988; Wolkoff 1992; Wolman 1988). Indeed, the flip side of the flexibility that this local funding source offers is a concomitant lack of accountability. TIF has been subject to misuse in certain instances, where expenditures have been made for golf courses, luxury car dealerships, fireworks displays, parades, marketing efforts, and the normal operating expenses of local governments. These kinds of project expenditures go beyond the intent of state legislation, but municipal agencies lacking uniform guidelines for funding choices have been known to resort to reactive deal making in their interactions with prospective developers.

TIF-Funded Redevelopment

States in which municipalities use TIF extensively tend to have fragmented fiscal structures and greater absolute numbers of taxing jurisdictions. In Maine, Illinois, and Indiana, fiscal pressures were found to be the most significant predictor of TIF adoption (Dye and Merriman 2000; LaPlante 2001; Man 1999). Other studies have found that TIF-adopting municipalities tend to have a greater share of nonresidential land uses and larger populations than nonadopters (Anderson 1990) and that they tend to be near other TIF-adopting municipalities (Byrne 2005).

Municipalities that adopt TIF use it to fund a wide range of redevelopment projects. Chicago spent approximately $60 million of TIF funds to rehabilitate and restore the historic buildings in its downtown theater district and, on a very different kind of project, used $11 million to help the Ford Motor Company build a supplier park on a brownfield site on the city's southwest side (Neighborhood Capital Budget Group 1999). Kansas City, Missouri wooed big-box retailers like Home Depot with land preparation and developer incentives, while San Diego built mixed retail-residential developments.

Smaller cities and towns are using TIF to revitalize the flagging main streets and downtown shopping areas depopulated by malls in the 1980s. New Ulm, Minnesota, helped Kraft Foods to expand its Velveeta facility in town (State of Minnesota 1996). Following Hurricane Andrew in 1993, the city of Homestead, Florida, was rebuilt using $54 million in TIF for everything from signage to a new community center (McEntee 1998).

Compared to most state and federal programs, TIF is a very flexible tool. The TIF process can be initiated any time a development opportunity presents itself, and TIF can be used for a variety of reimbursable costs (Paetsch and Dahlstrom 1990). In Chicago, for example, community-based economic development organizations have received TIF funding for workforce development to complement the city's focus on industrial retention and expansion.[2] One such organization, the Local Economic and Employment Development (LEED) Council, assisted Federal Express in securing $1.4 million of TIF funds to reconstruct a seawall on its property, after which the company signed an agreement that committed Federal Express to hiring its new employees through LEED's placement services (Barancik 1998). Federal Express front funded the money for job training, and the city agreed to reimburse the company when tax increments were generated. LEED was able to provide follow-up support and encouragement to program graduates to help ensure that they not only remained on the job but also advanced up the ladder to higher-paying jobs. TIF works especially well with these kinds of one-time allocations, especially when the employer is willing to commit its own funds up front and be paid back over time.

The design of TIF also works well with large, expensive projects that promise quick and substantial spikes in tax increment. Most municipalities are reluctant to use their bonding authority to sell revenue bonds for small (under $1 million) projects. This is because the amount of deficit financing needed for small projects—for a new roof or small parking lot for an existing business—is not likely to clear the minimum threshold for new issues or justify the high transaction costs (e.g., for bond counsel).

From the example of the new warehouse, it should be clear why TIF operates well in areas where property values are initially low relative to other parts of the municipality or are growing at a slower pace. Government-owned (i.e., tax exempt) property, abandoned buildings, or derelict sites in appreciating neighborhoods are especially ripe for TIF-financed in-fill development. TIF is also a useful tool in instances where land uses are upzoned—that is, when property moves from less-intensive usage to more-intensive usage. In these cases, the base value of the property (the value in the year of the TIF designation) is low enough so that when the property values start to grow in subsequent years, a substantial amount of increment can be generated. However,

TIF designation is also a signaling mechanism to developers and speculators that the municipality expects property values to increase in the designated district. If the municipality is unable to act quickly, developers may flock to the proposed district, purchasing property and driving up prices.

Evaluating Tax Increment Financing

Judging the success of TIF is difficult given the measurement problems involved. Municipal officials are quick to attribute new developments and increases in property values to their own economic development policies. Studies commissioned by municipalities simply add up the increases in property value since their program was initiated and either state or imply that the program caused the increases—an example of the kind of "credit-claiming" so prevalent in this realm of public policy (Bartik 1991; Rubin 1988). Local officials point to TIF-funded parking garages and office buildings, public improvements, and demolitions as evidence of the tool's success. Between 1984 and 1998, the city of Chicago, for example, attributed the creation of 9,500 jobs and retention of another 25,000 jobs to its aggressive use of TIF in industrial areas (City of Chicago Department of Planning and Development 1998).

In contrast, most scholars agree that determining the causal effect of TIF or any kind of economic development program is difficult because of the need to control, by reasonable assumption or appropriate statistical technique, for what would happen *without* the program (Bartik 1991; Persky, Felsenstein, and Wiewel 1997). Those studies that use appropriate methodology for dealing with causation have found mixed results. Man and Rosentraub (1998) found TIF had a positive effect on median housing values in Indiana. Comparing TIF-adopting and nonadopting municipalities, they showed how this economic development program was responsible for increasing the median owner-occupied housing value in their sample by 11.4 percent between 1980 and 1990. Man (2002) also finds statistically significant positive relationships between TIF and employment growth across 53 Indiana municipalities, growth that should also have a positive impact on housing values. Dardia (1998) found in his study of California that TIF had a substantial and positive impact on development.

However, Dye and Merriman's (2000) comparison of TIF-adopting and nonadopting municipalities in 247 municipalities around metropolitan Chicago found that TIF adoption had a negative impact on the growth of municipal-wide property values. They found that where property values within the TIF district rose, the rise was more than offset by a negative impact on the non-TIF portion of the same city. They hypothesize that TIF may induce an inefficient geographic allocation of investment; that is, TIF may subsidize growth in the TIF district at the expense of growth in the non-TIF portion of the same municipality. Dye and Merriman (2003) extended their results to cover municipalities throughout the state of Illinois and also ran separate analyses for industrial, commercial, and other types of TIF districts. Their evidence suggests that while commercial activity within TIF districts substitutes for other commercial activity within the same municipality, industrial activity within TIF districts does not appear to have relocated from elsewhere in the municipality. In other words, industrial TIF districts may be more likely to induce net new growth in a municipality relative to commercial land uses. Similarly, Byrne (2010) found that TIF adoption had no effect on employment growth, except for the case of industrial areas.

Regardless of whether the aggregate (i.e., municipality-wide) net impact is negative or positive, the local effects of TIF may be significant. In fact, viewed from the vantage point of an individual municipality, these seemingly contradictory results may be more consistent. It is possible that the TIF designation could increase property values within TIF districts in the same jurisdiction even if that increase is accompanied by a decrease in value in non-TIF areas located farther from these targeted areas. Indeed, Smith (2009), Dye and Merriman (2003), and Byrne (2005) found that the TIF increments grew at a faster rate than property in the rest of the TIF-hosting municipality. Although he did not control for potential selection bias, Smith (2006) found that appreciation rates for multifamily housing projects within TIF districts exceeded those of properties outside TIF boundaries.

In contrast, Weber, Bhatta, and Merriman (2003) found that, for industrial parcels in Chicago, location within a TIF area introduces a value penalty: industrial land and buildings within TIF districts sold for prices below those of similar properties outside of TIF districts. Weber, Bhatta, and Merriman (2007) tested the spillover effects of TIF on single-family home prices and found that while the effects were quite small, they were related to the land use within each district, with mixed-use TIF districts exerting a positive pull on home prices. Such contradictory findings at the level of the microgeography of urban neighborhoods raise the issue of whether TIF should be judged by how well it improves the blighted project area alone or by its impact on the entire municipality.

Debates about the independent influence of TIF on development and property values are at the heart of the controversies around the impact and benefit distribution of this financing mechanism. For example, if TIF has no independent effect on property values, then school districts and other overlapping tax jurisdictions are justified in arguing that TIF captures revenues that would otherwise be going to them. Property taxes support the operations of many taxing jurisdictions in addition to those of the municipality, including school, park, and library districts. Because TIF redirects property tax revenues away from overlapping jurisdictions for more than 20 years, these affected taxing bodies lose all the taxes derived from normal inflationary pressures and reinvestment. Weber (2003) found that school districts sharing their base with increment-rich TIF districts in Cook County, Illinois, experienced slower local revenue growth than school districts without TIF districts. On the other hand, without the use of TIF as a development incentive, there may not be any or much new revenue to distribute in the first place. Everything hinges on the "but for" question.

Even if TIF can be said to independently increase property values, it is possible that existing residents may not be prepared for the higher tax burden that comes with it. For example, small-business tenants may be unable to pay inflated rents; larger industrial users and big-box retailers may be the only ones that can afford the higher prices. Because there is no mechanism through which preexisting owners or renters may give or withhold their consent regarding the TIF designation, businesses gentrified out by spiraling property values and taxes may be forced to submit to a potentially coercive arrangement. Fear of rapid development, aggravated by the municipality's desire to move ahead on TIF designation quickly in order to lock in the lowest base, has prompted popular protest against the use of TIF. Residents in Richmond Heights, a middle-class suburb of St. Louis, attempted to stall a TIF-funded shopping mall project through voter referenda. Mexican immigrants waged protests against a proposed industrial TIF district in their Chicago neighborhood, fearing they would be displaced by rising property values.

TIF also influences the general fiscal health of municipalities. By encouraging municipalities to spend now for projects that will be paid off with future increments, TIF promotes risk taking that may not be rewarded if the hoped-for increments do not materialize. When the economy slows, the speculative roots of TIF are exposed. When the Kellogg Corporation announced plans to close its Battle Creek, Michigan, plant, for example, the city's Downtown Development Authority had to scramble to cover more than $60 million in TIF bonds it had issued (Ward 1999). In 2010, Bank of America foreclosed on downtown Cleveland's landmark Old Arcade shopping mall and hotel when it missed payments on $6 million of TIF debt (Devitt 2010). In California and Colorado, TIF bonds have defaulted (Johnson 1999). Even those TIF bonds secured with strong backup pledges may falter when the local economy starts to decline.

Suggestions for Reform

Although the early TIF legislation contained some very laudable goals, the actual administration of this financing tool has not always lived up to them. Several states have audited municipal use of TIF, and most have amended their enabling legislation to try to curb abuses (see Weber and Goddeeris [2007] for a lengthier description of reform efforts). Some have tightened their definitions of blight and have tried to restrict reimbursement for parking garages, ordinary municipal services, and poaching retail from adjacent localities (Redfield 1995). However, even in such cases, the ambiguity of most legislated criteria affords municipal officials substantial discretion in making increment allocation decisions.

Although it would slow the process down, it seems only fair that overlapping taxing jurisdictions should participate in TIF adoption and allocation decisions, given that TIF enables municipalities to shift part of the cost of financing development to these other overlapping jurisdictions. Municipalities are under no obligation to assess whether TIF would seriously harm a school or park district's financial condition, and, without state-granted rights, these districts lack legal authority to demand that their interests be taken into account. Some states require joint review boards on which representatives of all districts sit; however, in all but nine states, these boards have no official veto authority (Redfield 1995).[3] Schools in particular need to be compensated by the TIF when new residential development leads to a net increase in their student population.[4] Moreover, the 20-plus-year lifetime of a TIF is an arbitrary and lengthy period for jurisdictions to go without increases in tax revenues from the district. A shorter time frame would return increment to the municipality's general fund and to the other taxing bodies.

States may want to consider adding an inflation factor in the frozen base to allow overlapping districts to recapture some of the increment that is not attributable to the new development. The state of Minnesota, for example, requires that the original tax capacity (base assessed value) be adjusted by the inflation rate on property values in the district so that only increases above and beyond inflation will be captured (State of Minnesota 1996). Minnesota also attempts to distinguish between the incremental revenue attributable to TIF and increases in value due to other unrelated factors (e.g., low interest rates). If building permits were not issued in the 18 months before the assessment, if parcels were not redeveloped within four years of the district designation, or if the municipality never issued bonds or acquired property, then it cannot claim the full amount of the increment. In this way, the legislation requires municipalities to demonstrate responsibility for creating the value that is appropriated for economic development.

Municipalities also need to migrate more of the fiscal risks back to the developers and big-box tenants receiving generous TIF subsidies. Imperiling the public purse with bonds secured by uncertain future property tax growth makes less sense than asking developers to pay for the initial costs and paying them back as the increments are generated (Weber 2002). Some municipalities, like the city of Chicago, have taken a more cautious approach to bonding for TIF expenditures. In all but the largest and least risky projects, the city has opted for notes or pay-as-you-go arrangements, while suburban development agencies have compromised their bond ratings with excessive TIF debt.

As long as municipalities control the financing, they can also control the reciprocal obligations of those subsidized firms that partake of it. As is true with all public financial incentives, municipalities can require developers receiving TIF assistance to agree to certain standards of performance related, for instance, to employment (i.e., adherence to living-wage ordinances) or environmental conduct (Weber 2002). Local administrators can also structure deals so that TIF reimbursement is phased in as the company meets specified levels of performance. For example, no money changes hands until the developer-business hires and starts paying workers a designated minimum wage. Municipalities need to set up reporting systems to monitor the performance of TIF recipients and to determine if they have breached their contracts. A breach can trigger a host of remedies and damages. It may require recipient businesses to pay back all or part of TIF allocation ("clawback") or pay a penalty such as the interest accrued on a low-interest loan. It may prompt the municipality to terminate the subsidy, adjust its amount, or prohibit the noncompliant firm from receiving TIF assistance in the future.

Other suggestions for TIF reform involve looking to other kinds of incentives and public spending to further economic development goals. Despite evidence of a broad national trend toward TIF, the use of this device is by no means ubiquitous across the landscape of municipal governments. TIF districts are concentrated in certain cities and regions. Between 1986 and 1990, for example, TIF districts generated 43 percent of Minneapolis's revenues for economic development (Andrews 1999). In contrast, New York City and Durham, North Carolina, rely more on conventional property tax abatements, tax increases, and voluntary tax levies such as are instituted in business improvement districts. The decline of federal funding and the intensified competition for private investment need not translate the requirement to "do something" into a mandate to take risky or ill-advised action. TIF has serious fiscal implications for municipalities; such implications need to be considered before increasing dependence on this complex and controversial mechanism.

Notes

1. This amount can be represented mathematically as the present value of the future increment a project will produce until the termination of the TIF district:

$$PV = \sum \frac{(AV_n - AV_b) * TR_n}{(1+r)^n}$$

where

AV_n = assessed value of the individual property in year n (year following both the designation of the TIF district and construction of the proposed project),
AV_b = assessed value of the individual property in the base year (i.e., the year TIF was designated),
TR_n = consolidated property tax rate in year n, and
r = public sector discount rate.

2. Job training is considered a TIF-eligible activity in Illinois. State enabling legislation allows funds to be allocated toward "job training, advanced vocational education, and career education including but not limited to courses in occupational, semi-technical, or technical fields leading directly to employment in the TIF district" (Illinois Public Act 79–1525).

3. In Wisconsin and New Mexico, for example, state law requires that a majority of representatives of overlying districts approve the TIF district (Lemov 1994). In Kansas, a county or school board can veto the designation.

4. An amendment to the Illinois TIF statute allows school districts to demand reimbursement for new expenses caused by TIF-induced residential growth but does not mandate this reimbursement. Overlapping jurisdictions in Illinois can also sign intergovernmental agreements with municipalities to cover all or a portion of additional TIF-induced expenses.

References

Anderson, John E. 1990. Tax increment financing: Municipal adoption and growth. *National Tax Journal* 43(2): 155–63.

Andrews, James. 1999. The TIFs go on. *Planning* 65(1): 8–11.

Barancik, Marsha. 1998. TIF advocates link local labor with incoming businesses. *Illinois Real Estate Journal,* May 11.

Bartik, Tim. 1991. *Who Benefits from State and Local Economic Development Policies?* Kalamazoo, MI: Upjohn Institute.

Briffault, Richard. 1997. The law and economics of federalism: The rise of sublocal structures in urban governance. *Minnesota Law Review* 82: 503–34.

Byrne, Paul. 2005. Strategic interaction and the adoption of tax increment financing. *Regional Science and Urban Economics* 35(3): 279–303.

———. 2010. Does tax increment financing deliver on its promise of jobs? The impact of tax increment financing on municipal employment growth. *Economic Development Quarterly* 24(1): 13–22.

City of Chicago Department of Planning and Development. 1998. *Review of Tax Increment Financing in the City of Chicago*. Chicago, IL: Department of Planning and Development.

Clarke, Susan, and Gary Gaile. 1998. *The Work of Cities*. Minneapolis: University of Minnesota Press.

Dardia, Michael. 1998. *Subsidizing Redevelopment in California*. San Francisco: Public Policy Institute of California.

Devitt, Catilin. 2010. Failed Cleveland TIF on hot seat: Case could have wider implications. *The Bond Buyer*, August 18.

Dye, Richard, and David Merriman. 2000. The effects of tax increment financing on economic development. *Journal of Urban Economics* 47(2): 306–28.

———. 2003. The effect of tax increment financing on land use. In *The Property Tax, Land Use and Land Use Regulation,* ed. Richard Netzer, 37–61. Northampton, MA: Elgar.

Eisinger, Peter. 1988. *The Rise of the Entrepreneurial State*. Madison: University of Wisconsin Press.

Hissong, Rodney. 2001. Guest editor's symposium introduction. *Municipal Finance Journal* 22(1): iv–v.

Illinois Public Act 79–1525.

Indiana Administrative Code § 36–7–1–3. Planning and Development.

Johnson, Craig. 1999. TIF debt finance: An analysis of the mainstreaming of a fringe sector. *Public Budgeting and Finance* 19(1): 47–67.

Jolin, Marc, Sharon Legenza, and Matt McDermott. 1998. Tax increment financing: Urban renewal of the 1990s. *Clearinghouse Review,* July-August, 81–99.

LaPlante, Josephine. 2001. Who uses tax increment financing? Local government adoption catalysts. *Municipal Finance Journal* 22(1): 79–97.

Lemov, Penelope. 1994. Tough times for TIF. *Governing* 7: 18–19.

Man, Joyce. 1999. Fiscal pressure, tax competition and the adoption of tax increment financing. *Urban Studies* 36(7): 1151–67.

———. 2002. The effect of state and local tax incentive programs on job growth. In *Proceedings: Ninety-fifth Annual Conference on Taxation*, Orlando, Florida, November 14–16, and minutes of the annual meeting of the National Tax Association, November 14, pp. 316–22.

Man, Joyce, and Mark Rosentraub. 1998. Tax increment financing: Municipal adoption and effects on property value growth. *Public Finance Review* 26(6): 523–47.

McEntee, Christopher. 1998. Tips on TIFs: Panelists explain how to gain maximum benefits, quickly. *The Bond Buyer*, February 17, 34.

Meck, Stuart, and Stephen Friedman. 2005. Development finance and pro formas. AICP Training Materials CD. Chicago, IL: American Planning Association.

Molotch, Harvey. 1990. Urban deals in comparative perspective. In *Beyond the City Limits*, ed. John Logan and Todd Swanstrom, 175–98. Philadelphia, PA: Temple University Press.

Neighborhood Capital Budget Group (NCBG). 1999. *Chicago TIF Encyclopedia*. Chicago, IL: NCBG.

Paetsch, James, and Michael Dahlstrom. 1990. Tax increment financing: What it is and how it works. In *Financing Economic Development*, ed. Richard Bingham, Edward Hill, and Sammis White, 82–99. Newbury Park, CA: Sage.

Peddle, Michael. 1997. TIF in Illinois: The good, the bad, and the ugly. *Northern Illinois University Law Review* 17(3): 441–58.

Persky, Joe, Dan Felsenstein, and Wim Wiewel. 1997. How do we know that "but for the incentives" the development would not have occurred? In *Dilemmas of Urban Economic Development*, ed. Richard Bingham and Rob Mier, 28–55. Thousand Oaks, CA: Sage.

Redfield, Kent. 1995. *Tax Increment Financing in Illinois: A Legislative Issue*. Springfield, IL: Taxpayers Federation of Illinois.

Reese, Laura. 1991. Municipal fiscal health and tax abatement policy. *Economic Development Quarterly* 5: 24–32.

Rubin, Herbert. 1988. Shoot anything that flies; claim anything that falls. *Economic Development Quarterly* 2(3): 236–51.

Smith, Brent. 2006. The impact of tax increment financing districts on localized real estate: Evidence from Chicago's multifamily markets. *Journal of Housing Economics* 15(1): 21–37.

———. 2009. If you promise to build it, will they come? The interaction between local economic development policy and the real estate market: Evidence from tax increment finance districts. *Real Estate Economics* 37(2): 209–34.

State of Minnesota. 1996. *Tax Increment Financing*. Saint Paul, MN: Program Evaluation Division of the Office of the Legislative Auditor.

Ward, Andrew. 1999. Possible Kellogg plant closure imperils Michigan TIF bonds. *The Bond Buyer,* June 29, 1.

Weber, Rachel. 2002. Do better contracts make better economic development incentives? *Journal of the American Planning Association* 68(1): 43–55.

———. 2003. Equity and entrepreneurialism: The impact of tax increment financing on school finance. *Urban Affairs Review* 38(5): 619–44.

———. 2010. Selling city futures: The financialization of urban redevelopment policy. *Economic Geography* 86: 251–74.

Weber, Rachel, and Laura Goddeeris. 2007. *Tax Increment Financing: Process and Planning Issues*. Cambridge, MA: Lincoln Institute of Land Policy Working Paper.

Weber, Rachel, Saurav Bhatta, and David Merriman. 2003. Does tax increment financing raise urban industrial property values? *Urban Studies* 40: 2001–21.

———. 2007. Spillovers from tax increment financing districts: Implications for housing price appreciation. *Regional Science and Urban Economics* 37(2): 259–81.

Wisniewski, Mary. 2000. SmartZones: Michigan's plan to keep its geniuses at home. *The Bond Buyer,* August 16, 26.

Wolkoff, Michael. 1992. Is economic development decision making rational? *Urban Affairs Quarterly* 27(3): 340–55.

Wolman, Hal. 1988. Local economic development policy: What explains the divergence between policy analysis and political behavior? *Journal of Urban Affairs* 10(1): 12–28.

13
Development Exactions

Michael T. Peddle and Roger K. Dahlstrom

Paying for the costs associated with economic development is not always a straightforward proposition; it sometimes comes with unexpected twists, turns, and risks. Development exactions represent a popular response to paying for the costs of growth.

Several years ago, a small community in Illinois was approached by a residential developer seeking to build a subdivision proposed to include more housing units than the number of existing residents in the community. At build out, the subdivision was expected to triple or quadruple the community's population and to produce more than 500 new students who would need to be educated by the local school districts. Having no growth management plan in place, no comprehensive capital facilities plans for schools or other public infrastructure, no policies in place for development exactions, and no level of sophistication in development negotiations, the long-term ramifications of the development decisions faced by the community were hard to overstate. The amount of new public infrastructure required to support the new development was overwhelming, including the possible need for new school buildings. Large-scale infrastructure improvements were likely to require voter referenda for bond issues and corresponding real estate tax hikes. Under normal conditions, such a bond issue would be difficult to pass. Under conditions where much, if not all, of the need for the new infrastructure, and the vast majority of the benefits of the new infrastructure, flows from new development, a tax increase on existing residents may be even harder to swallow. The local school districts sought outside counsel and a short delay in the municipality's decision on the project, so as to better inform the village board of the potential ramifications of their decision on the fiscal health of the schools. Unfortunately, the district's pleas fell on deaf ears, and the development was approved with the stipulation that any future impact fees or development exactions that might otherwise apply to the project would be waived via the development/annexation agreement.

Fast forward a few years and the development playing field changed drastically. Residential and commercial developers, large and small, were victims of a severe economic downturn that touched all segments of the economy. Development projects were abandoned in unfinished form; developer-provided public improvements required by development agreements were left unbuilt, unfinished, or unfunded; debt service expected to be paid by impact fees or other forms of development exactions had to be paid via general property tax levies. The change in the playing field created a need to revisit the mechanisms used to pay for the costs of development.

The concept of sacrificing some of one's property or wealth to promote the greater good is at the heart of much charitable behavior. The adage that "you've got to spend money to make money" is also familiar advice given to fledgling businesses. Intellectually, development exaction systems are designed to capitalize on both of these sentiments, with the goal of providing greater amounts of high quality public infrastructure and services at a more affordable price for taxpayers. Politically, development exaction systems are designed to shift the burden of financing infrastructure away from the voters who have elected the community's leaders to groups not yet present (and therefore not yet voters) in the local community. What politician would not drool at the chance to provide improved public services and infrastructure and not have to burden his or her constituents with a tax increase to do it? Development exactions are often viewed by politicians and local residents as such a silver bullet.

A development exaction is a provision in the development approval process that requires a developer to give or provide something to, or on behalf of, a local government unit or service district. Development exactions include things like dedicating a parcel of land in a subdivision to be used as a park, building a fire station and then donating it to a municipality or fire district, or making cash donations/payments to a fund established for the purpose of funding open space land acquisitions. Development exactions are different from altruistic donations to local governments and traditional service districts in that the donation or payments made as part of a development exaction are required (legally, politically, or through moral suasion) in order for some form of development approval to take place. There is generally a clear quid pro quo relationship that underlies development exactions.

Impact fees represent one common and particular means by which development exactions are implemented. Impact fees are exactions that require a cash payment (as opposed to many other types of development exactions that provide an opportunity for the developer to make a land, building, or other type of in-kind donation in lieu of paying the exaction in cash) based upon a fixed-fee schedule that is published, available, and enforced through ordinance or resolution. Examples of impact fees are the cash payments required of builders or developers by many Chicago suburbs; these fees are based upon a schedule of fixed fees that vary by the number of bedrooms in a new home, are required to be paid in order to obtain a building permit for a new home, and are earmarked and escrowed by the municipality for disbursement to their local school district to help finance new school buildings that will service the residents of the home whose permit is being obtained. Impact fees are also charged for such things as building a new branch library, building a new fire station, expanding a wastewater treatment plant, and buying a new piece of fire equipment. Understanding development exactions and their use can be very important for economic developers, students of economic development, public policymakers, and resident taxpayers.

Development exactions are an increasingly popular means of financing the public costs associated with economic development projects and economic development activity (Peddle and Lewis 1996). They are also a rather unique and richly diverse financing tool whose use has been adapted over time to changing economic and political circumstances. Exactions provide a means by which public infrastructure and other capital projects can be built or provided without resorting to unpopular tax increases or cuts in alternative projects, or at least a means by which to reduce the necessary magnitude of those actions. Furthermore, negotiated exactions provide one of the few means by which infrastructure and government services can be paid for using revenue sources other than tools of compulsory finance like taxes and charges.

Like fees and charges, development exactions are generally linked to some form of benefit received by the person who pays them. However, unlike most other government and economic development finance tools, development exactions commonly are paid fully or in part through in-kind contributions or fee offsets. Depending on their form, development exactions often require a rational nexus to some form of development activity, a higher standard than is applied to just about any other form of government finance mechanism.

The Growing and Changing Use of Exactions

The use of development exactions has ebbed and flowed over time, both in terms of prevalence and in terms of the nature of the exactions with "most favored" status. Nevertheless, development exactions remain a much more major finance tool than they were 40 years ago. There are a number of reasons why the use of development exactions has exploded (Altshuler and Gómez-Ibáñez 1993). First, the late 1960s brought a significant increase in concern about the environment and quality of life. This concern continued into the twenty-first century and meant a more ambivalent attitude toward growth. Development exactions were often adopted as part of comprehensive growth management plans that were motivated by a desire to slow growth to a more manageable level. Development exactions are perceived to increase the costs of development, thereby slowing the rate at which development would be expected to occur (other things equal).

Second, development exactions provide a logical and focused means for newly empowered neighborhood groups to counteract the harsh effects of many types of local development projects (e.g., the building of a large new subdivision in DeKalb, Illinois, that will take forest lands, open space, and children's play areas away from existing, adjacent residents while adding more traffic, congestion, and drainage problems to the existing neighborhood). At a minimum, development exactions help price some of the negative externalities (spillover effects) associated with some types of development activities (e.g., in the DeKalb case, impact fees could be used to make road improvements, provide drainage enhancements, and build buffers to mitigate negative effects on the existing neighborhood).

Third, over time, stagnating incomes and the tax revolt movement have made reliance on traditional revenue sources like property taxes and sales taxes less popular and more difficult to obtain. In addition, changes in the municipal bond market have made some types of debt issues for infrastructure more problematic (e.g., changes in rules that resulted in limiting the use of industrial revenue and industrial development bonds). Development exactions have helped to fill the gap but are less reliable as a financing alternative to property, income, and sales taxes when development slows, as occurred in the early part of the twenty-first century.

Fourth, deferred maintenance and a backlog of capital improvement projects have created a financing bottleneck that has made it impossible to finance all critical projects out of traditional tax sources on a timely basis, despite the common occurrence and increased probability of infrastructure failures. Development exactions provide another means by which the financing bottleneck might be overcome, but exactions rely on a vibrant development market to produce sufficient revenues to finance desired projects.

Finally, some more sophisticated fiscal impact analysis has provided greater and more precise evidence that most forms of new development, particularly residential, do not pay for themselves, especially when one looks at both the capital and operating costs of government (see the seminal work of Robert Burchell and David Listokin). This is a controversial notion in the home building community: Critics maintain that this work neither reflects the property taxes that a home will pay over its useful life nor takes into account the commercial real estate that develops in the community because of the additional homes. However, few challenges to Burchell and Listokin's work appear to accurately reflect capital costs, operating costs, and the time value of money in the alternative calculation of the net fiscal effect of a new home or other development unit. Nevertheless, acceptance by local officials of the general conclusions of analysts like Burchell and Listokin created an even greater demand and incentive for local communities to shift some of the burden of infrastructure finance to new developments through exactions.

While the principle of shifting the burden to new development remains, the work of Burchell and Listokin has given way to more sophisticated approaches to fiscal impact analysis such as the Applied Planning Techniques (APT) approach discussed at the end of this chapter. The new fiscal impact models are more sensitive to changes in economic conditions and have a better ability to calculate the combined effects of developments (including redevelopment of abandoned properties) than did the theoretical, seminal, but now somewhat less useful work of Burchell and his collaborators.

Yet, while all of these developments have contributed to the growth in the use of exactions as a means of financing economic development, there are other reasons for the increased use of exactions that are grounded in economic, political, and social theory and practice.

Why Do Communities Adopt Exactions?

Communities adopt development exactions for a variety of reasons and in a variety of situations. However, there seem to be a few common reasons why communities choose to add development exactions to their economic development finance portfolio.

Perhaps the most important reason why development exactions are widely used by communities is that they help to hold property taxes down by providing an alternative revenue source for expenditures that would otherwise be financed through such taxes. This is particularly notable because property taxes have almost universally been found in citizen surveys over the past 30 years to be the least popular form of taxation at the state and local level. Lower property taxes will generally be perceived to make an area more attractive as a place of residence and a place to do business. Typically, any offsetting effect of development exactions is hidden from view, especially for existing properties. Furthermore, exactions usually are of a "one-payment" nature. Unlike property taxes or other "pay as you use" financing tools, the magnitude of the exaction is known and fixed up front, and the responsibility for further payments generally does not exist. Thus, past development exactions are invisible to future buyers of a given piece of property. This removes a great deal of uncertainty for the taxpayer, as compared with a property-tax-based system that passes on a future stream of property tax payments and the prospect of additions to that future stream as more infrastructure is brought on line. These effects make exactions that much more politically attractive to elected officials.

However, as many elected officials in the early twenty-first century found out, the lower property taxes produced by a development exaction system are intimately dependent on development projects proceeding in sufficient magnitude and at a sufficient pace; unless these conditions are met, too little revenue will be generated to significantly or fully offset property taxes committed to paying the debt service on infrastructure built in the name of concurrency. Concurrency refers to the principle that infrastructure should be online and available by the time initial users of the infrastructure are present in the community. (See Hillsborough County [2009] for one articulation of the principle of infrastructure concurrency in ordinance form.) One community in Illinois encountered this financing reality as they financed their brand new high school. In selling the referendum to voters, proponents provided figures reflecting the assumed increase in property taxes the average homeowner would incur if the referendum were to pass. These figures were heavily dependent on new growth-producing property tax revenues and development exaction revenues to significantly offset the burden on existing taxpayers. When the housing market in the area collapsed, and the anticipated new growth that made the need for a new high school so urgent failed to occur, the school district altered neither its plans for the high school nor its basic financing plan. The likely result is that existing taxpayers will bear nearly the entire burden of paying for the new high school and will do so at rates double or more than those promised during the referendum campaign. And the existing residents will do so in a housing market that has seen the average home's value drop by 25 percent or more since passage of the referendum.

Another related reason why development exactions are an increasingly popular local finance tool is that they add diversity to the revenue structure used to finance economic development. Over the years, there has been heavy reliance on the property tax to finance the local infrastructure and public services that support economic development activity and daily life in communities. Development exactions can help reduce reliance on the property tax and in the process provide a revenue structure that is more evenly divided among a diverse set of revenue tools.

Remember from the previous point that while the property tax remains a widely used form of local government finance, it also remains a flash point for tax revolt efforts and widespread resident dissatisfaction. As a result, tax and spending limitations have placed significant constraints on continued use of the property tax as the major source of funds for financing local infrastructure and services. This has contributed to fiscal stress at all levels of government, as cuts in the revenue available from property taxes have come at the same time as increased devolution of responsibility down the fiscal federalism chain. Such a combination has made local program cuts seem inevitable. It has also meant that the cries from communities for assistance from higher levels of government are more frequent, more urgent, and more fervent.

Development exactions often provide a way to help stem the downward slide for many growing communities, both in terms of the revenue stream they provide and in the way they improve the fiscal health of general funds (as well as other government funds) in these communities through their revenue diversification effects. For example, funds that otherwise would have been used to pay for the infrastructure and services supporting economic development can be freed up through development exactions and put to alternative uses. As a rule, revenue diversification aids in the stability and health of a government's finances. The effects are often seen in improved municipal bond ratings and the reduction in borrowing costs that comes with such improved ratings. While development exactions help to provide this valuable diversification, they are particularly sensitive to economic conditions. In a down economy, development exaction revenues often fall well short of their expected or planned level. To the extent that funds that would have been used to pay for infrastructure and capital projects are now irretrievably pledged to other projects, the development exaction system in some cases may exacerbate rather than ameliorate fiscal stress on governmental units and their communities.

Another reason why development exactions are popular with local governments is their perceived effectiveness as a tool of growth management. Development exactions have the reputation as a tool for helping "make growth pay for itself." In addition, development exactions raise the cost of developing a given piece of property, though some or all of these costs may be passed through to buyers or other participants in the development process (Skidmore and Peddle 1998). Development exactions are commonly expected to slow the growth that a community might expect to take place, and, therefore, can be an attractive tool for growth management. Empirical evidence of this was provided by Skidmore and Peddle (1998), who estimated that impact fees in DuPage County, Illinois, had been responsible for a 25 percent reduction in the residential growth rate in the county. It is notable that the county still experienced significant growth during the time period they studied, but that the fees that were imposed appeared to be an effective tool in dampening both the explosive growth of the county and the fiscal effects of that growth. In the early twenty-first century, focus shifted from dampening and managing growth to pulling out all stops to encourage growth. Development exaction systems were often perceived as a barrier to encouraging growth and in some cases were suspended by governments independently or at the behest of economically challenged developer and builders.

John Shannon, former executive director of the Advisory Commission on Intergovernmental Relations (a now defunct independent federal agency), coined the term "fend for yourself federalism" to describe the massive devolution of responsibilities from the federal and state governments down to the local level. Development exactions provide an attractive means of financing activities in such a setting because of their basis in the benefit principle of public finance. The benefit principle says that individuals should pay for government goods and services based on their degree of consumption of those goods and services. "Application of the benefit principle to growth management means that the costs of providing infrastructure should be borne by those economic units that create the need for that infrastructure" (Peddle and Lewis 1998). While the operating costs of government are generally difficult to attribute to individual households or businesses, infrastructure and capital costs are more discrete and attributable to individual economic units. Additionally, "by tying the costs of infrastructure more directly to the beneficiaries of the services provided by that infrastructure, economic efficiency in the allocation of public infrastructure investment dollars should be enhanced" (Peddle and Lewis 1998). Development exactions, and impact fees in particular, provide governmental units an opportunity to attribute and allocate certain capital costs to individual economic units. This provides a tangible justification for impact fees based on economic theory. Besides being economically efficient, it is also intuitively appealing to have the costs of government services and new infrastructure paid for by the people who use them. Yet, efficiency is not the only possible criterion by which the economic benefits of development exactions might be appropriately judged.

Equity Issues and Development Exactions

Because development exactions can be expected to alter the prevailing distribution of the costs of financing government services and infrastructure, one would expect that they might also have some effects on the income distribution and relative economic well-being in the community. While the potential efficiency gains from the use of development exactions are identifiable and attractive, the equity or fairness effects of development exactions—attributable generally to changes in the income distribution or living standards of different citizen groups in the community—are much more difficult to discern and generalize. These equity effects are not only important but also provide insight into another popular argument offered by existing community residents in favor of the adoption or enhancement of a development exaction system.

If they do nothing else, development exactions generally alter the distribution among economic actors of the costs of financing public infrastructure. In particular, development exactions are designed to increase the share of the cost of new infrastructure that is paid by new growth. Getting growth to "pay its own way" is one of the most common justifications offered for adopting a development exaction or impact fee system. In the absence of development exactions, the costs of infrastructure required to service new growth would typically be borne by the community's taxpayers as a whole, often through compulsory finance tools like the real property tax.

Development exactions are generally levied against the developer of projects that require building new infrastructure or that make use of excess infrastructure capacity built to accommodate or service new development projects. It is an empirical question as to which economic actors—the developers, builders, home buyers, or existing residents—bear the effective burden of any set of development exactions and how that burden is allocated among them.

The precise allocation of the burden of exactions is dependent on, among other things, the price elasticity of demand and the price elasticity of supply for a particular type of development (e.g., new, upscale, four-bedroom and larger homes) in a particular geographic market. In general, a particular set of economic actors will bear less of the burden when they have the ability to avoid the exactions by choosing to move their economic activity away from the jurisdiction that imposes them. For example, if home buyers can easily choose to go to an adjacent, nonexaction community to buy a comparable house, then, other things equal, a simple market reaction is likely to occur: Those home buyers will flee the fee by locating in another nearby community, thereby paying less of the impact fee or development exaction than if they had stayed put. However, a scenario in which development exactions do not shift at least some of the burden of infrastructure finance to developers and builders is very unlikely, as is a scenario where home buyers bear none of the burden of the exactions. These scenarios would presume absolute and total inability on the part of at least one type of economic actor to alter their economic behavior to avoid the development exaction—a situation of perfectly inelastic demand or supply in the housing or land market. Such a scenario borders on the impossible. Whether justified by reliable empirical evidence or not, perception among the general public is that development exactions help make sure that development pays for itself. Yet, in almost every community, much of the capital infrastructure was built at a time when development exactions were not used, or at least were not used extensively.

Thus, adopting a development exaction program typically begs the question of whether new residents and new businesses are being singled out for inequitable treatment. Assume that the infrastructure to support the existing homes and businesses in a community was financed by the community as a whole; without special exactions or assessments paid by the new development, one might perceive that new development is asked to bear an unfairly disproportionate share of financing the public infrastructure that is needed to support the new homes and businesses.

In addition, one can expect that the market price for housing, both existing and new dwelling units, will increase in the presence of a development exaction system, though the extent of that increase is again subject to the empirical conditions outlined earlier. Thus, one further equity issue raised by development exactions is the degree to which they decrease the affordability of housing in a community, thereby threatening the ability of lower- and moderate-income households to afford to buy or rent housing in that community. Some of the most sophisticated exaction systems have the provision of affordable housing as a required element of the donations made by developers of projects in the community (Altshuler and Gómez-Ibáñez 1993). Thus, one key issue for a community evaluating a development exaction system for adoption or continuation is the extent to which those development exactions are consistent with the community's values regarding the appropriate distribution of the costs of financing public infrastructure and public services, as well as the preservation of an affordable housing base in the community.

The Changing Playing Field of Development Exactions

The discussion thus far has presented a picture of development exactions primarily as they operated in the common environment of communities facing simultaneous growth pressure and fiscal stress in an era of property tax dissatisfaction and revolt. Development exactions and impact fees generally worked well in an environment where new growth occurred at a sufficiently fast pace to justify the significant investment in the infrastructure necessary to support the growth. Concurrency was a critical factor—would the needed new infrastructure be online in time to serve the new people and new businesses who created the need for it? In addition, growth occurred at a fast enough pace to produce sufficient exaction revenues or in-kind donations to take the pressure off revenue sources that were heavily reliant on existing residents and businesses (e.g., the real property tax). The playing field drastically changes in the midst of an economic slowdown like the one seen at the beginning of the twenty-first century.

Among the changes in the playing field observed during the start of the economic downturn in 2008 were the following: (1) moratoria on development exactions to help induce development activity (e.g., see Mullen 2010);

(2) greater developer preference for noncash development exactions as a means of improving their cash flow; (3) refinancing of infrastructure debt to stretch repayment schedules and allow the development market to find more reliable streams of revenues for debt service; (4) greater reliance on special service areas to finance infrastructure, allowing payments to be stretched out and making the statutory incidence fall on homeowners rather than developers with liens against property available as a tool for ensuring payment (e.g., see Sroka 2009); (5) more rigorous bonding requirements to assure that promised public improvements are made should a developer abandon a project; and (6) more effort by communities to rely on recapture agreements as a means of financing infrastructure. In the case of recapture agreements, developers agree to finance and build public infrastructure up front with the ability to recapture more than their investment by charging future users to hook up to the infrastructure system they provided. Recaptures are most commonly used in situations where water and sewer lines must be extended or expanded to service a developer's parcel or project, and the extension or expansion of infrastructure makes development of other nearby parcels a viable prospect. As one might imagine, the popularity of recapture agreements with communities is mirrored by a growing disinterest on the part of developers when they are being squeezed by a tough economy.

When a community is contemplating a reduction in exactions or impact fees in order to stimulate growth, careful consideration should be given to the underlying structure of the system. For example, if exaction levels have been determined based on a perception of what the market will bear, then a reduction may serve to correct an imbalance in the system. However, if payment levels have been established based on a thorough analysis of net negative impact, then an impact fee reduction will likely shift a portion of the burden of supporting new development onto the existing community.

Yet, even after a community has decided to implement a development exactions system, much work must be done to establish clear policies to guide the imposition and administration of the system. One key issue is how to calculate the costs of growth appropriately and allocate those costs among economic units.

General Approaches to Calculation

Development exactions are grounded in the notion that successful development in a community typically increases the need/demand for public infrastructure and services. Furthermore, the quantity or quality of adjustments in public services or infrastructure can often be attributed to a single development project. Finally, it is recognized that economic or community development projects generally result in some form of additional revenue stream for the community hosting those projects (e.g., real property taxes, sales taxes). Calculating an exaction requires that one investigate three components: (1) *demand,* or the increased need for infrastructure/services; (2) *cost,* or the outlay necessary to provide the newly demanded infrastructure/services; and (3) *revenue,* or the enhancement to the resources of the government provided through the new development. Taking these three elements into account produces an exaction amount that accurately reflects the appropriate net effects of a given development project on a community's infrastructure and public services.

In order to address the subject of exaction calculation, it is necessary to adopt definitions of various relevant terms. A *demand unit* is the discrete, identifiable entity whose addition will require improvements to capital facilities (e.g., an additional student requires additional school facilities; an additional family requires additional parks and active recreation facilities). A *service standard* is the quantity of capital facilities that will be required by new development (Nicholas, Nelson, and Juergensmeyer 1991). Further, for purposes of clarity, we will make a distinction between an exaction and an impact fee. An *exaction* is a condition of development approval that requires a builder or developer to give or provide something to (or on behalf of) a local government or service district. That something could include dedication of sites for common or public facilities; construction of common or public facilities; provision of vehicles and equipment for common or public use; payments to defray the costs of land, facilities, vehicles, and equipment; or some combination of these items (Frank and Rhodes 1987). In contrast, we define an *impact fee* as a form of cash-based development exaction based on a fixed-fee schedule and commonly published in an adopted ordinance or policy statement. In addition to a fixed-fee schedule, development impact fee programs are usually based on a specific calculation methodology that considers and then allocates the proportionate share of the impact on a facility that is generated by new development.

Although the actual calculation of appropriate exactions can take many forms and require rigorous investigation, the essential elements of analysis and calculation generally remain demand, cost, and revenue (Dahlstrom 1995). Therefore, if one accepts the definitions and distinctions we have provided regarding exactions and development impact fees, then the determination of an appropriate *negotiated* exaction (i.e., one not based on a fixed-fee schedule) may be influenced by the measurement of and balance among demand, cost, and revenue. In contrast, determination of an appropriate impact fee will be narrowly limited by the measurement and balance among demand, cost, and revenue reflected in some form of fixed-fee schedule.

Full consideration of demand, cost, and revenue is often overlooked in the rush to implement a development impact fee requirement to relieve capital cost burdens in rapidly growing communities. In general, demand and cost factors are easily determined, and while the revenue side of the equation can be more challenging, its importance should be apparent. We discuss each of the calculation components separately, and then develop a particular example of an impact fee methodology to illustrate how the calculation process might proceed in practice.

Demand

In order to sustain an active and vital community, some level of public infrastructure is required to support businesses, workers, and residents. That public infrastructure typically includes things like roads, water and sewer systems, police and fire protection, a judicial system, and schools. It may also include things like parks, recreation centers, community centers, hospitals, public libraries, convention centers, and a myriad of other local amenities. Despite the variety of forms that it can take, public infrastructure is typically characterized by two features: (1) investment must be in discrete large units that are "lumpy"; and (2) each unit has some finite capacity. These features have implications for the developing community.

First of all, public infrastructure, when first built, will have excess capacity that can be used to accommodate future development. The prudent community actively plans for the development and use of this excess infrastructure capacity. The best and most common way of planning is through a comprehensive capital improvement plan and program.

Second, a small change in the cumulative level of an area's development activity can trigger the need for a significant new investment in public infrastructure. The need for new infrastructure or the recapture of the costs of the excess capacity built into old infrastructure provide an important motivation for development exactions. At the most basic level, development increases the amount of demand for various types of public infrastructure and, therefore, the need for a way to pay for this infrastructure. The demand component of development exaction calculation allocates the capacity of infrastructure to a particular type of unit that is associated with the increased need for the particular type of public infrastructure. This unit, a "demand unit," is a single, discrete, identifiable entity that creates the need for—and uses of—public infrastructure.

Cost

Without costs, there would be no development exactions. In particular, development exactions exist to cover the cost of the public infrastructure required to service new developments. Typically, this infrastructure is financed up front through some form of debt finance (e.g., general obligation bonds, revenue bonds, tax increment financing bonds, installment contracts) or a leaseback arrangement.

In many ways, costs are the easiest of the key variables to estimate, especially if the infrastructure is built prior to the first demand units coming on line. The total capital cost of the infrastructure can then be reliably and objectively fixed (no contingencies should be necessary, since the project has been completed). Even in the case of infrastructure not yet built, but proposed in a comprehensive capital facilities plan, costs are typically estimable. Within an acceptable level of confidence, building costs are predictable from tables and experience, land costs can be hedged through banking and/or developer dedications, and the capacity of the infrastructure generally can be determined.

Of course, these costs must then be allocated to demand units, as well as revenue sources (since exactions may be only one of the financing sources for the infrastructure—more on this later). However, these issues are not issues of cost, but rather issues of demand and revenue structure.

Revenue

While proponents of development exactions often extol the virtues of having new growth pay for itself, most also recognize the need to not "overcharge" the new growth for community infrastructure. Furthermore, it should be recognized that particular development units might differ in their expected capacity to produce revenue for the local governments, even though as demand units their impact on the infrastructure can be expected to be the same. For example, a three-bedroom starter home and a more upscale three-bedroom home would be expected to generate roughly the same number of students for a school district over time, but the upscale home is likely to have a higher market value; therefore, those homeowners will pay more in property taxes that can be used to help pay for the services that its occupants require. Put another way, the upscale home is more likely to produce an excess of tax dollars above and beyond the services that it and its occupants consume: The higher the value of the home, the more likely this is to occur. That fiscal surplus then can be used to offset fiscal deficits created by other demand units. However, given that development exactions are designed solely to offset the capital, rather than the operating, costs attributable to new growth, calculations of a revenue offset must be done carefully and conservatively.

In effect, the revenue calculation attempts to credit new growth for the two separate contributions it makes to the fiscal health of the community. First, new growth should not be asked to simultaneously pay a disproportionate share of financing infrastructure to service its needs while also being asked to pay for the bond issues used to finance previous iterations of infrastructure built (solely) to service other areas of the community. Second, if the new growth will produce a fiscal surplus, that amount should be taken into account as a contribution to the community's finances and be credited against the exaction. One can quickly see the link between these analytical techniques and fiscal impact analysis.

There are obvious similarities between the methodologies employed in fiscal impact analysis and the calculation of development impact fees. Both should be based on a comprehensive analysis of an extensive array of relevant data. However, development impact fee analysis should be carried to higher levels of detail, because the objective is to determine an individualized assessment of impact. While fiscal impact analysis focuses on the effects of an entire development on an entire community, development impact fee analysis should focus on the effects of the development of an individual parcel of land on specific capital components of applicable community facilities. We present an example of an impact fee calculation later in this chapter.

Types of Exactions

As referenced earlier, communities adopt exactions in a wide variety of situations; as a result, it would be impossible to provide an exhaustive list. However, some forms of exactions are relatively common in high-growth situations, and some generalizations are achievable (Nicholas, Nelson, and Juergensmeyer 1991). Exactions may be applicable to residential development, to nonresidential development, or to both. Further, the majority of exactions fall into one of three categories that may be distinguished by the means of measurement of demand units. The first category uses residential population as the demand unit. This form of analysis is commonly applied to exactions for the following types of facilities:

- Schools
- Parks
- Libraries
- Water systems
- Sanitary sewer systems
- Police protection
- Emergency medical
- General governmental

In general, exactions based on residential population require an exact enumeration of dwelling units and conversion of those counts to an estimated population figure derived from a reliable source. That procedure considers the probable population load of the dwelling unit and allows the exaction to be sensitive to the demand unit that actually generates the need for the facility (population).

While sensitivity to population is desirable in the calculation of residential exactions, it is not always possible to accomplish, due to a lack of acceptable data. For example, data available from the Institute of Transportation Engineers (ITE) are widely cited for vehicle trip generation factors applied in the design of roadway exactions. ITE data for residential land uses are gathered and made available by basic dwelling-unit type. Consequently, a second category of residential exactions uses dwelling units for demand measurement rather than population. That form of analysis is commonly applied to exactions for the following types of facilities:

- Fire protection
- Roads
- Stormwater control systems

It should be noted that residential exactions might be based on dwelling units rather than on population in situations where reliable demographic data are not available.

Exactions for nonresidential land uses can be based on a broad range of demand unit measurements, depending upon the manner in which primary or secondary data are available. Most methodologies attempt to convert nonresidential demand to some population equivalent (PE) or use locally generated information regarding consumption by land area or floor area. That form of analysis is commonly applied for the following types of facilities:

- Sanitary sewer systems
- Water systems
- Stormwater control systems
- Public safety (police, fire, emergency medical)
- Roads
- General governmental

Calculating an Impact Fee: An Example

Exactions and development impact fees can be calculated in a variety of ways. The example that follows explains the data sources and basic calculations for the Applied Planning Techniques school district capital improvement development impact fee program. The APT program has been adopted in a number of annexation agreements in the State of Illinois. The program takes into account the state's "specifically and uniquely attributable" legal standard, first articulated in *Pioneer Trust and Savings Bank v. The Village of Mount Prospect* [176 N.E.2d 799, 801 (IL 1961)] for evaluation of such programs. Although it is not always entirely clear what is intended or required under the "specifically and uniquely attributable standard," it is acknowledged to be the most stringent standard for evaluating and judging exactions in that it implies a direct and material benefit in exchange for the exaction (Cope 2000).

The APT program is demand, cost, and revenue sensitive. Revenue sensitivity is achievable to extremely high levels of detail. The program requires a substantial amount of system-specific input data and can generate a substantial volume of unit-specific output data, which are often presented in tabular form. The required data for the APT school district capital improvement development impact program include details regarding the following:

1. District enrollment
2. Square footage of school facilities
3. School district operational and capital budgets
4. School district equalized assessed valuation and real estate tax factors
5. Capital facility projects completed by the district
6. Existing and projected debt for capital facilities

With respect to cost, the APT model is designed to recognize many of the unique qualities of individual school districts. For example, data input for the model is based generally on the prevailing service standard in the subject school district rather than on a regional, state, or national standard. In most instances, the service standard is measured in square footage of facilities per student, and the cost of delivering that service standard to a new student population is estimated from data on school facilities built in Illinois over several decades. Construction cost figures from the subject school district are introduced into the database and are over-weighted to reflect any unique circumstances that may affect that district. The intent is to produce locally sensitive yet broadly based construction cost factors. Historic cost information is updated to current levels through the application of a building construction cost index similar to those published regularly in *Engineering News Record.* The derived construction cost is compared to a national source of school construction data, *School Planning & Management,* from time to time as a monitoring measure (Planning4Education.com 2011).

The generation of demand factors for school district capital improvement impact fees is based on the specifics of dwelling unit type and number of bedrooms. Commonly, student generation data are obtained through the application of demographic factors from generally accepted, objective sources for single-family detached, single-family attached, and multifamily dwelling units. An example of a widely used source of demographic data and population tables in Illinois is the "Table of Ultimate Population per Dwelling Unit," published by the Illinois School Consulting Service/Associated Municipal Consultants (DeKalb County, IL 1996).

Because development generates value—and therefore revenue—in addition to demand, credits are applied in the overall impact analysis. Failure to consider credits may result in overcharging new residents for required capital facilities. The consideration of credits focuses on the extent to which a school district can direct revenue from new development to capital facilities. Generally, this revenue credit is based on projected participation in the retirement of capital debt. There are a number of ways to determine credits for school capital facilities. The APT model applies credits on a dollar-value basis. Although complex, that form of credit calculation produces a high degree of sensitivity (Nicholas, Nelson, and Juergensmeyer 1991).

A dollar-value credit calculation is based on the "spreading" of the debt service cost over the valuation of the taxing district's equalized assessed valuation, as modified by the proposed development. That is, the existing debt service of the taxing district is allocated to the expected total assessed valuation of the district after the development project is undertaken. For example, if the district has $4.5 million in debt service per year, a current assessed valuation of $400 million, and an expected increment to the assessed valuation of $50 million from a new subdivision (for a new total equalized assessed valuation of $450 million), the allocation would be $.10 per $1.00 of assessed valuation. A present value is calculated for the cumulative annual charge per dollar of valuation for the life of the debt service. If, in the previous example, the debt service were to continue for 30 years, the present value of a 30-year stream of allocated debt service payments would be taken. Due to variations in initial and effective bond terms and other individual qualities of the overall debt structure, a series of independent calculations must be made for each outstanding capital bond issue and for each property value. Depending upon the desired level of output detail, the methodology can require several thousand individual calculations.

However, a straightforward numerical example for a given home can provide a basic understanding of the concept of credits. A $300,000 home located in a school district in Cook County, Illinois, and subject to a real estate tax rate including a .5303 factor for bond debt would pay $548.99 annually for debt service, after adjusting for the assessment percentage, the equalization rate, and a homeowner's exemption. That is the amount the homeowner is contributing to paying for past capital projects in the district through the real property tax. In simple terms, since the homeowner is paying the impact fee for essentially the same or substitute capital facilities, asking them to pay a property tax bill for the facilities unfairly burdens them with disproportionate payments for the same facilities. Over time, these property taxes for capital facilities can add up. The present value of the amount in this example (over 30 years at a 5 percent rate of discount) is $8,439.29. In fact, some development impact fee programs employ a methodology for credit calculation that credits this full present value against the calculated impact fee. Most impact fee calculations credit a portion of this present value, recognizing the collective benefits of the infrastructure and services that should be shared by all, including those who also pay an impact fee. It should be noted that a form of credit calculation based on real estate tax is applicable only in those situations in which debt for capital facilities is funded through the property tax. However, regardless of credit calculation methodology, the intent is to produce a "net impact" measurement that considers the revenue generation attributable to the demand unit and is sensitive to not having the demand unit pay a disproportionate amount for the infrastructure or services.

The limitations of the APT program and similar programs are generally those associated with a lack of available local data. All development impact fee programs should be based on a careful evaluation of relevant service standards and identification of appropriate demand units. However, many local governments and service districts do not collect data in a form that facilitates analysis of service standards and demand units. For example, most communities can provide information regarding the daily pumping volumes of municipal water and give an estimate of the current population. As a result, these communities often believe that they have the necessary information (per capita water consumption) to implement a water-system-based capital-improvement development impact fee program. The problem is that nonresidential development also consumes water, and many water system engineering studies do not identify water consumption factors for nonresidential development to the level of detail required for accurate impact measurement.

Furthermore, supporting architectural and engineering studies should provide discrete cost data for the various components of the capital facility systems. Again, using a water system example, the system is usually comprised of elements for extraction, treatment, storage, and transmission. The distribution of cost for these elements may not be uniform throughout the system—a point of particular importance in large, complex water systems that may include multiple pressure zones due to elevation changes in the service area. In order to avoid the necessity of revising otherwise valid studies, future consideration of a development impact fee program should be an integral part of the capital improvement planning process rather than an afterthought.

In addition to the need for suitably detailed architectural and engineering studies for capital projects, comprehensive development impact fee programs should be supported by an up-to-date comprehensive plan and capital improvement program. These documents usually provide the projections that are essential to development impact fee program design and can be useful tools for explaining why such fees often are necessary components of a growth management program.

Conclusion

Although exaction programs come under pressure during difficult economic times, it is likely that development exactions will remain a popular means of financing the infrastructure costs associated with economic and community development. Exactions can be powerful growth management tools that improve the fiscal capacity and health of developing communities. However, exactions must be based on careful and predictable calculations of the costs imposed by growth and of the allocation of those costs to demand units in the community. When combined with a careful and comprehensive capital improvements program, development exactions provide a means for assuring infrastructure concurrency and fiscal solvency for communities.

References

Altshuler, Alan A., and José A. Gómez-Ibáñez. 1993. *Regulation for Revenue*. Cambridge, MA: Lincoln Institute of Land Policy.

Cope, Ronald S. 2000. *Impact Fees: Constitutional Calculations for Future Growth*. DeKalb: Illinois Association of School Business Officials.

Dahlstrom, Roger K. 1995. Development impact fees: A review of contemporary techniques for calculation, data collection, and documentation. *Northern Illinois University Law Review* 15 (Summer): 557–69.

DeKalb County, Illinois. 1996. Table of estimated ultimate population per dwelling unit. DeKalb: Illinois School Consulting Service, Associated Municipal Consultants. www.dekalbcounty.org/PDF_INTERNET/Zoning/TableEstdPopnPerUnit.pdf.

Frank, James E., and Robert M. Rhodes. 1987. *Development Exactions*. Chicago: American Planning Association.

Hillsborough County, Florida. 2009. Consolidated Impact Assessment Program Ordinance, as amended through July 2009.

Mullen, Caitlin. 2010. Sycamore considering short-term change to impact fees. *Daily Chronicle* (Sycamore, IL), August 28: 1.

Nicholas, James C., Arthur C. Nelson, and Julian C. Juergensmeyer. 1991. *A Practitioner's Guide to Development Impact Fees*. Chicago: American Planning Association.

Peddle, Michael T., and John L. Lewis. 1996. Development exactions as growth management and infrastructure finance tools. *Public Works Management and Policy* 1 (October): 129–44.

———. 1998. Would Illinois benefit from impact fee legislation? *Illinois Developer* 1 (March): 21–26.

Pioneer Trust and Savings. Bank v. The Village of Mount Prospect [176 N.E.2d 799, 801 (IL 1961)].

Planning4Education.com. 2011. *The 16th Annual 2011 School Construction Report.* Special report, *School Planning & Management,* February. www.peterli.com/spm/pdfs/SchoolConstructionReport2011.pdf (accessed March 15, 2012).

Skidmore, Mark, and Michael T. Peddle. 1998. Do development impact fees reduce the rate of residential development? *Growth and Change* 29 (Fall): 383–400.

Sroka, Diana. 2009. SSA battles get emotional, polarizing. *The Northwest Herald* (Crystal Lake, IL), November 15. http://nl.newsbank.com (accessed October 3, 2011). Video of an accompanying television program expanding on this story is also accessible through *The Northwest Herald.*

14
Financing Professional Sports Facilities

Robert A. Baade and Victor A. Matheson

The past 20 years have witnessed a massive transformation of professional sports infrastructure in North America and the rest of the world. In the United States and Canada alone, by 2012, 125 of the 140 teams in the five largest professional sports leagues, the National Football League (NFL), Major League Baseball (MLB), National Basketball Association (NBA), Major League Soccer (MLS), and National Hockey League (NHL), will play in stadia constructed or significantly refurbished since 1990. This new construction has come at a significant cost, the majority of which has been borne by taxpayers. Construction costs alone for major league professional sports facilities have totaled in excess of $30 billion in nominal terms over the past two decades, with over half of the cost being paid by the public. See Tables 14.1–14.5 for lists of newly constructed or refurbished stadia in various American sports leagues. It should be noted that these figures understate the total level of public subsidies directed toward spectator sports, as they exclude subsidies not directly related to infrastructure and also ignore minor league and collegiate sports as well as other popular professional sports such as golf, tennis, and auto racing.

North America is not alone in its largesse directed to sports facilities. South Africa spent $1.3 billion on building and upgrading 10 soccer stadia for the 2010 World Cup following on the heels of Germany's €2.4 billion investment in stadia and general infrastructure for the 2006 edition of the event. The Summer Olympic Games require the greatest financial commitment of all the mega-sports events, with the typical outlay in the neighborhood of $10 billion, but in some instances the sums have far surpassed that amount (Preuss 2004). China reportedly incurred costs in excess of $58 billion to host the event in 2008 (Upegui 2008). Such sums of direct public investment to

Table 14.1

New NFL Stadiums Since 1990

Team	Stadium	Built	Cost (000s) (nominal)	Public cost	Public percent
New Orleans	Superdome (repair and rehab)	2011	$505	$490	97
Giants/Jets	New Meadowlands Stadium	2010	$1,600	—	0
Kansas City	Arrowhead Stadium (rehab)	2010	$375	$250	67
Dallas	Cowboys Stadium	2009	$1,150	$325	28
Indianapolis	Lukas Oil Stadium	2008	$620	$620	86
Arizona	University of Phoenix Stadium	2006	$71	$267	72
Philadelphia	Lincoln Financial Field	2003	$285	$228	80
Green Bay	Lambeau Field	2003	$295	$251	85
Chicago	Soldier Field	2003	$600	$450	75
New England	Gillette Stadium	2002	$325	$33	10
Houston	Reliant Stadium	2002	$300	$225	75
Detroit	Ford Field	2002	$300	$219	73
Seattle	Qwest Field	2002	$300	$201	67
Pittsburgh	Heinz Field	2001	$230	$150	65
Denver	Invesco Field	2001	$365	$274	75
Cincinnati	Paul Brown Stadium	2000	$400	$400	100
Cleveland	Browns Stadium	1999	$283	$255	90
Tennessee	LP Field	1999	$290	$220	76
Buffalo	Ralph Wilson Stadium (rehab)	1999	$63	$63	100
Baltimore	M&T Bank Stadium	1998	$220	$176	80
Tampa Bay	Raymond James Stadium	1998	$169	$169	100
San Diego	Qualcomm Stadium	1997	$78	$78	100
Washington	FedEx Field	1997	$250	$70	28
Oakland	Oakland Coliseum (rehab)	1996	$200	$200	100
Carolina	Bank of America Stadium	1996	$248	$52	21
Jacksonville	Everbank Field	1995	$121	$121	100
St. Louis	Edward Jones Dome	1995	$280	$280	100
Atlanta	Georgia Dome	1992	$214	$214	100
	29 of 32 teams		$10,237	$6,281	61

build infrastructure for private businesses or events are generally rare in other sectors of the economy. For this level of public investment, it is reasonable to ask the extent to which professional sports serve to promote local economic development.

Professional Sports as a Mirror of Economic Development

Organized sports are as old as history itself. Typically, however, the construction of sports stadia and the creation of professional sports franchises have served as a reflection of economic development rather than as a means to it. The grandeur of the Roman Colosseum is a clear testament to the wealth and engineering skills

Table 14.2

New MLB Stadiums Since 1990

Team	Stadium	Built	Cost (000s) (nominal)	Public cost	Public percent
Miami	Marlins Field	2012	$525	$370	70
Minnesota	Target Field	2010	$544	$392	72
NY Mets	Citi Field	2009	$600	$164	27
NY Yankees	Yankee Stadium	2009	$1,300	$220	17
Kansas City	Kaufmann Stadium (rehab)	2009	$250	$175	70
Washington	Nationals Park	2008	$611	$611	100
Cardinals	Busch Stadium	2006	$365	$45	12
San Diego	PETCO Park	2004	$457	$304	66
Philadelphia	Citizens Bank Park	2004	$346	$174	50
Cincinnati	Great American Ball Park	2003	$325	$280	86
Pittsburgh	PNC Park	2001	$262	$262	100
Milwaukee	Miller Park	2001	$400	$310	78
Detroit	Comerica Park	2000	$300	$115	38
Houston	Minute Maid Park	2000	$265	$180	68
San Francisco	AT&T Park	2000	$357	$15	4
Seattle	Safeco Park	1999	$518	$392	76
Arizona	Chase Field	1998	$349	$238	68
Los Angeles Angels	Angel Stadium (rehab)	1998	$118	$30	25
Tampa Bay	Tropicana Field	1997	$208	$208	100
Atlanta	Turner Field	1997	$235	$165	70
Oakland As	Oakland Coliseum (rehab)	1996	$200	$200	100
Denver	Coors Field	1995	$215	$168	78
Cleveland	Progressive Field	1994	$175	$91	52
Texas Rangers	Ballpark at Arlington	1994	$191	$135	71
Baltimore	Camden Yards	1992	$110	$100	91
Chicago White Sox	U.S. Cellular Field	1991	$167	$167	100
	26 of 30 teams		$9,393	$5,511	59

of the Roman Empire, but it was certainly not designed to enhance local incomes. The Roman poet Juvenal coined the phrase "bread and circuses" around 100 C.E. to describe the use of food subsidies and lavish entertainment to distract and pacify the masses. This term has come to symbolize the decline of civic duty in the Roman Empire in favor of frivolity and shallow desires. According to Juvenal, Roman politicians decided that the most effective way to ascend to power was to buy the votes of the poor by giving out cheap food and entertainment, i.e., bread and circuses (Sperber 2001). Under the Roman emperors, the Colosseum was simply another way, albeit a costly one, to limit public dissent. There is no evidence that it was expected to promote local economic growth.

Rome was not alone in its pursuit of spectator sports. Ball games were played in ancient Egypt, the Greeks created the now famous Olympic Games in 776 B.C.E.,

Table 14.3

New MLS Stadiums Since 1990

Team	Stadium	Built	Cost (000s) (nominal)	Public cost	Public per-cent
Houston	Dynamo Stadium	2012	$110	$50	45
San Jose	Earthquakes Stadium	2012	$60	$0	0
Kansas City	Wizards Stadium	2011	$160	$80	50
Portland	PGE Park (rehab)	2011	$31	$31	100
Vancouver	BC Place Stadium	2011	$365	$365	100
New York	Red Bull Arena	2010	$190	$90	47
Philadelphia	PPL Park	2010	$120	$77	64
Salt Lake	Rio Tinto Stadium	2008	$115	$16	14
Colorado	Dick's Sporting Goods Park	2007	$131	$66	50
Toronto	BMO Field	2007	$63	$63	100
Chicago	Toyota Park	2006	$98	$98	100
Montreal	Saputo Stadium	2006	$14	$0	0
Dallas	Pizza Hut Park	2005	$80	$80	100
L.A. Galaxy/Chivas	Home Depot Center	2003	$150	$0	0
New England	Gillette Stadium	2002	$325	$33	10
Seattle	Qwest Field	2002	$300	$201	67
Columbus	Columbus Crew Stadium	1999	$29	$0	0
	17 of 18		$2,340	$1,249	53

and Native Americans played handball in the Mayan Empire and the forerunner of lacrosse in what is now the northeastern portion of the United States. Although many ancient sports such as archery, chariot racing, horseback riding, and wrestling can be seen as offshoots of professional military training, typically participants would have been considered amateur athletes. While contestants in these games may have been rewarded by government, religious leaders, or the spectators themselves for superior athletic performance, the rise of the truly professional athlete did not come about until the late 1800s (Matheson 2006).

The first sport in the United States to give rise to fully professional athletes was baseball. Following the codification of the rules by Alexander Cartwright in 1845, baseball grew in popularity both as a spectator and as a participatory sport. While some players on particular teams received compensation for their play, it was not until 1869 that the Cincinnati Red Stockings formed the first team comprised entirely of professional players. Their success on the field led other teams to adopt their strategy. By 1871, the National Association was formed with nine teams, including the Boston Braves, the forerunner of today's modern Atlanta Braves.

Not surprisingly, the rise of the professional athlete occurred during the time of the Industrial Revolution, which provided substantial increases in income

Table 14.4

New NBA Arenas Since 1990

Team	Stadium	Built	Cost (000s) (nominal)	Public cost	Public percent
Orlando	Amway Center	2010	$480	$430	90
Brooklyn Nets	Barclays Center	2010	$637	$150	24
Charlotte	Time Warner Cable Arena	2005	$265	$265	100
Memphis	FedEx Forum	2004	$250	$250	100
Phoenix	U.S. Air (construction and rehab.)	1992/ 2004	$157	$157	100
Houston	Toyota Center	2003	$235	$192	82
San Antonio	AT&T Center	2002	$186	$158	85
Oklahoma City	Ford Center	2002	$89	$89	100
Dallas	American Airlines Center	2001	$420	$210	50
Toronto	Air Canada Centre	1999	$265	—	0
Indianapolis	Conseco Fieldhouse	1999	$183	$183	100
Atlanta	Philips Arena	1999	$214	$63	29
Denver	Pepsi Center	1999	$160	$35	22
Lakers/Clippers	Staples Center	1999	$375	$59	16
New Orleans	New Orleans Arena	1999	$114	$114	100
Miami	American Airlines Arena	1998	$213	$213	100
Washington	Verizon Center	1997	$260	$60	23
Golden State	Oracle Arena (rehab)	1997	$121	$121	100
Philadelphia	Wells Fargo Center	1996	$206	—	0
Boston	TD Garden	1995	$160	—	0
Portland	Rose Garden	1995	$262	$35	13
Seattle	Key Arena (rehab)	1995	$75	$75	100
Cleveland	Quicken Loans Arena	1994	$152	$152	100
Chicago	United Center	1994	$175	—	0
New York	Madison Square Garden (rehab)	1991	$200	—	0
Salt Lake City	EnergySolutions Arena	1991	$93	—	0
Memphis	Memphis Pyramid	1991	$65	$65	100
Minneapolis	Target Center	1990	$104	$52	50
	27 out of 30		$6,115	$3,126	51

for the average worker. As the country grew wealthier, spectator sports rose in popularity, as people had both higher incomes to pay for these activities and an increased availability of leisure time. In addition, improvements in transportation allowed for the formation of intercity sports leagues.

Early stadium construction in the United States reflected the economic landscape. Playing facilities were located in the major population centers in the East. They offered few amenities compared to modern stadia, reflecting the lower income of the fan base and the concentration of population and economic power in the Midwest and Northeast. For 50 years between 1903

Table 14.5

New NHL Arenas Since 1990

Team	Stadium	Built	Cost (000s) (nominal)	Public cost	Public percent
Pittsburgh	Consol Energy Center	2010	$321	$130	40
New Jersey	Prudential Center	2008	$375	$210	56
Phoenix	Jobing.com Arena	2003	$180	$180	100
Dallas	American Airlines Center	2001	$420	$210	50
Columbus	Nationwide Arena	2000	$175	—	0
Minnesota	Xcel Energy Center	2000	$130	$130	100
Toronto	Air Canada Centre	1999	$265	—	0
Atlanta	Philips Arena	1999	$214	$63	29
Denver	Pepsi Center	1999	$160	$35	22
Los Angeles	Staples Center	1999	$375	$59	16
Carolina	RBC Center	1999	$158	$98	62
Ft. Lauderdale	BankAtlantic Center	1998	$212	$185	87
Washington	Verizon Center	1997	$260	$60	23
Nashville	Bridgestone Arena	1997	$144	$144	100
Philadelphia	Wells Fargo Center	1996	$206	—	0
Ottawa	Scotiabank Place	1996	$188	$6	3
Buffalo	HSBC Arena	1996	$128	$55	43
Tampa Bay	St. Pete Times Forum	1996	$160	$120	75
Montreal	The Bell Centre	1996	$230	—	0
Vancouver	Rogers Arena	1996	$160	—	0
Boston	TD Garden	1995	$160	—	0
Chicago	United Center	1994	$175	—	0
St. Louis	Scottrade Center	1994	$170	$35	20
Anaheim	Honda Center	1993	$123	$123	100
San Jose	HP Pavillion	1993	$163	$133	82
NY Rangers	Madison Square Garden (rehab)	1991	$200	—	0
	26 out of 30		$5,451	$1,974	36

and 1953, all 16 teams in Major League Baseball were located east of St. Louis and north of St. Louis and Washington, D.C. Similarly, except for a single season by a Los Angeles club, all 56 teams that played at least one season in the National Football League between its founding in 1920 and 1945 were located in the industrial Midwest or the Northeast corridor.

Large stadia, of course, were constructed during the early twentieth century to accommodate the growing number of fans of baseball, football, and other sports. While the franchises that these old stadia served still exist to this day, most succumbed to physical and economic obsolescence. Fans of the Boston Red Sox and Chicago Cubs, however, can watch their home games in the last two remaining professional baseball facilities from that era, Fenway Park and Wrigley Field, built in 1912 and 1914, respectively. In addition, several college football stadia from that time period are also still in current use, including Harvard Stadium (1903), Yale Bowl (1914), Rose Bowl (1922), and Los Angeles Coliseum (1923).

The relocation and expansion of sports leagues into the southern and western United States reflects the growing importance of these regions in the overall American economy. After half a century of stability, in the 1950s MLB franchises relocated from major cities on the East Coast to destinations far distant from the old centers of economic influence—the Philadelphia A's moved to Kansas City and then Oakland; the Brooklyn Dodgers and New York Giants headed west to Los Angeles and San Francisco, respectively; the Boston Braves went to Milwaukee and then south to Atlanta. Similarly, league expansion in the 1960s and 1970s created franchises in areas that had experienced rapid economic growth over the past half century, such as Southern California, Seattle, and Texas. The most recent wave of expansion in the 1990s brought new teams into the fast-growing Sunbelt regions of Florida and Arizona. Just as efficient railroad service allowed for travel between cities in the East, the advent of widespread passenger air service allowed for the development of truly nationwide sport leagues. Although this discussion has concentrated on the history of professional baseball, similar patterns of relocation and expansion can be observed in all of the other major sports. Again, stadium construction and franchise relocation reflected economic development in the country rather than the other way around.

Baade (2010) noted that geographic considerations were not the only factor in the construction of new sports facilities. Economy-wide fluctuations during the last century clearly influenced sports facility construction. Except for Yankee Stadium in New York and Soldier Field in Chicago, virtually no new stadia were constructed between World War I and 1946, a time dominated by the Great Depression and World War II. The pace of stadium construction accelerated from the 1950s through the mid-1970s, as growing prosperity and technological development enabled the construction of steel-and-concrete playing facilities during the ten years from 1965 through 1975, replacing many existing facilities.

Sports remain a very clear indicator of economic development to this day. Studies investigating national success at international sporting events such as the Olympics and World Cup suggest that economic factors play clear roles. For example, Bernard and Busse (2004) find that, all other things equal, a 1 percent increase in GDP per capita compared to the world average will increase the number of Olympic medals won by roughly the same amount. Similar results are found in other sports, for example, men's and women's international football (Hoffmann, Lee, and Ramasamy 2002; Hoffmann et al. 2006). In all cases, higher income is presumed to affect sporting success by providing athletes with better sports infrastructure, better access to specialized training, and more leisure time to pursue their athletic endeavors.

For individual professional teams, local market income is also an important factor in predicting both franchise location and team success. For professional leagues without significant limitations on team payrolls, such as Major League Baseball and most European soccer leagues, successful teams tend to be located in large metropolitan areas with high incomes. It comes as no surprise that MLB's New York Yankees, who reside in the country's largest and richest metropolitan area, have an unprecedented record of success over the past century. Similarly, English Premier League teams Arsenal and Chelsea, both of which call London home, are perennial contenders for their league's title. Wealthy, populous hometowns provide teams with a large potential revenue stream necessary for purchasing talented players.

While local economic development is clearly a factor in both the emergence of professional sports as well as sports success, from a public policy standpoint it is important to ask whether the reverse is also true. Does a healthy spectator sports environment lead to local economic development, or is it simply a by-product of normal economic development? The answer to such a question provides guidance on whether public subsidies for professional sports facilities are a wise investment. This question will be examined in the next section.

Economic Development Effects of Sports Leagues, Teams, and Events

If one believes the boosters, sports teams and so-called mega-events bring a substantial economic windfall to host cities. Promoters envision hordes of wealthy sports fans descending on a city's hotels, restaurants, and businesses and injecting large sums of money into the cities lucky enough to host these teams and events. In terms of one-off events, the NFL typically claims an economic impact from the Super Bowl of around $400 to $500 million (NFL 1999; W.P. Carey Business School 2008), and MLB attaches a $75 million benefit to the All-Star Game (Selig, Harrington, and Healey 1999) and up to $250 million for the World Series (Ackman 2000). Multiday events such as the Summer or Winter Olympics or soccer's World Cup produce even larger numbers. For example, consultants placed a $12 billion figure on the 2010 World Cup in South Africa (Voigt 2010) and estimated an economic impact of over $10 billion Canadian for the 2010 Winter Olympics in Vancouver (InterVISTAS Consulting 2002). See Table 14.6 for a list of published ex ante economic impact estimates for a variety of large sporting events.

Regular season games and year-round franchises also prompt eye-popping estimates of potential benefits. The St. Louis Regional Chamber and Growth

Table 14.6

Examples of Mega-Event ex ante Economic Impact Studies

Event	Year	Sport	Impact	Source
Super Bowl (Miami)	1999	Football	$393 million	Sports Management Research Institute, NFL 1999
Super Bowl (San Diego)	2003	Football	$367 million	Marketing Information Masters, NFL 2003
Super Bowl (Arizona)	2008	Football	$501 million	W.P. Carey Business School 2008
MLB All-Star Game	1999	Baseball	$75 million	Selig, Harrington, and Healey 1999
MLB World Series	2000	Baseball	$250 million	Comptroller of New York City, Ackman 2000
NCAA Men's Final Four (St. Louis)	2001	Basketball	$110 million	St. Louis Convention and Visitor's Bureau, Anderson 2001
U.S. Open	2001	Tennis	$420 million	Sports Management Research Institute, Williams 2001
World Cup (Japan)	2002	Soccer	$24.8 billion	Dentsu Institute for Human Studies, Finer 2002
World Cup (South Korea)	2002	Soccer	$8.9 billion	Dentsu Institute for Human Studies, Finer 2002
World Cup	2010	Soccer	$12 billion	Grant Thornton South Africa, Voigt 2010
Summer Olympics (Atlanta)	1996	Multiple	$5.1 billion 77,000 jobs	Humphreys and Plummer 2005
Winter Olympics (Vancouver, BC)	2010	Multiple	$10.7C billion 244,000 jobs	InterVISTAS Consulting 2002

Source: Matheson 2011.

Association estimated that in 2011 the St. Louis Cardinals baseball team brought $313 million in annual economic benefits to the region on top of the $52 million the area gained by the team's trip to the World Series (St. Louis Regional Chamber and Growth Association 2011). The New Orleans Saints of the NFL generated an estimated $402 million impact on the state of Louisiana in 2002 (Ryan 2003), while the NBA's Seattle Supersonics claimed that they pumped $234 million into the area's economy annually prior to their move to Oklahoma City (Feit 2006).

Of course, as noted by Baade, Baumann, and Matheson (2008), "leagues, team owners, and event organizers have a strong incentive to provide economic impact numbers that are as large as possible in order to justify heavy public subsidies." Sports leagues frequently utilize rosy economic impact statements and dangle mega-events such as the Super Bowl and baseball's All-Star Game in front of cities in order to encourage otherwise reluctant city officials and taxpayers to provide significant public funding for new stadia to the benefit of existing owners.

Unfortunately, the methodology used to formulate estimates of economic impact is fatally flawed, resulting in a consistent bias toward large, but unrealized, impacts. Economic impact predictions are done in a reasonably straightforward fashion. In the case of either an event or a franchise, the total number of visitors to the event or the team is estimated along with an average level of spending for each sports fan. The number of fans multiplied by the average spending results in an estimate of direct economic impact. Once the direct economic impact is determined, a multiplier is applied, which accounts for money recirculating in the local economy. For most sports-related spending, a multiplier around two is used, roughly doubling the direct economic impact.

Although this methodology is easy to understand, many researchers point to three primary flaws in most economic impact studies. The first is the failure to account for the *substitution effect*. While it is undeniable that sports fans around the country and around the world spend significant sums on spectator sports, in the absence of such entertainment opportunities, their spending would be directed elsewhere in the economy. A night at the ballpark means more money in the players' and team owner's pockets, but it also means less money in the pockets of local theater or restaurant owners. Most economists not associated with teams or event organizers advocate that any spending by local residents on local sporting events be eliminated from economic impact analyses.

The next common criticism is *crowding out*. The crowds and congestion associated with major sporting events tend to reduce other economic activity in the local area, as sports fans displace other individuals. As with the substitution effect, sports tend to affect the allocation of economic activity across businesses and different sectors of the economy—but not the total amount of activity that occurs. As a case in point, while Olympic visitors flocked to Beijing for the 2008 Summer Games, other visitors stayed away in droves. The number of tourist arrivals to the city in August 2008, the month of the Games, was the same as the number of visitors the previous year, and total visitor arrivals for the entire year was significantly lower than the previous year. Crowding out effects are clearly visible for major sporting events held in Hawaii as well. An analysis of flight arrival data by Baumann, Matheson, and Muroi (2009) shows that sporting events like the Honolulu Marathon and NFL Pro-Bowl, both of which attract tens of thousands of participants and spectators, lead to only small increases in the total number of tourists to the islands as the athletes and fans displace other vacationers.

Finally, money spent in local economies during either regular season games or special events may not stay in the local economy. The nature of professional sports is that the athletes generally command as wages a large share of revenues generated by sporting events. However, the athletes themselves are typically unlikely to live in the metropolitan area in which they play (Siegfried and Zimbalist 2002). Therefore, the income earned by athletes is *not likely to recirculate* in the local economy, leading to a *lower multiplier effect*. In the extreme, spending at a sporting event could actually reduce local incomes, as money is diverted from an activity with a high multiplier—for example, a dinner at a locally owned and operated restaurant—toward a sporting event—an activity with high leakages.

Researchers who have gone back and looked at economic data for localities that have hosted mega-events, attracted new franchises, or built new sports facilities have almost invariably found little or no economic benefits from spectator sports. Typically, ex post studies of the economic impact of sports have focused on employment (Baade and Matheson 2002; Feddersen and Maennig 2009), personal income (Baade and Matheson 2006a), personal income per capita (Coates and Humphreys 1999, 2002), taxable sales (Porter 1999; Coates and Depken 2009; Baade, Baumann, and Matheson 2008), or tourist arrivals (Lavoie and Rodriguez 2005; Baumann, Matheson, and Muroi 2009). These studies and a multitude of others generally find that the actual economic impact of sports teams or events is a fraction of that claimed by the boosters, and in some cases actually show a reduction in economic activity due to sports. See Table 14.7 for a list of published ex post economic impact estimates for a variety of large sporting events.

Even if the immediate direct economic impact of spectator sports is negligible, proponents of sports-based economic development suggest that the long-term effects may be large. Mega-events "put cities on the map," and new

Table 14.7

Examples of Mega-Event ex post Economic Impact Studies

Event	Years	Variable	Impact	Source
MLB All-Star Game	1973–1997	Employment	Down 0.38%	Baade and Matheson 2001
Super Bowl	1973–1999	Employment	537 jobs	Baade and Matheson 2000a
Summer Olympics (Atlanta)	1996	Employment	293,000 jobs	Hotchkiss et al. 2003
Summer Olympics (Atlanta)	1996	Employment	3,500–42,000 jobs	Baade and Matheson 2002
Summer Olympics (Atlanta)	1996	Employment	Approx. 75,000	Feddersen and Maennig 2009
World Cup	2006	Employment	Not statistically significant	Allmers and Maennig 2009
Super Bowl	1970–2001	Personal income	$91.9 million	Baade and Matheson 2006a
MLB playoffs and World Series	1972–2000	Personal income	$6.8 million/game	Baade and Matheson 2008
NCAA Men's BB Final Four	1970–1999	Personal income	Down $44.2–$6.4 million	Baade and Matheson 2004a
World Cup	1994	Personal income	Down $4 billion	Baade and Matheson 2004b
World Cup	2006	Personal income	Not statistically significant	Allmers and Maennig 2009
Multiple Events	1969–1997	Personal income/capita	Not statistically significant	Coates and Humphreys 2002
Daytona 500	1997–1999	Taxable sales	$32–$49 million	Baade and Matheson 2000b
Super Bowl	1985–1995	Taxable sales	No effect	Porter 1999
Multiple Events (Florida)	1980–2005	Taxable sales	Down $34.4 million (avg.)	Baade, Bauamann, Matheson 2008
Multiple Events (Texas)	1991–2005	Gross sales	Varied, pos. and neg.	Coates 2006
Multiple Events (Texas)	1990–2006	Sales tax revenue	Varied, pos. and neg.	Coates and Depken 2009
NFL Pro-Bowl	2004–2008	Tourist arrivals	6,726 visitors	Baumann, Matheson, and Muroi 2009
NHL regular season games	1990–1999	Hotel occupancy	Slight increase	Lavoie and Rodriguez 2005

Source: Matheson 2011.

stadia can serve as anchors in dilapidated areas to promote local growth. Here too, however, the data are not convincing. While tourists may flock to host cities during major sporting events, the surge in visitors tends to be short-lived. Matheson (2009) notes, "In Sydney, the host of the 2000 Summer Olympics, foreign tourism actually grew at a slower rate than in the rest of Australia in the three years following the Games. Lillehammer, Norway, the site of the 1994 Winter Olympics experienced a wave of bankruptcies in the years following their moment in the spotlight, as 40 percent of the full-service hotels in the town went bankrupt."

At least in part, a portion of the blame for the poor, long-term benefits of spectator sports is the fact that the capital used in staging sporting contests is not easily convertible to other uses. While the construction of general infrastructure, such as modern airports, highways, and mass transit systems, provides economy-wide benefits, such architectural and technological marvels as Beijing's "Water Cube," the 17,000 seat state-of-the-art swimming facility built for the 2008 Summer Olympics, has little use following the Games. The facility is now open to the general public for free swimming, making it the world's most expensive lap pool. Similarly, in South Korea most of the new stadia built for the 2002 World Cup sit unused today.

Giesecke and Madden (2007) have quantified the effects of infrastructure spending in Sydney for the 2000 Summer Olympics and have concluded that the "redirection of public money into relatively unproductive infrastructure, such as equestrian centers and manmade rapids, has since cut $2.1 billion from public consumption."

While the long-term benefits of sporting events and stadium construction may never arrive, the debts that localities incur in hosting professional sports must still be paid. Montreal was still paying off its debts from the 1976 Olympics three decades later, and the Astrodome in Houston still carried millions of dollars of debt despite being vacant for a nearly a decade.

Perhaps the most tragic tale is that of Greece, which suffered massive financial setbacks in 2010. Historically, Greece's federal government had been a profligate spender, but in order to join the euro currency zone, the government was forced to adopt austerity measures that reduced deficits from just over 9 percent of GDP in 1994 to just 3.1 percent of GDP in 1999, the year before Greece joined the euro. But the Olympics hosted by Athens broke the bank. Government deficits rose every year after 1999, peaking at 7.5 percent of GDP in 2004, the year of the Olympics, thanks in large part to the €9 billion price tag for the Games. For a relatively small country like Greece, the cost of hosting the Games equaled roughly 5 percent of the annual GDP of the country.

Unfortunately, as has been seen in other cases, the Olympics didn't usher in an economic boom. Indeed, in 2005 Greece suffered an Olympic-sized hangover with GDP growth falling to its lowest level in a decade. While it's hard to place all of the blame for the 2010 Greek meltdown on the Olympics, the lingering debts from the Games undoubtedly exacerbated an already difficult situation.

Even if commercial sport does induce an increase in economic activity, the efficacy of sport as a developmental tool needs to be considered. The litmus test arguably should not be whether sport induces an increase in economic activity, but whether it is the most efficient method for improving the economy. Focusing on employment, Baade and Sanderson (1997) observed that the cost of creating a full-time equivalent job through sports subsidies far exceeds the cost of job creation through other subsidies. More specifically, it was noted that the cost of job creation through sports is far greater than jobs created through the Public Works Capital Development and Investment Acts of the 1970s or Alabama's much maligned subsidies to convince Mercedes-Benz AG to locate some of their manufacturing in that state. It is also important to note that as many as 98 percent of the jobs created through sports subsidies are in the relatively low-paying, nonmanufacturing sector.

Numerous funding mechanisms have been used by local authorities for funding stadium construction. Table 14.8 shows the funding mechanisms for NFL stadia built between 1992 and 2006. While a variety of revenue sources are used for football stadium construction, three types are most common: personal seat licenses (PSLs), excise taxes on hotels or rental cars, and general funds including sales taxes.

PSLs involve a payment by a prospective season ticket buyer to the stadium builder in exchange for the purchaser gaining the right to buy a seat ticket in the new stadium. Personal seat licenses are a source of public works revenue unique to the sporting world, and they serve several purposes. First, they turn consumers' future willingness to pay for tickets into an immediate source of capital that can be used to defray current construction costs. Second, they allow teams to avoid revenue sharing agreements with the rest of the league. In the NFL, teams are required to share 40 percent of gate revenues with visiting teams while other revenue sources, such as PSLs, are not subject to the revenue sharing arrangement. All things equal, PSLs should raise nonshared revenue and lower ticket prices, reducing overall revenue sharing payments to the rest of the league. The other major sports leagues in the United States have lower revenue sharing percentages, and therefore PSLs are much less common in other sports. Finally, PSLs satisfy the "user pays" principle of public finance. A stadium financed by PSLs is a stadium that is financed by the very people who will be using the stadium and benefitting from the new team the stadium is designed to attract or from the enhanced amenities that new stadia provide.

Table 14.8

Sources of Public Funds for NFL Stadium Construction, 1992–2006

	Year built	Public contribution (%)	Referendum	Public funding source
Atlanta	1992	100	No	2.75 hotel tax
Jacksonville	1995	100	No	Sales tax, hotel tax, ticket charge, general funds
St. Louis	1995	100	No	2.5 hotel tax, general funds ($257 mil.)
Carolina	1996	21	No	Personal Seat License (PSL)
Oakland	1996	100	No	PSL
Washington	1997	28	No	
Baltimore	1998	80	No	Lottery
Tampa Bay	1998	100	Yes	0.5 sales tax
Buffalo	1999	100	No	General funds
Cleveland	1999	90	Yes	Hotel tax, car rental tax, sin taxes, PSL
Tennessee	1999	76	Yes	Hotel tax, PSL ($72 mil.)
Cincinnati	2000	200	Yes	0.5 sales tax, ticket charge, PSL ($25 mil.)
Denver	2001	75	Yes	Sales tax
Pittsburgh	2001	65	No	Ticket charge ($14 mil.), PSL ($42 mil.), other
Detroit	2002	73	Yes	1 hotel tax, $2 car rental tax
Houston	2002	75	Yes	Hotel tax, car rental tax, ticket charge, sin taxes, PSL
New England	2002	10	No	
Seattle	2002	67	Yes	Sales tax, 2 hotel tax, 10 ticket charge, lottery, PSL ($17 mil.)
Chicago	2003	75	No	2 hotel tax, PSL ($60 mil.)
Green Bay	2003	85	Yes	0.5 sales tax, ticket charge ($92.5 mil.)
Philadelphia	2003	80	No	
Arizona	2006	72	Yes	1 hotel tax, $3.50 car rental tax

Source: Baade and Matheson 2006b.

Other funding mechanisms used to finance events and stadium construction, however, more often violate commonly held principles of public finance. Taxes on rental cars, hotels, and central-city restaurants, the second common tool used to repay stadium bond issues, while seemingly shifting the expense of the stadium to out-of-town visitors, in fact, simply make those revenue sources unavailable for use elsewhere in the city. Furthermore, only a tiny fraction of the hotel rooms or rental cars used in a city over the course of a year are purchased by visitors engaging in sports tourism. Thus, restaurant goers, for example, may serve to simply subsidize better seating for football fans.

The use of general sales taxes or lottery proceeds, the third common source of funding for sports infrastructure, violates most people's notions of vertical equity by placing an undue burden on poorer residents. Both revenue sources are strongly regressive, while the benefits provided by subsidized stadium construction accrue primarily to the wealthy. Live attendance at major sporting events is dominated by wealthy individuals, and the revenue generated by sporting events for the most part ends up in the pockets of millionaire players and billionaire owners.

Even tax increment financing or ticket taxes or surcharges are not without their critics, as few other businesses are allowed to use taxes collected on their customers to pay for their own capital expenditures (Baade and Matheson 2006b).

The Final Justification: Quality of Life

If sports teams and events bring little in the way of direct economic benefits, do potential indirect benefits exist? Here, the evidence is much more favorable to athletic supporters. Clearly, sports are an entertainment option favored by many. Although the professional sports industry in the United States is roughly the same size as the cardboard box industry, cardboard boxes don't warrant multiple channels on cable television, they don't have a dedicated section in most newspapers, and they are not the focus of frequent discussions around the office watercooler. Sports serve as a municipal amenity that can create social capital and improve the quality of life.

Obviously, estimating a more esoteric measure such as societal well-being is more difficult than analyzing more concrete data such as employment or government revenues. Still, the data hint at clear quality-of-life benefits from sports. For example, the 2008 Olympics instilled a sense of pride in the Chinese people. Some 93 percent of the Chinese citizens surveyed by the Pew Research Center thought that the Games would improve the country's image (Matheson 2009). Similarly, Maennig's (2007) ex post analysis of the 2006 World Cup in Germany concludes that claims of "increased turnover in the retail trade, overnight accommodation, receipts from tourism and effects on employment [are] mostly of little value and may even be incorrect. Of more significance, however, are other (measurable) effects such as the novelty effect of the stadiums, the improved image for Germany and the feel-good effect for the population" (Maennig 2007, p. 1).

Numerous scholars, starting with Carlino and Coulsen (2004), have used hedonic-pricing techniques to attempt to quantify the quality-of-life aspects of sports. If the presence of an NFL franchise, for example, is a vital cultural amenity for residents in the area, then the value of the franchise to local citizens should be reflected in a higher willingness to pay for living in a city with a team. Carlino and Coulsen (2004) found that rental housing in cities with NFL franchises command 8 percent higher rents than units in other metropolitan areas after correcting for housing characteristics. Others such as Feng and Humphreys (2008) and Tu (2005) found localized effects of stadia and arenas on housing prices—but also that these effects fade quite quickly as the distance from the stadium grows. Conversely, Coates, Humphreys, and Zimbalist (2006) note that Carlino and Coulsen's results are highly dependent on model specification. According to Kiel, Matheson, and Sullivan (2010), the increase in housing costs does not extend to owner-occupied housing; in addition, the presence of stadium subsidies lowers housing values, a finding also uncovered by Dehring, Depken, and Ward (2007).

Other researchers have employed contingent valuation methods in an attempt to determine the "feel-good" effect that residents derive from spectator sports. While the existence of positive benefits from sports teams and events are more commonly identified in the contingent valuation literature than in the ex post examination of direct economic impact, here too the assessed value of sports tends to be smaller than the public subsidies that are handed out to professional sports (Johnson, Groothuis, and Whitehead 2001).

Improving citizens' quality of life is clearly an important goal for public policymakers, and there is evidence that sports are a valued amenity for local communities. Evidence of significant direct economic benefits from sporting events, franchises, and stadia is lacking, however. While public-private partnerships can be justified on quality-of-life grounds, voters and public officials should not be deluded by overoptimistic predictions of a financial windfall. Sports may make a city happy, but they are unlikely to make a city rich.

References

Ackman, D. 2000. In money terms, the subway series strikes out. *Forbes*, October 21.

Allmers, S., and W. Maennig. 2009. Economic impacts of the FIFA soccer World Cups in France 1998, Germany 2006, and outlook for South Africa 2010. *Eastern Economic Journal* 35(4): 500–19.

Anderson, P. 2004. *Business Economics and Finance with MATLAB, GIS and Simulation Models*, New York: Chapman & Hall/CRC, p. 131.

Baade, R. 2010. Getting into the game: Is the gamble on sports as a stimulus for urban economic development a good bet? In *Urban and Regional Policy and Its Effects,* ed. N. Pindus, H. Wial, and H. Wolman. Washington, DC: The Brookings Institution.

Baade, R., R. Baumann, and V. Matheson. 2008. Selling the game: Estimating the economic impact of professional sports through taxable sales. *Southern Economic Journal* 74(3): 794–810.

Baade, R., and V. Matheson. 2000a. An assessment of the economic impact of the American football championship, the Super Bowl, on host communities. *Reflets et Perspectives* 34(2–3): 35–46.

———. 2000b. High octane? Grading the economic impact of the Daytona 500. *Marquette Sports Law Journal* 10(2): 401–15.

———. 2001. Home run or wild pitch? Assessing the economic impact of Major League Baseball's All-Star Game. *Journal of Sports Economics* 2(4): 307–27.

———. 2002. Bidding for the Olympics: Fool's gold? In *Transatlantic Sport: The Comparative Economics of North American and European Sports,* ed. Carlos Pestanos Barros, Muradali Ibrahimo, and Stefan Szymanski, 127–51. London: Edward Elgar.

———. 2004a. An economic slam dunk or March Madness? Assessing the economic impact of the NCAA basketball tournament. In *Economics of College Sports*, ed. John Fizel and Rodney Fort, 111–33. Westport, CT: Praeger.

———. 2004b. The quest for the cup: Assessing the economic impact of the World Cup. *Regional Studies* 38(4): 341–52.

———. 2006a. Padding required: Assessing the economic impact of the Super Bowl. *European Sports Management Quarterly* 6(4): 353–74.

———. 2006b. Have public finance principles been shut out in financing new stadiums for the NFL? *Public Finance and Management* 6(3): 284–320.

———. 2008. Striking out: Estimating the economic impact of baseball's World Series. *International Journal of Sport Management and Marketing* 3(4): 319–34.

Baade, R., and A. Sanderson. 1997. Employment effect of teams and sports facilities. In *Sports, Jobs, and Taxes,* ed. Roger G. Noll and Andrew Zimbalist, 92–118. Washington, DC: The Brookings Institution Press.

Baumann, R., V. Matheson, and C. Muroi. 2009. Bowling in Hawaii: Examining the effectiveness of sports-based tourism strategies. *Journal of Sports Economics* 10(1): 107–23.

Bernard, A., and M. Busse. 2004. Who wins the Olympic Games: Economic resources and medal totals. *Review of Economics and Statistics* 86: 413–17.

Carlino, G., and E. Coulson. 2004. Compensating differentials and the social benefits of the NFL. *Journal of Urban Economics* 56(1): 25–50.

Coates, D. 2006. The tax benefits of hosting the Super Bowl and the MLB All-Star Game: The Houston experience. *International Journal of Sport Finance* 1(4): 239–52.

Coates, D., and C. Depken. 2009. The impact of college football games on local sales tax revenue: Evidence from four cities in Texas. *Eastern Economic Journal* 35(4): 531–47.

Coates, D., and B. Humphreys. 1999. The growth effects of sports franchises, stadia, and arenas. *Journal of Policy Analysis and Management* 14(4): 601–24.

———. 2002. The economic impact of post-season play in professional sports. *Journal of Sports Economics* 3(3): 291–99.

Coates, D., B. Humphreys, and A. Zimbalist. 2006. Compensating differentials and the social benefits of the NFL: A comment. *Journal of Urban Economics* 60(1): 124–31.

Dehring, C., C. Depken, and M. Ward. 2007. The impact of stadium announcements on residential property values: Evidence from a natural experiment in Dallas-Fort Worth. *Contemporary Economic Policy* 25(4): 627–38.

Feddersen, A., and W. Maennig. 2009. *Regional Economic Impact of the 1996 Summer Olympic Games—Wage and Employment Effects Reconsidered.* Working Paper 025, Chair for Economic Policy, University of Hamburg, Germany.

Feit, J. 2006. Key amendments: Council member Nick Licata challenges Sonics Subsidy. *The Stranger* (Seattle, WA), February 23–March 1.

Feng, X., and B. Humphreys. 2008. *Assessing the Economic Impact of Sports Facilities on Residential Property Values: A Spatial Hedonic Approach.* Working Paper 0812, International Association of Sports Economists & North American Association of Sports Economists.

Finer, J. 2002. The grand illusion. *Far Eastern Economic Review* 7: 32–36.

Giesecke, J., and J. Madden. 2007. *The Sydney Olympics, Seven Years On: An Ex-post Dynamic CGE Assessment.* CoPS/IMPACT Working Paper Number G-168, Monash University, Melbourne, Australia.

Hoffmann, R., C. G. Lee, and B. Ramasamy. 2002. The socio-economic determinants of international football performance. *Journal of Applied Economics* 5: 253–72.

Hoffmann, R., C. G. Lee, V. Matheson, and B. Ramasamy. 2006. International women's football and gender inequality. *Applied Economics Letters* 13(15): 999–1001.

Hotchkiss, J., R. Moore, and S. Zobay. 2003. Impact of the 1996 summer Olympic games on employment and wages in Georgia. *Southern Economic Journal* 69(3): 691–704.

Humphreys, J., and M. Plummer. 2005. *The Economic Impact on the State of Georgia of Hosting the 1996 Summer Olympic Games*. Athens: Selig Center for Economic Growth at the University of Georgia.

InterVISTAS Consulting. 2002. *The Economic Impact of the 2010 Winter Olympics and Paralympic Games: An Update*. Victoria: British Columbia Ministry of Competition, Science, and Enterprise.

Kiel, K., V. Matheson, and C. Sullivan. 2010. *The Effect of Sports Franchises on Property Values: The Role of Owners Versus Renters*. Department of Economics Working Paper No. 10–01, College of the Holy Cross, Worcester, Massachusetts.

Johnson, B., P. Groothuis, and J. Whitehead. 2001. The value of public goods generated by a major league sports team: The CVM approach. *Journal of Sports Economics* 2(1): 6–21.

Lavoie, M., and G. Rodríguez. 2005. The economic impact of professional teams on monthly hotel occupancy rates of Canadian cities: A Box-Jenkins approach. *Journal of Sports Economics* 6(3): 314–24.

Maennig, W. 2007. *One Year Later: A Re-appraisal of the Economics of the 2006 Soccer World Cup.* Working Paper 0723, International Association of Sports Economists & North American Association of Sports Economists.

Matheson, V. 2006. Professional sports. In *Encyclopedia of American Business History*, ed. Charles Geisst, 403–8. New York: Facts on File.

———. 2009. Bid's rejection could be for the best. *Chicago Tribune*, October 4.

———. 2011. Mega-events: The effect of the world's biggest sporting events on local, regional, and national economies. In *The Business of Sports*, vol. 1, ed. Dennis Howard and Brad Humphreys, 81–99. Westport, CT: Praeger Publishers, 2008. Revised tables from *Megaeventos deportivos. Estudios sociológicos y análisis de casos*, ed. Ramon Llopis-Goig. Valencia, Spain: Editorial UOC, S.L., 2011.

National Football League (NFL). 1999. Super Bowl XXXIII generates $396 million for south Florida. *NFL Report* 58(7).

———. 2003. Super Bowl XXXVII generates $367 million economic impact on San Diego County. May 14. www.nfl.com/news/ (accessed October 15, 2006).

Porter, P. 1999. Mega-sports events as municipal investments: A critique of impact analysis. In *Sports Economics: Current Research,* ed. J. Fizel, E. Gustafson, and L. Hadley. Westport, CT: Praeger.

Preuss, H. 2004. *Economics of the Olympic Games*. London: Edward Elgar.

Ryan, T. 2003. *The Economic Impact of the New Orleans Saints: 2002*. Working paper prepared for the State of Louisiana.

St. Louis Regional Chamber and Growth Association (RCGA). 2011. Cardinals' appearance in World Series shines spotlight on St. Louis Region's strong civic and economic renaissance. October 17. www.stlrcga.org/x4776.xml (accessed March 3, 2012).

Selig, B., J. Harrington, and J. Healey. 1999. MLB all-star game. Transcript, July 12. www.asapsports.com/show_interview.php?id=31050 (accessed August 29, 2000).

Siegfried J., and A. Zimbalist. 2002. A note on the local economic impact of sports expenditures. *Journal of Sports Economics* 3(4): 361–66.

Sperber, M. 2001. *Beer and Circus: How Big-Time College Sports Is Crippling Undergraduate Education.* New York: H. Holt.

Tu, C. 2005. How does a new sports stadium affect housing values? The case of FedEx Field. *Land Economics* 81(3): 379–95.

Upegui, O. 2008. The total cost of Beijing's summer Olympic games. Lingua Franca, August 3. http://epiac1216.wordpress.com/2008/08/03/the-total-cost-of-the-beijings-summer-olympic-games/.

Voigt, K. 2010. Is there a World Cup bounce? CNN, June 11. www.cnn.com/2010/BUSINESS/06/11/business.bounce.world.cup/index.html (accessed August 15, 2010).

W.P. Carey Business School. 2008. Economic impact study: Phoenix scores big with Super Bowl XLII. knowwpc, April 23. http://knowledge.wpcarey.asu.edu/article.cfm?articleid=1597 (accessed November 30, 2009).

Williams, Lena. 2001. Tennis: Roundup; Hevesi cities impact of open. *New York Times*, May 15. www.nytimes.com/2001/05/15/sports/tennis-roundup-hevesi-cites-impact-of-open.html?src=pm (accessed March 1, 2012).

15

Cobbling Together Funds for Mill Revitalization

John Mullin and Zeenat Kotval-K with Randolph Lyles

Over the past three decades, there has been a slow but steady interest in revitalizing older structures across the United States. Many of these structures, built as part of North America's Industrial Revolution, had fallen into neglect and decay due to changing technology, shifting markets, and lack of long-term capital reinvestment. In the Northeast, some industries fell prey to relocations to many southern states, which then suffered the same fate as those industries relocated overseas. Other industries were victims of the "electronic circuit silently replac[ing] the hiss and clank of moving parts" (Niesewand 1988, p. 9). Once the drivers of the economic engine of the country, these industries declined—often in a painfully slow way—and harmed not only the economies of the cities and towns that hosted them but also the social fabric and physical character of the surrounding community.

What seems to be needed is a sort of "land recycling," whereby derelict properties can be turned into economic resources for the community (Dull and Wernstedt 2010). Instead, the initial response to these problems was to ignore them and then, through urban renewal, city slum clearance, and blight removal programs, to demolish them with the hope that private-sector investment would occur. The 1980s saw a favorable new trend, as renewed investment interest in the older stock of buildings brought on revitalization efforts and partnerships between the public sector, the private sector, and the community.

Developers and Environmental Merchant Bankers (EMBs) play a critical role in this trend, taking on projects fraught with uncertainty and risks (Meyer and Lyons 2000). Regulatory and financial constraints remain a major deterrent (Alberini et al. 2005). To help, the government has created various incentives and policy instruments to offer developers some relief from the financial burden of revitalizing industrial structures, such as brownfield tax credits, TIFs, and renaissance zones (Heberle and Wernstedt 2006). Even so, funding remains difficult, as not all funding can be raised privately or through public money alone. It has to be pieced together in creative ways.

The town and community have a role to play as well. If the town becomes actively involved in the process, it can help turn older industrial sites into an integral part of redefining its community. The whole process starts when the town focuses on a structure to be revitalized. Its efforts to prepare the site are critical to the developer's success. This chapter starts with eight steps that towns and municipalities should take when preparing a site to attract developers. Then we address the issue of finding and combining various funding sources. Finally, the chapter concludes with three case studies that show different ways in which projects cobble together funding from various sources.

Eight Preparatory Steps

There are eight steps that towns and municipalities should take when preparing an old industrial site for redevelopment: (1) inventory older, obsolete buildings; (2) determine the needs of current owners; (3) conduct preliminary environmental testing; (4) recognize the value of infrastructure; (5) undertake price comparisons; (6) account for factors beyond sale values; (7) remember that the town or city can add value to the structure; and (8) plan for long-term financing.

Undertake an Inventory of Obsolete Structures

Not all old buildings are historic, and not all old buildings should be saved. Long-term residents of an area often are swayed by nostalgia for the past, and they may fail to recognize that how and where we work in the twenty-first century is fundamentally different from how and where we worked in the past. Therefore, a careful evaluation of the structure, its lands, its setting, and its supporting structures should be performed to gauge whether a revitalization effort is likely to be financially successful.

It is recommended that the inventory take place in stages to minimize the costs to the municipality. The process should begin with a review of property records to determine boundaries and the rights and privileges of ownership. This step is important because many derelict sites from the late nineteenth and first half of the twentieth century have protected water, sewer, or electrical rights, road or railroad access, or even control over dams that are upstream. Because of the nature of the industries that were located on these properties, in some cases these are decided rights and assets.

In the case of Holyoke, Massachusetts, for example, the local power company that serves the city's large industrial complexes has an agreement with the city's mill owners that enables the mill owners to purchase power at the lowest rate in the state. This low cost has stimulated interest from a number of high-technology companies (EMC, Cisco Systems) and universities (Massachusetts Institute of Technology, Harvard University, University of Massachusetts, Smith College) regarding the possibility of locating a high-speed computer facility in the city. In other cases, however, additional rights and assets can be high liabilities that discourage business. In Maynard, Massachusetts, a revitalization project of a 1.1 million-square-foot mill complex was nearly halted, because the dam associated with the site was in very poor shape and would have been prohibitively expensive to repair.

Determine the Needs of Current Owners

There is no pattern among owners of outmoded structures. Sometimes, owners are local citizens who have inherited the structures; other times, they are multinational corporations or speculators. Sometimes the structures may be held by banks or by the municipalities themselves. Different owners bring different issues to the table, and they must be addressed with sensitivity. Local owners, for example, may have sentimental attachment to the structures that make them unwilling to sell. And, if they are coming to a stage of life where they wish to collect the current returns (however small) from their structures, taking a risk on new investment may be of little interest. They also may have an unreasonable impression of its worth. Large corporations may be willing to sell quickly, if they are in a cash crunch. (The Digital Equipment Corporation, for example, sold its headquarters in an old mill in Maynard, Massachusetts, for $1.2 million when it was appraised for $12 million. Once the company started spiraling downward financially, it simply wanted a cash return.)

The phenomenon of outside speculators being interested in an old mill structure is relatively new. On the positive side, speculators see a potential positive return for their investment and are in a position to move a project forward. On the negative side, they are often more interested in short-term gains and in maximizing profits than in matching the visions of the community.

When banks hold the title, they generally have a great desire to remove nonperforming assets from their books, and, if a revitalization proposal is well thought out, they see an opportunity to invest. Municipal ownership of the property, on the other hand, can be particularly problematic. Municipalities have been extremely poor owners and maintainers of derelict properties, as there are often other, more pressing demands for their scarce financial resources. Regulatory requirements such as hearings increase "costs" to developers (Wernstedt, Meyer and Alberini 2006). Additionally, a staff that is inexperienced on brownfield redevelopment issues, deters potential investors and buyers for the site (Meyer and Lyons 2000). But in all these instances, understanding the needs of the owners is very important.

Conduct Preliminary Environmental Testing

If the property records are in order and the owners of the mill are willing to sell or participate in the revitalization of the structure, then a preliminary environmental assessment of the condition of the structure and land is in order. An initial scan in most states is not overly costly and should reveal if the property can be returned to economic vitality. Many older industrial buildings have contamination from the industrial processes that were used in the property, but many also contain substances like asbestos or lead, even if they are not contaminated by prior working conditions.

If the property is found to be contaminated, that fact will have an impact on its immediate worth and its potential for revitalization (Howland 2003). When owners are alerted to contamination, they inevitably undertake efforts to lower the property's assessed value. If, on the other hand, the property is not contaminated, then both the municipality and the owners will breathe a sigh of relief. The owner now knows that the structure is potentially valuable and may set a higher selling price. In short, the simple step of an environmental scan of the property has many ramifications and can sometimes decide its fate.

Recognize the Value of Infrastructure

One of the benefits of revitalizing old structures is that they typically require fewer large-scale capital expenditures than would be needed for new development. Nonetheless, there are some: Most notably, sufficient electric power and fiber-optic connectivity must be assured. How electrically well served a project is makes a huge difference in its costs. The fact that North Carolina has been able to keep its electrical costs so low has had a positive effect on its efforts to make its economy grow, and, as noted earlier, the low cost of electricity was the single greatest reason that Holyoke was able to attract a multi-university, local, high-speed computer initiative to its mill district.

Concerning fiber-optic and broadband connectivity, one frequently hears the phrase "be wired or be gone," signifying that any community without these services is unlikely to keep its economic base or develop new companies. Nowhere is this more evident than in Vermont, where twenty-first-century connectivity systems are so poor that economic expansion has virtually ceased. (The state is very much aware of the situation and is working aggressively to correct this shortcoming.) First-class connectivity is so important that the State of Connecticut's Southern New England Telephone (SNET) Company has developed a policy of funding the "last-mile" hookup: the company pays to assure that other companies close to the main trunk are connected. Interestingly, when old structures have smokestacks, these are often easily converted into transmission towers, an additional revenue generator for the developers and owners.

Beyond high-speed access, there are often issues related to water supply, sewer capacity, outdated heating and cooling systems, and transportation. Communities must be particularly careful regarding water use, as most municipalities' ability to find new sources of water is increasingly limited. Sewer issues most commonly center not on a community's ability to handle the amount of waste it generates but on whether it can process that waste: careful attention must be given to production systems to ensure that healthy conditions are maintained. Finally, there are road issues. Many older structures were built prior to the automobile revolution, and road access and parking solutions have had to be compromised.

The upgrade of roads and sewer and water systems alone will often provide enough of an incentive to spark investor interest. And when these improvements are combined with investments in electrical power, telecommunications, and parking improvements, the site begins to make the transition from a place that time forgot to one that will draw investment. A community's willingness to provide a standing lane at the entrance to the facility, upgrade water lines to meet future demands, and purchase a fire truck capable of providing services to a five-story mill are all examples of capital improvements that can tip the balance in favor of a project's success. While visioning, planning, and zoning activities do not typically require private-sector participation, a capital improvements program is often adopted specifically with investors in mind. In short, it can be used as an incentive.

Undertake Price Comparisons

As discussions continue, it is important to know about nearby communities' revitalization experiences in order to gauge the value of the buildings that have been renovated. This price comparison should focus as much as possible on the local market or connecting area—that is, the regional real estate market. It makes little sense to consider statewide or multicommunity trends when so often they are remarkably different. In Massachusetts, for example, although Boston and Springfield are less than 90 miles apart, the price differentials are huge: if a derelict building sold for $100,000 in Boston, it would sell for less than $50,000 in Springfield.

The price comparisons should follow real estate appraisal standards regarding the condition of the buildings and site, the state of utilities, and current privatizing rents, among other factors. Beyond this, it is critical to determine if other structures in the area are vacant, and, more generally, the condition of the neighborhood in which the structure is located. When only one mill is vacant and on the market, and it is in a small town with great amenities, its potential for revitalization is much higher than if the mill under consideration is one of several in a big city that is struggling. The Mansfield Mill, in Storrs, Connecticut, was a stand-alone structure located by a reservoir in a hot market: it was revitalized within months of being placed on the market. On the other hand, mills in declining cities across the Frost Belt may wait years—or forever—to be revitalized.

Take into Account Factors Beyond Sale Values

There are factors beyond price, location, and local characteristics that also have to be examined. These relate to the unique qualities of the structure—the "unique, specialty, and cachet" factor. Older structures that for one reason or another stand out tend to have a greater chance of capturing the attention of potential developers. For examples, during the heydays of the Digital Equipment Corporation (1957–1994), its world headquarters for its 90,000 employees was an old mill in Maynard, Massachusetts. By all accounts, the mill was quirky, drafty, noisy, and hardly representative of a then-twentieth-century multinational, cutting-edge, thriving, high-technology company. However, for Digital's executives, the mill matched the individuality of its workforce: they were free-spirited thinkers rather than standard manufacturers. And that mind-set carried through to the workforce: When asked to recall the experience of working in "Digital's mill," virtually all former workers spoke of it fondly. Later, after Digital was sold, Monster.com, an employment assistance corporation, successfully occupied some of its former space for many of the same reasons. Today, renamed "Clock Tower Place," the mill is home to approximately 40 different high-technology companies.

The former Quaker Oats complex in Akron, Ohio, included several tall silos at its facilities. Architects recognized that these structures provided an iconic symbol. Revitalized in the mid-1970s, those facilities are still fully occupied.

The town of Claremont, New Hampshire, once home to a textile mill, is a typical example of industrial displacement in northern New England. By any standard, it looks depressed. And yet, the owners of a New Hampshire-based hotel and restaurant chain saw that the mill's location (five minutes from an interstate), structure (a sturdy building), and its setting (by the Sugar River, with three falls of pounding water visible from all the hotel rooms) combined to form a unique set of positive factors. By all accounts, the resultant Common Man Inn has been remarkably successful.

The town of Concord, Massachusetts, is famous for its role in the American Revolution and, later, as the home of many of America's leading literary figures of the nineteenth century. In the present day, it is an affluent, well-planned suburban town approximately 20 miles outside of Boston. An address in Concord adds cachet to any company. When the old Damon textile mill in Concord became available, it was quickly revitalized and is now full of offices.

As the aforementioned examples show, it is not simply the state of the "bricks and mortar" of an old mill, but also other special characteristics that make a difference in whether revitalization is successful.

Remember That the Town or City Can Add Value to the Structure

In many parts of the United States, sales of older structures in derelict areas are approved at minimal values: the land is typically worth a small amount, but the aged structures—vacant, derelict, and often vandalized—are considered worthless. In short, the buildings themselves cannot be offered as equity in their present state for any privately motivated deal. Under such circumstances, the community can help in several ways without requesting the assistance of the owners. Investors are more likely to be attracted if a community expresses interest in the revitalization of these structures in its planning documents. If revitalization is part of the community's vision and economic strategy, and if the structures are referenced as being historically or culturally significant, potential investors know that the community will be supportive of their endeavors.

Plan for Long-term Financing

Mill revitalization often requires financial commitments for longer than a decade. The developers will be looking for financial help for each phase of the project. In the predevelopment phase, they will frequently ask the town to apply for planning grants, environmental analysis grants, and feasibility study funds. These grants are available from both state and federal sources. Once assistance has been gained and the project is feasible, the developers will then examine grants that will help them in the construction phase. They may be able to obtain funds for historic preservation, "green revitalization," or even bond financing to lower the cost of construction. For example, the State of Rhode Island provides developers who are revitalizing a building in a mill district with a tax credit of up to 30 percent. If the structure is eligible for historic preservation or new-market tax credits, these will also reduce the cost of construction or can be sold on the market, again lowering the redevelopment costs. There are also other financial tools available to position old structures for revitalization, such as tax increment financing (TIFs), one of the more powerful financing tools discussed in this book.

Piecing the Finance Puzzle Together

Once the city or town has deemed the structure fit for revitalization, it is up to the developers to see the project through. The developers will need expertise in brownfields and industrial revitalization. Equally important are drive, patience, and creativity. Developing a green site is easier and less financially burdensome than developing a brownfield site, but the unique attributes of older structures, the emotional equity, and the pride accruing from seeing a dying iconic structure get a new lease on life make revitalization worth the effort.

Revitalization projects typically receive funds by way of equity, debt financing, credits (tax credits), and grants and donations. Within these broad categories, there are various financing tools available that the developer can piece together in creative and ingenious ways. Projects may be funded extensively by government funds, or they might be funded extensively through private funds, but usually developers end up with a mix-and-match approach that uses both. A common rule is that developers look to generate about 70 percent of the total project financing through ways other than bank financing (since banks usually only give up to 30 percent of the overall project costs as loans). The bank financing typically helps to cover larger portions of the up-front costs, such as the initial purchase of buildings/structures.

Government Sources of Funding

Tax credits are allocated by state and federal governments for developments that further a public goal. Tax credits "induce owners to preserve and rehabilitate older properties rather than raze them. An incidental but important outcome is the stimulation of investment that would not otherwise occur because of the physical configuration of buildings and sites that are functionally obsolete" (Nelson and Talley 1991, p. 222). An example would be the low-income housing tax credit, which, as the name suggests, is aimed at developments providing affordable housing for low-income households (Baum-Snow and Marion 2009). Another would be the historic preservation tax credit, which is aimed at development that preserves and revitalizes historic structures. The latter has been very successful at preserving older structures that give their communities a unique character (Young 2008).

Apart from saving the developer money, these credits can be sold in a secondary market for about 75 percent of their value (giving the credits a cash value as well). Remember that the tax credits can be used only if (1) you pay taxes regularly, and (2) if you intend to make a profit that can be offset by the credits.

TIF agreements are also very beneficial for revitalization efforts. TIFs take many forms, depending upon the state. Most commonly, a TIF will reward developers with a tax reduction if they invest in a specific area. This enables developers to become competitive in the marketplace during the critical "rent-up" phase of the project. Where TIF districts are present, this competitiveness is enhanced if the site is within a mixed-use TIF district over an industrial TIF district (Weber, Bhatta and Merriman 2003). Moreover, the tax reduction becomes an asset to the developer in the form of equity, which reduces the amount of down payment that traditional lenders require. This financing source becomes even more effective if coupled with adequate knowledge and experience with the process of brownfield redevelopment (Bacot and O'Dell 2006). Additionally, incentives for larger projects that are stable are favored to those offered to labor-intensive enterprises and small businesses that are vulnerable in changing economic climates (Mueller and Oden 1999). In essence, tax abatements lower the taxes owed on a property by delaying the tax payments for a fixed number of years or by lowering the tax rate on the property for those years.

Equity and Bank Financing

Developers usually put some of their own funds into a project as equity, but they try to minimize this amount (and their risk) by using as much outside funding as they can muster. Bank financing comprises a large part of this outside funding (also known as debt financing). Bank loans are most common in development projects, but they are approved only with proof of sufficient equity and collateral. Even bank financing can be creative, as we will see with the Maynard mill renovation project, which obtained "phased financing" from its bank lenders.

Fund-raising Through the Community

Community funding includes donations, fund-raisers, and grants. The Whitinsville case study provides a good example of this type of financing.

Case Studies

In all the case studies that follow, the developers put in a lot of effort and creativity into sourcing funds and tenants for the redeveloped mill buildings.

However, the projects' individual circumstances, financing mix, and end goals were very different. For example, where the Whitinsville project was based more on grants and donations, the Ludlow project was based more on debt financing from the bank. Whitinsville's aim—to house mentally challenged individuals—was more of a community service objective, whereas the Maynard project was aimed solely at businesses, and the Ludlow project was a mixed-use development project.

Ludlow Mill Reuse Project

Ludlow was known as "jute town" historically, because it had a huge mill complex owned by the Ludlow Manufacturing Associates, along the Chicopee River, that made twine (end product of jute, a fiber imported from India) (O'Brien 2008). After the mill was shut down in 2005, there was a huge interest in its reuse or redevelopment as a mixed-use project. Not all mill buildings of the complex remain, but what does remain constitutes 1.6 million square feet of floor space on 170 acres of land. This redevelopment was considered a mix of brownfield and greenfield, because half the mill property was undeveloped. The WestMass Area Development Corporation (hereafter "WestMass"), part of the Economic Development Council of Western Massachusetts, acquired the mill property for redevelopment. WestMass adopted a debt-finance approach for this project. Seventy-eight percent of the initial purchase price of the mill was financed through a bank loan, while 22 percent was funded through equity contribution. Though initially loans covered a major part of the cost of the project, this portion decreased as other income increased—namely, when tenants were found for the redeveloped areas and certain parts of the mill were sold. One advantage this mill had was that it kept old tenants while redeveloping other parts of the mill. This allowed for a constant stream of rental income. Thus, during the first year of construction, rental income offset almost 2 percent of total expenditures, including acquisition costs.

The conventional loans, at 6.5 percent interest, had deferred interest payments and balloon payments at the end of the loan term. Another loan from MassDevelopment (the state economic development agency), with similar terms of interest and balloon payments, covered closing costs, permitting, engineering, demolition, and construction costs for the first year. In all, loans covered 90 percent of the costs of the project in the first year and a major portion of costs into the following years, with this share decreasing as the share from rental income increased.

The Ludlow Mill Redevelopment project took advantage of a number of tax credits, including those for low-income housing (the construction of housing units earned the developers $15,000 in tax credits per unit for 240 housing units), new markets, brownfields redevelopment, and historic preservation. To keep a check on costs, the developers were anticipating selling a portion of the historic preservation and new-markets tax credits on the secondary market.

The Whitinsville Mill Redevelopment Project

The approach undertaken by the not-for-profit "Alternatives" company in the renovation of their mill building in Whitinsville, Massachusetts, was different. The mission of the nonprofit was to integrate emotionally and developmentally challenged adults into the larger community. Alternatives undertook the renovation of the Whitinsville mill to provide a center for community life and economic growth in the region, as well as a place where the wider community could come to understand, collaborate with, and support the company's mission. The uniqueness of their project, together with their status as a nonprofit, enabled them to obtain loans, solicit individual donations, and apply for grants from foundations to fund their $9.8 million renovation. The developers were able to cover about 37 percent of their costs through those donations and grants. Additional corporate grants and donations for researching and implementing sustainable and green infrastructure increased the proportion of grant and contribution funds to 40 percent.

Alternatives was able to leverage that impressive funding figure to obtain the rest of its needed funds through bank loans. The developers took on $6.6 million of debt, half of which was a loan from the U.S. Department of Agriculture for rural development, since Whitinsville qualifies as a rural area. With the help of MassDevelopment, the developers then refinanced this debt by issuing tax-exempt bonds at 6.8 percent. This method of refinancing was less risky than conventional bank loan refinancing (and possible because of their tax-exempt status).

This project could not capitalize on tax credits to the full extent. Since Alternatives is tax exempt, the developers had to sell the credits on the secondary market for less than their worth and were not able to use them to their maximum advantage. The grants provided synergistic benefits: The fact that Alternatives was able to win them (due to the public's interest in sustainability and green building) further facilitated Alternatives' fund-raising efforts. The availability of grants and alternative-energy tax credits, along with drastically reduced energy costs, justified the additional costs of energy-efficient design (installing hydro, photovoltaic, and geothermal energy systems). The mill complex now generates 85 percent of its electrical needs and 100 percent of its heating and cooling needs, resulting in an estimated annual savings of $100,000, which can be funneled directly into services and programs provided to its clients.

Maynard Mill Redevelopment Project

The Mill in Maynard, Massachusetts, is 1.1 million square feet of floor space on 40 acres of land. The mill was built in the 1840s to manufacture carpets. During the Civil War, it produced blankets. The American Woolen Company purchased the mill in 1898, and it continued producing textiles until the 1950s, when it closed, only to be bought up again for the production of plastics. In the 1980s, it produced computers. The last owners, Digital Equipment Corporation, sold the mill to Franklin Lifecare Corporation for $1.2 million. Unable to make any progress toward effective revitalization due to a lack of investor support, Lifecare sold the mill to Wellesley Rosewood Maynard Mills LP (WRP).

WRP started to look for bank financing, but no U.S. banks were willing to invest in the project without any collateral. WRP then made a deal with Japan's Namura Bank for loans to fund part of the project through a unique, phased-funding scheme. The bank financed part of the project renovation as Phase 1, and when Phase 1 was completed, the bank used it as collateral to loan out funds for the next phase. This line of credit helped WRP secure small additional loans and provided a great incentive for timely completion of the phases in order to keep the project moving forward at a constant rate. The phased-in bank financing also meant that WRP was not dependent on rental income from tenants, giving them the leeway to concentrate on physical improvements to the facility that would attract more tenants. The bank benefited by giving out loans with collateral, which reduced its risk.

WRP had to come up with creative marketing strategies to attract realtors and tenants to the project. One of these strategies was to invite realtors to the new facility and, as an incentive, enter them into a drawing for the free use of a BMW for a year. This strategy paid off, as the winning realtor later secured the mill three new tenants. They also offered the use of a Mercedes for a year to any realtor who was able to bring in a tenant who rented more than 100,000 square feet of space.

Digital Equipment Corporation had spent a lot of money equipping the mill with state-of-the-art connectivity, which was a strong selling point with potential tenants. To close a deal with EDS Corporation, which was interested in leasing 70,000 square feet of space, WRP agreed to offer free shuttle bus service to and from the nearest Massachusetts Bay Transportation Authority commuter line. Even so, without financial help from government incentive programs, it would have been very difficult for WRP's project to see success.

The Maynard Mill project took advantage of a 10 percent abandoned-building tax credit and a 5 percent state investment tax credit. It also used tax increment funding: the Town of Maynard forgave taxation on 95 percent of all investments in improvements for five years and 50 percent of all investments in improvements for an additional 10 years. The developer then passed these tax savings on as rental discounts to attract tenants to the newly renovated spaces and also used them to continue to make improvements to the property. The tenants benefited from affordable lease rates and from substantial savings on fees related to common-area maintenance (CAM) rates. On average, CAM rates in the region increased the lease rates by 10–15 percent, but WRP was able to offer CAM rates at a negligible 2 percent.

The mill complex was named the Clock Tower Place due to the presence of a huge clock on one of the mill towers. The name symbolizes what the mill means to the community and has attracted a variety of tenants, including a Gold's Gym, a restaurant (whose rental fees were waived for a year so it could survive the lean time before the mill had a full complement of other tenants, a deal the developers felt was to their advantage because the restaurant's presence would help attract other tenants), and a web-based placement services company. By the year 2000, WRP had leased 1 million square feet of space to 85 companies (Kotval, Mullin, and Karamchandani 2008).

Conclusions

The recessions, global competition, and shifting markets hit the industrial and manufacturing sector hard and put additional pressure on the government to create policy instruments to redevelop and revitalize old mill properties (Greenberg and Issa 2005). Approaches that deal with the regulatory and financial deterrents to redevelopment and reuse are abundant. Adaptive rezoning can help change industrial areas to a mix of residential and commercial areas. Local expertise and experience with grant and funding sources is evident in a 2010 study that showed that a majority (67 percent) of applications to the EPA's brownfield redevelopment program were from local governments and local redevelopment authorities (Dull and Wernstedt 2010). However, lack of sufficient funding even for the programs themselves emphasizes the importance of sourcing funds through a mixture of private and public sources. Our three case studies show that public-private partnerships are very important to any revitalization project.

Tax incentives help bridge the gap between the costs of developing a greenfield site and redeveloping a brownfield site, and they help the developer acquire collateral for further market-based or conventional funding (Gose 2002). Demand for reused historical buildings is on the rise because many people like the idea of living or working in the urban core, occupying a charmingly retro former industrial structure, and paying lower mortgage rates. This demand, coupled with the available incentives and a favorable development climate, make for a viable and attractive project for a community and the developers alike (Lange and McNeil 2004). It's the rare mill revitalization project that can make it without the three-legged stool being built: It takes the strong presence of local government, the innovation of developer/investors, and the support of long-term risk takers in order for revitalization to happen. However, such projects can become central to the communities where they are located and are well worth the work required.

References

Alberini, A., A. Longo, S. Tonin, T. Francesco, and M. Turvani. 2005. The role of liability, regulation and economic incentives in brownfield remediation and redevelopment: Evidence from surveys of developers. *Regional Science and Urban Economics* 35(4): 327–51.

Bacot, H., and C. O'Dell. 2006. Establishing indicators to evaluate brownfield redevelopment. *Economic Development Quarterly* 20(2): 142–61.

Baum-Snow, N., and J. Marion. 2009. The effects of low income housing tax credit developments on neighborhoods. *Journal of Public Economics* 93(5–6): 654–66.

Dull, M., and K. Wernstedt. 2010. Land recycling, community revitalization, and distributive politics: An analysis of EPA brownfields program support. *The Policy Studies Journal* 38(1): 119–41.

Fisher, P., and A. Peters. 1997. Tax and spending incentives and enterprise zones. *New England Economic Review (*March-April): 109–30.

Gose, J. 2002. Rehab, reward, and remorse: Are the state historic tax credits that save doomed buildings doomed themselves? *Urban Land* 38 (October): 40–41.

Greenberg, M., and L. Issa. 2005. Measuring the success of the federal government's brownfields program. *Remediation* 15(3): 83–94.

Heberle, L., and K. Wernstedt. 2006. Understanding brownfields regeneration in the U.S. *Local. Environment* 11(5): 479–97.

Howland, M. 2003. Private initiative and public responsibility for the redevelopment of industrial brownfields: Three Baltimore case studies. *Economic Development Quarterly* 17(4): 367–81.

Kotval, Z., J. Mullin, and Z. Karamchandani. 2008. Partnerships and the fiscal implications of planning and development: A case study of Maynard, Massachusetts. *Planning, Practice & Research* 23(4): 461–78.

Lange, D., and S. McNeil. 2004. Clean it and they will come? Defining successful brownfield development. *Journal of Urban Planning and Development* 130(2): 101–08.

Meyer, P., and T. Lyons. 2000. Lessons from private sector brownfield redevelopers: Planning public support for urban regeneration. *Journal of the American Planning Association* 66(1): 46–57.

Mueller, E. and M. Oden. 1999. Distinguishing development incentives from developer give-aways: A critical guide for development practitioners and citizens. *Policy Studies Journal* 27(1): 147–64.

Neiesewand, N. 1988. *Converted Spaces*. London: Conran Octopus Limited.

Nelson, A., and J. Talley. 1991. Revitalizing minority commercial areas through commercial historic district designation. *Journal of Urban Affairs* 13(2): 222.

O'Brien, G. 2008. A new spin. *BusinessWest*, August 18. http://businesswest.com/2008/08/a-new-spin.

Weber, R., S. Bhatta, and D. Merriman. 2003. Does tax increment financing raise urban industrial property values? *Urban Studies* 40(10): 2001–21.
Wernstedt, K., P. Meyer, and A. Alberini. 2006. Attracting private investment to contaminated properties: The value of public interventions. *Journal of Policy Analysis and Management* 25(2): 347–69.
Young, R. 2008. Striking gold: Historic preservation and LEED. *Journal of Green Building* 3(1): 24–43.

Part V

Lessons Learned

16
Perspectives on Economic Development Financing

Sammis B. White

This chapter attempts to build on what the other contributors have said, tries to put finance tools into perspective, and discusses the case for using many of these tools. It also takes a step back to explore why it is we undertake economic development, how to measure what it is we are trying to do with economic development finance, and why we should make a case for assessing what we know about financing tools.

The two introductory chapters in this book offer a broad brush and a summary analysis of a number of economic development finance tools. Knowledge of these tools is important because an estimated $70 billion is allocated annually by state and local governments as business incentives, $50 billion of which is for location incentives (Thomas 2010). These chapters are followed by several that explore the common and not-so-common finance tools that governments use to generate economic development. Those in turn are followed by discussions of a few private financial mechanisms and then several examples of partnerships of public and private sectors. What should be evident beyond the variety of finance tools is the fact that there is no single answer to every situation in terms of finance, just as there is not one best way to stimulate growth.

Communities and states are unique. They differ in terms of the major industries in their economies, the investments they have made to date, the education levels of their citizens, their rates of population and labor-force growth, their tax structures, their provision of public services, the ages of their infrastructure, their politics, and their local challenges. It is in this setting that the key players in economic development must decide what steps, if any, are needed to create more and possibly better economic activity.

The words "more" and "better" raise additional issues. Some states and communities are faced with very slow economic growth; others that may be growing more rapidly seek even faster rates of development or the development of higher paying jobs. Whatever the case, it is clear that stimulating economic development most often requires financing. Several examples of actions that can contribute to economic growth but do not directly involve financing include (1) speeding up government decision making; (2) creating regulations that encourage development; (3) specifying outcomes that must be achieved but not dictating the methods that might be used to achieve them (e.g., air or water pollution levels); and (4) allowing for increased density or mixed-use development. While many of these initiatives don't directly involve cash transactions, they are considered to be money-saving incentives or ways to increase the rate of return for the developer. Most often, however, direct financing is a crucial element of economic development.

Each of the tools enumerated in the chapters in this book can be used successfully by developers and investors. But it is unlikely that a single tool can lead to the multiple goals that economic development is asked to accomplish. As we look across the spectrum of goals that economic development organizations seek to achieve, we see a wide range, indeed. Fundamentally, as Malpezzi notes in Chapter 1, the most common and most encompassing overall goal is to increase incomes—a goal generally achieved through the private-sector creation of jobs and the upgrading of those jobs. There are obviously many refinements to that statement, but it is the private sector that is responsible for generating the income that can then be used either privately or publicly.

Increases in incomes may be the ultimate goal, but many organizations have different objectives and a narrower focus. Two of us[1] participated in a 2011 survey on 20 non-random economic development organizations that had been identified by leaders of other agencies as among the better economic development entities in the United States. Responses to one question revealed that the various organizations were trying to accomplish a wide range of things, among them: creating jobs, creating new companies, positioning existing businesses globally, helping firms build capacity, improving the local business climate, attracting firms, incubating firms, marketing the region, and assisting new product development (Figure 16.1).

The ultimate goal of all of these objectives is to increase incomes. Some paths are more direct than others. Thus, what it is they do will vary, as will the techniques utilized.

Further complicating local and economic development decisions are the multiplicity of metrics used by organizations to measure their success. If jobs and income were the only choices, more attention could be paid to defining and measuring them with greater accuracy. But when these same economic

Figure 16.1 **Initiatives of Non-Random Sample of Local Economic Development Organizations**

- Business Incubator
- Business Retention Visits
- Capacity Building in Firms
- Change Local Business Climate
- Create Loan Funds (Micro, Pre-seed, Seed)
- Efforts to Better Position Businesses Globally
- Help with Research and Development
- Marketing of Area
- New Product Licensing
- Promote Entrepreneurship
- Revolving Loan Fund
- Site Selection Support
- Undertake Economic Research for Firms
- Workforce Development Connections

development organizations were asked how they measured their accomplishments, they revealed even more variety than they did in the stating of their initiatives. Examples of what they reported appear in Figure 16.2.

The 18 responses of the 20 agencies are listed alphabetically, with the most common being the number of jobs created. Half of those answering the question said it was simply "jobs added." Two organizations, however, collectively gave 41 different metrics by which they judge themselves. The three next most common measures were the number of business starts they saw, the number of revolving loans written, and the number of dollars invested in the local community. These imply job creation, but what is measured is often something else. As finance is examined, it is little wonder that there are many different approaches to analyzing the results.

Numerous options to finance economic development have developed over time. Some of these, such as tax incremental finance (TIFs), apply only at the local level. Several, such as industrial revenue bonds and other forms of public financing, can be either local or state initiated. And a few, such as Ohio's more comprehensive Third Frontier, are often limited to the state. Virtually all have worked in certain circumstances. Some have worked more consistently than others. Some are more ambitious than others. Some are more costly than others. Reese and Sands (Chapter 2) have reviewed a number of these, as have many others before them. And the authors of individual chapters have explained and assessed many of the individual finance tools.

What makes choosing the appropriate finance tool difficult is not only knowing where one is going but also understanding well what each tool can accomplish. As Reese and Sands contend in Chapter 2, this is difficult because "a general absence of analysis and evaluation, both before and after the applica-

Figure 16.2 **Metrics of Non-Random Sample of Economic Development Organizations**

- Businesses Retained
- Businesses Started
- Dollars Invested by Firms in the Community
- Dollars Invested in Small Businesses
- Increase in Incubator Space Available
- Incubator Successes
- Jobs Created
- Jobs Created per Discovery
- Local Unemployment Rate Decrease
- Patents Issued to New Companies
- Public/Private Partnerships Created
- Retail Tax Collection Gain
- Revolving Loans Issued
- SBIR/STTR Grants Awarded in Community
- Taxes Generated
- Technology Licensing Done Locally
- University/Industry Links Created
- Workforce Development for Multiple Jobs

tion of economic development tools, has served to trap local officials into these fads because they lack the information about which policies should be pursued and which should be stopped or forgone entirely." The two authors argue that we often use certain finance tools because we do not know any better.

We hope that this book has helped to increase the reader's understanding of several of the finance options. This chapter seeks to give the reader a few more insights into some of the dilemmas surrounding economic development finance.

What Works

Given that range of different goals, the variety of finance options, and the contention that we are not certain which economic development actions will actually generate new jobs, new firms, more growth-conducive environments, higher incomes, more innovation, and so forth, the reader may wonder why he or she has been asked to read the first 15 chapters of this book. This chapter explores "what really works." What must be noted at the outset is that all of the tools work some of the time, none of the tools work all of the time, and a few tools can be said to work only under special circumstances.

What really works is often the combination of financing mechanisms and other initiatives. There are no silver bullets that absolutely deliver in each and every case. Even one of the more promising approaches, the Ohio Third Frontier (OTF; see Chapter 8), can deliver a lot, but it is focusing on the creation and exploitation of technology as the source of economic growth. This means it is not delivering on other elements, such as real estate assembly and development, marketing, revolving loan funds, or public infrastructure investments that may also be needed for substantial success.

It is hard to pick winners at promoting economic development. Even the professionals do not do well. Angel investors (see Chapter 10 by Freear and Sohl) are advised to invest in 10 different new firms to come out ahead financially, because several of their choices will fail miserably, and a few will just break even. One is likely to be a home run, and a second and third may hit a single or double. The financing pros do not have any higher batting averages than do professional baseball players. Local communities are very similar; they struggle to hit singles and doubles, never mind the home runs. In many cases, they are not professionals in an investment sense, although they may be knowledgeable in many ways.

Reese and Sands ask the question: "Which policies appear to have the greatest promise for achieving sustainable local economies at acceptable costs in terms of forgone revenues or local investment?" They conclude, based on recent studies, that the best bet is "investments in policies and activities that make the community a better place to live: good local schools, safe streets, parks, libraries, and public buildings and spaces" (Reese 2010). They think that communities must have their acts together. With well-educated citizens, reasonably well-provided city services, and public amenities, communities have a good chance of attracting job-creating businesses. To be in these positions, almost all communities will use a variety of finance tools; they cannot just pay cash for the infrastructure improvements. And there may be times when they want to speed the development process, again requiring financing tools to allow for investments. But communities need not place bets on individual firms or industries; they let the businesses make their location decisions based on what is best for them.

Still others (Bartik 2011, p. 53) contend that a case can be made for the use of business incentives. Bartik argues that "for each dollar invested in a well-designed business incentive program, the present value of per-capita earnings of the original state residents will increase by $3.14." He goes on to explain that approximately three-fifths of the economic benefits occur because of increases in the employment rates of residents; the remaining two-fifths occur because of residents moving up to better-paying occupations. These benefits accrue when the program represents the "current best practice." The intervention must be targeted at export-based businesses that pay an above-average wage and have a larger than average multiplier effect. These conditions highlight the failure of many financial interventions and the substantial benefits of knowing what business incentives are among those that can deliver substantial value. Reese's negative assessment of business assistance comes from the many failures of the key players in economic development to learn and appreciate the forms of finance that are most appropriate.

Alternative Ways to Create Jobs

Since the main point of economic development is the creation of jobs, even if it might not be the best measure, we must explore job creation. Basically, a community has three options for expanding the number of jobs within its boundaries: attraction, starting new firms, or growing existing firms. Historically, attraction has been the most common approach for economic development organizations. Convincing existing firms from elsewhere to move to one's community appeared to be the best way to increase the number of jobs locally. Existing jobs in a community were already there and did not need much attention (or so it was believed). And new business starts were largely ignored because new businesses were thought to have too few jobs to be worthy targets. But times have been changing. All three options need to be reviewed. Economic development finance efforts should be better aimed at alternatives that will truly deliver the jobs that communities seek.

Attraction

The attraction of companies from other communities has been the major emphasis of economic development organizations for many decades. We are all aware of mills and other manufacturing plants that first moved from the Northeast and Midwest to the South because of lower labor costs. Firms then tended to move to Mexico. And finally the big push was to move production to China and other Southeast Asian countries. In each case, an aggressive effort was made by the receiving locations to attract the firms that subsequently moved.

A number of devices have been created to lure firms to new areas, among them land assembly, land cleanup, land development, infrastructure subsidy, marketing, site selection assistance, building construction, workforce development, road building, tax reduction, service rate reduction (water, sewer), and accelerated regulatory approvals. These examples give a sense of the tools that many communities have employed to convince existing businesses to relocate. Among the most powerful are those that reduce the costs of doing business in a particular location. This often involves reduced property taxes or income taxes, but it has also involved land and training subsidies, which need to be financed by someone. Finance plays a key role.

Attraction has appeal because the number of jobs potentially added, when successful, sounds impressive. It also does not take years of work to see results;

moves may take less than one year. Furthermore, the number of jobs being "created" (actually "located") in a community is quite well known from the outset. Those involved can generate an accurate cost-per-job-added assessment, assuming the initial numbers are accurate. That makes the concept of spending local dollars on attraction compelling; you can easily see the return. Of course, you do not know how long the businesses will stay nor whether they will actually create the number of jobs they've pledged to bring for the investment the community makes. But a good story can be told, and political support can be built, even if the special treatment of newcomers tends to upset the existing businesses in a community.

There are, however, several downsides to the emphasis on attraction. One is that many communities are competing for the same firms. That leads to bidding wars. At times, the price of attraction has been so high that there are questions about whether a community can ever generate sufficient benefits to offset the cost of the promises, like long-deferred taxation, free land, and substantial workforce development investments. Alabama's successful bid for Mercedes in the early 1990s has often been used as an example that will not work to Alabama's advantage. But continuing investments by Mercedes and its suppliers in that state have changed the math; the investments may well work. And it does work in some situations.

Downsides to Attraction

- Bidding wars increase the cost
- "Bought" firms have no allegiance
- Hard sell to convince firms to move
- Most firms will not move

Another issue is that firms that move for subsidies and lower-cost labor may not remain very long. That is why some communities have developed "clawback" provisions that are briefly discussed by Webster in Chapter 13. A third issue is that it is very hard to convince firms to move to certain locations. A fourth and very important consideration as communities examine which investments to make for economic development is that most firms do not want to move. Managers and owners typically like where they are located. A recent Brookings report (Muro and Fikri 2011) reveals that, on average, states generate about 2 percent of their employment growth through multiple schemes to attract employers from elsewhere. It is by far the least productive source of jobs.

Because of the low rate of success with job growth through attraction, those involved in economic development should expend their energies and resources on the other two options: the growth of existing firms and the creation of new firms. Local and state economic development agencies may still be able to use several of the economic development finance tools in their toolkit. But they also need to think more carefully about how these alternatives might create the scale of growth that the community seeks. The answer lies in analyzing which of the two—helping existing firms or helping start new firms—should receive greater emphasis.

There are conflicting interpretations of the role of existing and new firms. The Brookings study cited earlier claims that 42 percent of jobs come from the growth of existing firms and 56 percent comes from the establishment of new firms. Some of the discrepancy has to do with the definitions, but both approaches warrant attention and should be viewed in light of the conditions and assets in a given community or state.

The Case for Entrepreneurship

For a number of years there were many claims that most job growth was attributable to small firms, usually defined as firms with fewer than 500 employees. This started with Birch (1979). But the story is seldom clear. Over the 15 years between 1995 and 2010, small businesses have accounted for about 65 percent of the private-sector net job creation, according to BLS Business Employment Dynamics figures. Using the Census numbers from the Statistics of U.S. Businesses, small businesses accounted for about 90 percent of net new jobs through 2006 (Headd 2010).

A study by Haltiwanger, Jarmin, and Miranda (2009) reached a somewhat different conclusion. They showed that nearly all net job creation in the United States since 1980 has occurred in firms less than five years old. Small firms are not the source of most net job growth; young firms are. The researchers went beyond age to determine if other factors played a role in job creation (2010). Their main finding was that once they controlled for firm age, no systematic relationship existed between firm size and growth.

A concurrent study supported by the Kauffman Foundation (Stangler and Litan 2009) asserts that in the two and a half decades between 1980 and 2005, young firms (defined as one to five years old) accounted for roughly two-thirds of all job creation over the period. Of the 12 million new jobs that were added in the United States in 2007, young firms created almost 8 million of them. Over time, these young firms, on average, create nearly four jobs per firm per year. It is not that individually they are adding a large number of jobs; it is that there are so many of these new firms that they collectively account for about two-thirds of all job creation.

Haltiwanger, Jarmin, and Miranda (2010) further differentiated by years in business to learn that both start-ups (less than one-year old) and young businesses (one to five years old) played very important roles in both gross and net job creation. Start-ups often added a limited number of employees in their first year, but there are so many start-ups that they collectively are very important to job growth. Furthermore, some start-ups subsequently grew substantially. Thus, young firms also contribute substantially to job growth. In addition, they found an "up or out" dynamic of young firms, where such firms tend to either grow or close. These findings imply that it is critical to control for and understand the role of firm age in explaining U.S. job creation. The key to growth is the start, the survival, and the growth of new businesses.

Additional work by Stangler and Litan (2009) also showed in an analysis of 2007 Census data that without start-ups, net job creation in the U.S. economy would be negative in all but a handful of years over the last three decades. They conclude, "It is clear that new and young companies and the entrepreneurs that create them are the engines of job creation." But they go on to explain that the largest and oldest companies still matter for job growth, accounting for greater than 10 percent of net job creation. There is a dumbbell distribution of new job creation with the young end disproportionately larger.

Unfortunately for many parts of the United States, the distribution of these new firms is heavily skewed toward a limited number of states and even metropolitan areas. This means that many communities and many states have rates of new business starts that are well below those found in places like New York, Washington, or Massachusetts. Those communities that are lagging want to catch up; those that are leading want to stay ahead. The challenge is raising the rate of new business starts where the culture for doing so is lacking, as is the infrastructure of bankers, attorneys, accountants, business angels, venture capitalists, entrepreneurial mentors, education opportunities, and so forth that are found in places where entrepreneurship is thriving. The challenge for economic development organizations is to put into place all of the many pieces needed to encourage entrepreneurs. Heightening the challenge is evidence suggesting that entrepreneurship is higher when fixed costs are lower and when there are more entrepreneurial people (Glaeser, Kerr, and Ponzetto 2009).

More current economic development organizations do their best to encourage entrepreneurship. They try to increase the number of new businesses by publicizing entrepreneurial success. They assist tech companies by contributing to or providing support for Small Business Innovation Research (SBIR) grants or Small Business Technology Transfer (STTR) grants in the hopes that federal funding will fuel a given product or service's development and help demonstrate its commercial potential. These same organizations often try to link firms and individuals with universities to speed technology development. The organizations try to increase the transfer of tech licenses from local universities to local entrepreneurs. Economic development organizations sometimes even create business incubators to provide space and services that will help speed the development of new firms.

Many of these efforts require financial support. Convincing colleges and universities to offer an increasing number of entrepreneurship classes or organizing university/industry links does not cost an economic development organization money—only time. But some of the contributing steps by an economic development organization, such as offering an SBIR/STTR grant writer, space in an incubator, or access to experienced attorneys and accountants, would involve organizational operating costs. Finance interventions are necessary for developing early-stage seed funds, which then invest in some of the nascent firms; for gathering public finance for the operation of the economic development organization; and for seeking out governmental investment in venture capital funds aimed at local entrepreneurs.

Angel financing, or support from those with financial means for those who need money to move their ideas from concept to reality, is very important to the types of new businesses likely to create the most jobs (see Chapter 10 by Freear and Sohl). Angels invested $20.1 billion in 61,900 ventures in 2010 (Sohl 2011). Angel investors take risks. They know that they will lose all of their money on some investments and get modest returns on others. They hope to pick winners.

Many fewer new firms are funded by venture capitalists (VCs). VCs invest in between 2,700 and 4,200 companies a year (National Venture Capital Association 2011)—a very small number compared to the number of firms that seek their assistance, and even smaller when compared to the total number of new business starts annually. But the importance of access to venture capital in each location cannot be understated. VCs place their bets on firms that will likely grow rapidly. These are most often technology-based firms, be they in IT, telecommunications, or medical devices and pharmaceuticals. Both angel and venture investors have a strong tendency to invest in firms that are physically within 100 miles of their location. It is far easier for each of them to learn about those requesting their assistance. The result is that if an entrepreneur is located in an area with no venture capitalists and no angels, it is much harder to attract the capital needed to take one's business to the next level—that is, to grow the firms rapidly. That is why economic development organizations must make the effort to develop business angels and attract venture capital to their regions.

The expansion of interest in entrepreneurship does not just happen in most communities; it must be encouraged to happen. Missing ingredients must be created and supported. All of these activities take financing, whether public, private, or both. If entrepreneurship is to become more common, and it appears clear to many analysts that it must, many places will need funding to stimulate interest in starting businesses and supporting those individuals and teams that go down that path.

Among the states that have gone the furthest with the promotion of entrepreneurship, and especially entrepreneurship focused on technology, is Ohio. The chapter by Austrian and Auerbach (Chapter 8) provides a number of insights into how this program operates and describes some of the successes it has had to date. The scale of the activity is impressive. The Ohio Third Frontier (OTF) program has had some $2.3 billion in funding since 2002 to allocate to technology-based economic development across the state of Ohio. Some of these funds are tax dollars, but a large proportion is funds the state has borrowed to invest in expanding Ohio's economy.

The concept of using public bonding for economic development is also discussed by Crane (Chapter 3), Elmer (Chapter 6), and Robinson (Chapter 4). While these chapters are aimed at the local level, the concepts remain the same. Governments have the power to borrow and to invest. Governments also have to determine how they are to repay the borrowing, either through tax dollars earned by the expenditures of the borrowed funds or, if the governments relend the money, the interest and principal that are paid back over time. Few governments have been as involved in financing economic development as Ohio. But the citizens of the state approved two separate referendums that gave the state permission to borrow $1.2 billion for OTF. The majority of citizens clearly believed in the wisdom of using the state's fiscal power to stimulate Ohio's slumping economy.

Communities make the same decision, but they do so on a smaller scale and with more focused uses of their funds. Such borrowing has gone on for decades; over the years, the techniques have been refined. The tools are useful for several interventions, including tax increment financing (TIFs) (see Chapter 12 by Weber), revolving loans to businesses (see Chapter 4 by Robinson), portions of brownfield remediation (see Chapter 7 by De Sousa), or other steps that result in growing the local economy. It is harder to argue that local communities should use their financial resources to generate early-stage seed funds for new businesses. Such a proposition is likely too risky for most public officials. But local governments can contribute to the formation of such funds by supporting those individuals who attempt to create such funding sources, and communities can create revolving loan funds to assist businesses that are more established to help businesses access the capital they need to grow.

The private sector is different. There can be dramatic payoffs for those involved. Freear and Sohl discuss these to some extent in Chapter 10. Newberger and Berry (Chapter 9) write of the revised roles of banking institutions in community lending after the financial meltdown. In Chapter 15, Mullin and Kotval-K write of the challenges of pulling together the funds for the revitalization of mills and the role those older buildings commonly play in providing space for young firms.

Most of the emphasis on rekindling entrepreneurship in the United States has concentrated on metropolitan economies, usually where there are research universities that can spin out new technologies. But in Chapter 11, Renski and Wallace make the case that the push for entrepreneurship is not only for urbanites. The need to build the entrepreneurial culture across the country is substantial. The world has changed. China and several other economies have been growing rapidly. The United States is being challenged for economic leadership, and if it is to continue to provide jobs and incomes on the levels desired, it must start more companies and create opportunities for more of these new starts to succeed. Local and state economic development organizations have very important roles in making this happen.

New industries seldom appear overnight. For most, it takes decades for them to see growth, which is important to know as one seeks to add jobs. The largest number of jobs created in 2007 came from accommodations and food service, health care, and retail (Stangler and Litan 2009). Statistics for 2010 or 2011 are likely to be far different because of the downsizing of the role of retail, the drag on health care, and the partial revitalization of manufacturing. But the point is that it is the largest sectors of the economy—those with the most firms—are likely also to have the most *new* firms. In fact, the distribution of new firm starts by industry is found to be representative of the number of employers already in existence in those industries in a geographic area (Reynolds and White 1997). Yes, there are new industries developing, but none will grow dramatically in absolute number of jobs compared to what is already in existence.

Changing the culture to elevate the importance of and participation in the starting of new businesses does not happen overnight. Still, it is essential to a community's future health. Unfortunately, for a number of years, the contributions of entrepreneurs to net job creation will be minimal. The stronger the effort, however, the more the needed pieces—including financing—will be put into place. And the sooner entrepreneurship will be able to deliver the growth communities seek.

Existing Companies

Despite the robust argument just made for the support of entrepreneurship and the critical role new firms play in job growth, communities should not ignore existing firms, especially large ones. On any given day, existing firms account for almost all of the jobs in existence. Unless they are among a select few young firms or the oldest and largest firms, existing firms are unlikely to account for the bulk of the subsequent net job growth in a given geographic area any time soon. Existing firms are the source of most jobs for the foreseeable future in almost all communities. Therefore, existing firms should be a target of economic development organizations.

Communities do not want their employers to downsize, leave, or die. And if existing employers would grow, that would be highly desired. It is clear that economic development organizations must pay close attention to existing firms because they are the primary source of current jobs. Communities that have a limited number of new firms must rely on existing firms for growth until such time as they have developed a sufficient number of young firms that they collectively make a significant contribution to job growth.

Of the existing firms, those with fewer than 20 employees represent some 89 percent of all businesses but employ only 18 percent of all workers in firms and 15 percent of workers overall (Stangler and Litan 2009). Numerically, the small firms are important, but in terms of employment, small means collectively accounting for a limited portion of the total payroll. Large firms, those employing more than 500 workers, make up 0.3 percent of all firms, but they are responsible for nearly 50 percent of all employment in firms (Stangler and Litan 2009). (That phrasing of "employment in firms" is used to differentiate such workers from those who are self-employed with no firm affiliation.)

Picking Targets

Firms may receive incentives and attention in the form of TIF financing for their expansion or relocation, revolving loan fund money for operations or facilities, brownfield redevelopment assistance, and the like. In some cases, these incentives help to allow further growth, but quite often they are offered as a way to keep jobs in the state and especially in a particular community. Communities need to keep jobs as much as they need to be the home to new jobs. In many situations, finance tools are necessary to maintain the status quo, never mind stimulate job growth.

A common approach to economic development is to make a number of ad hoc decisions as to which companies to offer various forms of assistance. Companies that are better negotiators tend to win, as do those that appear to be offering more benefits for a community in the form of more jobs, higher paying jobs, more glamour, a better story, or whatever. The recent history in Wisconsin reveals that by far three large firms (Mercury Marine, Oshkosh Truck, and Harley Davidson) have received the bulk of the financial assistance made available by the state government. In the previous decade, the two largest state investments were in two automobile plants, neither of which remains open.

Some of these targeted investments work well. South Carolina, for example, placed a very good bet on the attraction of BMW. The state attracted not only the BMW jobs but also jobs from a number of suppliers that decided to locate near the BMW plant (Schunk and Woodward 2003). Moreover, the state won because the arrival of the new firms forced South Carolina to take workforce training far more seriously and stimulated much of the manufacturing sector to automate and require more sophisticated workers. The entire manufacturing sector was upgraded by the subsidized attraction of a single firm.

That said, Alabama's experience with Mercedes has taken far longer to justify the state's investment, in part because the state paid far more in subsidies per job created by the automaker than did South Carolina. The scale of those expenditures has not stopped other communities from spending extremely large sums for a limited number of jobs. For example, in the fall of 2010, Yahoo made a deal in Lockport, New York, for a new server farm. Yahoo is to receive $200 million in state and local tax breaks (including no property taxes), plus $58 million of cut-rate electricity from Niagara Falls and a $10 million stimulus grant. The total subsidy equals $268 million to create 125 jobs, or $2.1 million per job (Johnston 2011). Whether this is a worthwhile investment remains to be seen, but it should give pause.

The checkered history of states that have placed very risky bets on business attraction should be a lesson to others. The mixed returns raise the issue of whether states or local governments can do a good job at picking winners—companies that will pay off the public investments made in them. Picking company by company may not be the wisest route to take. Yet, just as with angel investors, communities occasionally hit home runs.

Ohio's Third Frontier (Austrian and Auerbach) has changed the approach by focusing attention not on individual firms but on specific target industry clusters. Within potential clusters, Ohio has focused on technology for two main reasons: the research strengths they have in the state, and the knowledge that innovation in technology can be a differentiator. Furthermore, Ohio has chosen to use third-party analysts to choose specific recipients of public funds. All three decisions appear to be wise. Ohio has spread the risk in one way (dealing with clusters), but it has reduced it in two others (choosing where the state has advantages and using nonpolitical, business standards to make investment decisions on specific firms in which to invest).

The Case for Industrial Clusters

Keeping and assisting existing businesses should be a high priority for communities. Whether it is supporting the Manufacturing Extension Partnership to help manufacturers become lean and green, assisting with land assembly for business expansion, or developing better focused workforce development training to aid efficiency improvements, communities need to be listening to and responding to the needs of businesses. This will help keep the economies going while they build the impacts of expanded entrepreneurship.

This assistance should not be random: There should be a focus. One of the key targets should be industrial clusters. The case for working with industrial clusters (i.e., a large presence of geographically concentrated, competitive, related companies)[2] rather than with scattershots across all industries has been gaining favor. After Porter (1990) started espousing the strengths of working with clusters, more and more communities have attempted to do so. Some of the initial evidence was not convincing, but with time, clusters have made increasing sense. What has changed is the strength of the profile of clusters and the understanding of why they work well. Moreover, clusters can involve all three targets: existing businesses on which a cluster is built, new firms that can be generated from the industry/university interaction and from the attraction of talent, and the attraction of firms that want to be where the action is in a given industrial cluster.

The clearest case for clusters can be made on the basis of the payoffs for the existing companies that benefit collectively from having more interaction, more innovation, and the likelihood of greater gains in productivity. But there is significant evidence of the positive impact of clusters on entrepreneurship. After controlling for convergence in start-up activity at the region-industry level, industries located in regions with strong clusters experience higher growth in new business formation and start-up employment (Delgado, Porter, and Stern 2010). If one wants to start an IT company, it is clear that the location of choice is the Silicon Valley. If one wants to start a biotech firm, the logical location choices are San Diego and Boston. If one wants to create a new financial enterprise, the location of choice is New York. Yes, there are exceptions, but these locations draw an outsized proportion of the new firm activity in these respective industries for two reasons—synergy and talent.

Clusters occur because they benefit from natural advantages or artificial efforts to strengthen the critical elements that are needed for success. The strongest clusters, such as Silicon Valley, are largely organic, at least initially. No one anointed this location to become the IT center of the world. It grew because of the presence of talent, a talent generator (Stanford University), and the growth over time of lawyers, bankers, business angels, venture capitalists, and others who understood the industry.

Orlando, conference center of the United States, explicitly brought together a number of the elements needed for the cluster's growth. This is an example of a more artificially induced growth. Unlike Anaheim, which houses the first Disney theme park, Orlando set aside land for further growth not only by Disney but also by other tourist attractions. It zoned for future supporting services, such as hotels and restaurants; it was very careful about land use decisions; it asked the University of Central Florida to create courses and degrees in hospitality and hotel management; and it built an airport with the capacity to accommodate the many visitors who would travel to the area. These are just some of the essential elements needed for the growth of the cluster. Many of these elements were identified early, and explicit steps were taken to put them in place.

Other communities are trying to take those lessons and build the growth of jobs and income around an initial cluster. One with which I am very familiar is Milwaukee and its efforts to build a larger sector around the historic and sizable presence of companies that deal with water. These companies treat water or wastewater; others produce pumps, valves, meters, filters, membranes, chemicals, controls, and other devices used in the treatment or delivery of water or wastewater. Still other firms manufacture dehumidifiers, garbage disposals, water heaters, water efficiency devices (for manufacturing industries, agriculture, or for the home), water recreation toys and tools (Jet Skis, boat docks, and floating trampolines, to name a few), and enzymes and other biocontrol devices. Engineering firms with long records of experiences in water and wastewater are also located here. All of these firms developed in Milwaukee because of several high-need industrial water users, namely breweries, tanneries, and food processors. These industries initially located here because of the ample presence of water. But the industry needs changed over time—they required better and more water, creating new opportunities for many other firms.

The existence of this core of firms was first recognized in 2007, and efforts were made to quantify them. Roughly130 water-related firms were identified, along with more than 100 freshwater researchers at colleges and universities in the region. Also present was the largest freshwater research center on the Great Lakes, a center that would soon be transformed into the nation's first School of Freshwater Sciences. With the academic and corporate strength, the effort to build on them was under way.

Surprisingly, the water firms had no knowledge and no contact with the universities in the region. The firms were unaware of the research that could help them develop new products and approaches to their businesses. Furthermore, the researchers were not aware of the water companies and their needs. It seemed that an opportunity for economic growth was waiting to be seized.

In 2008, White presented a paper that outlined the essential ingredients needed for such a cluster to grow. Among the ingredients identified were:

- A core of firms already in the industry
- Experienced talent in the region
- A talent development pipeline
- Collaboration among firms and water researchers
- Demand for solutions (money to support development)
- Desire by the private water firms to grow
- Recognition by the larger community of the assets and potential
- Resources and leadership to help bring the necessary ingredients together

The challenge was to enhance the resources that were present and create the elements that were not. The region set about filling the gaps and capitalizing on the elements that were already there.

Clearly, an organization was needed that could bring together the multiple actors needed and formulate a cohesive plan for moving forward. The Milwaukee Water Council was formally created in 2009 through the collaborative efforts of businesses, academia, and nonprofit environmental groups. The Water Council immediately emphasized bringing together area universities and businesses. To speed knowledge development, the Water Council ran mixers and a dating service, introducing each to the other. The Council encouraged sharing of information that heretofore had been held very close to the chest. After some courting, the academics and the businesses were much more open about what they wanted to do. Productive joint research began shortly thereafter.

In 2012, just five years after the initial exploration of the cluster, the Milwaukee Water Council and the water cluster are known across the world. Milwaukee has been present at Singapore International Water Week, Stockholm Water Week, the WATEC water industry show in Tel Aviv, and at international water discussions in Holland and elsewhere. It is one of only 14 cities in the world that is part of the UN Global Compact Cities Program and the only city chosen to demonstrate to others how to solve water problems. The visibility of the effort has grown dramatically. One company has moved to Milwaukee from California to be surrounded by the many others working in water. Two more firms are currently in discussions. University research in water has increased dramatically through a communal National Science Foundation effort to promote industry/university collaboration and efforts by individual firms that work directly with specific industry-funded university researchers.

Furthermore, there have been a number of initiatives to insure the continued growth of talent to work in the water cluster. Articulation agreements have proliferated between two-year and four-year colleges and universities. New faculty lines have been generated for water-related faculty positions.

A new degree program in business and water was created at the University of Wisconsin Whitewater, and a concentration in water law and policy was created at the Marquette University Law School. A new building for the University of Wisconsin–Milwaukee's School of Freshwater Sciences is in the design phase and will be completed by December 2013. More than 100 internships in water settings were arranged in 2011. Veolia Water has created a set of water-based explorations for fifth graders and is in the process of distributing it to all fifth grade classrooms in the region. Talent development is a critical component in the effort to strengthen the water cluster.

As the region and the state look for direction in where to invest and how to create jobs and income, they are increasingly making decisions to invest in clusters like the water cluster. The rationale is that there is identified strength in the number of firms in the cluster; a projected growth in demand both nationally and globally for water solutions; an organization that is helping give the project direction; and the opportunity to work with existing companies, new companies, and companies elsewhere that might be attracted by the activity and support given water companies in Milwaukee. The elements that will be strengthened by the Water Council, such as finance, further development of a talent pipeline, new business activity, global marketing, actor knowledge, and public support all contribute to the interest in the development of the cluster. It has also helped that the federal government has gotten behind this cluster in terms of support. The National Science Foundation, the Economic Development Administration, the Department of Labor, and the Small Business Administration have all invested in the further development of the cluster.

State and local governments are getting involved in financing cluster development. The state of Wisconsin is likely to fund the organizing entity, the Water Council, to speed its quest to grow the cluster. The City of Milwaukee is set to approve the creation of a TIF district to help promote the concentrated redevelopment of a 16-acre parcel so that the land is ready for the location and expansion of water companies near the new School of Freshwater Sciences. Other local governments in the region are also exploring explicit steps they can take to promote the growth of the water sector.

Milwaukee may be somewhat unique in its water emphasis and cluster development, but it is not unique in having industrial and academic strengths that can be built upon. Utilizing clusters for economic development makes sense for all participants. That is why there is increasing activity in identifying potential clusters and investing time and resources in their development. The basic underlying thinking is that progress can be better made in combinations of firms that have a history of success in an area and that share several common interests, such as talent development, marketing, banker understanding, and the like.

Other Considerations for Economic Development

Clusters have a compelling case for being the subject of concentrated economic development actions. A number of factors help to reduce the risk that public investments will be unsuccessful. Some analysts, like Reese noted earlier, argue that picking industries or even clusters to assist is not much better than picking individual firms in terms of risk reduction. Reese (Chapter 2) argues that what the available, reliable evidence strongly suggests is that "investments in policies and activities that make a community a better place to live" is the best option. That may be correct. But there is growing evidence that some interventions like OTF that focus on technology innovation in selected industries can have substantial payoffs and that well-constructed finance tools, chosen appropriately, can succeed. In fact, an SRI evaluation of OTF (2009) reported a return to Ohio of about $6 for every $1 the state invested.

Broadening the scope to consider investments beyond those that are targeted at specific industries or businesses opens the door to longer-term investment. One of the most intriguing is a subject explored by Bartik (2011). Bartik has done more examining of the costs and benefits of a wide range of business assistance programs than all other current economic development researchers. In recent years, he has been committed to examining an option that many have ignored as an economic development tool: early childhood education. Although it is clear that the economic development payoffs from early childhood education are not fully realized until the former child participants enter their prime earning years, there may be additional benefits to communities that invest in early childhood education. One potential savings is in a reduction of the need for special education classes on the scale that currently exists. Another is the benefit of increased property values in communities that offer the availability of universal, high-quality, early-childhood education. That experience would increase achievement levels across K–12 grades, making the schools more desirable to those making location decisions based on the quality of the schools, thus driving up property values.

Businesses will be increasingly interested in talent development, as talent shortages across the United States have already appeared and are projected to only worsen. Thus, businesses will be attracted to and willing to pay more for qualified talent. The economic development of growth in jobs and income will be better met. Unfortunately, the wisdom of these arguments is hard to sell to politicians because of the long wait for clearly defined payoffs, payoffs arriving far beyond most politicians' political lives.

The Need for Further Assessment

Another critical element is further assessment of the merits of alternative economic development tools. Given the mood of the U.S. public and its attitudes toward government, it is wise to explore in greater depth which of the many forms of intervention and financing make the most sense in particular situations. The chapters in this book offer the reader the best current insights. But as many authors have noted, the landscape keeps changing and our ability to tease new insights out of the interventions being employed continues to improve. We must take advantage of the opportunity to learn of refinements in financing techniques, improvements in outcomes, and improvements in our ability to discern what has happened and why. The reader needs to realize that the world is changing—and changing rapidly—and that what may have worked even 10 years ago may not work today and is even less likely to work tomorrow. That is, in part, the emphasis put on entrepreneurship in this book. Communities that are flexible and responsive are going to be healthier and more sustainable that those that are not.

Notes

1. I would like to thank Michael Slezak, a graduate student in urban planning at the University of Wisconsin–Milwaukee, for his efforts on this survey.

2. These consist of a number of rival companies around which are grouped complementary and supporting supplier companies and associated institutions. Geographical proximity allows interaction and efficient flows of goods, services, ideas, and skills. This yields high levels of productivity growth and rapid rates of innovation in both processes and products (Local Government Improvement and Development 2008).

References

Bartik, Timothy. 2011. *Investing in Kids: Early Childhood Programs and Local Economic Development.* Kalamazoo, MI: W.E. Upjohn Institute for Employment Research.

Birch, David. 1979. *The Job Generation Process.* Report. Cambridge, MA: MIT Program on Neighborhood and Regional Change.

Delgado, Mercedes, Michael Porter, and Scott Stern. 2010. Clusters and entrepreneurship. *Journal of Economic Geography* 10(4): 495–518.

Glaeser, Edward, William Kerr, and Giacomo Ponzetto. 2009. *Clusters of Entrepreneurship.* U.S. Census Bureau, Center for Economic Studies Paper No. CES-WP-09-36, October 1.

Haltiwanger, John, Ron Jarmin, and Javier Miranda. 2009. *Business Dynamics Statistics: An Overview.* Report, January 12. Kansas City, MO: Ewing Marion Kauffman Foundation. www.kauffman.org/uploadedFiles/BDS_handout_011209.pdf.

———. 2010. *Who Creates Jobs? Small vs. Large vs. Young.* Federal Reserve Bank of Atlanta. www.frbatlanta.org/documents/news/conferences/10smallbusiness (accessed March 11, 2012).

Headd, Brian. 2010. An analysis of small businesses and jobs. U.S. Small Business Administration, Office of Advocacy, March. http://archive.sba.gov/advo/research/rs359tot.pdf (accessed November 20, 2011), p. 10.

Johnston, David Cay. 2011. On the dole, corporate style. Tax.com, January 4. www.tax.com/taxcom/taxblog.nsf/Permalink/UBEN-8CSNLH?OpenDocument.

Local Government Improvement and Development. 2008. *Industrial Clusters and Their Implications for Local Economic Policy.* Paper, August 25. London: Local Government Improvement and Development Agency. www.idea.gov.uk/idk/core/page.do?pageId=8507296.

Muro, Mark, and Kenan Fikri. 2011. *Job Creation on a Budget: How Regional Industry Clusters Can Add Jobs, Bolster Entrepreneurship, and Spark Innovation.* Paper, January. Washington, DC: Brookings-Rockefeller Project on State and Metropolitan Innovation.

National Venture Capital Association (NVCA). 2011. Recent stats and studies. November 20. www.nvca.org/index.php?option=com_content&view=article&id=344&Itemid=103.

Porter, Michael. 1990.*The Competitive Advantage of Nations*. New York: Free Press.

Reese, L.A. 2010. Creative class or procreative class. Paper presented at the Making Cities Livable Conference, Charleston, SC, October.

Reynolds, Paul D., and Sammis B. White. 1997. *The Entrepreneurial Process: Economic Growth, Men, Women, and Minorities.* Westport, CT: Quorum Books.

Schunk, Donald, and Douglas Woodward. 2003. Incentives and Economic Development: The Case of BMW in South Carolina, in *Financing Economic Development in the 21st Century,* ed. Sammis B. White, Richard Bingham, and Edward W. Hill, 145–69, Armonk, NY: M.E. Sharpe.

Sohl, Jeffrey. 2011. The angel investor market in 2010: A market on the rebound. Paper, April. Durham, NH: Center for Venture Research. www.unh.edu/news/docs/2010angelanalysis.pdf.

SRI International. 2009. *Making an Impact: Assessing the Benefits of Ohio's Investment in Technology-Based Economic Development Programs* Menlo Park, CA.

Stangler, Daniel, and Robert Litan. 2009. *Where Will the Jobs Come From?* Kauffman Foundation Research Series Paper, November. www.kauffman.org/uploadedfiles/where_will_the_jobs_come_from.pdf.

Thomas, Kenneth P. 2010. *Investment Incentives and the Global Competition for Capital.* New York: Palgrave Macmillan.

White, Sammis B. 2008. *Water Summit White Paper*. Water Summit II, Milwaukee Water Council, Milwaukee, WI, July 14.

Index

About the Editors and Contributors

Eli Auerbach is a doctoral student in urban affairs and public administration at Ohio's Cleveland State University, where he earned master's degrees in urban planning and public administration and a bachelor's degree in urban affairs. Currently he is a research assistant for the Center for Economic Development at the Maxine Goodman Levin College of Urban Affairs. His research interests include economic development, regional development policy, and energy and sustainability.

Ziona Austrian is the director of the Center for Economic Development and a college fellow at the Maxine Goodman Levin College of Urban Affairs of Cleveland State University. She has over 25 years of experience in applied research, project management, and technical assistance. Dr. Austrian works with policymakers, civic leaders, and funders at the local, regional, state, and federal levels on projects and policy issues focusing on urban and regional economics, economic development, innovation and entrepreneurship, industrial clusters, the high-tech sector, regional indicators, and economic impact. She has taught graduate courses in economic development. She received her PhD and MA in economics from Case Western Reserve University.

Robert Baade is the Albert Blake Dick Professor of Economics at Lake Forest College in Lake Forest, Illinois. He received his PhD in economics from the University of Wisconsin–Madison. Professor Baade has published more than 50 scholarly articles, book chapters, and monographs about the economics of professional and amateur sports. In addition to his work as a scholar, Professor Baade has been involved in numerous country, state, county, and city deliberations relating to large public projects, including stadia, arenas, and convention centers. He is also the past president of the International Association of Sports Economists, a position he held from 2006 through 2010.

Michael V. Berry is the director of policy studies in the Federal Reserve Bank of Chicago's Community Development and Policy Studies division, and the managing editor of the Chicago Fed publication *Profitwise News and Views.* Prior to joining the Chicago Fed, Mr. Berry headed the market research group at RESCORP, a real estate development and consulting organization. His research interests include policy interventions to address the foreclosure crisis and the business models, roles, and impacts of community development financial institutions. Mr. Berry holds a BA in political science from Susquehanna University and an MBA from DePaul University.

Matt Brinkley is a senior planner for the Charter Township of Lansing, Michigan. He received his master's degree in urban and regional planning from Michigan State University in 2007. His thesis focused on the transfer of development rights in Michigan. Mr. Brinkley's current focus is on economic development, environmental planning, stormwater management, urban design, and Geographic Information Systems. He is an active member of the American Planning Association (APA) and the American Institute of Certified Planners (AICP).

Randall Crane studies the public finance, housing, transportation, and economic development challenges of cities, and the measure, meaning, and governance of sprawl. This work is mostly domestic, but his international experience includes projects in China, Colombia, Guyana, Indonesia, Kenya, the Philippines, Thailand, Vietnam, and Yemen, and a Fulbright professorship at the Colegio de México in Mexico City. He and Rachel Weber are editing the forthcoming *Oxford Handbook of Urban Planning*. Professor Crane is also the editor of the *Journal of the American Planning Association.*

Roger K. Dahlstrom is an assistant director and senior research associate with the Center for Governmental Studies at Northern Illinois University. He joined the University in 1999. He specializes in the preparation and coordination of community planning and development projects and programs. Mr. Dahlstrom has 32 years of professional city planning experience, including 17 years as the director of planning for the City of Elgin, Illinois. He has provided independent consulting and research assistance to numerous local governments and service districts throughout Illinois. He also serves as a local government representative, assisting the Illinois Municipal League in evaluating development impact fee issues.

Christopher A. De Sousa is an associate professor and the newly appointed director of the School of Urban and Regional Planning at Ryerson University.

Prior to joining Ryerson, he was the chair of Urban Planning at the University of Wisconsin–Milwaukee, as well as a member of the Geography and Urban Studies faculty. Professor De Sousa holds degrees in geography, urban planning, and environmental management from the University of Toronto. His research activities focus on various aspects of brownfield redevelopment, urban environmental management, and sustainability reporting in Canada and the United States. He has authored a book titled *Brownfields Redevelopment and the Quest for Sustainability,* as well as numerous journal articles, book chapters, and reports.

Vicki Elmer is the director of the Oregon Leadership in Sustainability graduate program at the University of Oregon. She has been a planning director and public works director in the City of Berkeley, a city manager in Eugene, Oregon, and a professor at the University of California at Berkeley. She taught science as a Peace Corps volunteer in Nepal from 1965 to 1967. Dr. Elmer holds a BA from the University of Michigan (1964), an MS from Columbia University (1970), and a PhD from the University of California (1991). Her book *Infrastructure Planning and Finance: A Guide for Local Practitioners* is forthcoming from Routledge Press.

John Freear is professor emeritus of accounting and finance, and a former associate dean of the Whittemore School of Business and Economics at the University of New Hampshire. He is a founding member and research associate in the Whittemore School's Center for Venture Research and has published extensively on the informal private equity capital market. Professor Freear joined the School in 1983, after serving as a member of the faculty of the University of Kent at Canterbury, England. He holds degrees from the Universities of Cambridge and Kent and is a fellow of the Institute of Chartered Accountants in England and Wales.

Zenia Kotval is a professor of urban and regional planning in the School of Planning Design and Construction at Michigan State University. Her teaching and research expertise is in economic development planning, community development practice, fiscal and economic impact assessments, and the development of underutilized areas. Her research has been published in leading international journals, and she has contributed chapters to several books. Professor Kotval also serves on the editorial boards of the ICMA Press and the *Journal of City and Town Management.* She is an active member of the Associated Collegiate Schools of Planning, the American Institute of Certified Planners, and the Planning Accreditation Board.

Zeenat Kotval-K is a doctoral candidate in urban geography at Michigan State University. She holds MS degrees in urban and regional planning and hospitality and tourism. Her research interests include sustainable development, built environments, transportation patterns and health, and global urban studies. Her dissertation on the Impacts of the Built Environment on Travel Behavior and Emissions in the Detroit Region is based on research conducted with Dr. Igor Vojnovic at MSU. Funds for this research were provided by an NSF grant on Accessibility, Travel and Health Impacts of the Built Environment in the Detroit Metropolitan Region. Ms. Kotval-K has published several papers and book chapters on her research.

Randolph Lyles, a graduate of Boston University School of Law, has more than 10 years' experience in the practice of corporate, environmental, and real estate law. After studying regional planning with a concentration on municipal zoning and land use planning at the University of Massachusetts, Amherst, he worked for UMass's Center for Economic Development. He is currently pursuing his MBA from the Isenberg School of Management with an emphasis on real estate development finance and municipal economic development. He also serves on the board of directors of A Better Chance, Amherst, an educational nonprofit serving young men of color from resource-disadvantaged school districts.

Patricia L. Machemer is an associate professor of urban and regional planning at Michigan State University and teaches within both the landscape architecture and urban and regional planning majors. Her research focuses on participatory design and planning, with a special interest in children's participation. Building on this research work and her work in the classroom, Professor Machemer's scholarship includes studies on teaching and learning. As a land use planner at the regional level, she explores the use of geographic information systems in both practice and teaching.

Stephen Malpezzi is the Lorin and Marjorie Tiefenthaler Distinguished Professor in the Wisconsin School of Business's Department of Real Estate and Urban Land Economics at the University of Wisconsin–Madison. He chairs that department and has also served as academic director of UW's James A. Graaskamp Center for Real Estate. Professor Malpezzi's research includes work on economic development, the measurement and determinants of real estate prices, housing demand, and the effects of regulation and other economic policies on real estate markets.

Victor A. Matheson is an associate professor in the Department of Economics at the College of the Holy Cross in Worcester, Massachusetts. He earned his PhD in economics from the University of Minnesota. He has published extensively in the field of the economics of collegiate and professional sports, including studies of the economic impact of the Super Bowl, the World Cup, and the Olympics. He has also worked as a referee in the top professional and intercollegiate soccer leagues in the United States.

John Mullin is a professor of urban planning and dean of the Graduate School at the University of Massachusetts, Amherst. He is also the founding partner of Mullin Associates, Incorporated, a planning consulting firm, and has worked as a practicing planner for more than 35 years. His research focuses on planning history and on the past and future of New England mill towns. He is a Fulbright Scholar, a National Endowment for the Arts grantee, and a charter member of the Fellows of the American Institute of Certified Planners. Dr. Mullin is a retired Brigadier General in the Massachusetts Army National Guard.

Robin Newberger is a senior business economist in the Community Development and Policy Studies department at the Federal Reserve Bank of Chicago. Ms. Newberger's areas of interest include banking and financial services for low- and moderate-income consumers and the growth and sustainability of community development finance institutions. Before working at the Chicago Fed, Ms. Newberger wrote for the Economist Intelligence Unit in Quito, Ecuador. She graduated from Columbia University and the John F. Kennedy School of Government at Harvard University. Ms. Newberger is a CFA charterholder.

Michael T. Peddle is an associate professor of public administration and the associate dean for academic administration at Northern Illinois University's College of Liberal Arts and Sciences. He has over 25 years' experience consulting with local and state governments on economic development and growth management issues, including the design of development exaction programs. Professor Peddle is an economist and accountant by training, but his primary expertise lies in public finance, economic development finance, and the use of negotiation and bargaining as a tool for improving the outcomes of public policy decisions. He currently serves as the chair of the Citizens Finance Advisory Committee in the City of DeKalb, Illinois.

Laura A. Reese is professor of political science and director of the Global Urban Studies Program at Michigan State University. Her main research and teaching areas are in urban politics and public policy, economic development, and local governance and management in both Canada and the United States.

She has conducted large-scale evaluations for the Economic Development Administration and substate economic development programs. Professor Reese has written several books and articles in these areas. She is also the editor-in-chief of the *Journal of Urban Affairs* and conducts training for local and state government officials on economic development incentives.

Henry Renski is an assistant professor in the Department of Landscape Architecture and Regional Planning at the University of Massachusetts, Amherst, and the associate director of the UMass Center for Economic Development. He teaches courses in state and local economic development policy, regional development analysis, quantitative methods, and Geographic Information Systems. His research interests include regional influences on entrepreneurship, changing knowledge and skill requirements in the labor force, industrial cluster analysis, applied analytical methods, and state and local economic development policy.

Kelly Robinson is interim director of the Joseph C. Cornwall Center for Metropolitan Studies at Rutgers University in Newark, New Jersey. Dr. Robinson's scholarly specialization is the study of regional economic development. With 25 years of experience in the field, he has conducted research in a variety of areas critical to the mission of the Cornwall Center, among them the redevelopment of public housing, the evaluation of community development activities, municipal contracting, hospital closings, and behavioral health. He also teaches graduate courses in evaluation methods and geographic information systems for public and nonprofit administrators.

Gary Sands is associate professor emeritus in the Department of Urban Studies and Planning at Wayne State University in Detroit, Michigan. His research and teaching have focused on the impact of public regulations and programs on urban development markets. He has been a consultant to government agencies at all levels, as well as to the private and not-for-profit sectors. Professor Sands has authored four books and numerous book chapters, journal articles, and research monographs.

Jeffrey E. Sohl is director of the Center for Venture Research and a professor of entrepreneurship at the University of New Hampshire. He currently serves on the advisory board of the New Hampshire Community Loan Fund, the United States Association for Small Business and Entrepreneurship, and the Babson College Entrepreneurship Research Conference Review Board. Professor Sohl also serves on the editorial board for *Venture Capital* and *Entrepreneurship Theory and Practice.* In 2006 he received the national Hans

Severiens Award from the Kauffman Foundation in recognition of his research on angel investing in the United States. He has written over 50 articles for publication in academic journals.

Ryan Wallace is a doctoral student in regional planning at the University of Massachusetts, Amherst, where he earned a master's degree in the same field. He received his bachelor's degree in finance from Bentley College (now University). His research interests within economic development planning relate to development finance, regional development policy, energy, and the dynamics within emerging economies.

Rachel Weber is an associate professor in the Urban Planning and Policy Program at the University of Illinois at Chicago, where she teaches courses and conducts research in the fields of economic development, urban policy, and real estate finance. Much of her recent work has focused on evaluating the design and effectiveness of property tax–based incentives for urban redevelopment. Professor Weber's articles on this topic have appeared in *Economic Geography, The Journal of the American Planning Association,* and *Regional Science and Urban Economics.* In 2011 she was appointed to the Task Force on TIF Reform by Chicago Mayor Rahm Emanuel.

Sammis B. White is associate dean of the School of Continuing Education, a longtime professor of urban planning, and director of the Center for Workforce Development at the University of Wisconsin–Milwaukee. He has written over 150 articles and reports and co-authored or co-edited five books. Dr. White co-founded and for ten years co-edited the leading economic development journal, *Economic Development Quarterly*. He has been a central actor in the building of a water technology cluster in southeast Wisconsin and has assisted the development of two other industrial clusters in the state. Dr. White is a graduate of Williams College and the University of Pennsylvania.